Rights and Wrongs under the ECHR

The prohibition of abuse of rights in Article 17 of the European Convention on Human Rights

SCHOOL OF HUMAN RIGHTS RESEARCH SERIES, Volume 78.

The titles published in this series are listed at the end of this volume.

Rights and Wrongs under the ECHR

The prohibition of abuse of rights in Article 17 of the European Convention on Human Rights

Paulien de Morree

intersentia

Cambridge – Antwerp – Portland

Intersentia Ltd
Sheraton House | Castle Park
Cambridge | CB3 0AX | United Kingdom
Tel.: +44 1223 370 170 | Fax: +44 1223 370 169
Email: mail@intersentia.co.uk
www.intersentia.com | www.intersentia.co.uk

Distribution for the UK and Ireland:
NBN International
Airport Business Centre, 10 Thornbury Road
Plymouth, PL6 7 PP
United Kingdom
Tel.: +44 1752 202 301 | Fax: +44 1752 202 331
Email: orders@nbninternational.com

Distribution for Europe and all other countries:
Intersentia Publishing nv
Groenstraat 31
2640 Mortsel
Belgium Tel.: +32 3 680 15 50 | Fax: +32 3 658 71 21
Email: mail@intersentia.be

Distribution for the USA and Canada:
International Specialized Book Services
920 NE 58th Ave. Suite 300
Portland, OR 97213
USA
Tel.: +1 800 944 6190 (toll free) | Fax: +1 503 280 8832
Email: info@isbs.com

Rights and Wrongs under the ECHR.
The prohibition of abuse of rights in Article 17 of the European Convention on Human Rights

Once upon a time, 2016, collage ca. 96 x 148 cm

The current state of the world troubles Dutch artist Charlotte Schrameijer. Our world is disrupted by wars, terrorism, social conflicts, and environmental and natural disasters. Yet we live life to the fullest as we dance on the edge of volcanoes.

These two extremes are what moves Schrameijer as she brings them together in her works of art: she cuts out photos of disaster areas, tainted by conflict, environmental or natural disasters, and transforms them into idyllic images of nature. The detailed cutting creates an intricate and fragile work of paper lace; rugged and full of reflections and shadows.

Once upon a time reveals a dissonant harmony created by the images of 'guilt-ridden' landscapes of the Second World War combined with a beautiful and unspoiled scenery.

Typesetting: Editing Department, School of Law, Utrecht University

ISBN 978-1-78068-418-5
D/2016/7849/164
NUR 828

British Library Cataloguing in Publication Data. A catalogue record for this book is available from the British Library.

Acknowledgements

Almost five years ago Professor Henk Kummeling and Professor Remco Nehmelman gave me the opportunity to return to my *alma mater* to start a PhD research on the prohibition of abuse of rights in Article 17 of the European Convention on Human Rights (ECHR). Ever since I first came across this provision while conducting research for my LLM thesis I have been fascinated by it. In 2012 I was given a chance to explore the rationale and interpretation of this provision. It was the start of an exciting academic adventure that has resulted in this book. This undertaking, however, would not have been possible without the help of a number of people.

First of all, I would like to thank my two PhD supervisors, Henk and Remco. Henk, you have been the calm and determined coach who never lost sight of the bigger picture. Despite your busy schedule and many travels abroad you always made sure that you had time to talk to me about the '*big Bertha*' in the ECHR and many other interesting issues. Remco, ever since you supervised the writing of my LLM thesis you believed in my academic qualities even when I had my doubts. You played an important role in creating the opportunity for me to work at Utrecht University, for which I am very grateful.

I also want to thank the members of the assessment committee, Professor Antoine Buyse, Professor Janneke Gerards, Professor Roel de Lange, Professor Yves Haeck and Wytze van der Woude, for taking the time to read my manuscript. Your suggestions and comments have given me the opportunity to make valuable improvements to the text.

I was lucky enough for my journey to take me abroad. In 2013 I spent a month at the European Court of Human Rights in Strasbourg, France, where I received great help from the employees at the registry and the library. Several Judges at the Court were kind enough to discuss their perception of Article 17 ECHR and the theoretical and practical issues surrounding it with me: Dean Spielmann, András Sajó, Angelika Nussberger, Dmitry Dedov and Johannes Silvis. The following year I also had the privilege of discussing my research with the Deputy Registrar at the time, Michael O'Boyle. I am grateful for their willingness to share their views with me.

Then, in 2014 my journey took me to Heidelberg, Germany. The scholarship that I received from the Max Planck Institute for Comparative Public Law and International Law allowed me to spend two months in the company of many inspiring researchers and to profit from the Institute's excellent library. I sincerely thank Professor Armin von Bogdandy and Professor Anne Peters for this experience. A special thanks to Professor Jochen A. Frowein for our inspiring meetings during which he was kind enough to share with me his thoughts on the prohibition of abuse of fundamental rights.

I also thank Peter Morris for editing my manuscript and Klaartje Hoeberechts for preparing it for publication. In addition I want to thank Tom Scheirs, Hans Kluwer, and Isabelle van Dongen at Intersentia for their assistance in the publication of this research. I am also indebted to Charlotte Schrameijer, who allowed me to use a photograph of one of her beautiful works of art for the cover of my book.

Even though the journey that lead to this book has at times been challenging, it was also a joyful experience thanks to all the wonderful people who have supported me along the way. While I cannot name them all, these include first of all my colleagues at the School of Law, present and past. It is a pleasure to work with people who are both academically inspiring and provide the welcome distractions one needs to stay sane during a PhD. I owe special thanks to my fellow PhD candidates at '*ASP*', in particular Sandra, Bettina, Daan, Elvis, Margot, Herman Kasper, Jasper, Mark, Hilke, Marloes, Willem, Marie Elske, Lukas, Hanneke, Pauline, Eduardo, Dayla, Katharine, Simone, Diana, Catherine and Leonie for their support and companionship.

I also want to thank my friends outside academia. These include the '*ASW girls*', with whom my academic adventure started years ago. I also thank my '*Nothing Toulouse*' buddies, who I am thrilled to still call my friends years after our semester in La Ville Rose. Thanks also to my fellow StuPa party members, with whom I shared an unforgettable experience that definitely contributed to my enthusiasm for constitutional law. Also my fellow board members of Stichting Initiatives for Peace and Human Rights deserve my thanks for embarking on the adventure of setting up an NGO with me. A special thanks to my friends Jorien, Iris, Marloes, Alyssa, Veerle, Rosanne and Nelleke for the many amazing moments we have shared together. Finally, I would like to thank all the wonderful people from all over the world that I have had the pleasure of meeting during the time of writing this book. You have all in your own way inspired and motivated me to continue on this journey and I am grateful to you all.

I want to express my heartfelt gratitude to my two paranymphs: Melissa and Loes. Melissa, we started out as colleagues but soon became close friends. The list of amazing places we have visited together and special moments we have shared continues to grow. With regard to finishing a PhD thesis you have showed me how it is done. Your enthusiasm, ambition and perseverance are truly inspiring. I hope you will continue to be in my life for many years to come. Loes, thank you for your endless moral support. The many coffees we enjoyed together were essential for me to blow off steam every now and then. Your understanding, creativity, and relativism helped me through my moments of despair. I am proud of you for following your own path and I hope to continue to be part of it. I could not have imagined this journey without the two of you. Especially during the challenges of the past year, your support has meant the world to me. I am eternally thankful for your friendship.

Finally, I want to thank my family, in particular my parents, Wim and Marjon, and my siblings Hester and Ruben. I consider myself lucky to have grown up in such a warm family. You have given me the confidence to find my own way in life and to explore the world. Whether we are near or far apart I know I can always count on you. Your unconditional love and support have been essential for the realisation of this book.

Utrecht, August 2016

Table of Contents

Chapter 3 The Strasbourg Case Law on Article 17 ECHR

Chapter 4 The Interpretation of Article 17 Echr in Legal Doctrine

Chapter 9 Militant Democracy in the Context of the ECHR

Chapter 10 Conclusions

List of Abbreviations

ACHR	American Convention on Human Rights
ADHR	American Declaration of the Rights and Duties of Man
BL	Basic Law (*Grundgesetz*)
CC	Civil Code (*Code Civil* or *Bürgerliches Gesetzbuch*)
CCPR	Human Right Committee
CESCR	Committee on Economic, Social and Cultural Rights
CHR	Commission on Human Rights
CJEU	Court of Justice of the European Union
CoE	Council of Europe
dec.	decision
ECHR	European Convention on Human Rights
EComHR	European Commission of Human Rights
ECOSOC	Economic and Social Council
ECtHR	European Court of Human Rights
EU	European Union
EU Charter	Charter of Fundamental Rights of the European Union
FCC	Federal Constitutional Court (*Bundesverfassungsgericht*)
GA	General Assembly
GC	Grand Chamber
GG	*Grundgesetz*
IAComHR	Inter-American Commission on Human Rights
IACtHR	Inter-American Court of Human Rights
ICERD	International Convention on the Elimination of All Forms of Racial Discrimination
ICESCR	International Covenant on Economic, Social and Cultural Rights
ICCPR	International Covenant on Civil and Political Rights
LFCC	Law on the Federal Constitutional Court (*Gesetz über das Bundesverfassungsgericht*)
OAS	Organization of American States
Rn.	Margin number (*Randnummer*)
SRP	Socialist Reich Party (*Sozialistische Reichspartei*)
TEU	Treaty on European Union
UDHR	Universal Declaration of Human Rights
UK	United Kingdom
UN	United Nations
UN Charter	Charter of the United Nations
US	United States (of America)
USSR	Union of Soviet Socialist Republics

Chapter 1
Introduction

1.1 Rights and wrongs under the ECHR

In 1956 the German Federal Constitutional Court held that the German Communist Party posed a threat to the 'free democratic basic order' and declared it unconstitutional. The party subsequently challenged its prohibition before the European Commission of Human Rights, arguing that it constituted a violation of its rights to freedom of expression and freedom of association. The Commission, however, found that advocating the establishment of a social communist society through a proletarian revolution was incompatible with the free operation of democratic institutions.[1]

In a hallmark case from the 1990s, the French philosopher, former politician and author of the book 'The Founding Myths of Modern Israel', Roger Garaudy, was convicted of disputing the existence of crimes against humanity, public defamation of a group of persons – in this case, the Jewish community – and incitement to racial hatred. In his book, Garaudy openly disputed the Holocaust and referred to the use of gas chambers by the Nazis as a myth. He argued that the criminal conviction amounted to an unjustified interference with his right to freedom of expression. The Court found that with the revisionist tenor of the book, the applicant attempted to deflect the right to freedom of expression from its real purpose by using it for ends which are contrary to the text and spirit of the Convention.[2]

In 2002 Mark Anthony Norwood, an active member of the extreme right-wing British National Party, was convicted of aggravated hostility towards a religious group for displaying in the window of his flat a large poster with a photograph of the Twin Towers in flames, the words *'Islam out of Britain – Protect the British People'* and a symbol of a crescent and a star in a prohibition sign. He complained before the European Court of Human Rights that the conviction violated his right to freedom of expression. The Court, however, found that *'such a general, vehement attack against a religious group, linking the group as a whole with a grave act of terrorism, is incompatible with the values proclaimed and guaranteed by the Convention, notably tolerance, social peace and non-discrimination'*.[3]

And in 2003 the German Federal Ministry of the Interior prohibited the activities of the international Islamic organisation Hizb Ut-Tahrir on German territory.

---

1 EComHR 20 July 1957, *German Communist Party v. Germany*, appl. no. 250/57.
2 ECtHR 24 June 2003 (dec.), *Garaudy v. France*, appl. no. 65831/01, par. 1.
3 ECtHR 16 November 2004 (dec.), *Norwood v. the United Kingdom*, appl. no. 23131/03.

This organisation promoted the unification of all Middle-Eastern states in one Islamic caliphate governed according to Sharia law and advocated the violent destruction of Israel and its inhabitants. The organisation brought the case to Strasbourg, claiming a violation of its right to freedom of association. The European Court of Human Rights found that advocating the violent destruction of Israel and its inhabitants was *'clearly contrary to the values of the Convention, notably the commitment to the peaceful settlement of international conflicts and to the sanctity of human life'*.[4]

What these divergent cases have in common is that the Strasbourg organs found that the applicants in question could not rely on the rights they invoked, because their exercise of these rights constituted an abuse of rights in the sense of Article 17 ECHR. Article 17 ECHR reads: *'[n]othing in this Convention may be interpreted as implying for any State, group or person any right to engage in any activity or perform any act aimed at the destruction of any of the rights and freedoms set forth herein or at their limitation to a greater extent than is provided for in the Convention'*.[5] Based on this provision, the Strasbourg organs have found that activities that run counter to democracy or democratic values are incompatible with the Convention and do not therefore warrant its protection.

Article 17 ECHR, also referred to as the Convention's abuse clause, touches upon the very foundations of the ECHR. The Convention came into being just after the Second World War when European leaders had the memories of the horrors of the Holocaust still fresh in their minds. The prime reason for the provision's existence is to give the Convention the legal means to defend itself against being overthrown in order to prevent a repeat of history. The *'object and purpose'* of the Convention have been identified in general terms as *'the protection of individual rights and freedoms'* and the maintenance and promotion of *'the ideals and values of a democratic society'*.[6] While the Convention essentially aims to promote freedom by affirming the fundamental rights and freedoms citizens enjoy vis-à-vis state authorities, Article 17 ECHR aims to protect democracy and democratic values against groups and individuals aiming to undermine them. The provision basically functions as a kind of

---

4 ECtHR 12 June 2012 (dec.), *Hizb Ut-Tahrir and others v. Germany*, appl. no. 31098/08, par. 74.

5 CoE, *European Convention for the Protection of Human Rights and Fundamental Freedoms*, as amended by Protocols Protocol No. 14 (*CETS* No. 194), signed on 4 November 1950, entered into force on 3 September 1953, *ETS* No. 5, available at: www.coe.int/en/web/conventions/full-list/-/conventions/treaty/005 (accessed 11 April 2016).

6 D.J. Harris et al. (eds.), *Harris, O'Boyle and Warbrick. Law of the European Convention on Human Rights*, 3rd ed., Oxford: Oxford University Press (2014), p. 7.

'boomerang' that effectively blocks *'those who seek to destroy the human rights of others... from successfully invoking those rights themselves'*.[7]

The provision touches upon a number of controversial issues. As Buyse pointed out, there unmistakably is an inherent tension between human rights protection and the abuse clause.[8] The question when the use of a right turns into abuse is a very complicated one, both for theorists and for courts required to adjudicate this question. This makes the application of the abuse clause a highly contentious and debatable matter. The cases referred to above illustrate that the abuse clause has been applied to a wide range of situations. In addition, as we will see later in Chapter two, there are similar cases in which Article 17 ECHR has been applied in a different way or was not applied at all without a clear justification for the difference in approach. This study argues that as long as uncertainties remain about when and how the abuse clause should be applied, its application will continue to be controversial. The aim of this study is therefore to clarify the interpretation of Article 17 ECHR.

1.2 Problem definition and research questions

The main objective of this study is to contribute to the body of knowledge concerning the prohibition of abuse of rights in Article 17 ECHR, especially in relation to the application of this provision. The prohibition of abuse of fundamental rights is one of the most fundamental, but at the same time controversial provisions of the Convention. For a long time the prohibition of abuse of rights in Article 17 ECHR led a relatively quiet existence. The provision was seldom invoked or applied in the case law of the Commission and the Court and in legal doctrine the issue generated little interest. In recent years, however, things have changed. Since the start of this research in 2012, issues related to the prohibition of abuse of human rights have increasingly received attention in legal and political debate. Also the Strasbourg Court seems to increasingly take an interest in Article 17 ECHR. The Court has openly evaluated the applicability of the provision in several recent high-profile cases.[9] Yet, the interpretation of Article 17 ECHR is far from unequivocal. Both theoretical and practical interpretations of

7 E. Brems, 'Democratie en zelfverdediging' ['Democracy and self-defence'], in: M.C. Snippe et al. (eds.), *Democratie op het einde van de 20ste eeuw. Onderzoek naar probleemgericht denken over de democratie bij jonge onderzoekers in Vlaanderen [Democracy at the end of the 20th century. Research into problem-oriented thinking about democracy among young research in Flanders]*, Brussels: Koninklijke Academie voor Wetenschappen, Letteren en Schone Kunsten, 1994, p. 320; J. Velaers, *De beperkingen van de vrijheid van meningsuiting [The restrictions on the freedom of expression]*, Antwerp: Maklu, 1991, p. 255.

8 A. Buyse, 'Contested contours. The limits of freedom of expression from an abuse of rights perspective – Articles 10 and 17 ECHR', in: E. Brems and J. Gerards (eds.), *Shaping Rights in the ECHR. The Role of the European Court of Human Rights in Determining the Scope of Human Rights*, Cambridge: Cambridge University Press, 2014, p. 184.

9 See e.g. ECtHR 15 October 2015 (GC), *Perinçek v. Switzerland*, appl. no. 27510/08, par. 26 and ECtHR 20 October 2015 (dec.), *M'Bala M'Bala v. France*, appl. no. 25239/13, par 39.

the abuse clause point in a variety of different directions. This is partly due to the broad wording of the provision itself. While Article 17 ECHR provides that activities that aim to destroy fundamental rights may be excluded from the protection of the Convention, it fails to stipulate any criteria for determining which activities fit this description. The inconsistent application of the abuse clause by the Strasbourg organs shows that there is a great need for clarification on this topic. This study therefore aims to shed light on the interpretation of the abuse clause in the Convention in order to contribute to the development of a more coherent interpretation of Article 17. The central question of this research is therefore:

How has the prohibition of abuse of rights in Article 17 of the European Convention on Human Rights to date been interpreted by the European Commission of Human Rights and the European Court of Human Rights and how can this provision be applied in the future?

The central research question is divided into the following six sub-questions:

1. *Why was the abuse clause included in the Convention?*
2. *How is Article 17 ECHR interpreted by the European Court of Human Rights and the European Commission of Human Rights (before the latter was abolished in 1998)?*
3. *How is Article 17 ECHR interpreted in contemporary legal doctrine?*
4. *What can we learn from the interpretation of other abuse clauses in human rights law for the understanding of Article 17 ECHR?*
5. *What can the doctrine on abuse of rights teach us about the interpretation of the prohibition of abuse of rights in Article 17 ECHR?*
6. *What can the concept of militant democracy teach us about the interpretation of Article 17 ECHR as a militant instrument of the ECHR?*

1.3 Research structure and methodology

The methodology followed in this research consists of legal, desk-based research. The approach of this study towards answering the central research question is threefold: to identify the current interpretation of Article 17 ECHR by the EComHR and the ECtHR and its complications; to explore different normative frameworks related to the concept of abuse of rights; and, based on the insights obtained from these different frameworks, to shed light on how the abuse clause can be interpreted in the future.

1.3.1 The current interpretation of Article 17 ECHR

The first step is to identify the current interpretation of Article 17 ECHR and the controversies involved. That is the purpose of the first two sub-questions. This part of the research is primarily descriptive in nature.

The purpose of the first sub-question is to examine what motivated the drafters of the Convention to include the abuse clause. Since the Convention is considered *'a living instrument which... must be interpreted in the light of present-day conditions'*, the *travaux préparatoires* only play a secondary role in the interpretation of the ECHR.[10] Article 17 ECHR, however, is very much a product of its time. The historical context in which the Convention came into being was crucial for the incorporation of an abuse clause. Some understanding of the context in which the provision saw the light of day is therefore crucial for understanding Article 17 ECHR and its interpretation by the Commission and the Court. It is therefore that this study starts with a short history of the creation of the Convention and the abuse clause in particular. This part of the research draws primarily on the *travaux préparatoires* to the Convention. In addition it draws on commentaries and academic literature interpreting the creation of the ECHR.

The second sub-question seeks to analyse the interpretation of Article 17 ECHR in the Strasbourg case law. In order to answer the second sub-question, this study examines the judgments and admissibility decisions (and occasionally also reports) of the Strasbourg Court and the Commission (before the latter was abolished in 1998).[11] Judgments and admissibility decisions that significantly contribute to the development, clarification, or modification of the interpretation of Article 17 ECHR, however, are not easily identified in the Court's online HUDOC database. A search based on the key words *'Article 17'* and *'Prohibition of abuse of rights'* yields almost a thousand hits. Within the context of this study, it was unfeasible to examine all these cases. Such a comprehensive scrutiny was also unnecessary, as a preliminary analysis

---

10 ECtHR 25 April 1978, *Tyrer v. the United Kingdom*, appl. no. 5856/72, par. 31. See also Article 32 of the Vienna Convention on the Law of Treaties, concluded on 23 May 1969, United Nations, Treaty Series, vol. 1155, p. 331. That the rules of interpretation in Articles 31 to 33 of the Vienna Convention are applicable to the ECHR was confirmed by the Court in ECtHR 21 February 1975, *Golder v. the United Kingdom*, appl. no. 4451/70, par. 29. See also J. Gerards, *EVRM – Algemene beginselen [ECHR – General principles]*, Den Haag: Sdu Uitgevers, 2011, p. 16-19 and 67-70.

11 Until the end of 1998 admissibility decisions were exclusively delivered by the European Commission of Human Rights. Only after an application was declared admissible by the Commission would the Court take on the case. With the entry into force of the 11th Protocol (*ETS* No. 155) on restructuring the Convention's control machinery on 1 November 1998, however, the structure of the Court changed drastically. The Commission was abolished and individuals were allowed to take cases directly to the Court. Since then, the Court assesses both the admissibility and the content of a complaint.

of these cases showed that Article 17 ECHR was often merely superficially referred to by one of the parties and did not play a significant role in the understanding of the case. For the selection of the relevant cases, therefore, this study draws primarily on the judgments and admissibility decisions that have been repeatedly cited in the Strasbourg case law and in legal doctrine. In addition, during this research the publication of new and relevant judgments and decisions was closely followed. This part of the research is descriptive, but also evaluative in the sense that it seeks to reveal the many difficulties and inconsistencies that exist in the interpretation of the abuse clause by the Court and the Commission. The analysis in this part of the study is based first and foremost on case law. It refers incidentally to academic literature and relevant non-binding standard-setting documents of the CoE when this is necessary to complete the picture.

1.3.2 Exploring potential solutions to the current controversies

As a second step, this study seeks to explore potential answers to the controversies surrounding the abuse clause from a broad range of perspectives. For that aim, this study first turns to the academic debate on Article 17 ECHR. The aim of the third sub-question is to identify the contemporary interpretation of Article 17 ECHR in legal doctrine. Because of its ambiguous nature, Article 17 ECHR has frequently been the subject of academic study. With the increase in references to Article 17 ECHR in the case law of the Court, the interest in the provision by legal scholars has also experienced an upsurge. This study therefore turns to the academic literature on Article 17 ECHR. This part of the research aims to expose the legal controversies surrounding the interpretation of the abuse clause and to bring attention to the various approaches that legal scholars have adopted towards the scope and interpretation of Article 17 ECHR. For that aim, it draws primarily on a literature study, and will include occasional references to case law in the event that this is necessary to illustrate the arguments made by legal scholars.

Subsequently, in the course of this book the approach to the issue under study is broadened. In the current debate on Article 17 ECHR solutions to its inconsistent interpretation are for the most part sought in the context of Article 17 ECHR itself. To develop a better and more thorough understanding, however, this study aims to add new angels to the discussion on the abuse clause in the ECHR. Three interesting perspectives that are closely related to the prohibition of abuse of rights in the ECHR will be examined: the interpretation of other abuse clauses in international and regional human rights law; the principle of abuse of rights; and the concept of militant democracy. This study will explore to what extent these perspectives may serve as frameworks for the understanding of Article 17 ECHR. The last three sub-questions are therefore more evaluative in nature.

1.3.2.1 Other abuse clauses in human rights law

The aim of the fourth sub-question is to find out whether the understanding of the abuse clauses in other human rights instruments provides relevant insights for the interpretation of Article 17 ECHR. Many scholars have pointed out that the ECHR is not the only human rights document that contains an abuse clause and that similar clauses are found in other human rights instruments. This study looks at the Universal Declaration of Human Rights, the International Covenant on Civil and Political Rights and the International Covenant on Economic, Social and Cultural Rights, the American Convention on Human Rights, and the Charter of Fundamental Rights of the EU, because these instruments can be considered as the Convention's counterparts at the international and regional level and contain abuse clauses that are similar – at least in wording – to Article 17 ECHR.[12] This part of the study will explore to what extent their interpretation is comparable and what we can learn from them for the understanding of Article 17 ECHR. It draws on the selected legislation, resolutions, recommendations and (quasi-)judicial decisions from the bodies that monitor the implementation of the above-mentioned instruments, and secondary sources in which these are interpreted, such as commentaries and academic literature.

1.3.2.2 The concept of abuse of rights

The fifth sub-question seeks to explore what we can learn from the general doctrine on abuse of rights. Article 17 ECHR is specified by the title *'prohibition of abuse of rights'*. The prohibition of abuse of rights is a legal principle that can be found in several legal disciplines, and that is most strongly developed in civil private law.[13] The principle has subsequently been increasingly accepted in a cross-border context, for instance in public international law and EU law. In the context of international human rights law, however, the doctrine on abuse of rights only recently started to receive attention.[14] To provide a comprehensive understanding of Article 17 ECHR,

---

12 The American Declaration of the Rights and Duties of Man, the African Charter on Human and Peoples' Rights, and the ASEAN Human Rights Declaration do not contain an abuse clause and are for that reason not included in this research. Also, since this study focuses on a selection of *general* international and regional human rights instruments equivalent to the ECHR, abuse clauses found in international treaties dealing with a particular human right or area of rights – such as Article 81(2) of the International Convention on Migrant Workers (ICMW) – are not taken into consideration.

13 J. Cueto-Rua, 'Abuse of Rights', *Louisiana Law Review*, vol. 35, no. 5, 1975, p. 967. See also, *inter alia*, J. Voyaume, B. Cottier and B. Rocha, 'Abuse of Rights in Comparative Law', in: *Abuse of Rights and Equivalent Concepts: the Principle and its Present Day Application*, 19th Colloquy on European Law, Strasbourg: CoE Publishing and Documentation Service, 1990, p. 26 and 43-44; H.C. Gutteridge, 'Abuse of Rights', *Cambridge Law Journal*, vol. 5, no. 1, 1933, p. 34 and V.G.A. Boll, *Misbruik van recht [Abuse of rights]*, Utrecht: A. Oosthoek, 1913, p. 6-7.

14 A. Spielmann, 'La Convention Européenne des droits de l'homme et l'abus de droit', in: *Mélanges en hommage à Louis Edmond Pettiti*, Brussels: Bruylant, 1998, p. 673.

this study explores how the principle of abuse of rights is understood in these other areas of law. It aims to describe the interpretation and development of this principle in these areas, but also pays attention to the accompanying academic debate. For this aim, a literature study is conducted of legal research and theories on the principle of abuse of rights in these areas. Case law will play an additional role to illustrate the functioning of the prohibition of abuse of rights in these legal areas.

1.3.2.3 The concept of militant democracy

The purpose of the sixth sub-question is to find out what the concept of militant democracy can teach us about the interpretation of Article 17 ECHR as a militant instrument of the ECHR. A militant democracy is a democratic system that is capable of defending itself against being overthrown from within. The abuse clause was included in the Convention in order to *'protect the signatory States against activities which threaten the preservation of the democratic rights and freedoms themselves'*.[15] It is the provision *par excellence* that articulates that within the system of the Convention it is not allowed for anti-democratic groups and individuals to profit from fundamental rights in order to suppress or destroy democracy or democratic values. Article 17 ECHR is consequently an explicit expression of the concept of militant democracy. The study of the concept of militant democracy consists of three parts: a study of the concept in general; a study of the implementation of this concept in Germany; and the role of this concept in the context of the ECHR and in the interpretation of Article 17 ECHR in particular.

First, the study of the concept of militant democracy focuses on the origin and on different interpretations of this concept in academic literature. The legal strife against anti-democratic actors aiming to destroy democracy is the principal focus of the concept of militant democracy. To better understand Article 17 ECHR, it is therefore important to learn more about the interpretation and implications of the concept of militant democracy. This part of the study takes a theoretical perspective and analyses the interpretation and evolution of the concept of militant democracy in legal doctrine. This part of the study is mainly descriptive in nature and draws on academic literature. This includes first and foremost publications by legal scholars.

Next, this study takes a look at the implementation of the concept of militant democracy in a specific legal context: Germany. The German constitutional order is particularly relevant for understanding the functioning of the concept of militant democracy, as the post-War German Basic Law (BL) is imbued with militant measures that aim to prevent the rise of another anti-democratic regime, including a prohibition

15 A. Robertson (ed.), *Collected edition of the 'Travaux Préparatoires'*, vol. IV, The Hague: Martinus Nijhof, 1975-1985, p. 26.

of abuse of rights in Article 18 BL.[16] This study explores the interpretation of the concept of militant democracy and the abuse clause in the context of the German constitutional order. Although some comparisons will be made, a true comparative method is not used in this study. Given the highly context-dependent nature of considerations of democratic self-defence, such an approach would be very difficult (if not impossible). The analysis of the German approach draws on legislation, predominantly Article 18 BL and looks at its drafting history. In addition it looks at the case law on Germany's interpretation of the concept of militant democracy and the abuse clause. It also draws on academic literature that comments on and interprets the German concept of militant democracy and the role of the abuse clause therein.

Finally, the research into the concept of militant democracy is brought back to the context of the ECHR. This part of the study explores the relevance of the concept of militant democracy for the ECHR and Article 17 ECHR in particular. This analysis is guided by the theories and perceptions on militant democracy discussed in the previous parts of this study. The analysis is based primarily on academic literature and case law relevant for understanding the militant nature of the ECHR.

1.3.3 Towards a more consistent approach to the interpretation of Article 17 ECHR

The third and final step of this research is to determine how Article 17 ECHR can be applied in the future. The central research question is normatively charged as it asks what shape the interpretation of the abuse clause can take against the background of the different angels that have been analysed in this study: the interpretation of Article 17 ECHR in legal doctrine, the interpretation of other abuse clauses in human rights law, the principle of abuse of rights and the concept of militant democracy. The outcome of this research is intended as an incentive for the ECtHR to have a closer look at its interpretation of Article 17 ECHR and to contribute to a more consistent approach to its application.

This study covers developments up until 1 March 2016 and the observations and conclusions in this book are based on that period.

16 Article 18 Basic Law provides: '*Whoever abuses the freedom of expression, in particular the freedom of the press (paragraph (1) of Article 5), the freedom of teaching (paragraph (3) of Article 5), the freedom of assembly (Article 8), the freedom of association (Article 9), the privacy of correspondence, posts and telecommunications (Article 10), the rights of property (Article 14), or the right of asylum (Article 16a) in order to combat the free democratic basic order shall forfeit these basic rights. This forfeiture and its extent shall be declared by the Federal Constitutional Court*', www.bundestag.de/blob/284870/ce0d03414872b427e57fccb703634dcd/basic_law-data.pdf (accessed 11 April 2016).

Furthermore, this study draws on sources originating from different legal areas and different national and international jurisdictions. As a result it includes documents, literature, and case law that were originally published in English, French, German, Spanish and Dutch. Whenever possible, this study refers to the official English language version of these sources. If suitable translations have been provided by others, these are adopted in this study, thereby mentioning where this translation can be found. If no suitable translations into English are available, this study refers to French and German texts in their original language. Other texts are translated by the author, of which mention is made in the footnotes.

1.4 Legal research on Article 17 ECHR

This study focuses on the interpretation of the prohibition of abuse of rights in Article 17 ECHR. Given the background and understanding of this provision as an instrument to protect democracy and democratic values, this study inevitably touches upon the question of how democracies should cope with anti-democratic actors. How democratic regimes should respond to threats that undermine democracy while at the same time upholding their commitment to democracy and democratic values has always been a fundamental question for constitutional lawyers. Intriguing as it may be, however, this specific question will not be answered in this study. The issue is only indirectly touched upon from the perspective of the understanding of the abuse clause in Article 17 ECHR.

Furthermore, this study approaches the abuse of fundamental rights from a legal perspective. Nevertheless, the issue not only has a legal dimension. The problem of subversive actors within (liberal) democracies has also been the subject of philosophy and political and social science.[17] Yet, philosophical, psychological, sociological, and empirical questions related to political extremism and democratic governance are not explicitly addressed in this study. This does not mean, however, that it does not occasionally draw on works from other disciplines. Still, these references are not intended as an autonomous research within these disciplines, but will merely draw on the insights provided by these disciplines to the extent that they influence the legal framework.

1.5 Focus on the ECHR

This study primarily focuses on the abuse clause in the European Convention on Human Rights. This provides a specific normative setting through which questions of abuse of fundamental rights are evaluated. Questions related to the restriction of the

17 See e.g. W. Downs, *Political Extremism in Democracies. Combating Intolerance*, New York: Palgrave Macmillan, 2012; P. Norris, *Radical Right. Voters and Parties in the Electoral Market.* Cambridge: Cambridge University Press, 2005.

rights of those that may pose a threat to the system are not exclusive to the ECHR. Nor are these issues confined to the European continent. By focussing merely on these issues in a European context, this study risks following a Eurocentric approach. As a result, the conclusions of this study may not be automatically applicable outside of the European context. At the same time, however, by also including insights from other legal areas and other human rights systems, this study may contribute to the understanding of the concept of abuse of rights beyond the context of the ECHR. Whether it is in private law, German constitutional law, or the International Covenant on Civil and Political Rights, for example, the prohibition of abuse of rights has to be balanced versus liberal principles such as pluralism, the protection of individual freedom and the demands of democratic government. The processes and criteria taken into account with regard to the interpretation and application of Article 17 ECHR may therefore also play a role in the context of the evaluation of similar issues in other national and international contexts.

1.6 Terminology

A few preliminary points on the terminology used in this study are worth elaborating upon.

First, the term *abuse of rights* plays a key role in this study. The understanding of abuse in the context of this study differs from what is commonly referred to as abuse of rights, namely the violation of human rights by state authorities.[18] This study focuses on abuse in the sense of misuse by the right holder. In general, the term 'abuse of rights' in this context refers to the exercise of a subjective right contrary to the aim of that right. Yet, the exact understanding of the term depends on the specific legal context in which it operates. Within human rights law it does not focus on what states do in defiance of their obligations to protect human rights law, but on the responsibilities of individuals and groups as rights holders under international human rights law. In addition, the term *abuse clause* refers in this context to clauses in general international or regional human rights instruments or national constitutions prohibiting any abuse of the rights and freedoms set forth therein.

Second, *fundamental rights* are to be understood in this study as those subjective rights and freedoms guaranteed in the ECHR and its accompanying protocols. *Human rights* refer to the basic subjective rights and freedoms guaranteed in the different general international and regional human rights instruments, such as the UDHR, the ICCPR and the EU Charter. Furthermore, the term *constitutional rights* refers to

18 See also A. Sajó, 'Preface', in: A. Sajó (ed.), *Abuse: The Dark Side of Fundamental Rights*, Utrecht: Eleven International Publishing, 2006, p. 1.

the basic subjective rights that are guaranteed in a specific national constitution, for instance in the German BL.

Third, *human rights bodies* are those permanent bodies, agencies, and organs belonging to either the UN or to regional organisations that are specifically mandated to regulate and monitor state compliance with human rights instruments, such as the HRC, the IACtHR and the ECtHR. In the context of the CoE, the notion of *Strasbourg organs* refers specifically to the EComHR and the ECtHR as the organs that supervise the enforcement of the ECHR in the States Parties to the Convention.

Finally, the concept of *militant democracy* included in this book refers to a democratic system that has adopted and applies pre-emptive, *prima facie* undemocratic legal instruments to defend itself against the risk of being overthrown by anti-democratic actors that make use of democracy with the aim of abolishing it. In German this concept is referred to as '*wehrhafte Demokratie*' or '*streitbare Demokratie*'.[19] *Anti-democratic actors* can subsequently be defined as those who are opposed to the democratic system or to democratic values. These definitions rely on the dichotomy between democracy and its anti-democratic opponents. This study recognises, however, that these notions are highly abstract and subjective in character. There is no objective interpretation of democracy as an international norm and consequently there is no objective understanding of what is anti-democratic. Also under the ECHR there is no clear-cut definition of the notion of democracy.[20] This study does not aim to settle the ongoing discussion on the interpretation of these notions and does not therefore provide a uniform definition of these terms. Yet, when referring to democracy, the concept of militant democracy, and anti-democratic actors, this study will go into the understanding of these notions in the context in which they come up. Already worth mentioning is that within the context of the ECHR the concept of democracy is understood very broadly and refers not only to the formal framework for democratic decision-making in the sense of 'rule by the people' and majority rule, but also to substantive values and principles that ought to be respected by decision-

19 See for more on the interpretation of this concept in the context of the German Basic Law Chapter eight.

20 P.E. de Morree, 'Het Europees Hof voor de Rechten van de Mens als hoeder van de democratie' ['The European Court of Human Rights as a guardian of democracy'], in: M. Duchateau and P. Kingma (eds.), *Regt spreken volgens de wet? Bijdragen over de staatsrechtelijk positie van de (Europese) rechter [Adjudication in accordance with the law? Contributions regarding the constitutional position of the (European) judge]*, Nijmegen: Wolf Legal Publishers, 2013. See also A. Logeman, *Grenzen der Meschenrechte in demokratischen Gesellschaften, die 'demokratische Gesellschaft' als Determinante der Grundrechtsschranken in der Europäischen Menschenrechtskonvention*, Baden-Baden: Nomos Verlagsgesellschaft, 2004, p. 298-299.

making authorities, such as (political) pluralism, tolerance, the principle of non-discrimination and respect for the rule of law.[21]

1.7 Structure of this book

The research structure introduced above forms the backbone of this book. The structure of this book is subsequently as follows.

First, *Chapter two* describes the introduction of Article 17 ECHR into the Convention from a historical perspective. It explains the context and intentions behind the creation of the Convention in general and the prohibition of abuse of rights in particular. *Chapter three* is a rather lengthy chapter that is devoted to the interpretation of Article 17 ECHR in the case law of the European Commission of Human Rights and the European Court of Human Rights.

Next, *Chapter four* examines the interpretation of Article 17 ECHR in legal doctrine. Then, *Chapter five* looks into the interpretation of several other abuse clauses in human rights law. *Chapter six* will subsequently analyse the prohibition of abuse of rights as a legal principle that is found in multiple legal disciplines. *Chapter seven* of this book is devoted to analysing the interpretation and evolution of the concept of militant democracy. The German Basic Law is widely recognised as the archetype of a militant convention and is therefore studied in more detail in *Chapter eight*. Subsequently, *Chapter nine* is a reflective chapter, which focuses on the interpretation of the ECHR as a militant Convention.

Finally, *Chapter ten* presents the overall conclusions of the present study. It brings together the relevant insights gained by exploring the different frameworks. Based on these insights, it will provide a comprehensive answer to the main research question and put forward a proposal for the future interpretation of Article 17 ECHR.

21 See on different interpretations of the notion of democracy (procedural versus substantive) Chapter seven. For the interpretation of the concept of militant democracy in the context of the ECHR see Chapter nine.

Chapter 2
The Creation of the European Convention on Human Rights

2.1 Introduction

The prohibition of abuse of rights in Article 17 ECHR is very much a product of its time. Before the second half of the 20th century, such a formula had not been recognised in any of the principal human rights texts.[1] But the historical context in which the Convention came into being – just after the Second World War – was crucial for the creation of the abuse clause. This chapter explores what motivated the drafters to include Article 17 ECHR in the Convention. It will move through the different stages of the drafting of the Convention, from the first steps in creating a European human rights treaty by the European Movement in 1948 to the final signing of the Convention by the Member States of the Council of Europe in 1950. The drafting of the Convention, even though it took only roughly two years, was a complex and arduous process. This chapter will not elaborate at length on this process, but instead focuses on aspects of the drafting of the Convention that form the background of the prohibition of abuse of rights in Article 17 ECHR.

2.2 First steps by the European Movement

The ECHR was developed during the turbulent first years following the Second World War. On the one hand, the atrocities committed by the Nazi regime had shaken up the international community and through international cooperation European democracies wanted to prevent such a tragedy from ever happening again. On the other hand, the immediate post-war period was dominated by rising tensions between 'East' and 'West' and the Soviet Union under Stalin was considered a severe and immediate threat to Western European democracies.[2] In the midst of all of this, the first steps towards a European human rights convention were taken by the International Committee of the Movement of European Unity, or the 'European Movement'.[3]

During the first half of 1949 the European Movement started to prepare a draft European human rights convention. Set against the experience of totalitarianism during the Second World War, they attached great significance to democracy. They

---

1 P. le Mire, 'Article 17', in: L.E. Pettiti, E. Decaux and P.H. Imbert (eds.), *La Convention Européenne des Droits de l'Homme. Commentaire Article par Article*, 2nd ed., Paris: Economica, 1999, p. 509.

2 E. Bates, *The Evolution of the European Convention on Human Rights. From its Inception to the Creation of a Permanent Court of Human Rights*, Oxford: Oxford University Press, 2010, p. 46.

3 Bates, p. 47.

believed respect for human rights and a democratic form of government to go hand in hand. The Convention to be drafted would therefore embody Europe's *'ardent belief in human rights and democracy'*.[4] But Western European states also realised at the time of the drafting of the Convention that their newly reclaimed democratic status was fragile. The *travaux préparatoires* echo the fear that their post-war democratic constitutions would (again) be overthrown by anti-democratic forces. And so the European Movement took on its task from the assumptions that European democracies shared *'the same conception of freedom and share[d] the same danger of losing it'*.[5] The Convention was, therefore, first and foremost a defensive reaction on the part of European democracies to any potential danger of the emergence or re-emergence of totalitarianism.[6] The main idea behind the first draft was, in other words, to create *'a collective pact against totalitarianism'*.[7] The compliance of this treaty would be supervised by a European Court of Human Rights, which would serve as an '*alarm bell*' for democratic Europe.[8]

For that purpose the drafters initially had a rather minimalist Convention in mind that would merely protect the very basis of democracy: democratic institutions and the rights and freedoms directly associated with them. According to the preamble to the first draft Convention produced by the European Movement, the Member States of the Council of Europe wished *'[t]o preserve the moral values and democratic principles which are their common heritage'*.[9] Accordingly, the European Movement draft offered a Convention that was meant to primarily guarantee those fundamental rights deemed *'essential for a democratic way of life'*.[10] As demonstrated by Bates, a '*political liberties clause*', which required the States Parties to regularly hold free elections and to allow political opposition, lay at the heart of the European Movement draft.[11] Ironically enough, though, it was this fundamental provision

4 Bates, p. 5.

5 Bates, p. 53.

6 A. Spielmann and D. Spielmann, 'The Concept of Abuse of Rights and the European Convention for the Protection of Human Rights and Fundamental Freedoms', in: *Abuse of Rights and Equivalent Concepts: the Principle and its Present Day Application* (Proceedings of the nineteenth Colloquy on European Law), CoE: Strasbourg, 1990, p. 79.

7 Bates, *The Evolution of the ECHR*, p. 7.

8 Bates, p. 54.

9 A. Robertson (ed.), *Collected edition of the 'Travaux Préparatoires' (hereafter referred to as 'TP')*, vol. I, The Hague: Martinus Nijhof, 1975-1985, p. 296 (Appendix).

10 Robertson, *TP*, vol. I, p. 43-44 (Teitgen). See also S. Marks, 'The European Convention on Human Rights and its "Democratic Society"', in: *British Yearbook of International Law*, London: Oxford University Press, 1995, p. 211.

11 This clause read: *'Every State a party to this Convention undertakes faithfully to respect the fundamental principles of democracy, and in particular, within its metropolitan territory: a) to hold at reasonable intervals free elections by universal suffrage and secret ballot, so that governmental action and legislation may accord with the expressed will of the people; b) to take no action which will interfere with the right of political criticism and the right to organise a political opposition'*. See also Bates, *The Evolution of the ECHR*, p. 55.

that was most vigorously debated at the time of the Convention's creation.[12] While Teitgen, one of the founding fathers of the Convention, stressed that the relevance of this provision stemmed from the indissoluble link between democracy and human rights protection,[13] its opponents objected to the vagueness of the reference to *'the fundamental principles of democracy'* and argued that the issues concerned were of a *'constitutional and political character'*[14] and went *'outside the traditional domain of human rights'*.[15] Eventually, the drafters did not manage to come to an agreement before the Convention was signed and the *'political liberties clause'* did not make it into the final text of the Convention. However, a similar provision providing that the States Parties agree to hold free and fair elections, yet without a reference to the fundamental principles of democracy, was later incorporated in Article 3 of the First Protocol to the Convention.[16]

2.3 The work of the Consultative Assembly

In July 1949, the European Movement had completed its draft Convention and it was sent to the Council of Europe. At the Council of Europe, the Convention went through several drafting stages, starting with deliberations in the Consultative Assembly. Even though other fundamental issues, such as the right to individual petition and the jurisdiction of the Court, dominated the debate, the question of the Convention's self-defence was undeniably a moot point. Also in the Consultative Assembly it was stressed that the purpose of the Convention was to *'ensure that the states of the Members of the Council of Europe are democratic, and remain democratic'*.[17] During the first plenary debate in the Consultative Assembly Teitgen stressed that besides the threat of regimes violating the rights of their citizens there was a second threat that deserved the attention of the drafters. *'Radicalism'*, he warned, *'did not die out*

---

12 Marks, *British Yearbook of International Law*, p. 221.

13 Robertson, *TP*, vol. V, p. 288 (Teitgen). See Robertson, *TP*, vol. V, p. 210 (Layton).

14 Robertson, *TP*, vol. III, p. 182 (Dowson).

15 Robertson, *TP*, vol. IV, p. 140 (Patijn). See also Marks, *British Yearbook of International Law*, p. 222.

16 Nonetheless, given *'the heightened political sensitivity of questions surrounding the design and implementation of electoral systems'*, the Court is generally reluctant to pass a judgment on the way states manage their electoral affairs: D.J. Harris et al. (eds.), *Harris, O'Boyle and Warbrick. Law of the European Convention on Human Rights*, 3rd ed., Oxford: Oxford University Press (2014), p. 946. See e.g. ECtHR 2 March 1987, *Mathieu-Mohin and Clerfayt v. Belgium*, appl. no. 9267/81, par. 52; ECtHR 6 October 2005 (GC), *Hirst v. the United Kingdom (no. 2)*, appl. no. 74025/01, par. 61; ECtHR 9 April 2002, *Podkolzina v. Latvia*, appl. no. 46726/99, par. 33; ECtHR 8 July 2008 (GC), *Yumak and Sadak v. Turkey*, appl. no. 10226/03, par. 109(ii); ECtHR 8 July 2008, *Vajnai v. Hungary*, appl. no. 33629/06, par. 48-50; ECtHR 6 January 2011 (GC), *Paksas v. Lithuania*, appl. no. 34932/04, par. 96; and ECtHR 16 March 2006 (GC), *Ždanoka v. Latvia*, appl. no. 58278/00, par. 103. See also R. de Lange, Case note to ECtHR 6 January 2011 (GC), *Paksas v. Lithuania*, appl. no. 34932/04, *EHRC* 2011/47, par. 12.

17 Robertson, *TP*, vol. II, p. 60 (Ungoed-Thomas).

with Hitler'.[18] Radical movements from the extreme left or the extreme right might continue to put in jeopardy the very principles of democracy.

Later during that same session the issue of democratic self-defence was raised again. A member of the Greek delegation, Maccas, warned that the issue of the abuse of rights had so far been neglected and stressed that: *'human freedom, just because it is sacred, must not become an armoury in which the enemies of freedom can find weapons which they can later use unhindered to destroy this freedom'*. The freedom of European democracies and their citizens, he claimed, depended on their capacity to defend themselves. *'Otherwise freedom would perish in suicide'*. Maccas therefore proposed, *'[w]hen stating our rights, let us also state our duties; when proclaiming our freedom, let us also proclaim our will to defend and to safeguard it. When inscribing the European Charter of mankind on granite, let us not be one-sided: let us write a true gospel, which shall include equally sacred obligations. In drawing up this code let us not think – and let us not frame sanctions – only against the tyrannic acts of those who misuse power, but also against those who misuse freedom'*.[19] Maccas was not alone in this. One of the other founding fathers of the Convention, Sir David Maxwell-Fyfe, relied on the same fears when he held that *'[w]e do not desire by sentimentality in drafting to give evilly disposed persons the opportunity to create a totalitarian government which will destroy Human Rights altogether'*.[20] Yet, the majority of the Consultative Assembly was not convinced of the need to incorporate an abuse clause.[21]

Nevertheless, during the following, second plenary debate in the Consultative Assembly, the issue of abuse of rights was brought up again by the Turkish member Düsünsel. He feared that individuals or groups with totalitarian aims would take advantage of the fundamental rights guaranteed by the Convention to infiltrate the democratic legal order and attempt to wipe out or abolish democracy. Perhaps disappointed with the absence of an abuse clause, he asked Rapporteur Teitgen to what extent the draft Convention allowed States to legitimately fight Nazism, fascism and communism: *'if one day in a democratic country, some party, and I am going to use plain words, of either nazi, fascist or communist tendency, were to take advantage of the declarations of human rights and insinuate itself, thanks to the freedom which every democratic State, in its constitution, must ensure to all its nationals; if such an agitator, like a wolf in sheep's clothing, were to attempt to wipe out and abolish*

18 Robertson, *TP*, vol. I, p. 40 (Teitgen).

19 Robertson, *TP*, vol. I, p. 108-110.

20 Robertson, *TP*, vol. I, p. 118.

21 In the deliberations of the Assembly's Committee on Legal and Administrative Questions an abuse clause similar to the one in Article 30 UDHR was proposed (Robertson, *TP*, vol. I, p. XXVI and 170). An amendment proposed by the British member Lord Layton to leave out this provision, however, was adopted unanimously, removing this proposal from the draft text (ibid, p. 180). As a result, in the *Teitgen Report* that was eventually presented to the Consultative Assembly on behalf of the Committee on Legal and Administrative Questions the abuse clause was still absent.

democracy; if then the laws of each country contain measures for the protection of democracy and State sovereignty against people who would above all be acting on orders from abroad, would this country be legally regarded as being in a state of legitimate defence of its rights and of democracy?'.[22] The reply of Teitgen to this question was quite simple, recalling that the justification could be found in Article 6 of the resolution that allowed States to define, limit and restrain fundamental rights when public order and security are threatened. According to Teitgen, this provision satisfactorily guaranteed that *'there can be no conceivable freedom at the expense of the common interest, the common good, and the order and security of the citizen'*.[23] However, during the same debate the Italian member Benvenuti argued that the Convention had to *'prevent totalitarian currents from exploiting in their own interests the principles enunciated by the Convention; that is to invoke the rights of freedom in order to suppress Human Rights'*.[24] He, therefore, stressed the need for incorporating an abuse clause corresponding to the one in Article 30 of the Universal Declaration of Human Rights.[25] An amendment he had drafted to this effect however, was submitted to the Bureau after the expiration of the time limit and was not considered during the debate.[26] So, despite the attention that was repeatedly drawn at this stage to safeguarding the Convention against abuse, Recommendation 38 delegating the drafting of the Convention to the Committee of Ministers contained no reference to a provision corresponding to Article 17 ECHR.[27]

22 Robertson, *TP*, vol. II, p. 28 (Düsünsel).

23 Article 6 of the draft resolution of the Legal Committee contained a general clause authorising limitations *'Each country shall have the right to determine the means whereby the guaranteed freedoms shall be exercised, but the conditions, limitations and restrictions which it has to place upon each of these freedoms shall be directed only to securing the rights and freedoms of others, and to satisfy the rightful demands of morality, law and security in a democratic society'*. See Robertson, *TP*, vol. II, p. 32.

24 Robertson, *TP*, vol. II, p. 136. See also A.M. Williams, 'The European Convention on Human rights: a new use?', *Texas International Law Journal*, vol. 12, 1977, p. 281.

25 The text of the proposed amendment was: *'No provision of the proposed Convention may imply the recognition of the right of a State or of an individual to undertake activity aimed at the destruction of the freedoms which are contained in it'*. Robertson, *TP*, vol. II, p. 140.

26 Robertson, *TP*, vol. II, p. 142. See also Preparatory work on Article 17 of the European Convention on Human Rights, Information document prepared by the Secretariat of the Commission, Strasbourg, 5 March 1975, CDH(75)7 (Doc A. 38.797), p. 8 footnote 1.

27 Preparatory work on Article 17 of the European Convention on Human Rights, Information document prepared by the Secretariat of the Commission, Strasbourg, 27 April 1957, DH(57)4 (Doc A. 33.551), p. 7.

2.4 Final decisions by the Committee of Ministers

The drafting process was then continued by the governments of the Member States of the Council of Europe in the Committee of Ministers.[28] More than questions concerning democratic self-defence, however, the Committee was concerned about the curtailment of their sovereignty that a European human rights instrument would entail.[29] The Committee of Ministers amended the draft Convention considerably. Nevertheless, even though the issue of an abuse of the Convention by anti-democratic actors was primarily discussed in the Consultative Assembly, it was at this stage that a provision prohibiting the abuse of fundamental rights and freedoms was incorporated in the Convention. In preparation for the work by the Committee, the Secretariat General of the Council of Europe had compared the Assembly's text with the draft International Covenant by the UN and noted that a provision equivalent to the abuse clause included in the UN drafts was absent in the draft ECHR.[30] Subsequently, at the request of the Turkish representative in the Committee of Experts, a Committee that was convened by the Committee of Ministers for the purpose of drafting the Convention, an abuse clause was inserted in an article consisting of four provisions of a more general nature on the limitation of rights.[31] The commentary to this draft explained that the aim of this clause was *'to protect the signatory States against activities which threaten the preservation of the democratic rights and freedoms themselves'*.[32] The text of this abuse clause was practically identical to that of the abuse clause in the Draft International Covenant on Human Rights, including the prohibition of the excessive limitation of rights that was not included in any of the earlier proposals.[33]

2.5 The signing of the Convention

Ultimately, the Convention was signed by the Member States of the Council of Europe in Rome on 4 November 1950 and the *'foundations on which to base the defence of human personality against all tyrannies and against all forms of totalitarianism'*, as

28 Unfortunately, the *travaux préparatoires* for this stage – and therefore also the information available on the Committee's points of view on the issue of democratic self-defence – are less illuminating. The exact how and why the abuse clause was included in the Convention therefore remains something of a mystery. See also Bates, *The Evolution of the ECHR*, p. 79.

29 Bates, p. 77-78.

30 An abuse clause was found in Article 22, paragraph 1, of the Draft International Covenant on Human Rights, see Preparatory work on Article 17 of the European Convention on Human Rights, Information document prepared by the Secretariat of the Commission, Strasbourg, 27 April 1957, DH(57)4 (Doc A. 33.551), p. 8; Preparatory work on Article 17 of the European Convention on Human Rights, Information document prepared by the Secretariat of the Commission, Strasbourg, 5 March 1975, CDH(75)7 (Doc A. 38.797), p. 9 footnote 1. See Robertson, *TP*, vol. III, p. 32.

31 Robertson, *TP*, vol. IV, p. 26.

32 Robertson, *TP*, vol. IV, p. 26.

33 Robertson, *TP*, vol. IV, p. 26.

Schuman described it, became a reality.[34] The Convention subsequently came into force in 1953 after the receipt of the tenth instrument of ratification and in 1959 the European Court of Human Rights was set up to monitor States' respect for the fundamental rights set forth therein.

Looking back at the development of Article 17 ECHR, it is interesting to see that the final text does not differ much from the abuse clause nowadays found in Article 5 of both of the International Covenants (ICCPR and ICESCR) that served as the example for the amendment proposed by the Committee of Experts.[35] The first abuse clause proposed by Teitgen, on the other hand, had more in common with the abuse clause in the UDHR.[36] The most important difference between these two is that in the UDHR's abuse clause the prohibition of limiting rights and freedoms to a greater extent than provided for is absent.

2.6 Conclusions

In this chapter we have seen how the Convention came into being at the end of the 1940s. The *travaux préparatoires* show that the creation of the Convention was motivated by the terrible experiences of the Second World War. With the defeat of totalitarian Nazi dictatorship, democracy had triumphed in Western Europe and a major, if not the major, impetus for the creation of the Convention was to keep things that way.[37] Since experience had shown that totalitarian regimes were a danger to democracy and human rights, self-defence was at this stage predominantly framed in terms of the democratic 'we' versus the totalitarian 'they'.[38] At the time especially political actors with a Nazi, fascist or communist tendency were considered a threat to the democratic orders of the States Parties. When the Convention was signed, as Bates argues, it was therefore generally considered *'more of an inter-State pact against totalitarianism than anything else, with the international system of control unlikely to be invoked other than in extreme cases'*.[39]

---

34 Schuman quoted by Benvenuti (at that time the Secretary-General of the CoE) in his speech at the ceremony held on 18th September 1963 to mark the 10th anniversary of the entry into force of the Convention. See A. Robertson, *Yearbook of the European Convention on Human Rights: the European Commission and European Court of Human Rights*, Dordrecht: Springer Science and Business Media, 1963, p. 82.

35 Article 5(1) of both UN Covenants reads: *'Nothing in the present Covenant may be interpreted as implying for any State, group or person any right to engage in any activity or to perform any act aimed at the destruction if any of the rights or freedoms recognized herein, or at their limitation to a greater extent than provided for the present Covenant'*.

36 Article 30 of the Universal Declaration of Human Rights reads: *'Nothing in this Declaration may be interpreted as implying for any State, group or person any right to engage in any activity or to perform any act aimed at the destruction of any of the rights and freedoms set forth herein'*.

37 Marks, *British Yearbook of International Law*, p. 210.

38 Robertson, *TP*, vol. II, p. 90 (Sweetman).

39 Bates, *The Evolution of the ECHR*, p. 104.

This political context formed the background of the abuse clause that was included in the Convention. In fact, the abuse clause in Article 17 ECHR is the most explicit expression of the Convention's ambition to protect European democracies against the threat of totalitarianism. The purpose of Article 17 ECHR is to *'protect the signatory States against activities which threaten the preservation of the democratic rights and freedoms themselves'*.[40] In that context, Article 17 ECHR aims *'to prevent totalitarian currents from exploiting in their own interests the principles enunciated by the Convention'*.[41] The text of Article 17 ECHR was largely copied from the abuse clauses in the UDHR, which had been adopted just before the drafting process of the ECHR had officially began, and in the draft International Covenants (ICCPR and ICESCR), which were being prepared simultaneously. During the drafting of the Convention, the abuse clause was eventually accepted without much debate.[42] This shows how uncontested and self-evident the need to incorporate such a clause seemingly was to the Committee of Ministers at that time.[43] Apparently, the terrifying memory of National Socialism as practised by Hitler was enough in itself to convince the drafters of the necessity to include an abuse clause.

In the introduction we learned that the text of the abuse clause in Article 17 ECHR is rather ambiguous. The abuse clause clearly reflects the high ambitions and ideals harboured by the drafters of the Convention. The objective of creating a European system that would ensure the protection of human rights and the maintenance of democracy was at the time, and still is, appealing. Yet, as predominantly an expression of the abstract and idealistic moral ambitions of its creators, questions regarding when and how the abuse clause should be applied in practice were not addressed. The prohibition of abuse of rights was only discussed in broad terms during the drafting of the Convention, leaving it up to the Commission and the Court as the Convention's supervisory organs to give an interpretation of the provision. The following chapter will therefore explore the interpretation of Article 17 ECHR according to the case law of the EComHR and the ECtHR.

---

40 Robertson, *TP*, vol. IV, p. 26.

41 Robertson, *TP*, vol. II, p. 136 (Benvenuti).

42 S. Van Drooghenbroeck, 'L'Article 17 de la Convention Européenne des Droits de l'Homme est-il indispensable?', *Revue trimestrielle des droits de l'homme,* vol. 12, no. 46, 2001, p. 542-543; M.E. Villiger, 'Article 17 ECHR and freedom of speech in Strasbourg practice', in: J. Casadevall et al. (eds.), *Freedom of Expression. Essays in Honour of Nicolas Bratza*, Oisterwijk: Wolf Legal Publishers, 2012, p. 322; H. Cannie and D. Voorhoof, 'The Abuse Clause and Freedom of Expression in the European Human Rights Convention: an Added Value for Democracy and Human Rights Protection?', *Netherlands Quarterly of Human Rights,* vol. 29, no. 1, 2001, p. 56.

43 A. Buyse, 'Contested contours. The limits of freedom of expression from an abuse of rights perspective – Articles 10 and 17 ECHR', in: E. Brems and J. Gerards (eds.), *Shaping Rights in the ECHR. The Role of the European Court of Human Rights in Determining the Scope of Human Rights*, Cambridge: Cambridge University Press, 2014, p. 187.

Chapter 3
The Strasbourg Case Law on Article 17 ECHR

3.1 Introduction

In the previous chapter we have seen that the abuse clause in Article 17 ECHR was included in the Convention with the aim of preventing *'totalitarian currents from exploiting in their own interests the principles enunciated by the Convention'*.[1] The provision is the most explicit expression of the ambition of the Convention as a whole: preventing the emergence or re-emergence of totalitarian regimes in Western Europe. At the same time we have also seen that the text of the abuse clause in Article 17 ECHR is rather ambiguous. Neither the wording of the provision nor the *travaux préparatoires* make clear how it should be interpreted in practice. Who, exactly, can abuse the rights in the Convention? Can all the rights and freedoms in the Convention be abused? Which activities and acts are considered to aim at the destruction of rights and freedoms? What does the destruction of rights and freedoms actually mean? And what are the legal consequences of the abuse of fundamental rights and freedoms?

It is the role of the European Court of Human Rights (and of the European Commission of Human Rights until its dissolution in 1998) to interpret the Convention. This chapter seeks to identify the interpretation of Article 17 ECHR by the Court and the Commission. It analyses the judgments and admissibility decisions that have significantly contributed to the development, clarification, or modification of the interpretation of Article 17 ECHR. With a yearly case law running into thousands of judgments and decisions[2], the Strasbourg supervision has developed into a strong enforcement system. Yet, judgments and decisions in which the scope and interpretation of Article 17 ECHR are defined are rare. Especially in the first years after the entry into force of the Convention Article 17 ECHR led a relatively quiet existence. The American scholar Weil, writing in 1960, believed that Article 17 ECHR was one of criteria related to the admissibility of complaints *'which have not been used excessively in the past and those which by virtue of the passage of time are likely to be less important'*.[3] Over the years, however, the interest in Article 17

---

1 A. Robertson (ed.), *Collected edition of the 'Travaux Préparatoires' (hereafter referred to as 'TP')*, vol. II, The Hague: Martinus Nijhof, 1975-1985, p. 136 (Benvenuti).

2 In 2015, for example, the Court delivered 2,441 judgments and 43,135 applications were declared inadmissible or struck out of the list of cases by a Single Judge, a Committee or a Chamber: www.echr.coe.int/Documents/Stats_analysis_2015_ENG.pdf (accessed 11 April 2016).

3 G.L. Weil, 'Decisions on Inadmissible Applications by the European Commission of Human Rights', *American Journal of International Law*, vol. 54, no. 4, 1960, p. 880.

ECHR has increased and the provision seems less dormant than Weil predicted. In some of the cases discussed, the abuse clause was invoked by one of the parties. In other cases, however, the Commission and the Court referred to Article 17 ECHR *ex officio*, without the request of one of the parties.[4]

This chapter starts with the interpretation of the scope of the abuse clause: which rights and freedoms can be abused and what are the consequences of a finding of abuse for the exercise of the rights and freedoms in the Convention? Subsequently, it investigates the interpretation of the abuse clause in relation to the obligations of State Parties under the Convention. Next, it analyses the interpretation of Article 17 ECHR vis-à-vis groups and individuals according to a number of key judgments and admissibility decisions which are categorised by themes.

3.2 The scope of application of Article 17 ECHR

The wording of the prohibition of abuse of rights in Article 17 ECHR is rather broad, potentially covering all the rights and freedoms enshrined in the Convention. In the case *Lawless v. Ireland*, however, the Court has limited its application to those fundamental rights that directly contribute to the destruction of the rights guaranteed in the Convention. Earlier in the case against the German Communist Party (which will be discussed further on in this chapter), the Commission had found that because the party had engaged in activities aimed at the destruction of any of the rights and freedoms set forth in the Convention, it could not *'rest upon any provision of the Convention, least of all on Articles 9, 10 and 11'*.[5] Even though the Commission singled out Articles 9, 10 and 11 ECHR, this sentence suggests that the abuse of one of the rights or freedoms in the Convention would cause the applicant to be completely excluded from the protection of the Convention. The Irish government argued accordingly in the *Lawless* case that since the applicant had been involved with the anti-democratic IRA he should not be able to benefit from the protection of Articles 5, 6, and 7 ECHR or any other right guaranteed by the Convention for that matter.[6]

The Court, for its part, recalled that the aim of Article 17 ECHR is to prevent totalitarian groups from exploiting in their own interest the rights and freedoms set forth in the Convention. Yet, in order to achieve that aim, the Court found that *'it is not necessary to take away every one of the rights and freedoms guaranteed in the*

4 Y. Arai (rev.), 'Prohibition of abuse of the rights and freedoms set forth in the convention and of their limitation to a greater extent than is provided for in the convention (Article 17)', in: P. van Dijk et al. (eds.), *Theory and Practice of the European Convention on Human Rights*, 4th ed., Antwerp/Oxford: Intersentia, 2006, p. 1085; Y. Haeck, 'Artikel 17 Verbod van rechtsmisbruik' ['Article 17 Prohibition of Abuse of rights'], in: Vande Lanotte, J. and Haeck, Y. (eds.), *Handboek EVRM. Deel 2. Artikelsgewijze commentaar, volume II [Handbook ECHR. Part 2. Commentary by article, volume II]*, Antwerp/Oxford: Intersentia, 2004, p. 253, footnote 38.

5 EComHR 20 July 1957, *German Communist Party v. Germany*, appl. no. 250/57.

6 ECtHR 1 July 1961, *Lawless v. Ireland (no. 3)*, appl. no. 332/57.

Convention from persons found to be engaged in activities aimed at the destruction of any of those rights and freedoms'.[7] Article 17 ECHR *'covers essentially those rights which, if invoked, would facilitate the attempt to derive therefrom a right to engage personally in activities aimed at the destruction of 'any of the rights and freedoms set forth in the Convention'*.[8] From this perspective, Lawless had not *'relied on the Convention in order to justify or perform acts contrary to the rights and freedoms recognised therein'* but merely to complain about having been deprived of the protection of the right to liberty (Article 5 ECHR) and the right to a fair trial (Article 6 ECHR).[9] Even though Lawless had been arrested for his involvement in IRA activities, Article 17 ECHR did not therefore preclude him from claiming the protection of Articles 5 and 6 ECHR.[10] So, the Court's judgment in the *Lawless* case shows that only those rights and freedoms that have been abused with the aim of destroying rights and freedoms can be subject to forfeiture.[11]

Earlier the Commission had already narrowed down the interpretation of Article 17 ECHR by asserting that the provision does not allow for the permanent deprivation of rights and freedoms based on the mere fact that at one point the applicant acted upon totalitarian beliefs.[12] In the case *De Becker v. Belgium* the applicant complained about the forfeiture of his civil and political rights, owing to his pro-Nazi activities during the Second World War. The forfeiture made it impossible for him to continue his work as a journalist in Belgium. This, he claimed, constituted a violation of his right to freedom of expression guaranteed in Article 10 ECHR. Despite De Becker's (former) Nazi sympathies, the Commission refused to declare the application inadmissible on the basis of Article 17 ECHR.[13] In its report on this case it emphasised that Article 17 ECHR has a restricted scope and that its application should be strictly proportionate to the gravity and duration of the threat to democracy.[14] Even though the applicant's

7 Ibid, par. 6.
8 Ibid.
9 Ibid.
10 Recently, the Court came to a similar conclusion in the case *Varela Geis v. Spain*. This case was instigated by a bookshop owner who was convicted of selling books about the Holocaust. He complained under Article 6 ECHR (the right to a fair trial) that he had been sentenced for an offence that corresponded neither to the charges against him nor to his conviction at first instance. The Spanish government invited the Court to declare the application inadmissible based on Article 17 ECHR by referring to its standing case law regarding publications that aim to trivialise or justify the Holocaust. Endorsing its findings in *Lawless*, however, the Court observed that the applicant had not invoked the Convention to justify or perform acts contrary to the rights and freedoms guaranteed, but to complain about being deprived of the guarantees provided in Article 6 ECHR. Consequently, the Court did not consider it appropriate to apply Article 17 ECHR: ECtHR 5 March 2013, *Varela Geis c. Espangne*, appl. no. 61005/09, par. 40.
11 Haeck, *Handboek EVRM. Deel 2*, p. 258.
12 A.M. Williams, 'The European Convention on Human rights: a new use?', *Texas International Law Journal*, vol. 12, 1977, p. 282.
13 Williams, *Texas International Law Journal*, p. 282-283.
14 EComHR 8 January 1960 (report), *De Becker v. Belgium*, appl. no. 214/56, par. 279.

past pro-Nazi activities would have justified the application of Article 17 ECHR at the time they occurred, there were no indications that he was abusing his right to freedom of expression at the time of the proceedings. In sum, there was no proof that De Becker posed a threat to the democratic system at that time. The Commission therefore did not consider it necessary to declare the complaint in relation to Article 10 ECHR inadmissible based on Article 17 ECHR.

3.3 Article 17 ECHR invoked vis-à-vis a State Party

Article 17 ECHR does not only address groups and persons, but also states. In the Strasbourg case law, however, this aspect of the abuse clause plays a marginal role. In a number of cases before the Commission and the Court applicants have relied upon Article 17 ECHR. Although these claims are habitually barely substantiated, they can be read as a complaint that the respondent state party has used its power to interfere with a right in a manner beyond that permitted by the Convention.[15] Yet, the Commission and the Court have generally managed to avoid reaching a decision on this issue.[16] Commentators have noted that the absence of a violation of the right of the applicant generally releases the Court from any additional review under Article 17 ECHR.[17] Moreover, when the Court finds a violation of a right, it does not consider it necessary to examine the case under Article 17 ECHR.[18] So far, therefore, no state has ever been condemned for nullifying the rights set forth in the Convention by restricting them further than is provided for.[19]

The only time the prohibition to invoke restrictions with a view to undermining the Convention values played a (slight) role was in one of the rare inter-state procedures: the *Greek case*. Based on Article 33 ECHR any State Party may refer to the Court any alleged breach of the Convention and the protocols thereto by any other State Party. By submitting an inter-state complaint, the state is *'fulfilling its role as one of the collective guarantors of Convention rights'*.[20] In the Greek case, the applicant governments invoked Article 17 ECHR to challenge the applicability of Article 15 ECHR. After the 'Greek colonels' had seized power in a military coup

15 D.J. Harris et al. (eds.), *Harris, O'Boyle and Warbrick. Law of the European Convention on Human Rights*, 3rd ed., Oxford: Oxford University Press, 2014, p. 856.

16 Harris, p. 856.

17 A. Buyse, 'Contested contours. The limits of freedom of expression from an abuse of rights perspective – Articles 10 and 17 ECHR', in: E. Brems and J. Gerards (eds.), *Shaping Rights in the ECHR. The Role of the European Court of Human Rights in Determining the Scope of Human Rights*, Cambridge: Cambridge University Press, 2014, p. 188; Arai, *Theory and Practice of the ECHR,* p. 1089; J.E.S. Fawcett, *The Application of the European Convention on Human Rights*, Oxford: Clarendon Press, 1987, p. 315; J.A. Frowein, 'Artikel 17', in: J.A. Frowein and W. Peukert, *Europaïsche MenschenRechtsKonvention*, 3rd ed., Kehl am Rhein: N.P. Engel Verlag, 2009, p. 433.

18 Fawcett, *The Application of the ECHR*, p. 315; Buyse, *Shaping Rights in the ECHR*, p. 188.

19 Haeck, *Handboek EVRM. Deel 2*, p. 246.

20 Harris et al., *Law of the ECHR*, p. 115.

in April 1967, they suspended several key constitutional provisions.[21] According to the States Parties that brought the case before the Commission the totalitarian regime in Greece was destroying the fundamental rights enshrined in the Convention. The Greek government could not therefore rely on Article 15 ECHR, which allows states to derogate from some of its Convention obligations in a time of war or public emergency. The applicant governments *'while agreeing with the respondent Government that Article 15 and 17 were designed to protect democratic regimes against totalitarian conspiracies, maintained that the respondent Government had itself introduced a totalitarian regime in Greece and destroyed human rights and fundamental freedoms; it was therefore prevented from invoking Article 15 as a justification of its measures of derogation'*.[22] The Commission did not get to answer this question, because it had already found that the requirements of Article 15 ECHR had not been met.[23] Nevertheless, in his dissenting opinion Commission member Ermacora explicitly argued that Article 17 ECHR applied in this case. In his opinion, by causing a totalitarian situation the Greek government had engaged in activities or had performed acts aiming at the limitation of rights to a greater extent than is provided for in the Convention. He therefore considered the appeal to Article 15 ECHR by Greece incompatible with Article 17 ECHR.[24]

3.4 Article 17 ECHR applied vis-à-vis groups and individuals

The dominant role of the abuse clause in the Strasbourg case law is that of a rampart to prevent anti-democratic groups and individuals from relying on the Convention for the justification of subversive activities that threaten democracy or democratic values. We have seen in the previous chapter that the drafters of the Convention included Article 17 ECHR with the aim of preventing anti-democratic actors from *'from exploiting in their own interests the principles enunciated by the Convention'*.[25] So, even though the provision is also directed towards states, practically all significant judgments and decisions that contribute to the interpretation of Article 17 ECHR deal with the application of this provision vis-à-vis individuals and groups that rely on the Convention to complain about state interferences with the rights they enjoy under the Convention. These judgments and admissibility decisions are therefore the main focus of the remainder of this chapter.

---

21 Bates, *The Evolution of the ECHR*, p. 264.

22 EComHR 5 November 1969 (report), *Denmark, Norway, Sweden and the Netherlands v. Greece (The Greek case)*, appl. nos. 3321/67, 3322/67, 3323/67, 3344/67, par. 149.

23 Ibid, par. 150.

24 Dissenting opinion by Ermacora (Austria), see *Yearbook of the European Convention on Human Rights. The Greek case 1969*, The Hague: Martinus Nijhof, 1972, p. 102-103.

25 Robertson, *TP*, vol. II, p. 136 (Benvenuti).

In search of clarity, the judgments and admissibility decisions in which the Court and the Commission clarified the interpretation of Article 17 ECHR are in this chapter organised according to the main themes they deal with. These consist of: (i) revisionist speech, (ii) the promotion of a totalitarian ideology, (iii) hate speech, (iv) incitement to violence, and (v) challenges to the notion of secularism. Finally, an interesting case will be discussed, *Paksas v. Lithuania*, that does not fit within one of these categories.

There is a certain overlap between these categories. Holocaust denial, for example, is often referred to as a common feature of the promotion of a totalitarian ideology (Nazism) and can also be labelled as hate speech. Any categorisation is necessarily a simplification of a complex reality. Realising that alternative classifications are possible, however, these categories have been identified because they allow for an overview of the relevant case law that effectively demonstrates the difficulties and inconsistencies involved in the interpretation of Article 17 ECHR.

3.4.1 Revisionist speech

Cases concerning Holocaust denial are a dominant category in the case law on Article 17 ECHR. According to long-standing Strasbourg case law individuals in a democratic society have the right to express their views, even if these run counter to the views of the majority and may be perceived as unwelcome.[26] Yet, this protection is not so broad as to cover the denial of the historical events of the Holocaust. The Commission and the Court have consistently ruled that Holocaust denial constitutes an abusive exercise of the right to freedom of expression, which based on the prohibition of abuse of rights in Article 17 ECHR fall outside the scope of the protection of the fundamental rights guaranteed in the Convention.[27]

Holocaust denial is (explicitly or implicitly) recognised as a criminal offence in many European states.[28] Furthermore, the issue of Holocaust denial has also been addressed at the international level. In 2007 the UN General Assembly passed a resolution condemning Holocaust denial and urging member states to *'reject any denial of the Holocaust as a historical event, either in full or in part, or any activities to this end'*.[29] In addition, several intergovernmental organisations have passed resolutions and concluded agreements *'commemorating the Holocaust and condemning its denial or trivialization'*.[30] Also within the framework of the Council of Europe member

26 ECtHR 7 December 1976, *Handyside v. the UK*, appl. no. 5493/72, par. 49.

27 See for a similar conclusion ECtHR 13 December 2005 (dec.), *Witzsch v. Germany*, appl. no. 7485/03.

28 L. Pech, 'The Law of Holocaust Denial in Europe', in: L. Hennebel and T. Hochmann, *Genocide Denials and the Law*, Oxford: Oxford University Press, 2011, p. 185.

29 UN Resolution on Holocaust denial adopted by the General Assembly on 22 March 2007, *UN Doc.* A/RES/61/255.

30 M. Whine, 'Expanding Holocaust Denial and Legislation Against It', in: I. Hare and J. Weinstein (eds.), *Extreme Speech and Democracy*, Oxford: Oxford University Press, 2009, p. 541-543.

states have repeatedly condemned Holocaust denial and have undertaken to fight it, often within the context of the fight against anti-Semitism.[31] The most recent manifestation of the Council of Europe's denunciation of Holocaust denial is found in the 2007 Parliamentary Assembly Resolution No. 1563 on Combating Anti-Semitism in Europe, which called upon the Member States to *'make a criminal offence the public denial, trivialisation, justification or praise, with racist intentions, of crimes of genocide, crimes against humanity or war crimes in accordance with ECRI General Policy Recommendation No. 7 on national legislation to combat racism and racial discrimination, adopted in December 2002'*.[32]

For their part, the Court and the Commission have repeatedly held that the Holocaust is a *'clearly established historical fact'*.[33] The extermination of millions of Jews during the Holocaust, the Commission held, is *'common knowledge established beyond any doubt by overwhelming evidence of all kind'*.[34] Hence it held that, these crimes cannot be a matter of debate within the framework of the Convention. As a consequence, activities whereby the applicant denied the Holocaust or any historical circumstances related to it are categorically excluded from the protection of the freedom of expression in Article 10 ECHR.

3.4.1.1 Early Commission cases regarding Holocaust denial

During the 1980s and the 1990s the Commission was repeatedly faced with applications lodged by applicants who had been convicted of denial of the Holocaust and related

---

31 See e.g. CoE, Committee of Ministers, *Recommendation No. R(97)20 on 'hate speech'*, Strasbourg, 30 October 1997; CoE, ECRI, *General Policy Recommendation No. 7 on national legislation to combat racism and racial discrimination*, Strasbourg, 13 December 2002 (CRI(2003)8); and CoE, *Additional Protocol to the Convention on Cybercrime, concerning the criminalisation of acts of a racist and xenophobic nature committed through computer systems*, 28 January 2003. So far, 24 Member States of the CoE have ratified this Additional Protocol: www.coe.int/en/web/conventions/full-list/-/conventions/treaty/189/signatures?p_auth=xaLukj0Y (accessed 11 April 2016]. According to Article 6(2)(sub b), however, states are allowed to make reservations with regard to the requirement in Article 6(1). Four Member States (Denmark, Finland, Montenegro and Norway) did that: www.coe.int/en/web/conventions/full-list/-/conventions/treaty/189/declarations?p_auth=xaLukj0Y (accessed 11 April 2016).

32 Article 12.3 of the CoE, Parliamentary Assembly, *Resolution No. 1563 on Combating Anti-Semitism in Europe*, Strasbourg, 27 June 2007.

33 ECtHR 23 September 1998 (GC), *Lehideux and Isorni v. France*, appl. no. 24662/94, par. 47.

34 EComHR 16 July 1982, *X v. Germany*, appl. no. 9235/81, par. 5.

crimes.[35] Around that time Europe was increasingly faced with Holocaust deniers and states had progressively taken legal measures to curtail their freedom to spread their views.[36] This eventually led to a number of cases in which the Commission was asked to rule on the legitimacy of these convictions in the light of the right to freedom of expression in Article 10 ECHR. The line of reasoning regarding the interpretation of Article 17 ECHR followed by the Commission in these cases is very similar.

In these cases the Commission generally started by considering that there had been an interference with the applicant's freedom of expression as protected in Article 10(1) ECHR and that such an interference constitutes a violation of the Convention unless it is justified under the second paragraph of Article 10 ECHR. In respect of the question whether the interference was necessary in a democratic society the Commission turned to Article 17 ECHR and recalled that no one should be allowed to derive from the Convention *'a right to engage in activities aimed at the destruction of any of the rights and freedoms set forth in the Convention, inter alia the right to freedom of expression'*.[37] The Commission subsequently focussed on the applicant's attempt to incite hatred against Jews. In that context it found that the public interest in the prevention of crime and disorder and the protection of the reputation and the rights of Jews outweigh in a democratic society the freedom to deny the Holocaust.[38] An applicant who tries to rely on Article 10 ECHR to justify denying the genocide against the Jews by the Nazi regime essentially seeks to use the freedom of expression *'as a basis for activities which are contrary to the text and spirit of the Convention and which, if admitted, would contribute to the destruction of the rights and freedoms set forth in the Convention'*.[39] Under those circumstances the Commission found that the interference with the applicant's freedom of expression could be considered as 'necessary in a democratic society' within the meaning of Article 10(2) ECHR. In a

35 See e.g. EComHR 29 March 1993, *F.P. v. Germany*, appl. no. 19459/92; EComHR 11 January 1995, *Walendy v. Germany*, appl. no. 21128/92; EComHR 6 September 1995, *Remer v. Germany*, appl. no. 25096/94; EComHR 18 October 1995, *Honsik v. Austria*, appl. no. 25062/94; EComHR 29 November 1995, *Nationaldemokratische Partei Deutschlands, Bezirksverband München-Oberbayern v. Germany*, appl. no. 25992/94; EComHR 16 January 1996, *Rebhandl v. Austria*, appl. no. 24398/94; EComHR 24 June 1996, *Marais v. France*, appl. no. 31159/96; EComHR 26 June 1996, *D.I. v. Germany*, appl. no. 26551/95; EComHR 9 September 1998, *Herwig Nachtmann v. Austria*, appl. no. 36773/97; EComHR 20 April 1999, *Witzsch v. Germany*, appl. no. 41448/98.

36 R.A. Kahn, *Holocaust Denial and the Law: A Comparative Study*, New York: Palgrave Macmillan, 2004, p. 1.

37 See e.g. EComHR 6 September 1995, *Remer v. Germany*, appl. no. 25096/94, par. 1.

38 EComHR 6 September 1995, *Remer v. Germany*, appl. no. 25096/94, par. 1; EComHR 29 November 1995, *Nationaldemokratische Partei Deutschlands, Bezirksverband München-Oberbayern v. Germany*, appl. no. 25992/94; EComHR 16 January 1996, *Rebhandl v. Austria*, appl. no. 24398/94, par. 3.

39 EComHR 2 September 1994, *Ochensberger v. Austria*, appl. no. 21318/93, par. 1; EComHR 18 October 1995, *Honsik v. Austria*, appl. no. 25062/94; EComHR 24 June 1996, *Marais v. France*, appl. no. 31159/96, par. 1; EComHR 16 January 1996, *Rebhandl v. Austria*, appl. no. 24398/94, par. 3.

couple of other cases the Commission came to a similar conclusion after finding that denial of the Holocaust ran *'counter [to] one of the basic ideas of the Convention, as expressed in its preamble, namely justice and peace'*.[40] Accordingly, the Commission concluded that the facts did not disclose any appearance of a violation of Article 10 ECHR. Eventually, the Commission declared all these applications inadmissible as manifestly ill-founded.

Interestingly, the Commission had earlier come to the same conclusion in a couple of cases concerning Holocaust denial, yet without mentioning Article 17 ECHR. The 1982 case *X. v. Germany*, for example, concerned an applicant who was convicted of displaying pamphlets in his garden describing the Holocaust as a Zionistic swindle.[41] The Commission held that by describing the Holocaust in these terms, *'the pamphlets in question not only gave a distorted picture of the relevant historical facts but also contained an attack on the reputation of all those who were described as liars or swindlers, or at least as persons profiting from or interested in such lies or swindles'*.[42] The restriction of his right to freedom of expression was therefore necessary in a democratic society, because, as the Commission put it, *'[s]uch a society rests on the principles of tolerance and broadmindedness which the pamphlets in question clearly failed to observe'*.[43] For that reason it considered the complaint manifestly ill-founded and declared the application inadmissible.

3.4.1.2 Garaudy v. France

Yet, the hallmark case on Holocaust denial is the 2003 case *Garaudy v. France*. In his book *Les Mythes fondateurs de la politique Israelienne* the French philosopher, writer and former politician Roger Garaudy had openly disputed the crimes committed by the Nazis against the Jews and referred to the Holocaust and the use of gas chambers as a myth. Based on Article 24*bis* of the Law on the Freedom of the Press of 1881, which was amended by the 'Gayssot Act' in 1990, Garaudy was convicted of denying crimes against humanity, public defamation of the Jewish community and incitement to discrimination and racial hatred. He argued before the Court that *'his book did not deny that the Nazis had committed crimes against the Jews or that these were crimes against humanity, but was a political work whose main purpose had been to criticise*

40 EComHR 6 September 1995, *Remer v. Germany*, appl. no. 25096/94, par. 1. See also EComHR 18 October 1995, *Honsik v. Austria*, appl. no. 25062/94; EComHR 29 November 1995, *Nationaldemokratische Partei Deutschlands, Bezirksverband München-Oberbayern v. Germany*, appl. no. 25992/94; EComHR 24 June 1996, *Marais v. France*, appl. no. 31159/96, par. 1; EComHR 26 June 1996, *D.I. v. Germany*, appl. no. 26551/95, par. 2.

41 EComHR 16 July 1982, *X. v. Germany*, appl. no. 9235/81. See for a similar line of reasoning also EComHR 14 July 1983, *T. v. Belgium*, appl. no. 9777/82.

42 EComHR 16 July 1982, *X. v. Germany*, appl. no. 9235/81, par. 4.

43 Ibid, par. 4.

the State of Israel's policies... In his view, it followed that his criminal convictions amounted to unjustified interference with the exercise of his right to freedom of expression'.[44] The French government, for its part, submitted that the application should be declared inadmissible in accordance with Article 17 ECHR. If the Court would not follow this argument, the government subsidiarily argued that at the very least the limitation clause in Article 10(2) ECHR would have to be read in the light of the obligations of the applicant under Article 17 ECHR.

The Court's ruling started by recalling that notwithstanding the *'overriding and essential nature'* of the right to freedom of expression in a democratic society, this right has its limits.[45] In that regard the Court reiterated its earlier findings in the case *Lehideux and Isorni*, which will be discussed later in this chapter, that there is a *'category of clearly established historical facts – such as the Holocaust – whose negation or revision would be removed from the protection of Article 10 by Article 17'*.[46] With regard to Garaudy's conviction for denying crimes against humanity, the Court referred to the purpose of Article 17 ECHR as set out in the *Lawless* case, which *'in so far as it refers to[...] individuals is to make it impossible for them to derive from the Convention a right to engage in any activity or perform any act aimed at destroying any of the rights and freedoms set forth in in the Convention; [...] no person may be able to take advantage of the provisions of the Convention to perform acts aimed at destroying the aforesaid rights and freedoms'*.[47] The Court subsequently found that Garaudy, far from confining himself to criticising Zionism, systematically denied the crimes against humanity perpetrated by the Nazis. The real purpose of that approach, according to the Court, was to rehabilitate the Nazi regime, and as a consequence, accusing the victims of the Holocaust of falsifying history. The Court therefore considered that '*the main content and general tenor of the applicant's book, and thus its aim, are markedly revisionist and therefore run counter to the fundamental values of the Convention, as expressed in its Preamble, namely justice and peace. It considers that the applicant attempts to deflect Article 10 of the Convention from its real purpose by using his right to freedom of expression for ends which are contrary to the text and spirit of the Convention. Such ends, if admitted, would contribute to the destruction of the rights and freedoms guaranteed by the Convention. Accordingly, the Court considers that, in accordance with Article 17 of the Convention, the applicant cannot rely on the provisions of Article 10 of the Convention regarding his conviction for denying crimes against humanity'*.[48] For that reason, the Court declared the application incompatible *ratione materiae* with the Convention pursuant to Article 35(3) ECHR.

44 ECtHR 24 June 2003 (dec.), *Garaudy v. France*, appl. no. 65831/01, par. 1.
45 Ibid, par. 1.
46 Ibid, par. 1.
47 ECtHR 24 June 2003 (dec.), *Garaudy v. France*, appl. no. 65831/01, par. 1. See also ECtHR 1 July 1961, *Lawless v. Ireland (no. 3)*, appl. no. 332/57, par. 7.
48 ECtHR 24 June 2003 (dec.), *Garaudy v. France*, appl. no. 65831/01, par. 1.

Contrary to the earlier Commission cases in which the Commission referred to Article 17 ECHR in the context of the necessity of the conviction under Article 10(2) ECHR, the Court applied Article 17 ECHR at the admissibility stage of the proceedings. Based on this approach, the Court ruled that the applicant could not benefit from the protection of Article 10 ECHR.[49] Accordingly, the Court was exempted from evaluating this part of the application on its merits in the light of the limitation clause in paragraph 2 of Article 10 ECHR.[50] Buyse has suggested that this change in approach to the application of Article 17 ECHR *'may be explained by an increasing awareness in the 1980s and 1990s of the pernicious nature of Holocaust denial'*.[51] Others, however, have argued that the aim to rehabilitate a totalitarian regime played a crucial role in the decision to apply Article 17 ECHR and to exclude Garaudy's revisionist utterances from the protection of the Convention.[52]

3.4.1.3 Witzsch v. Germany

Worth mentioning in this context are also the cases of the German teacher and politician Witzsch, who appeared before the Strasbourg Court twice after being convicted of revisionism. The reason for the first case were the letters written by Witzsch to several Bavarian politicians in which he complained about the planned amendment of the German Penal Code that would punish incitement to hatred, expressly intended to penalise denial of the Holocaust.[53] To these letters he had attached a statement in which he denied the mass killing of Jews and others in gas chambers. He was subsequently convicted of disparaging the dignity of the deceased. He complained before the Court that his conviction constituted a violation of his freedom of expression protected in Article 10 ECHR. The Court recalled that the

---

49 See for a similar approach in a case concerning Holocaust denial ECtHR 13 December 2005, *Witzsch v. Germany*, appl. no. 7485/03.

50 This part of the application concerned Garaudy's conviction for denying crimes against humanity. With regard to his complaint about his conviction for racially defamatory statements and incitement to racial hatred, however, the Court seems to revert to its initial indirect approach to Article 17 ECHR. With regard to that part of the application the Court held that it *'has had serious doubts as to whether the expression of such opinions could attract the protection of the provisions of Article 10 of the Convention. Indeed, although political criticism of the State of Israel, or any other State, does indisputably fall under that provision, the Court finds that the applicant does not limit himself to such criticism, but in fact pursues a proven racist aim'*. Next, the Court went on to conclude that it *'does not consider it necessary to decide that issue in the present case, as it considers that this part of the complaint is in any event manifestly ill-founded'*, an approach similar to that in earlier Commission cases.

51 Buyse, *Shaping Rights in the ECHR*, p. 195.

52 See in more detail S.G. Hinghofer-Szalkay, 'Extreme Meinungen und Meinungsäußerungsfreiheit: Die Schranke des Artikel 17 EMRK. Die Straßburger Rechtsprechung und ihre Struktur', *Journal für Rechtspolitik*, vol. 20, no. 2, 2012, p. 111.

53 See Chapter eight on the German legislation on Holocaust denial.

negation or revision of clearly established historical facts, such as the Holocaust, would be removed from the protection of Article 10 ECHR by Article 17 ECHR.[54] Still, the Court continued to examine the case under Article 10(2) ECHR. In this regard, it held that the public interest in the prevention of crime and disorder and the protection of the reputation and the rights of Jews outweigh in a democratic society the freedom of the individual to deny the Holocaust.[55] The Court subsequently found that the facts in the case demonstrated that the reasons for the applicant's conviction were relevant and sufficient and the interference could therefore be regarded as being necessary in a democratic society. There was accordingly no appearance of a breach of Article 10 ECHR and the Court declared the application manifestly ill-founded.

Six years later Witzsch again appeared before the Court. This time he had written a letter to a well-known professor of history in reply to an article of the latter in a German magazine about the responsibility of Hitler and the Nazis in the mass killing of the Jews. In his letter Witzsch qualified these statements as *'false and historically unsustainable'*.[56] He was again convicted of disparaging the dignity of the deceased. Before the Court he complained of an infringement of his right to freedom of expression. This time the Court's approach differed from that of six years earlier. After asserting that the applicant had denied an established historical fact relating to the responsibility of Hitler and the NSDAP for the Holocaust and had thereby disparaged the dignity of the deceased, the Court immediately turned to Article 17 ECHR. In that context the Court found that the applicant's statements showed disdain towards the victims of the Holocaust. The Court therefore found *'that the views expressed by the applicant ran counter to the text and the spirit of the Convention. Consequently, he cannot, in accordance with Article 17 of the Convention, rely on the provisions of Article 10 as regards his statements at issue'*.[57] The Court accordingly considered the application incompatible *ratione materiae* with the provisions of the Convention and declared it inadmissible.

3.4.1.4 Broad interpretation of Article 17 ECHR with regard to Holocaust denial

The case law of the Commission and the Court shows that the prohibition of a denial of the Holocaust pursuant to Article 17 ECHR is rather broad. The exclusion of Holocaust denial from the protection of Article 10 ECHR not only refers to the *'bare denial'* of the Holocaust, but also to other forms of revision, apologia, justification,

---

54 ECtHR 20 April 1999 (dec.), *Witzsch v. Germany*, appl. no. 41448/98. See also ECtHR 23 September 1998 (GC), *Lehideux and Isorni v. France*, appl. no. 24662/94, par. 47.

55 ECtHR 20 April 1999 (dec.), *Witzsch v. Germany*, appl. no. 41448/98, par. 1. See also EComHR 6 September 1995, *Remer v. Germany*, appl. no. 25096/94, par. 1; EComHR 29 November 1995, *Nationaldemokratische Partei Deutschlands, Bezirksverband München-Oberbayern v. Germany*, appl. no. 25992/94; EComHR 16 January 1996, *Rebhandl v. Austria*, appl. no. 24398/94, par. 3.

56 ECtHR 13 December 2005 (dec.), *Witzsch v. Germany*, appl. no. 7485/03, par. A.

57 ECtHR 13 December 2005 (dec.), *Witzsch v. Germany*, appl. no. 7485/03, par. 3.

or trivialisation of any of the historical events related to the Holocaust.[58] In the case *Witzsch v. Germany* from 2005 that was previously discussed, for example, the Court noted that *'the applicant denied neither the Holocaust as such nor the existence of gas chambers. However, he denied an equally significant and established circumstance of the Holocaust considering it false and historically unsustainable that Hitler and the NSDAP had planned, initiated and organised the mass killing of Jews'*.[59] Also the fact that the statements were made in a private letter and not before a larger audience was irrelevant in the eyes of the Court. The Court therefore found that in accordance with Article 17 ECHR the applicant could not rely on the protection of Article 10 ECHR.

Recently, the Court again gave a rather extensive interpretation of the role of Article 17 ECHR in Holocaust-related cases in the case *M'Bala M'Bala*. The cases concerned the French comedian and political activist Dieudonné, who was convicted in 2009 of public insults directed at persons of Jewish origin or faith. At the end of a comedy show Dieudonné had invited Robert Faurisson, who has been repeatedly convicted of Holocaust denial, to join him on stage to receive a *'prize for unfrequentability and insolence'*.[60] The prize, a three-branched candlestick with an apple on each branch, was awarded to him by an actor dressed as a Jewish deportee in a concentration camp. Even though neither Dieudonné nor Faurisson explicitly mentioned the Holocaust in their speeches, based on the circumstances of the scene the Court concluded that the facts demonstrated hatred and anti-Semitism and called the Holocaust into question.[61] In that context, the Court held that even though it had so far only applied Article 17 ECHR to explicit and direct denials or trivialisations of the Holocaust that did not require any further interpretation, a hateful and anti-Semitic attitude disguised as an artistic production is just as dangerous as a frontal and direct attack. The disturbing scene was therefore also excluded from the protection of the right to freedom of expression in Article 10 ECHR.[62]

Then again, when the Holocaust is referred to without elements of glorification, the Court does not consider it appropriate to apply Article 17 ECHR. For example, when two Germans protested against a doctor performing abortions by associating his work with the Holocaust (*'then: Holocaust, today: Babycaust'*)[63], the Court

---

58 M. Oetheimer, 'Protecting freedom of expression: the challenge of hate speech in the European Court of Human Rights case law', *Cardozo Journal of International and Comparative Law*, vol. 17, no. 3, 2009, p. 432.

59 ECtHR 13 December 2005 (dec.), *Witzsch v. Germany*, appl. no. 7485/03, par. 3.

60 Press release, 'European Convention on Human Rights does not protect negationist and anti-Semitic performances', 10 November 2015, ECHR 354(2015), http://hudoc.echr.coe.int/eng?i=003-5219244-6470067 (accessed 11 April 2016).

61 ECtHR 20 October 2015 (dec.), *M'Bala M'Bala c. France*, appl. no. 25239/13, par 39. See also the case note to this case by P.E. de Morree, *EHRC* 2016/45, par. 4-6.

62 ECtHR 20 October 2015 (dec.), *M'Bala M'Bala c. France*, appl. no. 25239/13, par 40.

63 ECtHR 13 January 2011, *Hoffer and Annen v. Germany*, appl. nos. 397/07 and 2322/07, par. 8.

held that the applicants *'by comparing the performance of abortions to the mass-homicide committed during the Holocaust, had violated the physician's personality rights in a particular[ly] serious way'* and found no violation of Article 10 ECHR, without any reference to Article 17 ECHR.[64] And when the animal rights organisation PETA was prevented from referring to the Holocaust in an advertising campaign under the heading *'The Holocaust on your plate'*, even though the Court observed that '*the intended poster campaign did not pursue the aim to debase the depicted concentration camp inmates, as the pictures merely implied that the suffering inflicted upon the depicted humans and animals was equal'*, it respected that a reference to the Holocaust was particularly sensitive in the context of the German past and found no violation of Article 10 ECHR, yet again without any mention of Article 17 ECHR.[65]

3.4.1.5 The Court's approach to other historical debates

In contrast with the broad interpretation of Article 17 ECHR in cases concerning Holocaust denial, the Court adopted a much more restrictive approach when asked to rule on debates concerning other major historical human rights violations. In cases regarding other historical events, the Court has repeatedly stressed that *'it is an integral part of freedom of expression to seek historical truth'*.[66] The Court considers that its own role in such debates should be modest: *'it is not the Court's role to arbitrate the underlying historical issues, which are part of a continuing debate between historians that shapes opinion as to the events which took place and their interpretation'*.[67] It is *'essential in a democratic society that a debate on the causes of acts of particular gravity amounting to crimes against humanity should be able to take place freely'*.[68]

In the case *Lehideux and Isorni v. France*, for example, the Court made a distinction between the negation of the Holocaust as *'a clearly established historical fact'* that is excluded from the protection of the Convention and ongoing debates regarding historical events that are protected by the Convention.[69] The case concerned a

64 Ibid, par. 45-50.
65 ECtHR 8 November 2012, *PETA Deutschland v. Germany*, appl. no. 43481/09, par. 48-51.
66 ECtHR 29 June 2004, *Chauvy and others v. France*, appl. no. 64915/01, par 69. See also ECtHR 14 September 2010, *Dink v. Turkey*, app. nos. 2668/07, 6102/08, 30079/08, 7072/09 and 7124/09, par. 135; ECtHR 31 January 2006, *Giniewski v. France*, appl. no. 64016/00, par. 51.
67 ECtHR 29 June 2004, *Chauvy and others v. France*, appl. no. 64915/01, par 69; ECtHR 21 September 2006, *Monnat v. Switzerland*, appl. no. 73604/01, par. 57; ECtHR 22 April 2010, *Fatullayev v. Azerbaijan*, appl. no. 40984/07, par. 87; ECtHR 31 January 2006, *Giniewski v. France*, appl. no. 64016/00, par. 51; ECtHR 15 October 2015 (GC), *Perinçek v. Switzerland*, appl. no. 27510/08, par. 214.
68 ECtHR 31 January 2006, *Giniewski v. France*, appl. no. 64016/00, par. 51. See also ECtHR 17 December 2013, *Perinçek v. Switzerland*, appl. no. 27510/08, par. 103.
69 Hennebel and Hochmann, *Genocide Denials and the Law*, p. 185 and xxxv.

publication on the role of the former Marshal Pétain, in which this chief of state of France during the Second World War who collaborated with Nazi Germany was presented in a favourable light. Presumably with the case law on Holocaust denial in mind, the French Government claimed that the publication *'infringed the very spirit of the Convention and the essential values of democracy'*.[70] The Court, for its part, concluded that the role of Pétain *'does not belong to the category of clearly established historical facts – such as the Holocaust – whose negation or revision would be removed from the protection of Article 10 by Article 17'*. The Court went on to find that *'it does not appear that the applicants attempted to deny or revise what they themselves referred to in their publication as 'Nazi atrocities and persecutions' or 'German omnipotence and barbarism'*.[71] The publication was therefore not *a priori* excluded from the protection of Article 10 ECHR. With regard to the necessity of the interference in a democratic society, the Court found that the applicants were not in fact praising Pétain's policy, but calling for the revision of his conviction.[72] Subsequently, the Court stressed that the events referred to in the publication had occurred more than forty years previously. Even though remarks such as those of the applicants were likely to reopen controversy and bring back painful memories the Court argued that *'the lapse of time makes it inappropriate to deal with such remarks, forty years on, with the same severity as ten or twenty years previously. That forms part of the efforts that every country must make to debate its own history openly and dispassionately'*.[73]

Nonetheless, the Court was divided over the issue as six of the twenty-one judges voted against the opinion of the majority. All five judges that wrote a dissenting opinion in this case stressed, among other things, *'that such issues should be left within France's margin of appreciation, since they concerned an issue peculiar to that country's history, which could be better decided by national than by international courts'*.[74] At the same time, out of feelings of guilt and shame states may be inclined to suppress the memory of painful historical events and silence the public debate on such issues. Gerards, for example, has argued that all societies have a logical inclination to keep silent about cruelties committed by their ancestors. Here an international authority, such as the Strasbourg Court, may be better capable of

70 ECtHR 23 September 1998, *Lehideux and Isorni v. France*, appl. no. 24662/94, par. 35.

71 Ibid, par. 47. See also ECtHR 29 June 2004, *Chauvy and others v. France*, appl. no. 64915/01, par. 69, regarding alleged defamatory statements accusing a leader of the French resistance of treason in which the Court repeated this conclusion.

72 ECtHR 23 September 1998, *Lehideux and Isorni v. France*, appl. no. 24662/94, par. 53.

73 Ibid, par. 55.

74 Buyse, *Shaping Rights in the ECHR*, p. 199. See the joint dissenting opinion by Judge Foighel (Denmark), joined by Judges Loizou (Cyprus) and Freeland (United Kingdom), par. 5-6; the dissenting opinion by Judge Casadevall (Andorra), par. 1; and the dissenting opinion Judge Morenilla (Spain), par. 3.

judging whether the national legal order should give latitude to discussions regarding its past.[75]

The line of argumentation of the majority in the *Lehideux and Isorni* case was subsequently confirmed in two other French cases. First, in the case *Chauvy and others v. France* the Court had to decide on a debate about the alleged double role played by a member of the French resistance. In a book the applicants had accused the leader of the French resistance, Aubrac, of treason during the Second World War. The Court emphasised that *'it is an integral part of freedom of expression to seek historical truth and it is not the Court's role to arbitrate the underlying historical issues, which are part of a continuing debate between historians that shapes opinion as to the events which took place and their interpretation'*. With regard to the role of Aubrac, the Court concluded that the issue in question also did *'not belong to the category of clearly established historical facts – such as the Holocaust – whose negation or revision is removed from the protection of Article 10 by Article 17 of the Convention'*.[76]

Subsequently, in the case *Orban and others v. France* the Court was faced with a debate regarding the memoires of the French general Aussaresses, who had served in Algeria during its war of independence against France. In his memoires, Aussaresses described the shocking war crimes in Algeria in which he took part, such as torturing and summary executions. He declared that he did not regret the things he had done, because they were an efficient way to satisfy the orders from France.[77] The Court, for its part, stressed that there is no doubt that expressions that aim to justify war crimes other than those committed during the Second World War are in principle equally characterised as deviating Article 10 ECHR from its purpose and are therefore excluded from the protection of the right to freedom of expression.[78] But, according to the Court, the aim of the publication in question was not the revision of the alleged war crimes committed by the French military during the Algerian war for independence. On the contrary, the applicants aimed to contribute to a historical debate on this topic that, although sensitive and polemical, is of general interest: *'[i]l ressort en effet du contenu dudit ouvrage que son auteur, affecté en Algérie entre la fin de l'année 1954 et l'automne 1957 en qualité d'officier des services de renseignement, entendait contribuer à un « débat historique » – selon les mots des requérants – et apporter son témoignage direct sur un sujet qui, bien que sensible et polémique, relevait sans aucun doute de l'intérêt général : la question de l'usage de la torture et du recours aux exécutions sommaires par les autorités françaises durant*

75 J.H. Gerards, Case note to ECtHR 15 January 2009, *Orban and others v. France*, appl. no. 20985/05, *EHRC* 2009/30.

76 ECtHR 29 June 2004, *Chauvy and others v. France*, appl. no. 64915/01, par. 69.

77 Gerards, Case note to *Orban and others v. France*, *EHRC* 2009/30.

78 ECtHR 15 January 2009, *Orban and others v. France*, appl. no. 20985/05, par. 35.

la guerre d'Algérie'.[79] The Court did not therefore consider it appropriate in this case to apply Article 17 ECHR.[80]

Furthermore, in the case *Leroy v. France* the Court refused to apply Article 17 ECHR to what the French government considered the glorification of the 9/11 terrorist attacks on the World Trade Center in New York. A cartoon by the cartoonist Denis Leroy representing the attack on the Twin Towers with the caption *'We have all dreamt of it... Hamas did it'*, was published in a newspaper two days after the attacks. France claimed that the cartoon should be excluded from the protection of the right to freedom of expression. Referring to the Commission's and the Court's case law regarding Holocaust denial and hate speech the French government suggested that terrorism apologia should likewise fall within the scope of Article 17 ECHR.[81] The Court, however, held that the cartoon did not belong to the category of publications that would be withdrawn from the protection of Article 10 ECHR by Article 17 ECHR.[82] The underlying message of the caricature, the destruction of American imperialism, was not aimed at the repudiation of fundamental rights and was therefore not to be compared with racism, anti-Semitism and Islamophobia, themes that have been attacked under Article 17 ECHR in the case law referred to by the French government.[83]

Finally, in the case *Fatullayev v. Azerbaijan* the Court found that also the ongoing debate regarding the '*Khojaly events*' was not removed from the protection of Article 10 ECHR by virtue of Article 17 of the Convention.[84] Azerbaijan had invoked the abuse clause against the applicant who had been convicted of expressing a reading of the events at the town of Khojaly during the war in Nagorno-Karabakh that differed from the generally accepted version, according to which hundreds of Azerbaijani civilians had been killed by the Armenian armed forces in the early 1990s.[85] The Court found that many aspects and details of these events are still unclear. The Court held that these matters *'still appear to be open to ongoing debate among historians, and as such should be a matter of general interest in modern Azerbaijani society. In this connection, the Court also reiterates that it is essential in a democratic society that a debate on the causes of acts of particular gravity which may amount to war crimes or crimes against humanity should be able to take place freely'*.[86] The Court

79 Ibid, par. 35.
80 Ibid, par. 35.
81 ECtHR 2 October 2008, *Leroy v. France*, appl. no. 36109/03, par. 23-24.
82 Ibid, par. 27.
83 ECtHR 2 October 2008, *Leroy v. France*, appl. no. 36109/03, par. 27.
84 ECtHR 22 April 2010, *Fatullayev v. Azerbaijan*, appl. no. 40984/07, par. 81.
85 See also Buyse, *Shaping Rights in the ECHR*, p. 206.
86 ECtHR 22 April 2010, *Fatullayev v. Azerbaijan*, appl. no. 40984/07, par. 87.

continued that the applicant had not denied the mass killings or expressed contempt for the victims of these events. The applicant was in fact merely *'supporting one of the conflicting opinions in the debate concerning the existence of an escape corridor for the refugees and, based on that, expressing the view that some Azerbaijani fighters might have also borne a share of the responsibility for the massacre. By doing so, however, he did not seek to exonerate those who were commonly accepted to be the culprits of this massacre, to mitigate their respective responsibility or to otherwise approve of their actions'*.[87] The Court therefore did not consider it appropriate to apply Article 17 ECHR and dealt with the case under Article 10(2) ECHR. Eventually the Court unanimously concluded that the conviction of the applicant constituted a violation of Article 10 ECHR.

3.4.1.6 Perinçek v. Switzerland

Of particular interest in this regard is the Grand Chamber's judgment in the case *Perinçek v Switzerland*. The applicant in this case was a Turkish politician who was convicted in Switzerland of publicly expressing the view that the mass deportations and massacres of Armenians by the Ottoman Empire in 1915 and the following years did not amount to genocide. The question as to how the mass deportations and massacres are to be qualified is part of an ongoing political debate in which Turkey, considered as the successor to the Ottoman Empire, has always argued against the qualification of these events as genocide. Article 261bis of the Swiss Criminal Code makes it a criminal offence to intentionally and publicly deny, trivialise, or seek justification for genocide or other crimes against humanity guided by motives of racial discrimination.[88] The Swiss Federal Court had held, among other things, that this provision does not exclusively apply to a denial of the Holocaust but also to the renunciation of other genocides. It subsequently found that *'there was a general consensus, particularly among academics, as to the classification of the events of 1915 as genocide'* and that the local court was right not to *'allow the appellant's attempt to open a historical and legal debate on this issue'*.[89] Worth mentioning is

87 Ibid, par. 81.

88 Article 261bis of the Swiss Criminal Code (Strafgesetzbuch/Code penal/Codice penale) reads *'any person who publicly denigrates or discriminates against another or a group of persons on the grounds of their race, ethnic origin or religion in a manner that violates human dignity, whether verbally, in writing or pictorially, by using gestures, through acts of aggression or by other means, or any person who on any of these grounds denies, trivialises or seeks justification for genocide or other crimes against humanity... is liable to a custodial sentence not exceeding three years or to a monetary penalty'*, www.admin.ch/ch/e/rs/3/311.0.en.pdf (accessed 11 April 2016).

89 ECtHR 15 October 2015 (GC), *Perinçek v. Switzerland*, appl. no. 27510/08, par. 26. See also the original judgment of the Swiss Federal Court (*Bundesgericht/Tribunal fédéral/Tribunale federale*), 12 December 2007, 6B_398/2007, par. 4.6, http://relevancy.bger.ch/php/aza/http/index.php?lang=de&zoom=&type=show_document&highlight_docid=aza%3A%2F%2F12-12-2007-6B_398-2007 (accessed 11 April 2016).

also that the Swiss National Council in December 2003 passed a non-binding motion (*Postulat*) to recognise the events of 1915 and the following years as genocide.[90]

Before the Court, the applicant, amongst other things, relied on the right to freedom of expression in Article 10 ECHR. Considering the Court's line of case law with regard to Holocaust denial, it is to be applauded that the Grand Chamber, just like the Chamber had done in 2013, decided on its own motion to assess the applicability of Article 17 ECHR. The Grand Chamber confirmed that Article 17 ECHR is *'only applicable on an exceptional basis and in extreme cases'*.[91] It subsequently held that in cases concerning the right to freedom of expression in Article 10 ECHR this means that *'it should only be resorted to if it is immediately clear that the impugned statements sought to deflect this Article from its real purpose by employing the right to freedom of expression for ends clearly contrary to the values of the Convention'*.[92] The Grand Chamber did not consider that such a threat had been demonstrated in the case concerned and concluded that *'[s]ince the decisive point under Article 17 – whether the applicant's statements sought to stir up hatred or violence, and whether by making them he attempted to rely on the Convention to engage in an activity or perform acts aimed at the destruction of the rights and freedoms laid down in it – is not immediately clear and overlaps with the question whether the interference with the applicant's right to freedom of expression was "necessary in a democratic society", the Court finds that the question whether Article 17 is to be applied must be joined to the merits of the applicant's complaint under Article 10 of the Convention'*.[93]

Next, the Grand Chamber went on to address the case on its merits. In the context of the necessity of the interference with the applicant's right to freedom of expression, the Grand Chamber found that it had to strike a balance between the applicant's right guaranteed in Article 10 ECHR and the right to respect for private life of the Armenian community under Article 8 ECHR.[94] The Grand Chamber made a detailed evaluation of all the relevant aspects of the case and eventually concluded, just like the Chamber had done in 2013, that *'[t]aking into account all the elements analysed above – that the applicant's statements bore on a matter of public interest and did not amount to a call for hatred or intolerance, that the context in which they were made was not marked by heightened tensions or special historical overtones in Switzerland, that the statements cannot be regarded as affecting the dignity of the members of the Armenian community to the point of requiring a criminal law*

90 National Council (*Nationalrat/Conseil National/Consiglio Nazionale*), Motion No. 02.3069, passed on 16 December 2003 by 107 votes to 67, with 11 abstentions, www.parlament.ch/e/suche/Pages/geschaefte.aspx?gesch_id=20023069 (accessed 11 April 2016).

91 ECtHR 15 October 2015 (GC), *Perinçek v. Switzerland*, appl. no. 27510/08, par. 114. See also ECtHR 6 January 2011 (GC), *Paksas v. Lithuania*, appl. no. 34932/04, par. 87.

92 ECtHR 15 October 2015 (GC), *Perinçek v. Switzerland*, appl. no. 27510/08, par. 114. See also ECtHR 6 January 2011, *Paksas v. Lithuania*, appl. no. 34932/04, par. 87.

93 ECtHR 15 October 2015 (GC), *Perinçek v. Switzerland*, appl. no. 27510/08, par. 115.

94 Ibid, par. 228.

response in Switzerland, that there is no international law obligation for Switzerland to criminalise such statements, that the Swiss courts appear to have censured the applicant for voicing an opinion that diverged from the established ones in Switzerland, and that the interference took the serious form of a criminal conviction – the Court concludes that it was not necessary, in a democratic society, to subject the applicant to a criminal penalty in order to protect the rights of the Armenian community at stake in the present case.... There has therefore been a breach of Article 10 of the Convention'.[95] Finally, the Court decided by thirteen votes to four that it found no grounds to apply Article 17 ECHR.

3.4.1.7 Restrictive application of Article 17 ECHR to other historical debates

Case law shows that when it comes to the denial or revision of controversial topics of historical debate, the Strasbourg approach to Article 17 ECHR has not been uniform.[96] The discrepancy between the Strasbourg approach to the application of Article 17 ECHR between Holocaust denial, on the one hand, and the denial of other genocides, war crimes and crimes against humanity, on the other, has also been criticised by Judge Nussberger in her dissenting opinion in the case *Perinçek*: *'[w]hy should criminal sanctions for denial of the characterisation of the massacres of Armenians in Turkey in 1915 as "genocide" constitute a violation of freedom of expression, whereas criminal sanctions for Holocaust denial have been deemed compatible with the Convention?'*[97] Even though the Court's sensitivity when it is faced with issues related to the horrors of the Second World War may be explicable considering the context in which the Convention came into being, Buyse rightly argues that it *'is not easy to defend why the line should be drawn there'*.[98]

3.4.2 Promotion of totalitarian ideologies

Article 17 ECHR has also played an important role in cases regarding the promotion of National Socialism by neo-Nazi groups and their members. The fight against Nazi ideology is a constant matter of concern to European democracies. Europe's tragic experience with the German Nazi regime was one the major motivating forces for the

95 Ibid, par. 280-281.

96 Additional dissenting opinion of Judge Silvis (the Netherlands), joined by Judges Casadevall (Andorra), Berro (Monaco) and Kūris (Lithuania) in the case ECtHR 15 October 2015 (GC), *Perinçek v. Switzerland*, appl. no. 27510/08, par. 2.

97 Partly concurring and partly dissenting opinion of Judge Nussberger (Germany). Also dissenting Judge Silvis (the Netherlands), joined by Judges Casadevall (Andorra), Berro (Monaco) and Kūris (Lithuania), have criticised the Court's inconsistent approach to the application of Article 17 in cases concerning the denial or trivialisation of historical events in their additional dissenting opinion.

98 Buyse, *Shaping Rights in the ECHR*, p. 205-206.

creation of the Convention.[99] A reading of the *travaux préparatoires* of the Convention confirms that the drafters of the Convention believed that a revival of National Socialism had to be prevented at all times, an idea that considerably influenced the creation and interpretation of the Convention. The Council of Europe has also repeatedly drawn attention to the worrying phenomenon of the resurgence of Nazism. In 2006, the Council of Europe's Parliamentary Assembly adopted a resolution in which it referred to National Socialism as *'the most cruel and barbaric regime that Europe had ever known'*.[100] Post-war Europe, the Parliamentary Assembly held, *'has been conceived on the basis of a total rejection of the Nazi ideas and principles, to ensure that such horrendous crimes as those committed by the Nazi regime in the name of "racial superiority" will never be repeated. The Council of Europe, as the oldest European political organisation aimed at protecting and furthering democracy, human rights and the rule of law, has a special responsibility in preventing the resurgence of the Nazi ideology'*.[101] It therefore called for coordinated action to resist the revival of this ideology, whereby the Council of Europe should play a leading role. In the same line of thought, the Commission and the Court have held that activities related to neo-Nazism are activities in the sense of Article 17 ECHR and are therefore excluded from the protection of Article 10 ECHR. The risk of Nazi dictatorship actually being restored in the future thereby seems to be irrelevant.[102]

3.4.2.1 Kühnen v. Germany

The first case on this issue, *Kühnen v. Germany*, dealt with the criminal conviction of the leader of a neo-Nazi organisation that advocated the reinstitution of the NSDAP, Hitler's Nazi party. This case is illustrative for the Strasbourg approach in cases concerning National Socialism. The Commission examined this case under Article 10 ECHR. With regard to the necessity of the interference in accordance with Article 10(2) ECHR, the Commission's assessment in fact consisted of nothing more than a reference to the prohibition of abuse of rights in Article 17 ECHR.[103] By advocating National Socialism, the Commission argued, Kühnen had aimed to impair *'the basic order of freedom and democracy'*.[104] The Commission continued that *'the applicant's proposals thus ran counter to one of the basic values underlying the Convention, as*

---

99 Bates, *The Evolution of the ECHR*, p. 44.

100 CoE, Parliamentary Assembly, *Recommendation No. 1495 on combating the resurrection of Nazi ideology*, Strasbourg, 12 April 2006, par. 1.

101 *Recommendation No. 1495 on combating the resurrection of Nazi ideology*, par. 8.

102 See also M. van Noorloos, *Hate Speech revisited. A comparative and historical perspective on hate speech law in the Netherlands and England and Wales*, Antwerp: Intersentia, 2011, p. 70.

103 The same applies to several other cases related to organisations advocating National Socialist ideas. See e.g. with regard to ECtHR 1 February 2000 (dec.), *Schimanek v. Austria*, appl. no. 32307/96. See also Buyse, *Shaping Rights in the ECHR*, p. 199.

104 EComHR 12 May 1988, *Kühnen v. Germany*, appl. no. 12194/86, par. 1.

expressed in its fifth preambular paragraph, namely that the fundamental freedoms enshrined in the Convention "are best maintained... by an effective political democracy"'.[105] In addition, as noted by the domestic court, Kühnen's publications could revive anti-Semitic sentiments, and clearly contained elements of racial and religious discrimination. Accordingly, the Commission held that the applicant was essentially seeking to use the freedom of information enshrined in Article 10 ECHR as a basis for activities that are contrary to the text and spirit of the Convention and which, if admitted, would contribute to the destruction of the fundamental rights set forth in the Convention. Yet, instead of declaring the application incompatible *ratione materiae* with the Convention, the Commission concluded that the interference was necessary in a democratic society within the meaning of Article 10(2) ECHR and declared the application manifestly ill-founded.

This approach has later been repeatedly confirmed by both the Commission and the Court in cases concerning the sanctions against leaders of a number of Austrian National Socialist-inspired organisations.[106] Some applicants complained that they were being discriminated against as adherents of National Socialism, as no similar sanctions were imposed on those belonging to other political groups. They referred to Article 14 ECHR, which prohibits discrimination on any grounds, including political opinion. Nonetheless, according to the Commission this difference in treatment had *'an objective and reasonable justification'* in the light of the Austrian experience with Nazism and the danger this ideology may pose to Austrian society.[107] The Commission therefore concluded that *'National Socialism is a totalitarian doctrine incompatible with democracy and human rights and that its adherents undoubtedly pursue aims of the kind referred to in Article 17... There is therefore no appearance of discrimination contrary to Article 14... of the Convention'.*[108]

3.4.2.2 Fáber v. Hungary

In the neo-Nazi-related cases discussed above, the Commission and the Court have structurally found, without further ado, that applicants engaging in activities inspired by Nazism do not enjoy the protection of the Convention and declared their applications inadmissible. These decisions were primarily based on the National

105 Ibid.

106 EComHR 12 October 1989, *B.H., M.W., H.P. and G.K. v. Austria,* appl. no. 12774/87; EComHR 2 September 1994, *Ochensberger v. Austria*, appl. no. 21318/93; ECtHR 1 February 2000 (dec.), *Schimanek v. Austria*, appl. no. 32307/96.

107 EComHR 12 October 1989, *B.H., M.W., H.P. and G.K. v. Austria,* appl. no. 12774/87, par. 2.

108 Ibid. See also Haeck, *Handboek EVRM. Deel 2,* p. 254; H. Cannie and D. Voorhoof, 'The Abuse Clause and Freedom of Expression in the European Human Rights Convention: An Added Value for Democracy and Human Rights Protection?', *Netherlands Quarterly of Human Rights*, vol. 29, no. 1, 2011, p. 59.

Socialist intentions of the applicants.[109] Yet, the case *Fáber v. Hungary* shows that it may sometimes be difficult to assess the intentions of the applicant. The topic of discussion in this case was the Árpád-striped flag, which is considered a historical symbol referring to the founding dynasty of Hungary, the House of Árpád. However, since the pro-Nazi Arrow Cross regime that ruled Hungary by the end of the Second World War used it in its flag it is also associated with Hungarian Nazism. Fáber was fined for displaying the flag on a day that both anti-racist and right-wing organisations demonstrated in Budapest. He complained before the Court, among other things, that his prosecution amounted to a violation of Article 10 ECHR. In this regard the Court stressed that *'[w]hen the right to freedom of expression is exercised in the context of political speech through the use of symbols, utmost care must be observed in applying any restrictions, especially if the case involves symbols which have multiple meanings. In this connection the Court emphasises that it is only by a careful examination of the context..., that one can draw a meaningful distinction between shocking and offensive language which is protected by Article 10 and that which forfeits its right to tolerance in a democratic society'*.[110] Given that the Árpád-striped flag has multiple meanings, the Court observed that *'it is only by a careful examination of the context in which the offending expressions appear that one can draw a meaningful distinction between shocking and offensive expression which is protected by Article 10 and that which forfeits its right to tolerance in a democratic society'*.[111] In this regard the Court stressed that *'where the applicant expresses contempt for the victims of a totalitarian regime as such, this may amount – in application of Article 17 of the Convention – to an abuse of Convention rights'*.[112] In this case, however, the Court did not find such an abusive element. The Court went on to conclude that the restriction of Fábers' right to freedom of expression did not meet a pressing social need and could therefore not be considered necessary in a democratic society. Subsequently, the Court found a violation of Article 10 ECHR.

The judgement, however, was not adopted unanimously. Judge Keller in her dissenting opinion strongly disagreed with the opinion of the majority. She agreed that the freedom of expression also protects expressions that annoy, cause offence or even shock. But, in her view *'this threshold is passed in the present case. What message [...] other than a racist and fascist one could be conveyed by a flag that is associated in public opinion with the 1944/45 Nazi Regime in Hungary and is raised at a place where grave human rights violations were committed during the Second World War? In the light of Article 17 of the Convention [...], I have serious doubts*

109 Buyse, *Shaping Rights in the ECHR*, p. 202.
110 ECtHR 24 July 2012, *Fáber v. Hungary*, appl. no. 40721/08, par. 36.
111 Ibid, par. 54.
112 Ibid, par. 58.

as to whether the expression of such an opinion could attract the protection of [...] Article 10'.[113]

3.4.2.3 Communist ideology

The *travaux préparatoires* demonstrate that the creation of the ECHR was a response not merely to Europe's past experience with Nazism, but also to the fears of a communist future.[114] The 1957 hallmark decision of the Commission concerning the prohibition of the German Communist Party clearly symbolizes this cold-War mind-set. This political party had been considered a threat to the German 'free democratic basic order' (*die freiheitliche demokratische Grundordnung*) and was declared unconstitutional by the German Federal Constitutional Court in 1956.[115] Before the Commission the party relied on Articles 9, 10 and 11 ECHR. The Commission, however, found no difficulty in concluding that in accordance with Article 17 ECHR *'there is no need to consider the application of the second paragraphs of Articles 9, 10 and 11'.*[116] The German Communist Party advocated the establishment of a social communist society through a proletarian revolution and a period of dictatorship of the proletariat during which the fundamental rights protected under the Convention would be nullified. Turning to the *travaux préparatoires*, the Commission held that Article 17 ECHR was *'designed to safeguard the rights listed therein by protecting the free operation of democratic institutions'.*[117] The fact that the German Communist Party merely tried to reach their political aims through the constitutional means provided by the German Basic Law was irrelevant. Irrespective of the actual threat posed by the party, the Commission found that the recourse to dictatorship to install a regime is incompatible with the Convention because this would imply the destruction of multiple fundamental rights guaranteed in the ECHR.[118] The organization and functioning of the German Communist Party according to the Commission constituted an act in the sense of Article 17 ECHR. Rather drastically, the Commission subsequently concluded that *'it is clear from the foregoing that the application by the German Communist Party cannot rest upon any provision of the Convention, least of all on Article 9, 10 and 11'.*[119] Nowadays this decision may seem rather exaggerated and

---

113 Dissenting opinion of Judge Keller (Switzerland) in the case *Fáber v. Hungary*, ECtHR 24 July 2012, appl. no. 40721/08, par. 12.

114 Bates, *The Evolution of the ECHR*, p. 5.

115 See for the decision of the German Federal Constitutional Court (*Bundesverfassungsgericht*) Chapter eight on the notion of the '*wehrhafte Demokratie*' in Germany.

116 EComHR 20 July 1957, *German Communist Party v. Germany*, appl. no. 250/57.

117 Ibid.

118 See also Buyse, *Shaping Rights in the ECHR*, p. 193.

119 EComHR 20 July 1957, *German Communist Party v. Germany*, appl. no. 250/57.

it is safe to assume that the Court would declare this case admissible if it would be lodged today.[120]

Subsequently, the admission of a large number of former communist states from Eastern and Central Europe and the Baltics to the Council of Europe in the 1990s raised new issues as regards the communist heritage of these new States Parties.[121] For many of these states the years of communist control symbolise a dark page in their history. After the fall of the Soviet Union, they have undergone a process of 'decommunisation'.[122] Besides a ban on neo-Nazism, many of these states have banned communist ideology in a similar way. In several Eastern and Central European and Baltic states, for example, any denial of the crimes committed in the name of communism is prohibited.[123] Moreover, in many of these states communist symbols are prohibited. Also at the international level awareness has been raised with regard to the crimes committed by communist regimes.[124] In several cases brought before the Court concerning their communist history, the defending States Parties set up an argument with respect to Article 17 ECHR similar to that in cases related to Nazism. The Court, however, has not interpreted these issues in analogy to Neo-Nazism by excluding them from the protection of the Convention pursuant to the prohibition of abuse of rights in Article 17 ECHR.

An example is found in the case *Vajnai v. Hungary* that dealt with the public display of a five-pointed red star, a controversial symbol with multiple meanings that is prohibited in Hungary. As vice president of the Hungarian Workers' Party, the applicant wore the five-pointed red star during a lawful demonstration in Budapest in 2003, resulting in a conviction for the use of a totalitarian symbol in public. Before the Court, the applicant relied on the freedom of expression in Article 10 ECHR. The Government, for its part, argued that the application was incompatible *ratione materiae* with the provisions of the Convention in the light of Article 17 ECHR.[125] The government compared the use of the five-pointed red star to the use of Nazi

120 Bates, *The Evolution of the ECHR*, p. 218.

121 Including Hungary (1990), Poland (1991), Bulgaria (1992), Estonia, Lithuania and Slovenia, the Czech Republic, Slovakia and Romania (1993), Latvia, Albania, Moldova, Ukraine, 'the Former Yugoslav Republic of Macedonia' (1995), and Russia and Croatia (1996).

122 H.A. Welsh, 'Dealing with the Communist Past: Central and East European Experiences after 1990', *Europe-Asia Studies*, vol. 48, no. 3, 1996, p. 414.

123 Hungary, Lithuania and Poland: C. Closa Montero, *Study on how the memory of crimes committed by totalitarian regimes in Europe is dealt with in the Member States*, 2010, p. 296, http://ec.europa.eu/justice/fundamental-rights/files/totalitarian_regimes_final_study_en.pdf (accessed 11 April 2016).

124 See e.g. CoE, Parliamentary Assembly, *Resolution No. 1481 on the need for international condemnation of crimes of totalitarian communist regimes*, Strasbourg, 25 January 2006; OSCE, Parliamentary Assembly, *Vilnius Declaration*, Vilnius, 29 June-3 July 2009; *Declaration on Crimes of Communism*, Prague, 25 February 2010.

125 ECtHR 8 July 2008, *Vajnai v. Hungary*, appl. no. 33629/06, par. 20.

symbols and claimed that *'...the red star symbolises totalitarian ideas and practices directed against the Convention's underlying values'* and that *'to wear it – being conduct disdainful of the victims of the Communist regime – meant the justification of a policy aimed at the destruction of the rights and freedoms under the Convention'.* Even though the cases that the Government relied on concerned the expression of racist and anti-Semitic ideas related to Nazi ideology, *'the Government submitted that all ideologies of a totalitarian nature (including bolshevism symbolised by the red star) should be treated on an equal footing, and their expression should thus be removed from the protection of Article 10'.*[126] The Court, however, held that, due to the multiple meanings of the symbol, displaying the five-pointed red star was different from the use of Nazi symbols. In this case the Court was therefore not convinced that the displaying of the red star *'was intended to justify or propagate totalitarian oppression serving "totalitarian groups". It was merely the symbol of lawful left-wing political movements. Unlike in the above-cited cases, the expression which was sanctioned in the instant case was unrelated to racist propaganda'.*[127] Displaying the five-pointed red star was hence not excluded from the protection of the Convention pursuant to Article 17 ECHR. The Court's judgment can be read as a conclusion that there was no *'real and present'* danger of the installation of a new communist dictatorship, as a result of which the application of Article 17 ECHR was not appropriate.[128]

3.4.3 Hate speech

The Commission and the Court have continuously emphasised that the freedom of expression is one of the cardinal rights protected under the Convention.[129] It *'constitutes one of the essential foundations'* of a democratic society and it is therefore *'it is applicable not only to "information" or "ideas" that are favourably received or regarded as inoffensive or as a matter of indifference, but also to those that offend, shock or disturb the State or any sector of the population. Such are the demands of that pluralism, tolerance and broadmindedness without which there is no "democratic society"'.*[130] The Court repeatedly stressed in particular that under

---

126 Ibid, par. 22.

127 ECtHR 8 July 2008, *Vajnai v. Hungary*, appl. no. 33629/06, par. 25-26.

128 A. Buyse, 'Dangerous expressions: the ECHR, Violence and Free Speech', *International and Comparative Law Quarterly*, vol. 63, no. 2, 2014, p. 501. See in this regard also ECtHR 3 November 2011, *Fratanoló v. Hungary*, appl. no. 29459/10, par. 25.

129 Y. Arai, 'Article 10: Freedom of Expression', in: D.J. Harris et al. (eds.), *Harris, O'Boyle and Warbrick. Law of the European Convention on Human Rights*, 3rd ed., Oxford: Oxford University Press, 2014, p. 613.

130 ECtHR 7 December 1976, *Handyside v. the UK*, appl. no. 5493/72, par. 49. See also ECtHR 23 September 1998 (GC), *Lehideux and Isorni v. France*, appl. no. 24662/94, par. 55.

Article 10(2) ECHR there is little scope for restrictions on debates on matters of public interest.[131]

On the other hand, the Convention attaches great importance to the fight against hate speech. Whereas the Strasbourg Court attaches great importance to free participation in public and political debate, it has also repeatedly stressed that minorities have to be protected against hateful forms of expression.[132] As Cannie and Voorhoof put it, within the European human rights framework, the core values of human dignity and equality have been translated into a firm right of non-discrimination that curtails hate speech.[133] Article 14 ECHR provides that the enjoyment of the fundamental rights set forth in the Convention shall be secured without discrimination on any ground, including race, colour, religion, national origin, or association with a national minority.[134] In the past, the Commission has even held that discrimination based on race may, under extreme circumstances, amount to degrading treatment within the meaning of Article 3 ECHR.[135] In some cases, the Court also referred to provisions prohibiting racial discrimination in a number of international instruments, in particular Article 4(a) of the International Convention on the Elimination of All Forms of Racial Discrimination, which has been ratified by a large majority of the States Parties to the ECHR.[136]

---

131 ECtHR 25 November 1996, *Wingrove v. the United Kingdom*, appl. no. 17419/90, par. 58.

132 R. de Lange, 'Gutmann's Dilemma: democratie, minderheden en fundamentele Rechten' ['Gutmann's Dilemma: democracy, minorities and fundamental rights'], in: C.W. Noorlander et al. (eds.), *Het volk regeert. Beschouwingen over de (Nederlandse) democratie in de 21e eeuw [The people rule. Reflections on the (Dutch) democracy in the 21st century]*, Nijmegen: Wolf Legal Publishers, 2008, p. 202-204.

133 Cannie and Voorhoof, *Netherlands Quarterly of Human Rights*, p. 65-66; Hare, *Extreme Speech and Democracy*, p. 76-77. See e.g. CoE, Parliamentary Assembly, *Recommendation No. 1222 on the fight against racism, xenophobia and intolerance*, Strasbourg, 29 September 1993; CoE, Committee of Ministers, *Vienna Declaration*, Vienna, 9 October 1993; CoE, Parliamentary Assembly, *Recommendation No. 1275 on the fight against racism, xenophobia, anti-Semitism and intolerance*, Strasbourg, 28 June 1995; CoE, Parliamentary Assembly, *Recommendation No. 1438 on the threat posed to democracy by extremist parties and movements in Europe*, Strasbourg, 25 January 2000; CoE, Parliamentary Assembly, *Recommendation No. 1543 on racism and xenophobia in cyberspace*, Strasbourg, 8 November 2001; CoE, Parliamentary Assembly, *Resolution No. 1308 on restrictions on political parties in the CoE member states*, Strasbourg, 18 November 2002; CoE, ECRI, *General Policy Recommendation No. 9 on the fight against anti-Semitism*, Strasbourg, 25 June 2004.

134 In addition, the Twelfth Protocol to the Convention aims to provide protection against discrimination in all those activities the states chooses to regulate. To date, however, this protocol has not been widely ratified (19 States Parties out of 47: www.coe.int/en/web/conventions/full-list/-/conventions/treaty/177/signatures?p_auth=L2Gr5bkl (accessed 11 April 2016). See also Harris et al., *Law of the ECHR*, p. 783.

135 EComHR 14 December 1973 (report), *East African Asians v. the United Kingdom*, appl. nos. 4403/70 et al., par. 207-208.

136 See e.g. EComHR 11 October 1979, *Glimmerveen and Hagenbeek v. the Netherlands*, appl. nos. 8348/78 and 8406/78; ECtHR 23 September 1994 (GC), *Jersild v. Denmark*, appl. no. 15890/89, par. 21.

The Court's – rather wide – definition of hate speech is based on Recommendation No. R(97)20 on hate speech adopted by the Committee of Ministers of the Council of Europe according to which this notion encompasses *'all forms of expression which spread, incite, promote or justify racial hatred, xenophobia, anti-Semitism, or other forms of hatred based on intolerance, including intolerance expressed by aggressive nationalism and ethnocentrism, discrimination, and hostility towards minorities, migrants, and people of immigrant origin'*.[137] Despite the fundamental importance of the right to freedom of expression in a democratic, pluralistic society, therefore, the Court has stressed that *'as a matter of principle it may be considered necessary in certain democratic societies to sanction or even prevent all forms of expression which spread, incite, promote or justify hatred based on intolerance (including religious intolerance)'*.[138] Consequently, the Court has shown itself to be *'particularly conscious of the vital importance of combating racial discrimination in all its forms and manifestations'*.[139] Racially discriminatory utterances therefore hardly deserve the protection of Article 10 ECHR.[140] Yet, as we will see, not all hate speech falls under the scope of Article 17 ECHR.[141]

3.4.3.1 Hate speech excluded from the protection of the Convention

In an early decision in the case *Glimmerveen and Hagenbeek v. the Netherlands* the Commission set out an exclusive approach to racial discrimination under the Convention. The applicants in this case were leading members of a nationalist political party (the *Nederlandse Volks Unie* or NVU). They were convicted of incitement to discrimination on the basis of race for distributing leaflets addressed to the *'white Dutch people, white fellow citizens, our white people'* claiming that, when in power, the NVU would remove all immigrants from the Netherlands.[142] In addition, the Central Voting Board had refused their candidacy for the local elections because of their racist agenda. Before the Commission Glimmerveen and Hagenbeek

---

137 CoE, Committee of Ministers, *Appendix to Recommendation No. R(97)20 on 'hate speech'*, Strasbourg, 30 October 1997, p. 107. See also Cannie and Voorhoof, *Netherlands Quarterly of Human Rights*, p. 66.

138 ECtHR 6 July 2006, *Erbakan v. Turkey*, appl. no. 59405/00, par. 56; ECtHR 4 December 2003, *Gündüz v. Turkey*, appl. no. 35071/97, par. 40.

139 ECtHR 23 September 1994 (GC), *Jersild v. Denmark*, appl. no. 15890/89, par. 30.

140 See e.g. ECtHR 10 July 2008, *Soulas et autres c. France*, appl. no. 15948/03, par. 42-45; ECtHR 4 November 2008, *Balsytė-Lideikienė v. Lithuania*, appl. no. 72596/01, par. 78-80; ECtHR 16 July 2009, *Willem c. France*, appl. no. 10883/05, par. 36-38. See also D. Voorhoof, Case note to ECtHR 16 July 2009, *Féret c. Belgique*, appl. no. 15615/07, *ECHR* 2009/111, par. 4.

141 Cannie and Voorhoof, *Netherlands Quarterly of Human Rights*, p. 65. See also A. Nieuwenhuis, Case note to ECtHR 9 February 2012, *Vejdeland and other v. Sweden*, appl. no. 1813/07, *ECHR* 2012/85, par. 5-6.

142 EComHR 11 October 1979, *Glimmerveen and Hagenbeek v. the Netherlands*, appl. nos. 8348/78 and 8406/78, par. 4.

complained about a violation of their right to freedom of expression as guaranteed in Article 10 ECHR and their right to stand for election protected in Article 3 First Protocol to the ECHR. The Commission, for its part, stressed that Article 10(2) ECHR provides that *'whoever exercises his freedom of expression undertakes "duties and responsibilities" the scope of which depends on his situation and the technical means he uses'*.[143] Interestingly, the Commission added that these duties and responsibilities *'find an even stronger expression in a more general provision, namely Article 17 of the Convention'*.[144] According to the Commission, the policy advocated by Glimmerveen and Hagenbeek clearly contained elements of racial discrimination, which is *inter alia* prohibited under Article 14 of the Convention. That the party had few sympathisers and that the chances of it bringing its racist agenda in practice were small did not seem to play a role in the Court's considerations.[145] The mere justification of such a policy *'clearly constitutes an activity within the meaning of Article 17 of the Convention. The applicants are essentially seeking to use Article 10 to provide a basis under the Convention for a right to engage in these activities which are, as shown above, contrary to the text and spirit of the Convention and which right, if granted, would contribute to the destruction of the rights and freedoms referred to above'*.[146] Consequently, the application was declared incompatible with the provisions of the Convention.

Another example of a clear-cut application of Article 17 ECHR is found in the famous case *Norwood v. the United Kingdom*. In this case the Court held that displaying a poster showing a photograph of the Twin Towers in flames and the words *'Islam out of Britain – Protect the British People'* followed by a symbol of a crescent and star in a prohibition sign amounted to a public attack on all Muslims in the United Kingdom. *'Such a general, vehement attack against a religious group, linking the group as a whole with a grave act of terrorism, is incompatible with the values proclaimed and guaranteed by the Convention, notably tolerance, social peace and non-discrimination. The applicant's display of the poster in his window constituted an act within the meaning of Article 17, which did not, therefore, enjoy the protection of Articles 10 or 14'*, the Court concluded.[147] Buyse has noted that the particularities of the context of the case were not really taken into account. In fact, the Court immediately turned to the abuse clause, without any discussion of the applicability of Article 10 ECHR. The poster had not provoked any violence, the countryside where Norwood lived did not suffer from racial or religious tensions and

143 ECtHR 7 December 1976, *Handyside v. the United Kingdom*, appl. no. 5493/72, par. 49.
144 EComHR 11 October 1979, *Glimmerveen and Hagenbeek v. the Netherlands*, appl. nos. 8348/78 and 8406/78.
145 See also Buyse, *Shaping Rights in the ECHR*, p. 194.
146 EComHR 11 October 1979, *Glimmerveen and Hagenbeek v. the Netherlands*, appl. nos. 8348/78 and 8406/78.
147 ECtHR 16 November 2004 (dec.), *Norwood v. the United Kingdom*, appl. no. 23131/03.

no Muslim had actually seen the poster. Yet, for the Court these facts were irrelevant and *'intentions rather than consequences seem to have been decisive'*.[148]

Later, the Court came to a similar conclusion with regard to anti-Semite utterances in the case *Ivanov. v. Russia*. The case concerned the publication of a series of articles portraying Jews as the source of all evil in Russia and calling for their exclusion from social life. The Court ruled that it *'had no doubt as to the markedly anti-Semitic tenor of the applicant's views and it agrees with the assessment made by the domestic courts that he sought his publication to incite hatred towards the Jewish people. Such a general and vehement attack on one ethnic group is in contradiction with the Convention's underlying values, notably tolerance, social peace and non-discrimination. Consequently, the Court finds that, by reason of Article 17 of the Convention, the applicant may not benefit from the protection afforded by Article 10 of the Convention'*.[149] The Court therefore concluded that this part of the application is incompatible *ratione materiae* with the Convention.[150]

3.4.3.2 Hate speech dealt with under the scope of the right to freedom of expression

Even though the Court has maintained that racial discrimination is unacceptable under the Convention, in recent years it seems to increasingly deal with hate speech cases under Article 10 ECHR.[151] Instead of applying Article 17 ECHR and declaring an application incompatible *ratione materiae* with the provisions of the Convention, the Court dealt with these cases according to the 'normal' limitation requirements in Article 10(2) ECHR.

In some of these cases the Court seems to avoid having to judge on the application of Article 17 ECHR. This was the case, for example, in the Court's decision in the case *Seurot v. France*. Seurot was a schoolteacher who had written an article for the school newspaper in which he spoke of unassimilated Islamic masses that besieged France. Referring to Article 17 ECHR and the cases *Lehideux and Isorni* and *Garaudy*, the Court recalled that there is no doubt that expressions directed against the basic values of the Convention, by virtue of Article 17 ECHR are withdrawn from the protection of Article 10 ECHR: *'[e]nfin, la Cour rappelle qu'il ne fait aucun doute que tout propos dirigé contre les valeurs qui sous-tendent la Convention se verrait soustrait*

148 Buyse, *Shaping Rights in the ECHR*, p. 196.

149 ECtHR 20 February 2007 (dec.), *Pavel Ivanov v. Russia*, appl. no. 35222/04, par. 1.

150 See also ECtHR 2 September 2004 (dec.), *W.P. and others v. Poland*, appl. no. 42264/98, concerning the refusal by the Polish authorities to allow the registration of an association whose statutes included anti-Semite statements, in which the Court was *'satisfied that the evidence in the present case justified the need to bring Article 17 into play'* and found that the applicants could not rely on Article 11 ECHR to challenge the prohibition of the formation of the association.

151 Buyse, *International and Comparative Law Quarterly*, p. 496.

par l'article 17 à la protection de l'article 10'.[152] In accordance with this observation, the Court subsequently wondered whether the utterances of the applicant should not be excluded from the protection of Article 10 ECHR by virtue of the prohibition of abuse of rights in Article 17 ECHR.[153] The Court, however, responded to this question by concluding that it did not consider it necessary to further elaborate on this point, because this part of the application was in any case inadmissible as the interference complied with the requirements of Article 10(2) ECHR and therefore considered the application manifestly ill-founded.[154]

In other cases, such as the case *Féret v. Belgium*, the Court explicitly rejected the claim that Article 17 ECHR would be applicable. The applicant, who was the president of the right-wing political party *Front National* in Belgium, was convicted of the distribution of racist leaflets during election campaigns. Before the Court, Féret relied on the freedom of expression guaranteed in Article 10 ECHR. The Belgian government had urged the Court to declare the application inadmissible on the grounds of an abuse of rights. Yet, the Court for its part considered that the applicability of this provision had to be discussed in the light of Article 10 ECHR, in particular the question regarding the necessity of the interference in a democratic society.[155] In that regard the Court, among other things, held that incitement to hatred does not necessarily require a call for violence or a criminal act. The damage caused by harming, insulting or discriminating against certain groups in society, like in the case concerned, constitutes a sufficient justification for restricting racist speech. According to the Court, *'[l]es discours politiques qui incitent à la haine fondée sur les préjugés religieux, ethniques ou culturels représentent un danger pour la paix sociale et la stabilité politique dans les Etats démocratiques'*.[156] So, even though the Court considers that the political discourse enjoys a higher level of protection in a democratic society, it is of the opinion that politicians should avoid incitement to racial discrimination and refrain from hurtful or humiliating utterances, which risk raising reactions among the public that are incompatible with a tranquil social climate and undermine the confidence in democratic institutions.[157] Since the language used by Féret clearly incited racial discrimination and hatred, the Court considered that the conviction met a pressing social need and was necessary in a democratic society.[158]

152 ECtHR 18 May 2004 (dec.), *Seurot c. France*, appl. no. 57383/00.
153 Ibid.
154 Ibid.
155 ECtHR 16 July 2009, *Féret c. Belgique*, appl. no. 15615/07, par. 52.
156 Ibid, par. 73.
157 Ibid, par. 77.
158 Ibid, par. 78.

Accordingly, the Court did not find a violation of Article 10 ECHR.[159] Finally, after having completed the examination under Article 10(2) ECHR, the Court rather puzzlingly noted at the very end that the content of the applicant's utterances did not justify the application of Article 17 ECHR.[160]

A year later, in the case *Le Pen v. France*, the Court declared the application of the president of the French *Front National* inadmissible, yet without any reference to Article 17 ECHR. In an interview with a daily newspaper Jean-Marie Le Pen had argued that an increase in Muslims in France would result in the domination and humiliation of the French. He was convicted of incitement to discrimination, hatred and violence towards a group of persons because of their origin, their (non-) membership of an ethnic group, nation, race or religious group. Before the Court he complained under Article 10 ECHR that his conviction constituted a violation of his right to freedom of expression. The Court considered that the applicant had presented Muslims in a disturbing light. In the context of a complex political and social debate regarding the challenges of immigration and integration, this was likely to give rise to feelings of rejection and hostility. Having regard to these facts, the Court considered the interference with the applicant's freedom of expression to be necessary in a democratic society. The Court declared the application manifestly ill-founded.[161]

Worth mentioning in this regard is also the case *Vejdeland v. Sweden*. The applicants in this case had distributed leaflets printed by an organisation called National Youth at a secondary school by leaving them in the pupils' lockers. In the leaflets they claimed, inter alia, that homosexuality was a *'deviant sexual proclivity'*, had *'a morally destructive effect on the substance of society'* and was to blame for the development of the *'modern-day plague'* of HIV and AIDS.[162] Stressing that discrimination based on sexual orientation is as serious as discrimination based on '*race, origin or colour*',[163] the Court concluded that there had been no violation of Article 10 ECHR.[164] Interesting is that even though neither the parties involved nor the Court referred to the prohibition of abuse of rights, several judges in their

159 Yet, the judgment was not decided unanimously (four votes to three). The dissenters supported a more tolerant approach to the right to freedom of expression and argued that the right to freedom of expression should not be sacrificed to a politics of non-discrimination: Dissenting opinion by Judge Sajó (Hungary), joined by Judges Zagrebelsky (Italy) and Tsotsoria (Georgia) in the case *Féret c. Belgique*, ECtHR 16 July 2009, appl. no. 15615/07.

160 ECtHR 16 July 2009, *Féret c. Belgique*, appl. no. 15615/07, par. 82. See for a similar approach in a case concerning the publication of a book in which the author argued that Islamic civilisation from a specific geographical area was incompatible with European civilisation: ECtHR 10 July 2008, *Soulas et autres c. France*, appl. no. 15948/03, par. 48.

161 ECtHR 20 April 2010 (dec.), *Le Pen c. France*, appl. no. 18788/09.

162 ECtHR 9 February 2012, *Vejdeland and others v. Sweden*, appl. no. 1813/07, par. 8.

163 Ibid, par. 55.

164 Ibid, par. 60.

concurring opinions questioned the admissibility of the application in the light of Article 17 ECHR. In particular Judges Yudkivska and Villiger without a doubt went further than the majority in this respect. Nieuwenhuis suggests that their definition of hate speech coincides with the notion of abuse of rights.[165] Referring to the Court's decision in the case *Norwood v. UK*, in which the Court rejected the application of an applicant who linked Muslims in the UK to the terrorist attack on the World Trade Center, they held that *'[l]inking the whole group in the present case to the 'plague of the twentieth century' should not be granted the protection of Article 10 either'*.[166] In their opinion, the statements by Vejdeland and the others were clearly abusive in the sense of Article 17 ECHR and therefore fell outside of the scope of protection of Article 10 ECHR.[167]

Finally, the Court refused to apply Article 17 ECHR in the case *Vona v. Hungary* concerning the dissolution of an association on account of enabling the organisation of anti-Roma rallies. Even though this case was dealt with under Article 11 ECHR (the right to freedom of association), the findings of the Court in this case are interesting in the light of the fight against racial discrimination and hate speech. The applicant was the chairman of the Hungarian Guard Association, an organisation founded in 2007 by some members of the Hungarian nationalist political party *Jobbik*. This organisation subsequently created the Hungarian Guard Movement, which aimed to defend the Hungarian culture and traditions. Dressed in uniforms reminiscent of the Arrow Cross Party – the National Socialist party that led Hungary between October 1944 and March 1945 – the guardsmen of the Hungarian Guard Movement held several rallies and demonstrations throughout Hungary, in particular in villages with large Roma populations, calling for the defence of ethnic Hungarians against so-called '*Gipsy criminality*'.[168] In 2008 the Hungarian Guard Association was dissolved. Drawing attention to the international concerns about the Hungarian Guard Movement, the Hungarian government held that '*the application should be declared inadmissible as being incompatible* ratione materiae *with the provisions of the Convention in the light of Article 17, because the Association provided an institutional framework for expressing racial hatred against Jewish and Roma citizens*'.[169]

The Court, for its part, found that the case law on Article 17 ECHR relied on by the Hungarian government did not apply to the Hungarian Guard Association. Those cases concerned the justification of Nazi-like policies. *'Consequently, the finding of an abuse under Article 17 lay in the fact that Article 10 had been relied on*

165 Nieuwenhuis, Case note to *Vejdeland and other v. Sweden*, *ECHR* 2012/85, par. 10.
166 Concurring opinion of Judge Yudkivska (Ukraine), joined by Judge Villiger (Lichtenstein) to ECtHR 9 February 2012, *Vejdeland and others v. Sweden*, appl. no. 1813/07, par. 10.
167 Nieuwenhuis, Case note to *Vejdeland and other v. Sweden*, *ECHR* 2012/85, par. 5-6.
168 ECtHR 9 July 2013, *Vona v. Hungary*, appl. no. 35943/10, par. 10.
169 Ibid, par. 33.

by groups with totalitarian motives', the Court recalled.[170] The Court went on to hold that *'it has not been argued by the Government that the applicant expressed contempt for the victims of a totalitarian regime... or belonged to a group with totalitarian ambitions'*[171] and concluded that *'the application does not constitute an abuse of the right of petition for the purposes of Article 17 of the Convention'*[172] and declared the application admissible. Quite remarkably, the Court seems to ignore the case law in which also the expression of racist political ideas was considered *'an activity within the meaning of Article 17 of the Convention'*.[173] Yet, even though the Court rejected the application of Article 17 ECHR, it did consider the dissolution of the Hungarian Guard Movement justified, given that *'the State is also entitled to take preventive measures to protect democracy vis-à-vis such non-party entities if a sufficiently imminent prejudice to the rights of others threatens to undermine the fundamental values on the basis of which a democratic society exists and functions... Even if that movement has not made an attempt to seize power and the risk of its policy to democracy is not imminent, the State is entitled to act preventively if it is established that such a movement has started to take concrete steps in public life to implement a policy incompatible with the standards of the Convention and democracy'*.[174]

3.4.4 Incitement to violence

Besides hate speech aimed at denying the Holocaust, promoting pro-Nazi policies or inciting (racial) discrimination, in the past decades the Court has also found that calls for the use of violence fall outside the scope of the Convention's rights by virtue of Article 17 ECHR. This is not surprising as the prohibition and sanctioning of calls for violence are *'prima facie one of the few limitations on free speech on which most people would agree'*.[175]

In the case *Hizb Ut-Tahrir v. Germany* the Court made clear that calls for violence fall within the scope of Article 17 ECHR and are therefore excluded from the protection of the Convention.[176] Hizb Ut-Tahrir is an international Islamic organisation that promotes the unification of all Middle Eastern states in one Islamic caliphate governed according to Sharia law and advocates the violent destruction of Israel and its inhabitants. In 2003 the German Federal Ministry of the Interior proscribed the activities of Hizb Ut-Tahrir on German territory. Hizb Ut-Tahrir complained before the Court, among other things, about a violation of its right to freedom of association

170 Ibid, par. 36.
171 Ibid, par. 37.
172 Ibid, par. 39.
173 EComHR 11 October 1979, *Glimmerveen and Hagenbeek v. the Netherlands*, appl. nos. 8348/78 and 8406/78.
174 ECtHR 9 July 2013, *Vona v. Hungary*, appl. no. 35943/10, par. 57.
175 Buyse, *International and Comparative Law Quarterly*, p. 492.
176 Buyse, *Shaping Rights in the ECHR*, p. 197.

provided in Article 11 ECHR. The German government argued that the organisation could not rely on the protection of this provision, because *'[n]o less than denying the Holocaust, such violent propaganda constituted an abuse of rights under the Convention (Article 17 of the Convention). In this context, the government considered that it also had to be taken into account that the first applicant ultimately wished to abolish the rights and freedoms of the Convention by establishing the worldwide dominance of the Caliphate and Sharia'*.[177] In the context of its assessment under Article 11 ECHR, the Court immediately referred to Article 17 ECHR. The Court confirmed that the applicant advocated the violent destruction of Israel and the killing of its Jewish inhabitants. For that reason, the Court found that Hizb Ut-Tahrir *'attempts to deflect Article 11 of the Convention from its real purpose by employing this right for ends which are clearly contrary to the values of the Convention, notably the commitment to the peaceful settlement of international conflicts and to the sanctity of human life'*.[178] The Court consequently found that in accordance with Article 17 ECHR the organisation may not benefit from the protection afforded by Article 11 ECHR. Consequently, the Court found that the application was incompatible *ratione materiae* with the provisions of the Convention and had to be rejected.

A year later the Court confirmed this conclusion in a case brought before it by two members of Hizb Ut-Tahrir who were convicted in Russia based on their membership of a prohibited organisation: *Kasymakhunov and Saybatalov v. Russia*. The applicants relied, among other provisions, on Articles 9 (freedom of religion), 10 (freedom of expression), and 11 ECHR (freedom of association). The Court started its assessment by examining whether the activities of the applicants fell within the scope of Article 17 ECHR. In that context the Court stressed that from its earlier case law it *'necessarily follows that a political organisation whose leaders incite to violence or put forward a policy which fails to respect democracy or which is aimed at the destruction of democracy and the flouting of the rights and freedoms recognised in a democracy cannot lay claim to the Convention's protection against penalties imposed on those grounds'*.[179] Turning to the circumstances of the present case, the Court first reaffirmed that it was not convinced that the organisation rejected the possibility of recourse to violence.[180] The organisation clearly aspired to gain political power, but rejected any possibility of participating in the democratic political process. Based on these facts the Court therefore saw no reason to depart from its earlier findings

177 ECtHR 12 June 2012 (dec.), *Hizb Ut-Tahrir and others v. Germany*, appl. no. 31098/08, par. 63.
178 Ibid, par. 74.
179 ECtHR 14 March 2013, *Kasymakhunov and Saybatalov v. Russia*, appl. nos. 26261/05 and 26377/06, par. 105. See also ECtHR 25 May 1998 (GC), *Socialist Party and Others v. Turkey*, appl. no. 21237/93, par. 46-47; ECtHR 9 April 2002, *Yazar v. Turkey*, appl. nos. 22723/93, 22724/93 and 22725/93, par. 49; ECtHR 13 February 2003 (GC), *Refah Partisi (the Welfare Party) and other v. Turkey*, appl. nos. 41340/98 et al., par. 97-98.
180 ECtHR 14 March 2013, *Kasymakhunov and Saybatalov v. Russia*, appl. nos. 26261/05 and 26377/06, par. 106-108.

regarding the incompatibility of the ideology of Hizb Ut-Tahrir with the Convention. Second, the Court held that the legal and constitutional changes proposed by Hizb Ut-Tahrir were incompatible with the fundamental democratic principles underlying the Convention.[181] Here the Court also took into account that Hizb Ut-Tahrir challenged the secular organisation of democracies and advocated a theocratic regime, an element that was not taken into consideration in the case *Hizb Ut-Tahrir v. Germany* for that matter. The Court held that under the regime proposed by the organisation there is no respect for political freedoms. The regime that Hizb Ut-Tahrir intends to set up is based on the rules of the Sharia, a system the Court had earlier already identified as incompatible with the fundamental principles of democracy.[182] By spreading the ideas of this organisation, the applicants had engaged in an activity that falls within the scope of Article 17 ECHR.[183] The complaint was therefore considered incompatible *ratione materiae* with the provisions of the Convention.

Yet, even with regard to speech that calls for violence the Court's approach is not uniform. A decade earlier, in the case *Kaptan v. Turkey*, the Court adopted a different approach. In this case, the Court found that the distribution of pro-Kurdish propaganda which *'advocated and glorified violence and aimed at winning over as many persons as possible for the armed struggle against the Turkish authorities'* was *'not covered by Article 10 of the Convention'*.[184] Article 17 ECHR was not mentioned in this regard. Paradoxically, however, the Court subsequently continued to assess the case under Article 10(2) ECHR and concluded that the interference with the applicant's right to freedom of expression could reasonably be considered necessary in a democratic society.[185] Eventually, the Court declared the complaint manifestly ill-founded.[186]

In other cases in which the applicant called for violence, however, the Court did consider the activities in question to be covered by the right to freedom of expression and dealt with the cases on their merits in the light of Article 10(2) ECHR. In these cases Article 17 ECHR was again not mentioned and the cases were not declared manifestly ill-founded. In another case concerning pro-Kurdish propaganda, for example, the Court found that the letters that were published by the applicant expressed that recourse to violence would be a necessary and justified measure of self-defence in the face of the Kurdish fight for independence. The Court therefore found that the letters in question amounted *'to an appeal to bloody revenge*

181 ECtHR 14 March 2013, *Kasymakhunov and Saybatalov v. Russia*, appl. nos. 26261/05 and 26377/06, par. 109-112.

182 See also ECtHR 13 February 2003 (GC), *Refah Partisi (the Welfare Party) and other v. Turkey*, appl. nos. 41340/98 et al., par. 117-128.

183 ECtHR 14 March 2013, *Kasymakhunov and Saybatalov v. Russia*, appl. nos. 26261/05 and 26377/06, par. 113.

184 ECtHR 12 April 2001 (dec.), *Kaptan* v. *Switzerland*, appl. no. 55641/00, par. 1.

185 See also Buyse, *Shaping Rights in the ECHR*, p. 199.

186 ECtHR 12 April 2001 (dec.), *Kaptan* v. *Switzerland*, appl. no. 55641/00, par. 1.

by stirring up base emotions and hardening already embedded prejudices which have manifested themselves in deadly violence'. Especially in the context of the already tense situation between the PKK and the Turkish state, *'the content of the letters must be seen as capable of inciting to further violence in the region by instilling a deep-seated and irrational hatred against those depicted as responsible for the alleged atrocities. Indeed, the message which is communicated to the reader is that recourse to violence is a necessary and justified measure of self-defence in the face of the aggressor'*.[187] In those circumstances, the Court considered that the interference at issue was proportionate to the legitimate aims pursued and did not disclose a breach of Article 10 ECHR.[188]

3.4.5 Challenges to the notion of secularism

The Court has repeatedly emphasised that individuals or groups with totalitarian aims that want to put an end to democracy can be denied the protection of the Convention pursuant to Article 17 ECHR.[189] The question is whether this also applies to groups or political parties that aim to replace the free and pluralistic democratic system with a theocratic system. Under such a system, in which there is no separation of Church and state, the suspicion is inevitable that the human rights standards developed in the context of the ECHR will not be met. As Buyse rightly points out, this issue *'strikes at the heart of the original purpose of Article 17: to protect democracy and thereby fundamental rights'*.[190]

The Court was confronted with the applicability of the prohibition of abuse of rights to the advocacy of a theocratic regime in the hallmark case *Refah Partisi v. Turkey*. The political party Refah Partisi was founded in 1983 and had become a political actor to be reckoned with in Turkish politics. It had become the largest party in the Turkish Parliament and in 1996 had formed a coalition government in which it

187 ECtHR 8 July 1999 (GC), *Sürek v. Turkey (no. 1)*, appl. no. 26682/95, par. 62.

188 Ibid, par. 65. See for a similar line of reasoning ECtHR 30 June 2009, *Herri Batasuna and Batasuna v. Spain*, appl. nos. 25803/04 and 25817/04. With regard to the two political parties in question, which were said to support the Basque terrorist organisation ETA, the Court found that their conduct *'bears a strong resemblance to explicit support for violence and the commendation of people seemingly linked to terrorism'* (par. 86). The Court therefore could not accept that *'the impugned conduct was covered by the protection afforded to freedom of expression, as claimed by the applicant parties, since the methods used fell outside the bounds set by the Court's case-law, namely the lawfulness of the means used to exercise that right and their compatibility with fundamental democratic principles'* (par. 87), a reasoning that shows a resemblance to that of Article 17 ECHR. This provision, however, was not mentioned by either the defending government or by the Court. Eventually the Court concluded that the dissolution of the parties was necessary in a democratic society and did not find a violation of Article 11 ECHR (par. 94-95).

189 See e.g. ECtHR 1 July 196, *Lawless v. Ireland (no. 3)*, appl. no. 332/57, par. 6.

190 Buyse, *Shaping Rights in the ECHR*, p. 201.

was the dominant player.[191] Nonetheless, Turkey's Constitutional Court dissolved the party in 1998 on the ground of having become a *'centre of activities contrary to the principle of secularism'*, a pillar of Turkish democracy enshrined in its Constitution.[192] The first controversial aspect of the applicant's political agenda was its proposal to establish a plurality of legal systems, which means that each religious community in Turkey would be governed according to the laws of its own faith.[193] Yet, even more controversial was the party's declared *'commitment to sharia as the source of all basic law'*.[194] In its decision to ban the party, the Turkish Constitutional Court had referred to both Article 11(2) and Article 17 ECHR and *'pointed out in that context that Refah's leaders and members were using democratic rights and freedoms with a view to replacing the democratic order with a system based on sharia'*.[195] Refah Partisi complained about this ban before the Strasbourg Court. In 2001 the Court's Chamber decided by a slight majority of four votes to three that there had been no violation of Article 11 ECHR.[196]

In an extensive judgment, the Grand Chamber eventually unanimously confirmed the Chamber's conclusion that the ban on this political party had been justified. With regard to the right to freedom of association, the Grand Chamber in the first place reaffirmed the primordial role played in a democratic regime by political parties that enjoy the right to freedom of association in Article 11 ECHR and the right to freedom of expression in Article 10 ECHR. At the same time, however, these rights *'cannot deprive the authorities of a State in which an association, through its activities, jeopardises that State's institutions, of the right to protect those institutions'*.[197] Nevertheless, the protection of democratic institutions must be in accordance with the requirements set out in paragraph 2 of Article 11 ECHR. The Grand Chamber – rather confusingly – held that *'[o]nly when that review is complete will the Court be in a position to decide, in the light of all the circumstances of the case, whether Article 17 of the Convention should be applied'*.[198] Paradoxically, however, the test applied by the Grand Chamber to assess the necessity of the measure in a democratic society clearly echoes the logic of the abuse clause in Article 17 ECHR.[199]

---

191 S. Issacharoff, 'Fragile Democracies', *Harvard Law Review*, vol. 120, no. 6, 2007, p. 1443.
192 ECtHR 13 February 2003 (GC), *Refah Partisi (the Welfare Party) and other v. Turkey*, appl. nos. 41340/98 et al., par. 23.
193 Issacharoff, *Harvard Law Review*, p. 1444-1445.
194 Issacharoff, p. 1444-1445.
195 ECtHR 13 February 2003 (GC), *Refah Partisi (the Welfare Party) and other v. Turkey*, appl. nos. 41340/98 et al., par. 40.
196 ECtHR 31 July 2001, *Refah Partisi (the Welfare Party) and others v. Turkey*, appl. nos. 41340/98 et al.
197 ECtHR 13 February 2003 (GC), *Refah Partisi (the Welfare Party) and other v. Turkey*, appl. nos. 41340/98 et al., par. 96.
198 Ibid, par. 96.
199 See also Haeck, *Handboek EVRM. Deel 2*, p. 245; Buyse, *Shaping Rights in the ECHR*, p. 202.

In the light of the scrutiny of the party ban under Article 11 ECHR, the Court recalled that according to its earlier case law, political parties *'may promote a change in the law or the legal and constitutional structures of the State on two conditions: firstly, the means used to that end must be legal and democratic; secondly, the change proposed must itself be compatible with fundamental democratic principles'*.[200] Yet, while referring to the Commission's admissibility decision in the German Communist Party case, the Court also stressed that the possibility exists that a political party may use the rights in the Convention for activities *'intended to destroy the rights or freedoms set forth in the Convention and thus bring about the destruction of democracy'*.[201] *'In view of the very clear link between the Convention and democracy'*, the Court brought to mind that *'no one must be authorised to rely on the Convention's provisions in order to weaken or destroy the ideals and values of a democratic society. Pluralism and democracy are based on a compromise that requires various concessions by individuals or groups of individuals, who must sometimes agree to limit some of the freedoms they enjoy in order to guarantee greater stability of the country as a whole'*.[202] Where political parties are concerned, however, the conditions for restricting the right to freedom of association have to be interpreted restrictively. Furthermore, a party's constitution and programme alone are not sufficient to determine its objectives and intentions and therefore have to be compared with the actions and discourse of the party's leaders. In the case of Refah Partisi, the Grand Chamber found that the party's aim to set up a theocratic regime based on Sharia law was incompatible with democracy.[203] Moreover, the fact that the party *'had the real potential to seize political power without being restricted by the compromises inherent in a coalition'* made the danger to democracy more tangible and more immediate.[204] The Court therefore held that it *'cannot criticise the national courts for not acting earlier, at the risk of intervening prematurely and before the danger concerned had taken shape and become real. Nor can it criticise them for not waiting, at the risk of putting the political regime and civil peace in jeopardy, for Refah to seize power and swing into action, for example by tabling bills in Parliament, in order to implement its plans'*.[205] Several commentators have noted that this reveals that, contrary to the older cases regarding the prohibition of Nazi parties and the German Communist Party, not just the party's intent matters but also

200 ECtHR 13 February 2003 (GC), *Refah Partisi (the Welfare Party) and other v. Turkey*, appl. nos. 41340/98 et al., par. 98.
201 Ibid, par. 99.
202 Ibid, par. 99.
203 Ibid, par. 125.
204 Ibid, par. 108-110.
205 Ibid, par. 110.

the imminence of the risk it poses to the democratic regime.[206] The Grand Chamber, just like the Chamber and the Turkish Constitutional Court before it[207], considered these plans incompatible with the concept of a democratic society. Sharia law, the Court found, *'is incompatible with the fundamental principles of democracy, as set forth in the Convention'*.[208] The Court therefore concluded that Refah's dissolution was necessary in a democratic society and there had accordingly been no violation of Article 11 ECHR.[209]

3.4.6 Paksas v. Lithuania

A somewhat odd case in the list of Article 17 ECHR case law is that of *Paksas v. Lithuania*. This case did not deal with any of the usual Article 17 ECHR topics: the banning of extreme political parties and expressions. On the other hand, given that it allegedly concerned the protection of the constitutional order, it is understandable why that the issue of Article 17 ECHR came up. The central question with respect to the application of Article 17 ECHR in this case was whether the former Lithuanian President, Paksas, who had been removed from public office through an impeachment procedure, was allowed to rely on the right to stand for election guaranteed in Article 3 First Protocol ECHR to challenge the prohibition to apply for public office for a second time. Paksas had been brought into discredit after issuing a decree granting Lithuanian citizenship by way of an exception to a Russian businessman. Upon a

206 S. Sottiaux, 'Anti-democratic Associations: Content and Consequences in Article 11 Adjudication', *Netherlands Quarterly of Human Rights*, vol. 22, no. 4, 2004, p. 599; Buyse, *Shaping Rights in the ECHR*, p. 202.

207 ECtHR 31 July 2001, *Refah Partisi (the Welfare Party) and others v. Turkey*, appl. nos. 41340/98 et al., par. 72.

208 ECtHR 13 February 2003 (GC), *Refah Partisi (the Welfare Party) and other v. Turkey*, appl. nos. 41340/98 et al., par. 123.

209 In this regard it is also worth referring to the Court's admissibility decision regarding the Dutch Christian political party SGP. According to this party's basic tenets *'Government should govern as God's servant according to the Word of God'*. The party accordingly believes that men and women have different roles in society and that women, unlike men, should not be eligible for public office (par. 6-8). The Court recalled that *'not only is democracy a fundamental feature of the European public order but the Convention was designed to promote and maintain the ideals and values of a democratic society'* (par. 70) and that a political party may pursue its political aims on two conditions: 1) the means used towards those ends must be legal and democratic; 2) the changes proposed must themselves be compatible with fundamental democratic principles (par. 71). Based on Article 3 First Protocol in conjunction with Article 14 ECHR, the Court confirmed the domestic court's conclusion that *'the SGP's position is unacceptable regardless of the deeply-held religious conviction on which it is based'* (par. 77). Consequently, the Court found that *'the application is manifestly ill-founded and must be rejected'* (par. 79). Even though the firm reasoning of the Court with regard to the incompatibility of the discriminatory policy of the SGP with the principles of democracy shows a resemblance to the logic of Article 17 ECHR, this provision was not mentioned in the decision.

request by the Lithuanian Parliament, the Constitutional Court concluded that the decree was not in compliance with the Constitution and the Citizenship Act and that the decision to grant the Russian businessman Lithuanian citizenship was not based on his worthiness to become a citizen, but on his significant contribution to Paksas' election campaign. In April 2004 Paksas was removed from the office of President. Nevertheless, Paksas sought to run for president again in June 2004. Quickly, the relevant legislation was amended to make sure that a person who had been impeached could not be re-elected as president[210] nor be elected as a member of parliament.

Before the Strasbourg Court, the Lithuanian government held that with regard to the application of Article 17 ECHR that *'it would be contrary to the general principles set forth in the Court's case-law concerning protection of democracy for the applicant to be able to stand in parliamentary elections after having breached his constitutional oath'*.[211] The Court referred to the purpose of Article 17 ECHR and emphasised that it is *'applicable only on an exceptional basis and in extreme cases, as indeed is illustrated by the Court's case-law'*.[212] Subsequently, the Court held that it found no indication that the applicant was pursuing totalitarian aims. Eventually, the Court concluded that the applicant had *'relied legitimately on Article 3 of Protocol No. 1 to challenge his disqualification from elected office [...]. In other words, he is seeking to regain the full enjoyment of a right which the Convention in principle secures to everyone, and of which he claims to have been wrongly deprived by the Lithuanian authorities, the Government's allegation that the applicant's real aim is to be re-elected President of Lithuania being immaterial in this context. Article 17 of the Convention cannot therefore apply'*.[213]

3.5 Conclusions

This chapter examined the interpretation of Article 17 ECHR by the EComHR and the ECtHR. Judgments and admissibility decisions in which the interpretation of Article 17 ECHR has been clarified are rare. Buyse has noted that the *'lack of prominence of Article 17 ECHR in the case law of the Convention's supervisory institutions has been called paradoxical, considering how important is the underlying idea of protecting democracy'*.[214] For a long time, the prohibition of abuse of rights seemed

210 Because the Court – not completely convincingly – considered the office of president not to fall under the definition of legislature in Article 3 First Protocol, the complaint regarding this aspect was declared inadmissible and the Court confined its evaluation to Paksas' disqualification for being elected a member of parliament. See also De Lange, Case note to *Paksas v. Lithuania*, *EHRC* 2011/47, par. 11.

211 ECtHR 6 January 2011 (GC), *Paksas v. Lithuania*, appl. no. 34932/04, par. 85.

212 Ibid, par. 87.

213 Ibid, par. 89.

214 Buyse, *Shaping Rights in the ECHR*, p. 191-192. See also Van Drooghenbroeck, *Revue trimestrielle des droits de l'homme*, p. 542.

to play a passive role. During the early years of the Convention the abuse clause was sporadically referred to in relation to extreme political views related to the totalitarian threats identified at the time of drafting of the Convention: Communism and neo-Nazism. This overview has shown, however, that over the past decade the Court has increasingly taken an interest in the prohibition of abuse of rights. As a result, the scope of Article 17 ECHR has been broadened and Article 17 ECHR has increasingly been applied to issues that go beyond the original interpretation of the provision as a rampart against totalitarianism. The Court has progressively identified activities that are contrary to the '*basic*', '*underlying*' or '*fundamental*' '*values*' or '*ideas*' or the '*text and spirit*' of the Convention, such as racial discrimination or hostility towards a religious group, to be abusive in the sense of Article 17 ECHR.[215] In these cases the decision to apply Article 17 ECHR seems to have been primarily provoked by the intolerance that resonates from these racist and discriminatory statements.[216]

Furthermore, the case law makes very clear that the Commission and the Court have failed to stipulate clear criteria for the application of Article 17 ECHR. This makes an analysis of the case law particularly difficult. In the case *Paksas v. Lithuania*, the Court stressed that this provision '*is applicable only on an exceptional basis and in extreme cases*'.[217] Still, it is far from clear which cases fit this description, as the case law analysis reveals an obscure and inconsistent case-to-case approach.

First, the case law demonstrates that the Court failed to clearly define the material scope of Article 17 ECHR. On the one hand, the judgments and admissibility decisions in which Article 17 ECHR was applied cover a wide variety of activities, ranging from Holocaust denial, support for communist ideology, hate speech, challenges to the principle of secularism, and incitement to violence. On the other hand, however, the Commission and the Court refused to apply Article 17 ECHR in relation to other extreme activities. Moreover, the reasoning why the circumstances of a certain case justify a different approach often fails to be convincing. For example, while the Court has consistently and without much ado found that Holocaust denial is covered by Article 17 ECHR, it has been reluctant to apply the provision to revisionist speech concerning other historical events. With regard to the mass deportations and massacres of Armenians by the Ottoman Empire in 1915, for example, the Court found that it was '*not immediately clear*' that the applicant '*sought to stir up hatred*

215 See e.g. EComHR 6 September 1995, *Remer v. Germany*, appl. no. 25096/94, par. 1; EComHR 18 October 1995, *Honsik v. Austria*, appl. no. 25062/94; EComHR 29 November 1995, *Nationaldemokratische Partei Deutschlands, Bezirksverband München-Oberbayern v. Germany*, appl. no. 25992/94; EComHR 24 June 1996, *Marais v. France*, appl. no. 31159/96, par. 1; ECtHR 16 November 2004 (dec.), *Norwood v. the United Kingdom*, appl. no. 23131/03; ECtHR 14 March 2013, *Kasymakhunov and Saybatalov v. Russia*, appl. nos. 26261/05 and 26377/06, par. 113.

216 See e.g. ECtHR 20 February 2007 (dec.), *Ivanov v. Russia*, appl. no. 35222/04; ECtHR 16 November 2004 (dec.), *Norwood v. the United Kingdom*, appl. no. 23131/03.

217 ECtHR 6 January 2011 (GC), *Paksas v. Lithuania*, appl. no. 34932/04, par. 87.

or violence' and therefore did not consider it appropriate to apply the abuse clause,[218] a criterion that has not been used in cases concerning Holocaust revisionism. Also with regard to the purpose of Article 17 ECHR to uphold the democratic system, the principal aim of the abuse clause according to its drafters, the Strasbourg approach fails to be convincing. While the core purpose of Article 17 ECHR is the protection of the democratic regime, the Court abstained from referring to Article 17 ECHR in the *Refah Partisi* case in relation to a political party whose *'aim to set up a theocratic regime based on sharia was incompatible with democracy'*.[219] Moreover, the Commission and the Court have in some cases considered that racist hate speech *'clearly constitutes an activity within the meaning of Article 17 of the Convention'*[220] while in other cases they found that the racist utterances of the applicant were not sufficiently serious to justify the application of Article 17 ECHR.[221]

Second, the case law is not clear as to how Article 17 ECHR should be applied. The Court's approach to the form in which Article 17 ECHR is applied has been rather irregular with the result that over the years a wide range of different applications has evolved. In some cases the Commission and the Court have used Article 17 ECHR to declare applications inadmissible as being incompatible *ratione materiae* with the rights and freedoms enshrined in the Convention. This suggests that once it has been established that the activities of the applicant fall within the scope of Article 17 ECHR, this results in the inadmissibility of the application exempting the Commission or the Court from examining the case under the relevant provisions of the Convention. In other cases, however, activities that were identified as falling within the scope of Article 17 ECHR were still examined in accordance with the second paragraphs of Articles 10 and 11 ECHR. In a number of early admissibility decisions regarding Holocaust denial, for example, the Commission referred to Article 17 ECHR in the context of the necessity of the interference with the applicant's right to freedom of expression. Even though the Commission found that the denial of the Holocaust was an activity *'contrary to the text and spirit of the Convention and which, if admitted, would contribute to the destruction of the rights and freedoms set forth in the Convention'*, it continued to assess these cases under Article 10(2) ECHR.[222] Yet, in some cases these two approaches seem to be downright confused. In the *Refah Partisi* case, for example, the Court held that only when the review of the case in the light of

218 ECtHR 15 October 2015 (GC), *Perinçek v. Switzerland*, appl. no. 27510/08, par. 115.

219 ECtHR 13 February 2003 (GC), *Refah Partisi (the Welfare Party) and other v. Turkey*, appl. nos. 41340/98 et al., par. 125.

220 EComHR 11 October 1979, *Glimmerveen and Hagenbeek v. the Netherlands*, appl. nos. 8348/78 and 8406/78.

221 ECtHR 16 July 2009, *Féret v. Belgium*, appl. no. 15615/07. See also Buyse, *Shaping Rights in the ECHR*, p. 202-203.

222 EComHR 2 September 1994, *Ochensberger v. Austria*, appl. no. 21318/93, par. 1; EComHR 18 October 1995, *Honsik v. Austria*, appl. no. 25062/94; EComHR 24 June 1996, *Marais v. France*, appl. no. 31159/96, par. 1; EComHR 16 January 1996, *Rebhandl v. Austria*, appl. no. 24398/94, par. 3.

the requirements set out in paragraph 2 of Article 11 ECHR is complete will it be *'in a position to decide, in the light of all the circumstances of the case, whether Article 17 of the Convention should be applied'*.[223] Furthermore, in a number of cases the EComHR and the ECtHR followed a reasoning comparable to that adopted under Article 17 ECHR without openly referring to this provision. In addition, in a few cases they even completely ignored the abuse clause and the accompanying case law in cases where the provision logically could have seemed relevant.

In sum, as Judge Silvis critically noted in his dissenting opinion in the *Perinç*ek case, it seems that the Court *'has kept its options open'* when it comes to the application of Article 17 ECHR.[224] Since Article 17 ECHR covers a wide variety of activities and has been applied in different forms in comparable cases, it is almost impossible to distinguish clear criteria for the application of Article 17 ECHR.[225] This inconsistent and obscure approach makes it highly unpredictable whether a case will be examined under Article 17 ECHR or under the limitation clauses in Article 10(2) or 11(2) ECHR. As a result, applicants are unable to foresee whether the abuse clause will play a role in their case, and if so, whether that will result in the inadmissibility of the case or not. Given the fundamental nature of the abuse clause and the fact that the provision is increasingly applied these uncertainties are highly undesirable. The provision's ambiguous nature has also repeatedly drawn the attention of legal scholars. In order to further clarify the abuse clause, the next chapter will therefore analyse the interpretation of Article 17 ECHR in legal doctrine.

---

223 ECtHR 13 February 2003 (GC), *Refah Partisi (the Welfare Party) and other v. Turkey*, appl. nos. 41340/98 et al., par. 96. See also ECtHR 16 July 2009, *Féret c. Belgique*, appl. no. 15615/07, par. 82 and ECtHR 10 July 2008, *Soulas et autres c. France*, appl. no. 15948/03, par. 48.

224 Dissenting opinion in the case ECtHR 15 October 2015 (GC), *Perinçek v. Switzerland*, appl. no. 27510/08 of Judge Silvis (the Netherlands), joined by Judges Casadevall (Andorra), Berro (Monaco) and Kūris (Lithuania) par. 8.

225 See also Harris et al., *Law of the ECHR*, p. 854 at footnote 21.

Chapter 4
The Interpretation of Article 17 ECHR in Legal Doctrine

4.1 Introduction

In the previous chapter we have seen how the ECommHR and the ECtHR have interpreted Article 17 ECHR. We have seen that their approach is inconsistent and raises many questions regarding the functioning of the abuse clause in the context of the ECHR. Because of a lack of clear criteria for the interpretation of Article 17 ECHR, the provision has increasingly been applied to a wide range of allegedly abusive activities. In addition, case law revealed ambiguity about how Article 17 ECHR should be applied. Over the course of time a wide range of different applications have evolved that seem to be applied unsystematically.

This chapter turns to the academic debate on Article 17 ECHR. Notwithstanding its limited practical relevance in the decisions and judgments of the Commission and the Court, Article 17 ECHR has been the subject of academic debate since the Convention entered into force. The provision's ambiguous nature has repeatedly drawn the attention of legal scholars. And with the increase of references to Article 17 ECHR in the case law of the Court, the interest in the provision by legal scholars has also experienced an upsurge. This chapter will examine the contemporary interpretation of Article 17 ECHR in legal doctrine. It will discuss how they read the scope and legal consequences of the provision and the methods of its application. Subsequently, it will discuss the academic debate that has unfolded on the current interpretation and application of Article 17 ECHR by the Strasbourg organs. Every now and then references will be made to relevant case law on Article 17 ECHR when legal scholars have explicitly cited these cases to substantiate their claims. To a great extent, these cases will overlap with the cases discussed in the previous chapter, but occasionally they may not.

4.2 Different addressees of Article 17 ECHR

Article 17 ECHR is unique in the sense that it is the only provision that addresses both the States Parties that have to guarantee the fundamental rights in the Convention and individuals and groups who enjoy these rights.[1] Several legal scholars have argued that

1 Y. Arai (rev.), 'Prohibition of abuse of the rights and freedoms set forth in the convention and of their limitation to a greater extent than is provided for in the convention (Article 17)', in: P. van Dijk et al. (eds.), *Theory and practice of the European Convention on Human Rights*, 4th ed., Antwerp/Oxford: Intersentia, 2006, p. 1085.

the different addressees in Article 17 ECHR – states, groups and persons – are subject to different norms that stem from the provision.[2] Article 17 ECHR not only refers to abuse with the aim of destroying the rights and freedoms set forth in the Convention, but also to the abuse of the competence to limit these rights. Van Drooghenbroeck points to the fact that the relation between the different addressees of Article 17 ECHR and the two norms laid down in the provision was not discussed during the creation of the Convention.[3] Nevertheless, commentators generally seem to assume that the last part of the sentence is aimed at the States Parties to the Convention, while the first part of Article 17 ECHR is primarily directed at groups and individuals.

So, according to legal doctrine, states would be subject to the second norm laid down in Article 17 ECHR, which prohibits any excessive restriction of fundamental rights (i.e. activities or acts aimed at the limitation of any of the rights and freedoms set forth in the Convention *'to a greater extent than is provided for in the Convention'*).[4] The *travaux préparatoires* do not explain why states are included in Article 17 ECHR. Yet, we do know that during the drafting of the ECHR the Committee of Ministers of the CoE closely followed the preparation of the International Covenants at the UN level.[5] In fact, the text for the abuse clause was taken from the draft of the ICCPR.[6] In this draft states had by then been included in the abuse clause, because in the past they had frequently been the chief offenders against human rights.[7] In the Strasbourg practice, scholars have observed, this aspect of the provision hardly seems to play

2 Y. Haeck, 'Artikel 17 Verbod van rechtsmisbruik' ['Article 17 Prohibition of Abuse of rights'], in: Vande Lanotte, J. and Haeck, Y. (eds.), *Handboek EVRM. Deel 2. Artikelsgewijze commentaar, volume II [Handbook ECHR. Part 2. Commentary by article, volume II]*, Antwerp/Oxford: Intersentia, 2004, p. 245; S. Van Drooghenbroeck, 'L'Article 17 de la Convention Européenne des Droits de l'Homme est-il indispensable?', *Revue trimestrielle des droits de l'homme*, vol. 12, no. 46, 2001, p. 543-550; Arai, *Theory and practice of the ECHR*, p. 1084; J.E.S. Fawcett, *The Application of the European Convention on Human Rights*, Oxford: Clarendon Press, 1987, p. 315; D.J. Harris et al. (eds.), *Harris, O'Boyle and Warbrick. Law of the European Convention on Human Rights*, 3rd ed., Oxford: Oxford University Press, 2014, p. 852-857.

3 Van Drooghenbroeck, *Revue trimestrielle des droits de l'homme*, p. 545.

4 Van Drooghenbroeck, *Revue trimestrielle des droits de l'homme*, p. 543-550; Arai, *Theory and practice of the ECHR*, p. 1084; Fawcett, *The Application of the ECHR*, p. 315.

5 A. Robertson (ed.), *Collected edition of the 'Travaux Préparatoires' (hereafter referred to as 'TP'), vol. II*, The Hague: Martinus Nijhof, 1975-1985, p. 302. See also E. Bates, *The Evolution of the European Convention on Human Rights. From its Inception to the Creation of a Permanent Court of Human Rights*, Oxford: Oxford University Press, 2010, p. 80.

6 A.M. Williams, 'The European Convention on Human rights: a new use?', *Texas International Law Journal*, vol. 12, 1977, p. 281. See also Robertson, *TP*, vol. III, p. 32. Preparatory work on Article 17 of the European Convention on Human Rights, Information document prepared by the Secretariat of the Commission, Strasbourg, 5 March 1975, CDH(75)7 (Doc A. 38.797), p. 9.

7 UN ECOSOC, Commission on Human Rights, second session, 41st meeting, 16 December 1947, *UN doc. E/CN.4/SR.41*, p. 7-9.

any role. In fact, no state has ever been condemned for nullifying the fundamental rights set forth in the Convention by restricting them further than is provided for.[8]

It has been argued that excessively restricting the rights in the Convention is also prohibited by Article 18 ECHR and the limitation clauses in the second paragraphs of Articles 8 to 11 ECHR.[9] The limitation clauses in the second paragraphs of Articles 8 to 11 ECHR provide that interferences with these rights are only justified if they are proscribed by law and necessary in a democratic society in the interest of one of the legitimate objectives listed in these provisions. Commentators have observed that the absence of a violation of the right of the applicant generally releases the Court from any additional review of state action under Article 17 ECHR.[10] Moreover, when the Court finds a violation of a right, it does not consider it necessary to examine the case under Articles 17 ECHR.[11] In addition, Article 18 ECHR prohibits a misuse of power (*détournement de pouvoir*) by the States Parties by providing that the restrictions permitted under the Convention may not be applied for any purpose other than those for which they have been prescribed.[12] If the prohibition on limiting rights beyond what is provided for in the Convention also includes the requirement that the limitation must serve one of the legitimate aims provided in the limitation clause, there is a certain overlap between the two provisions. Commentators have therefore argued that Article 17 ECHR merely confirms the norms to which states are already bound based on the general limitation requirements of the specific rights and freedoms and Article 18 ECHR.[13] This leaves little room for an autonomous role of

---

8 Haeck, *Handboek EVRM. Deel* 2, p. 246. The only time the prohibition to invoke restrictions with the aim of undermining the Convention's underlying values played a (slight) role was in the inter-state procedures in the *Greek case*: EComHR 5 November 1969 (report), *Denmark, Norway, Sweden and the Netherlands v. Greece (The Greek case)*, appl. nos. 3321/67, 3322/67, 3323/67, 3344/67, par. 149, see Chapter three.

9 Haeck, *Handboek EVRM. Deel* 2, p. 248; J.A. Frowein, 'Artikel 17', in: J.A. Frowein and W. Peukert, *Europaïsche MenschenRechtsKonvention*, 3rd ed., Kehl am Rhein: N.P. Engel Verlag, 2009, p. 431; J.F. Flauss, 'L'abus de droit dans le cadre de la Convention européenne des droits de l'homme', *Revue Universelle des Droits de l'Homme*, vol 4, no. 12, 1992, p. 461, footnote 5; A. Buyse, 'Contested contours. The limits of freedom of expression from an abuse of rights perspective – Articles 10 and 17 ECHR', in: *Shaping Rights in the ECHR. The Role of the European Court of Human Rights in Determining the Scope of Human Rights*, E. Brems and J. Gerards (eds.), Cambridge: Cambridge University Press, 2014, p. 188.

10 Frowein, *Europaïsche MenschenRechtsKonvention*, p. 433; Buyse, *Shaping Rights in the ECHR*, p. 188; Arai, *Theory and practice of the ECHR*, p. 1089; Fawcett, *The Application of the ECHR*, p. 315.

11 Frowein, *Europaïsche MenschenRechtsKonvention*, p. 433.

12 Article 18 ECHR reads: *'[t]he restrictions permitted under this Convention to the said rights and freedoms shall not be applied for any purpose other than those for which they have been prescribed'*. See on Article 18 ECHR Harris et al., *Law of the ECHR*, p. 857.

13 Frowein, *Europaïsche MenschenRechtsKonvention*, p. 431; Haeck, *Handboek EVRM. Deel 2*, p. 248; Harris et al., *Law of the ECHR*, p. 856.

the abuse clause vis-à-vis States Parties. Buyse therefore argues that *'the provision seems rather superfluous as a protection against state abuse'*.[14]

Groups and individuals, on the other hand, would primarily be subject to the norm that prohibits them from relying on the Convention to justify activities that are aimed at destroying the fundamental rights guaranteed in it (i.e. activities or acts *'aimed at the destruction of any of the rights and freedoms set forth [in the Convention]'*).[15] That is to say that states may invoke Article 17 ECHR essentially as a justification for restrictions or sanctions against individuals and groups that engage in subversive activities.[16] It has been noted that if the EComHR or the ECtHR has found that an applicant abused his fundamental right, this inevitably indicates that the state concerned did not violate the Convention.[17] Both in legal doctrine and in case law it is this application vis-à-vis individuals and groups that has received the most attention.

4.3 The relation between the two norms in Article 17 ECHR

There is uncertainty in legal doctrine regarding the relation between the two norms provided in Article 17 ECHR. Some scholars have argued that the two norms – one stating that the rights in the Convention are not to be interpreted as justifying the exercise of rights aimed at their destruction and one prohibiting their limitation to a greater extent than is provided for in the Convention – are contradictory and incompatible.[18] On the one hand, it has been pointed out that the beneficial effect of Article 17 ECHR is that it permits states to subject anti-democratic actors to restrictions that surpass the limitation clauses by denying them the protection of a right. In that sense, Article 17 ECHR would allow for limitations that go beyond those tolerated by the other provisions in the Convention. On other hand, however, the second part of the provision prohibits states from applying limitations that go further than those provided for in the limitation clauses of several fundamental rights. Some commentators have argued that this contradiction would be resolved if the

---

14 Buyse, *Shaping Rights in the ECHR*, p. 188.

15 Van Drooghenbroeck, p. 543-550; Arai, *Theory and practice of the ECHR*, p. 1084; Fawcett, *The Application of the ECHR*, p. 315; Harris et al., *Law of the ECHR*, p. 852-857.

16 Haeck, *Handboek EVRM. Deel 2*, p. 248.

17 Arai, *Theory and practice of the ECHR*, p. 1086-1088.

18 P. le Mire, 'L'Article 17', in: L.E. Pettiti, E. Decaux and P.H. Imbert (eds.), *La Convention Européenne des Droits de l'Homme: commentaire article par article*, 2nd ed., Paris: Economica, 1999, p. 521-522; J. Velu and R. Ergec, *La Convention européenne des droits de l'homme*, Brussels: Bruylant, 1990, p. 138-139; Flauss, *Revue Universelle des Droits de l'Homme*, p. 464; See also Fawcett, who argues that because *'Nothing in the Convention' also includes Article 17 ECHR itself, states may not transgress the limitations allowed under the Articles 8(2) until 11(2) ECHR when countering the activities of those who rely on the Convention to undermine it'*: Fawcett, *The Application of the ECHR*, p. 315.

provision would be interpreted as a simple interpretation clause that respects the limitation clauses of these fundamental rights.[19]

Nevertheless, Van Drooghenbroeck is of the opinion that this alleged antinomy is illusory. Focussing on the potential incompatibility of the two norms, he argues, attaches too much weight to the – clumsy – letter of the provision over its spirit.[20] Given that the abuse clause in the ECHR is based on Article 30 of the Universal Declaration of Human Rights, which exclusively corresponds to the first part of the sentence in Article 17 ECHR, Van Drooghenbroeck argues that the crucial purpose of the provision is to give democracy the additional means to defend itself. The second part of the provision must therefore in his view not be read so as to limit the state's powers under the first part of the sentence. Besides, he believes that the two parts of the provision will never apply simultaneously.[21] The first part of the provision limits the scope of application of the fundamental rights protected in the ECHR. Activities that constitute an abuse of rights, therefore, do not benefit from the protection of the Convention and thus fall *outside* the scope of its application. Alternatively, the second part of the provision refers exclusively to the limitation of rights with respect to activities that do fall *within* the scope of the Convention. Therefore, when an activity does not fall within the scope of application of the Convention, restrictions on the limitation of rights are no longer relevant and the second part of the provision does not apply.

4.4 Does Article 17 ECHR impose a positive obligation on states?

Ambiguity also exists as to whether Article 17 ECHR imposes a positive obligation on states to counter anti-democratic tendencies in society. In general, the Convention is interpreted as imposing both negative and positive obligations upon states. Negative obligations are those by which a state is required to abstain from interference with a right or freedom – typical for civil and political rights – , while positive obligations require a state to take action to secure fundamental rights.[22] A few scholars see the potential for such positive obligations arising from Article 17 ECHR.[23] Given that Article 17 ECHR can only be applied in connection with another right, positive

---

19 Flauss, *Revue Universelle des Droits de l'Homme*, p. 464; Velu and Ergec, *La Convention européenne des droits de l'homme*, Brussels: Bruylant, 1990, p. 139.

20 Van Drooghenbroeck, *Revue trimestrielle des droits de l'homme*, p. 546.

21 Van Drooghenbroeck, p. 547.

22 Harris et al., *Law of the ECHR*, p. 21-22. See extensively on the positive obligations of states under the ECHR e.g. D. Xenos (ed.), *The positive obligations of the state under the European Convention on Human Rights*, London/New York: Routledge, 2012; A.R. Mowbray, *The development of positive obligations under the European Convention on Human Rights by the European Court of Human Rights*, Oxford: Hart Publishing, 2004.

23 Williams, *Texas International Law Journal*, p. 287; Flauss, *Revue Universelle des Droits de l'Homme*, p. 465.

obligations would only derive from this provision read in conjunction with one of the fundamental rights, for example a positive obligation under Article 17 ECHR in conjunction with Article 11 ECHR to ban the assembly of a group whose activities are covered by Article 17 ECHR.[24] Williams believes that a positive obligation to restrain the activities of individuals and groups exercising fundamental rights to destroy the rights and freedoms guaranteed in the Convention could be derived from Article 17 ECHR read in conjunction with Article 1 ECHR. Under Article 1 ECHR, the States Parties have committed themselves to *'secure to everyone within their jurisdiction the rights and freedoms defined in Section I of this Convention'*. From this pledge, Williams derives that *'[s]tates, upon ratifying the Convention, have an affirmative duty to protect the rights enumerated in section I in such a way that these rights cannot be destroyed by anyone'*.[25] This positive obligation includes the adoption of specific national legislation, such as outlawing totalitarian political parties, and the active prosecution of individuals and groups threatening to destroy the protection of rights under the Convention.[26] *'Consequently'*, she argues, *'when a state permits individuals or groups to destroy or limit these rights, the state violates article 1, since it is not securing these rights to everyone within its jurisdiction'*.[27] A similar logic is found in Fox and Nolte. By becoming party to a human rights treaty that includes the obligation to hold genuine periodic elections, they argue, states have committed themselves vis-à-vis the international community to uphold democracy. The international community, as a kind of contractual guarantor of this commitment, *'may protect the democratic entitlement whether or not a majority of citizens at a particular moment chooses to reject its democratic institutions'*.[28] This also means that states are under the obligation to adopt measures of self-protection if this is necessary to ensure the continuation of democracy.[29]

Yet, such a broad interpretation of the abuse clause that imposes positive obligations on States Parties to the Convention is rejected by other scholars.[30] The critics of this reading argue that even though states can rely on Article 17 ECHR to take militant measures to protect freedom and democracy, this does not imply that states are under an obligation to take positive action in order to prevent an abuse of the Convention. As put by Harris *et al.*, even though Article 17 ECHR confers a power on states to act, it does not impose a positive duty to do so.[31] Buyse, however, points out that a positive obligation to counter groups or individuals with anti-democratic

24 This is what Fawcett appears to suggest: Fawcett, *The Application of the ECHR*, p. 275-276.
25 Williams, *Texas International Law Journal*, p. 287.
26 Williams, p. 287.
27 Williams, p. 287.
28 G.H. Fox and G. Nolte, 'Intolerant democracies', *Harvard International Law Journal*, vol. 36, no. 1, 1995, p. 61.
29 Fox and Nolte, p. 59-68.
30 Harris et al., *Law of the ECHR*, p. 856; Buyse, *Shaping Rights in the ECHR*, p. 189-190.
31 Harris et al., *Law of the ECHR*, p. 856.

aims may in fact arise from other international human rights treaties, such as the International Convention on the Elimination of All Forms of Racial Discrimination.[32] Under this Convention States Parties have agreed to condemn all forms of racial discrimination, undertake to pursue all reasonable measures to eliminate it, and to ensure that human rights are secured for all without such discrimination.[33] Under Article 4 of the ICERD, in particular, States Parties are required to enact and implement specific legislation on racial discrimination.[34] Yet, even if states based on other international treaties are required to counter anti-democratic groups and individuals, this does not create any positively obligation under Article 17 ECHR.

4.5 The relation between Article 17 ECHR and other provisions in the Convention

Article 17 ECHR provides that *'[n]othing in this Convention'* may be interpreted as justifying activities that seek the abolition or excessive limitation of fundamental rights. Commentators have stressed that the provision does not have an independent character and that it should always be applied in combination with one or more of the rights and freedoms guaranteed in the Convention or its accompanying protocols.[35] Yet, how the prohibition of abuse of rights exactly relates to the protection of

---

32 Buyse, *Shaping Rights in the ECHR*, p. 190.

33 Articles 2 to 5 of the International Convention on the Elimination of All Forms of Racial Discrimination, *UN doc.* A/6014, 660 *UNTS* 195, entered into force on 4 January 1969. See on this Conventiuon I. Hare, 'Extreme Speech Under International and Regional Human Rights Standards', in: I. Hare and J. Weinstein (eds.), *Extreme Speech and Democracy*, Oxford: Oxford University Press, 2009, p. 64-65 and 71-72.

34 Article 4 ICERD reads: '*States Parties condemn all propaganda and all organizations which are based on ideas or theories of superiority of one race or group of persons of one colour or ethnic origin, or which attempt to justify or promote racial hatred and discrimination in any form, and undertake to adopt immediate and positive measures designed to eradicate all incitement to, or acts of, such discrimination and, to this end, with due regard to the principles embodied in the Universal Declaration of Human Rights and the rights expressly set forth in article 5 of this Convention, inter alia:*
(a) Shall declare an offence punishable by law all dissemination of ideas based on racial superiority or hatred, incitement to racial discrimination, as well as all acts of violence or incitement to such acts against any race or group of persons of another colour or ethnic origin, and also the provision of any assistance to racist activities, including the financing thereof;
(b) Shall declare illegal and prohibit organizations, and also organized and all other propaganda activities, which promote and incite racial discrimination, and shall recognize participation in such organizations or activities as an offence punishable by law;
(c) Shall not permit public authorities or public institutions, national or local, to promote or incite racial discrimination'.

35 Arai, *Theory and practice of the ECHR*, p. 1084; H. Cannie and D. Voorhoof, 'The Abuse Clause and Freedom of Expression in the European Human Rights Convention: an Added Value for Democracy and Human Rights Protection?', *Netherlands Quarterly of Human Rights*, vol. 29, no. 1, 2001, p. 58; Haeck, *Handboek EVRM. Deel 2*, p. 247.

fundamental rights the provision does not say. Referring to the decision in the *German Communist Party* case, Spielmann recalls that the Commission's initial interpretation of the legal consequences of the application of Article 17 ECHR was a rather extensive one.[36] In this case, which has been discussed in more detail in the previous chapter, the Commission found that because the party had engaged in activities aimed at the destruction of any of the rights and freedoms set forth in the Convention, it could not *'rest upon* any *provision of the Convention, least of all on Articles 9, 10 and 11'*.[37] Even though the Commission singled out Articles 9, 10 and 11 ECHR that were invoked by the applicant, the decision appears to suggest that the abuse of one of the rights or freedoms in the Convention would cause the applicant to be completely excluded from the protection of the Convention. Such a broad interpretation of Article 17 ECHR has been rejected in legal doctrine. In the words of Spielmann, this approach implies that the competences of the States Parties under Article 17 ECHR would go beyond Article 15(2) ECHR and allow infringements of the *'hard core'* of human rights.[38] Such an interpretation would be incompatible with the Convention. It would basically render the applicant *'Vogelfrei'*, or outlawed, under the Convention, as Frowein put it.[39]

In a number of later cases, however, the EComHR and the ECtHR have placed important constraints on the application of Article 17 ECHR to justify restrictive measures. Based on this case law, commentators have asserted that the application of Article 17 ECHR always has to be linked to a specific Convention right or freedom that is deemed to be used with the intention of destroying other fundamental rights enshrined in the Convention.[40] In particular the *Lawless* case, which has been discussed in the previous chapter, is often cited in this regard. In this case the Court found for the first time that Article 17 ECHR *'covers essentially those rights which, if invoked, would facilitate the attempt to derive therefrom a right to engage personally in activities aimed at the destruction of "any of the rights and freedoms set forth in the Convention"'*.[41] Thus, Article 17 ECHR only applies to fundamental rights that entitle

36 A. Spielmann, 'La Convention Européenne des droits de l'homme et l'abus de droit', in: *Mélanges en hommage à Louis Edmond Pettiti*, Brussels: Bruylant, 1998, p. 683; Frowein, *Europaïsche MenschenRechtsKonvention*, p. 431-432.

37 EComHR 20 July 1957, *German Communist Party v. Germany*, appl. no. 250/57 [emphasis added].

38 Spielmann, *Mélanges en hommage à Louis Edmond Pettiti*, p. 683.

39 Frowein, *Europaïsche MenschenRechtsKonvention*, p. 431.

40 Cannie and Voorhoof, *Netherlands Quarterly of Human Rights*, p. 58; Arai, *Theory and practice of the ECHR*, p. 1088; Harris et al., *Law of the ECHR*, p. 853; Van Drooghenbroeck, *Revue trimestrielle des droits de l'homme*, p. 547.

41 ECtHR 1 July 1961, *Lawless v. Ireland (no. 3)*, appl. no. 332/57, par. 6, p. 18. See also more recently ECtHR 5 March 2013, *Varela Geis v. Spain*, appl. no. 61005/09, par. 40.

a group or a person to engage in subversive activities.[42] Arai has referred to as this criterion as the *'linkage requirement'*. This requirement sets out that *'the applicability of Article 17 depends on the requirement of linkage between Convention rights and the destructive aims pursued'*.[43] Yet, the next question that arises is whether all the fundamental rights guaranteed in the Convention can contribute to the pursuit of the destruction of democracy. In other words, which rights and freedoms enshrined in the Convention qualify for the application of Article 17 ECHR?

4.5.1 Which rights are eligible for the application of Article 17 ECHR?

While the wording of Article 17 ECHR suggests that the provision is applicable to all the rights and freedoms protected in the Convention, legal doctrine argues that only a small number of fundamental rights are actually apt for the application of Article 17 ECHR. Based on the required link between the exercise of a right and the destructive aims pursued, the nature of the majority of the provisions in the Convention and the protocols would make them unsuitable to facilitate an attempt to destroy the fundamental rights protected in the Convention.

4.5.1.1 Rights and freedoms that can be abused

In legal doctrine, the prohibition of abuse of rights has in particular been discussed in relation to the freedom of expression in Article 10 ECHR, since this is the right to which most Article 17 ECHR cases are linked.[44] Keane notes that the right to

---

42 B. Rainey, E. Wicks and C. Ovey, *Jacobs, White and Ovey. The European Convention on Human Rights*, 6th ed., Oxford: Oxford University Press, 2014, p. 122.

43 Arai, *Theory and practice of the ECHR*, p. 1088. Yet, when a part of the application is declared inadmissible based on Article 17 ECHR, another part of the application that is based on another right or freedom may still be admissible. In the case *Kasymahkunov and Saybatalov v. Russia*, for example, the Court held that based on Article 17 ECHR the applicants could not rely on Article 9, 10 or 11 of the Convention, but found a violation of Article 7 ECHR in respect of the second applicant: ECtHR 14 March 2013, *Kasymakhunov and Saybatalov v. Russia*, appl. nos. 26261/05 and 26377/06. See also Harris et al., *Law of the ECHR*, p. 853.

44 Cannie and Voorhoof, *Netherlands Quarterly of Human Rights*, p. 58; Buyse, *Shaping Rights in the ECHR*, p. 185. See on Article 17 ECHR in relation to Article 10 ECHR also D. Keane, 'Attacking hate speech under Article 17 of the European Convention on Human Rights', *Netherlands Quarterly of Human Rights*, vol. 25, no, 4, 2007; M. Oetheimer, 'Protecting freedom of expression: the challenge of hate speech in the European Court of Human Rights case law', *Cardozo Journal of International and Comparative Law*, vol. 17, no. 3, 2009; F. Tulkens, 'Les Relations entre le Négationnisme et les Droits de l'Homme. La Jurisprudence de la Cour Européenne des Droits de l'Homme', in: *Law in the Changing Europe, Liber Amicorum Pranas Kuris*, Vilnius: Mykolo Romerio universietas, 2008; A. Buyse, 'Dangerous expressions: the ECHR, Violence and Free Speech', *International and Comparative Law Quarterly*, vol. 63, no. 2, 2014; M.E. Villiger, 'Article 17 ECHR and freedom of speech in Strasbourg practice', in: J. Casadevall et al. (eds.), *Freedom of Expression. Essays in Honour of Nicolas Bratza*, Oisterwijk: Wolf Legal Publishers, 2012.

freedom of expression in Article 10(1) ECHR basically seems to protect all types of expression.[45] Contributions to the public debate, an essential feature of the democratic society, receive particular protection under Article 10 ECHR. In fact, Flauss has argued, *'freedom of expression is not only a subjective right of the individual against the State, but is also an objective fundamental principle for life in a democracy. That is, it is not an end unto itself, but a means toward the establishment of a democratic society; freedom of speech is necessary for the full development of social democratic ideals'*.[46] Several commentators recall in that regard that the Court stated in the case *Handyside v. the United Kingdom* that the right to freedom of expression constitutes *'one of the essential foundations'* of a democratic society and that it is *'one of the primary conditions of its progress and for the development of every man'*.[47] Consequently, *'it is applicable not only to 'information' or 'ideas' that are favourably received or regarded as inoffensive or as a matter of indifference, but also to those that offend, shock or disturb the State or any sector of the population'*.[48] Subsequently, it is generally up to the state to show that an interference with this right was justified under paragraph 2 of Article 10 ECHR.[49] Article 10(2) ECHR requires in that regard that an interference is prescribed by law[50] and necessary in a democratic society in the interests of national security, territorial integrity or public safety, for the prevention of disorder or crime, for the protection of health or morals, for the protection of the reputation or rights of others, for preventing the disclosure of information received in confidence, or for maintaining the authority and impartiality of the judiciary. This includes that any interference has to correspond to a pressing social need and is proportionate to the legitimate aim pursued.[51]

---

45 Keane, Netherlands Quarterly of Human Rights, p. 642. Article 10(1) ECHR reads: *'Everyone has the right to freedom of expression. This right shall include freedom to hold opinions and to receive and impart information and ideas without interference by public authority and regardless of frontiers. This Article shall not prevent States from requiring the licensing of broadcasting, television or cinema enterprises'*. See on the broad scope of Article 10(1) ECHR also Harris et al., *Law of the ECHR*, p. 614-617.

46 JF. Flauss, 'The European Court of Human Rights and the Freedom of Expression', *Indiana Law Journal*, vol. 84, no. 3, 2009, p. 814.

47 ECtHR 7 December 1976, *Handyside v. the United Kingdom*, appl. no. 5493/72, par. 49; Oetheimer, *Cardozo Journal of International and Comparative Law*, p. 427; Tulkens, *Law in the Changing Europe*, p. 809-849.

48 ECtHR 7 December 1976, *Handyside v. the United Kingdom*, appl. no. 5493/72, par. 49.

49 Article 10(2) reads: '*The exercise of these freedoms, since it carries with it duties and responsibilities, may be subject to such formalities, conditions, restrictions or penalties as are prescribed by law and are necessary in a democratic society, in the interests of national security, territorial integrity or public safety, for the prevention of disorder or crime, for the protection of health or morals, for the protection of the reputation or rights of others, for preventing the disclosure of information received in confidence, or for maintaining the authority and impartiality of the judiciary*'.

50 For an interpretation of this requirement see ECtHR 26 April 1979, *Sunday Times v. the United Kingdom (no. 1)*, appl. no. 6538/74, par. 49.

51 ECtHR 24 March 1988, *Olsson v. Sweden (no. 1)*, appl. no. 10465/83, par. 67.

The application of Article 17 ECHR has to a lesser extent also been linked to the right to freedom of association in Article 11 ECHR.[52] Like the freedom of expression, the freedom of association is central to the effective working of the democratic system.[53] Freedom of political opinion and freedom of association, including political parties, are *'primordial elements of any genuine democracy as envisaged by the Statute of the Council of Europe'*.[54] Although Article 11(1) ECHR does not specifically mention the freedom to form political parties, the provision is considered to provide for the creation and operation of such associations.[55] A political party has been defined by the Venice Commission as *'a free association of persons, one of the aims of which is to participate in the management of public affairs, including through the presentation of candidates to free and democratic elections'*.[56] Interferences with this right are only justified if they meet the criteria set out in paragraph 2 of the provision.[57] These require that any interference is prescribed by law and is necessary in a democratic society in the interests of national security or public safety, for the prevention of disorder or crime, for the protection of health or morals or for the protection of the rights and freedoms of others. Given the vital role of political parties in a democracy, restrictions on their creation and organisation should be applied with the utmost restraint. Before resorting to the prohibition or dissolution of a political party, therefore, the relevant state authorities should asses *'whether the party really represents a danger to the free and democratic political order or to the rights of individuals and whether other, less radical measures could prevent the said danger'*.[58]

---

52 Cannie and Voorhoof, *Netherlands Quarterly of Human Rights*, p. 58; Buyse, *Shaping Rights in the ECHR*, p. 185.

53 Harris et al., *Law of the ECHR*, p. 710.

54 CoE, Venice Commission, *Guidelines on prohibition and dissolution of political parties and analogous measures*, Venice, 10-11 December 1999, CDL-INF(2000)001, p. 4.

55 Harris et al., p. 710. Article 11(1) reads *'Everyone has the right to freedom of peaceful assembly and to freedom of association with others, including the right to form and to join trade unions for the protection of his interests'*.

56 CoE, Venice Commission and OSCE/ODIHR, *Guidelines on Political Party Regulation*, Venice, 15-16 October 2010, CDL-AD(2010)024, p. 8.

57 *Article 11(2) ECHR reads: 'No restrictions shall be placed on the exercise of these rights other than such as are prescribed by law and are necessary in a democratic society in the interests of national security or public safety, for the prevention of disorder or crime, for the protection of health or morals or for the protection of the rights and freedoms of others. This Article shall not prevent the imposition of lawful restrictions on the exercise of these rights by members of the armed forces, of the police or of the administration of the State'*.

58 CoE, Venice Commission, *Guidelines on prohibition and dissolution of political parties and analogous measures*, Venice, 10-11 December 1999, CDL-INF(2000)001, p. 5.

In addition, several commentators have asserted that Article 3 First Protocol can also be abused.[59] Hamilton, however, has suggested that the Court seems hesitant to accept claims of abuse of Article 3 First Protocol, due to the vital importance of this right for the democratic order of the state.[60] Article 3 First Protocol contains an obligation for the States Parties to *'hold free elections at reasonable intervals by secret ballot, under conditions which will ensure the free expression of the opinion of the people in the choice of the legislature'.* Article 3 First Protocol does not use the term 'democracy', but the provision is clearly an expression of the Convention's commitment to democratic ideals. By guaranteeing the right to free elections Article 3 First Protocol directly contributes to an *'effective political democracy'*.[61] The provision is not phrased in terms of a particular right or freedom, but the Court has found that it guarantees the individual rights to vote and to stand for election.[62] The prohibition of abuse of rights in Article 17 ECHR has so far been exclusively relevant to the right to stand for election and not for the right to vote. Even though the provision does not contain specific limitation requirements, the Court has insisted that this does not mean that the rights in question are absolute. They are subject to implied limitations on the basis of which certain individuals may be excluded from the electorate.[63]

Furthermore, some scholars have argued that also the right to right to respect for private and family life in Article 8 ECHR and the right to freedom of thought, conscience and religion in Article 9 ECHR fall within the scope of Article 17 ECHR.[64] It has also been suggested that the right to property protected in Article 1 First Protocol can be abused in the sense of Article 17 ECHR.[65] Other authors claim that Article 17 ECHR might also apply to the freedom of movement within or out of the state where

59 Van Drooghenbroeck, *Revue trimestrielle des droits de l'homme*, p. 548; Haeck, *Handboek EVRM. Deel 2*, p. 259; Flauss, *Revue Universelle des Droits de l'Homme*, p. 463, footnote 25; Harris et al., *Law of the ECHR*, p. 921; Cannie and Voorhoof, *Netherlands Quarterly of Human Rights*, p. 58, footnote 11.

60 M. Hamilton, 'Transition, political loyalties and the order of the state', in: A. Buyse and M. Hamilton (eds.), *Transitional Jurisprudence and the European Convention on Human Rights. Justice, Politics and Rights*, Cambridge: Cambridge University Press, 2011, p. 155-156.

61 ECtHR 16 March 2006 (GC), Ždanoka v. Latvia, appl. no. 58278/00, par. 98.

62 Harris et al., *Law of the ECHR*, p. 920. See e.g. ECtHR 2 March 1987, *Mathieu-Mohin and Clerfayt v. Belgium,* appl. no. 9267/81, par. 46-51.

63 ECtHR 2 March 1987, *Mathieu-Mohin and Clerfayt v. Belgium,* appl. no. 9267/81, par. 52.

64 Van Drooghenbroeck, *Revue trimestrielle des droits de l'homme*, p. 547-548. Haeck, *Handboek EVRM. Deel 2*, p. 259; Cannie and Voorhoof, *Netherlands Quarterly of Human Rights*, p. 58, footnote 11.

65 C.J. Staal, *De vaststelling van de reikwijdte van de rechten van de mens [The definition of the scope of human rights]*, Nijmegen: Ars Aequi Libri, 1995, p. 122. Nevertheless, Jacobs and White have expressed doubts as to whether Article 17 ECHR can be invoked in relation to a claim based on Article 1 First Protocol: F.G. Jacobs and R.C.A. White, *The European Convention on Human Rights*, 2nd ed., Oxford: Clarendon Press, 1996, p. 311.

one resides lawfully according to Article 2 Fourth Protocol.[66] Moreover, Villiger has pointed out that during the drafting of the First Protocol to the Convention in 1951 a long discussion ensued on the relationship between Article 17 ECHR and Article 2 First Protocol on the right to education.[67] Some of the drafters feared that this right *'could be construed to mean that parents whose 'philosophical convictions' are fundamentally opposed to the conceptions of democracy and human rights would have the right to educate their children in the same beliefs'*.[68] This would suggest that also the right to education would fall within the scope of Article 17 ECHR. Finally, several commentators are of the opinion that also the prohibition of discrimination in Article 14 ECHR can be abused in the sense of Article 17 ECHR.[69] Here the position of Haeck and Van Drooghenbroeck is most convincing. They argue that since Article 14 ECHR is a complementary right that can only be invoked in combination with a fundamental right,[70] this provision can only be abused if it is invoked in relation to one of the rights that are liable to abuse and not when invoked with one of the procedural guarantees.[71]

4.5.1.2 Rights and freedoms that cannot be abused

Several authors have suggested that the rights that cannot be derogated from in time of war or other public emergency threatening the life of the nation according to Article 15(2) ECHR cannot be abused in the sense of Article 17 ECHR.[72] These include the right to life (Article 2 ECHR), the prohibition of torture (Article 3 ECHR), the prohibition of slavery (Article 4(1) ECHR), and the right not to be punished for an action that did not constitute a crime under the law at the time it was

---

66 Flauss, *Revue Universelle des Droits de l'Homme*, p. 463, footnote 25; Velu and Ergec, *La Convention Européenne des Droits de l'Homme*, p. 140; Van Drooghenbroeck, *Revue trimestrielle des droits de l'homme*, p. 547-548.

67 Villiger, *Freedom of Expression*, p. 322.

68 Preparatory work on Article 17 of the European Convention on Human Rights, Information document prepared by the Secretariat of the Commission, Strasbourg, 27 April 1957, DH(57)4 (Doc A. 33.551), p. 14. At that time the drafters particularly feared Communist propaganda (p. 16.)

69 Cannie and Voorhoof, *Netherlands Quarterly of Human Rights*, p. 58, footnote 11. Others, however, are of a different opinion: see e.g. Flauss, *Revue Universelle des Droits de l'Homme*, p. 463, footnote 26; Velu and Ergec, *La Convention Européenne des Droits de l'Homme*, p. 140.

70 Harris et al., *Law of the ECHR*, p. 784.

71 Haeck, *Handboek EVRM. Deel 2*, p. 261; Van Drooghenbroeck, *Revue trimestrielle des droits de l'homme*, p. 548, footnote 33.

72 A. Spielmann and D. Spielmann, 'The Concept of Abuse of Rights and the European Convention for the Protection of Human Rights and Fundamental Freedoms', in: *Abuse of Rights and Equivalent Concepts: the Principle and its Present Day Application* (Proceedings of the nineteenth Colloquy on European Law), CoE: Strasbourg, 1990, p. 67. See also Velu and Ergec, *La Convention Européenne des Droits de l'Homme*, p. 140; Haeck, *Handboek EVRM. Deel 2*, p. 260 and 262.

committed (Article 7 ECHR).[73] Without claiming a hierarchy between the rights in the Convention, these rights can be considered essential for the exercise of all the other rights. Accepting that these rights can be abused, it has been argued, would be contrary to Article 15(2) ECHR.[74]

In addition, procedural guarantees, such as the right to liberty (Article 5 ECHR), the right to a fair trial (Article 6 ECHR), and the right not to be punished for an action that did not constitute a crime under the law at the time it was committed (Article 7 ECHR), are generally not considered to qualify for the application of Article 17 ECHR.[75] Because of their procedural nature, these rights cannot serve as instruments for destructive activities.[76] In the previous chapter we have seen that the Court indeed concluded in the case *Lawless v. Ireland* that the applicant could not be deprived of the procedural guarantees protected by Articles 5 and 6 ECHR based on Article 17 ECHR.[77] By analogy, it has been argued that also the procedural guarantees in Article 13 ECHR and Articles 1, 2 3 and 4 of the Seventh Protocol to the Convention fall outside of the scope of application of Article 17 ECHR.[78]

Finally, some scholars have argued that also the right to marry and to found a family guaranteed in Article 12 ECHR cannot be abused.[79]

4.5.2 Derogations in time of emergency

Article 17 ECHR provides a rather drastic instrument that can be used against rights holders when they threaten to overthrow democracy and destroy fundamental rights. In the doctrine on Article 17 ECHR some scholars have wondered whether there is a certain overlap between this provision and Article 15 ECHR on states' competences

---

73 Article 15(2) ECHR reads: *'No derogation from Article 2, except in respect of deaths resulting from lawful acts of war, or from Articles 3, 4 (paragraph 1) and 7 shall be made under this provision'.*

74 Frowein, *Europaïsche MenschenRechtsKonvention*, p. 431; Spielmann and Spielmann, *Abuse of Rights and Equivalent Concepts*, p. 67.

75 Van Drooghenbroeck, *Revue trimestrielle des droits de l'homme,* p. 548; Velu and Ergec, *La Convention Européenne des Droits de l'Homme*, p. 140; Flauss, *Revue Universelle des Droits de l'Homme*, p. 463, footnote 26. With regard to Article 5 and 6 ECHR, see Frowein, *Europaïsche MenschenRechtsKonvention*, p. 431; Haeck, *Handboek EVRM. Deel 2*, p. 260.

76 Velu and Ergec, *La Convention Européenne des Droits de l'Homme*, p. 140.

77 ECtHR 1 July 1961, *Lawsless v. Ireland (no. 3)*, appl. no. 332/57, p. 18.

78 Flauss, *Revue Universelle des Droits de l'Homme*, p. 463, footnote 26; Velu and Ergec, *La Convention Européenne des Droits de l'Homme*, p. 140; Van Drooghenbroeck, *Revue trimestrielle des droits de l'homme*, p. 549; Haeck, *Handboek EVRM. Deel 2*, p. 261.

79 J. Velaers, *De beperkingen van de vrijheid van meningsuiting*, Antwerp: Maklu, 1991, p. 256, footnote 105, cited by Haeck, *Handboek EVRM. Deel 2*, p. 261.

to derogate from their obligations under the Convention in times of emergency.[80] Although the number of occasions on which states have relied on Article 15 ECHR is small, the Strasbourg Court has addressed some of these situations, such as derogations introduced by Ireland and the United Kingdom in respect of terrorism in relation to the Northern Irish conflict,[81] derogations made by Turkey in respect of Kurdish separatist violence[82] and the derogation made by the United Kingdom shortly after the events of 9/11 in order to deal with suspected terrorists.[83] These issues demonstrate that some parallels indeed exist between this emergency clause and the abuse clause in Article 17 ECHR. Fox and Nolte have therefore argued that derogations from the rights guaranteed by the Convention under Article 15 ECHR may under exceptional circumstances be inevitable if *'the life of the nation'*, including its democratic form of government, is at risk.[84]

Yet, legal doctrine does not suggest that Article 15 ECHR is an alternative to the application of Article 17 ECHR. Commentators have held that the two provisions come into play at different stages on the 'slide downwards towards totalitarianism'. Declaring a state of emergency is only possible when an anti-democratic individual or political group has almost succeeded in coming to power in order to avert the danger at the very last moment. Fox and Nolte give the example of preventing an anti-democratic party from assuming power *after* an electoral victory by declaring a state of emergency.[85] Article 17 ECHR, on the other hand, appears to be of a more preventive nature and may come into play at an earlier stage to avert the rise of totalitarian groups. As Buyse puts it, Article 17 ECHR occupies *'a place halfway between 'ordinary violations' and states of emergency'*.[86] In other words, Article 17 ECHR can be relied upon by states in situations that pose a threat to the democratic

---

80 Fox and Nolte, *Harvard International Law Journal*, p. 54-59; Van Drooghenbroeck, *Revue trimestrielle des droits de l'homme*, p. 565; Buyse, *Shaping Rights in the ECHR*, p. 190-191. Article 15 ECHR reads: *'In time of war or other public emergency threatening the life of the nation any High Contracting Party may take measures derogating from its obligations under this Convention to the extent strictly required by the exigencies of the situation, provided that such measures are not inconsistent with its other obligations under the Convention'*.

81 ECtHR 1 July 1961, *Lawless v. Ireland (no. 3)*, appl. no. 332/57; ECtHR 18 January 1978, *Ireland v. the United Kingdom*, appl. no. 5310/71; ECtHR 25 May 1993, *Brannigan and McBride v. the United Kingdom*, appl. nos. 14553/89 and 14554/89.

82 ECtHR 18 December 1996, *Aksoy v. Turkey*, appl. no. 21987/93.

83 ECtHR 19 February 2009 (GC), *A. and others v. the United Kingdom*, appl. no. 3455/05. See for a description of the Article 15 case law J.P. Loof, 'On Emergency-proof Human Rights and Emergency-proof Human Rights Procedures', in: A. Ellian and G. Molier (eds.), *The State of Exception and Militant Democracy in a Time of Terror*, Dordrecht: Republic of Letters Publishing, 2012, p. 152-158.

84 Fox and Nolte, *Harvard International Law Journal*, p. 54-59.

85 Fox and Nolte, p. 54.

86 Buyse, *Shaping Rights in the ECHR*, p. 191. See also Van Drooghenbroeck, *Revue trimestrielle des droits de l'homme*, p. 565.

society that are not yet so severe as to justify the proclamation of a state of emergency under Article 15 ECHR.[87]

4.5.3 The prohibition of an abuse of the right to individual petition

Several commentators have noted that Article 17 ECHR is not the only prohibition of abuse of rights in the Convention. Article 35(3)(a) ECHR provides that the Court shall declare inadmissible any individual applications that it considers *'an abuse of the right of individual application'*.[88] According to the Court's own admissibility guide 'abuse' within the meaning of Article 35(3)(a) ECHR *'must be understood in its ordinary sense according to general legal theory – namely, the harmful exercise of a right for purposes other than those for which it is designed'*.[89] Applications considered abusive in the sense of Article 35(3)(a) ECHR include applications which are knowingly based on untrue information with a view to deceiving the Court, applications in which the applicant uses offensive language, applications that intentionally breach the duty of confidentiality of friendly-settlement negotiations (Articles 39(2) ECHR and 62(2) Rules of the Court) and repeatedly lodged vexatious and manifestly ill-founded applications.[90] In general, the Commission and the Court have been reluctant to declare an application inadmissible based on an abuse of the right to individual recourse under Article 35(3)(a) ECHR based on the political motives of the applicant. In general, therefore, legal doctrine considers the two prohibitions of abuse in the Convention to cover different abusive applications. The prohibition of an abuse of the right of individual petition in Article 35(3)(a) ECHR refers to situations of a different kind than the exercise of rights with the aim of destroying the fundamental rights guaranteed in the Convention as prohibited in Article 17 ECHR. While Article 17 ECHR refers to the abusive use of

87 Harris et al., *Law of the ECHR*, p. 856-857. It is important to note, though, that Article 17 ECHR is also applied in cases that do not necessarily lead up to a state of emergency, such cases concerning Holocaust denial.

88 Article 35(3)(a) reads: *'The Court shall declare inadmissible any individual application submitted under Article 34 if it considers that: (a) the application is incompatible with the provisions of the Convention or the Protocols thereto, manifestly illfounded, or an abuse of the right of individual application'.*

89 The Court's Admissibility guide: *Practical Guide on Admissibility Criteria*, p. 37, www.echr.coe.int/Documents/Admissibility_guide_ENG.pdf (accessed 11 April 2016). For an analysis of the general principle of abuse of rights see Chapter six.

90 The Court's Admissibility guide: *Practical Guide on Admissibility Criteria*, p. 37-40. See also ECtHR 15 September 2009, *Miroļubovs and other v. Latvia*, appl. no. 798/05, par. 62-65. See also Y. Haeck and H. De Vylder, 'Art. 35 EVRM' ['Article 35 ECHR'], in: J.H. Gerards et al. (eds.), *SDU Commentaar EVRM, Deel II – Procedurele Rechten [SDU Commentary ECHR, Part II – Procedural Rights]*, The Hague: SDU Uitgevers, 2014, p. 205-206.

the rights (*'substantive abuse'*), Article 35(3)(a) ECHR refers to the abusive use of the protection mechanism of the Convention (*'procedural abuse'*).[91]

4.6 Methods of application of Article 17 ECHR

Article 17 ECHR itself does not prescribe how the provision should be applied. In the previous chapter we have seen that a wide range of different applications have been developed in the Strasbourg case law. Legal doctrine on Article 17 ECHR traditionally distinguishes between two forms of application: direct application and indirect application.[92] The first refers to the application of Article 17 ECHR to declare an application inadmissible as being incompatible with the Convention, while according to the second the case is examined on its merits according to the requirements of the limitation clause in Article 10(2) or 11(2) ECHR.[93] Whereas the direct application of Article 17 ECHR is quite rare, the indirect approach is more common in the Strasbourg case law.[94]

Yet, given the great variety of ways in which the Commission and the Court have applied Article 17 ECHR these two categories do not suffice to satisfactorily describe the practice of the prohibition of an abuse of rights. Villiger distinguishes four different ways of applying Article 17 ECHR: (i) Article 17 is directly applied and the application is declared inadmissible, (ii) Article 17 ECHR is applied indirectly when assessing whether the interference was necessary in a democratic society, (iii) Article 17 ECHR could have been applied, but instead is ignored, and (iv) Article 17 ECHR is not applied because the facts are not considered to be sufficiently serious.[95] Hereafter these categories will be looked at more closely.

---

91 Haeck, *Handboek EVRM. Deel 2*, p. 245, footnote 8. See also Spielmann, *Mélanges en hommage à Louis Edmond Pettiti*, p. 675-676; L. Zwaak (rev.), 'Chapter 2 The procedure before the European Court of Human Rights' in: P. van Dijk, F. van Hoof, A. van Rijn and L. Zwaak (eds.), *Theory and practice of the European Convention on Human Rights*, 4th ed., Antwerp/Oxford: Intersentia, 2006, p. 193; Rainey, *The ECHR*, p. 40-41. In the admissibility guide, abuse of the right of application is indeed categorised under the procedural criteria: the Court's Admissibility guide: *Practical Guide on Admissibility Criteria*, p. 37ff.

92 Cannie and Voorhoof, *Netherlands Quarterly of Human Rights*, p. 67; Haeck, *Handboek EVRM. Deel 2*, p. 249. Van Drooghenbroeck refers to vertical and horizontal application, *Revue trimestrielle des droits de l'homme*, p. 550 ff.

93 Harris et al., *Law of the ECHR*, p. 854.

94 Buyse, *Shaping Rights in the ECHR*, p. 198.

95 Villiger, *Freedom of Expression*, p. 326. In fact, others have also distinguished these categories, but they often merged classifications (iii) and (iv) under one category 'Article 17 ECHR not applied'. See e.g. Buyse, *Shaping Rights in the ECHR*, p. 202-203; Haeck, *Handboek EVRM. Deel 2*, p. 253-254.

4.6.1 (i) Direct application of Article 17 ECHR

The direct approach means that the application is declared inadmissible as being incompatible with the scope of protection of the Convention on the basis of Article 17 ECHR.[96] The direct application of Article 17 ECHR should therefore be read in the light of the scope of the Convention as such. What the direct application of Article 17 ECHR actually does is that it places acts that threaten to destroy fundamental rights outside of the scope of protection of the Convention. As Buyse has aptly put it, Article 17 ECHR defines the *'outer limit'*[97] of the protection offered by the Convention in the sense that *'[t]he scope of each substantive ECHR right is meant to metaphorically shrink in order to exclude 'liberticidal' activities (acts aimed at destroying liberties)'*.[98] Because the direct application of Article 17 ECHR results in the inadmissibility of the complaint, the Commission or the Court are exempted from further examining the compatibility of the interference of the applicant's right with the limitation criteria in the second paragraph of Articles 10 and 11 ECHR. Haeck has used the term *'guillotine application'* in this regard to emphasise that the direct application of Article 17 ECHR abruptly results in the end of the proceedings in Strasbourg.[99]

4.6.2 (ii) Indirect application of Article 17 ECHR

Under the indirect application a case is considered in the light of the justified limitations under Article 10(2) or 11(2) ECHR and Article 17 ECHR merely plays a role in the light of the balancing of the various interests under the limitation clauses in the second paragraph of these articles. In this context, Article 17 ECHR has frequently been resorted to when establishing whether the interference was *'necessary in a democratic society'*.[100] In these cases *'Article 17 serves as a strong magnetic pole that often draws the judicial compass-needle towards the conclusion that no violation of the right has occurred'*.[101] In a number of cases this eventually brought

---

96 E.g. EComHR 20 July 1957, *German Communist Party v. Germany*, appl. no. 250/57; EComHR 11 October 1979, *Glimmerveen and Hagenbeek v. the Netherlands*, appl. nos. 8348/78 and 8406/78; ECtHR 2 September 2004 (dec.), *W.P. and others v. Poland*, appl. no. 42264/98; ECtHR 24 June 2003 (dec.), *Garaudy v. France*, appl. no. 65831/01; ECtHR 16 November 2004 (dec.), *Norwood v. the United Kingdom*, appl. no. 23131/03; ECtHR 13 December 2005 (dec.), *Witzsch v. Germany*, appl. no. 7485/03; ECtHR 20 February 2007 (dec.), *Ivanov v. Russia*, appl. no. 35222/04; ECtHR 12 June 2012 (dec.), *Hizb Ut-Tahrir and others v. Germany*, appl. no. 31098/08; ECtHR 14 March 2013, *Kasymakhunov and Saybatalov v. Russia*, appl. nos. 26261/05 and 26377/06.

97 Buyse, *International and Comparative Law Quarterly*, p. 494.

98 Buyse, *Shaping Rights in the ECHR*, p. 204.

99 Haeck, *Handboek EVRM. Deel 2*, p. 249. See also Flauss, *Revue Universelle des Droits de l'Homme*, p. 464.

100 Villiger, *Freedom of Expression*, p. 325.

101 Buyse, *Shaping Rights in the ECHR*, p. 198.

the Commission or the Court to conclude that the interference was manifestly ill-founded and to declare the application inadmissible.[102] In these cases the Commission initially suggested that the activities engaged in by the applicant fell outside the scope of the right to freedom of expression, to subsequently, rather paradoxically, reframe its decision in terms of Article 10(2) ECHR and conclude that the interference had been necessary in a democratic society and declare the application manifestly ill-founded.[103] In his additional dissenting opinion in the case *Perinçek v. Switzerland*, Judge Silvis described this application as the *'combined approach'*, because *'the case is subjected to the standard Article 10 § 2 analysis'*. Yet, *'at the 'necessity' stage, Article 17 is invoked, leading to the conclusion that the application is manifestly ill-founded (without merit, but not outside the scope of Article 10)'*.[104] In a few cases, the Court strangely enough left the question regarding the applicability of Article 17 ECHR open until after the examination of the merits of the case. In the case *Féret v. Belgium*, for instance, the Court considered that the arguments put forward by the government with regard to Article 17 ECHR, and consequently the applicability of Article 10 ECHR, were so closely linked to the evaluation of the necessity of the interference under Article 10(2) ECHR that it joined the examination of the two. Finally, after having reached the conclusion that the interference was necessary in a democratic society the Court added that the expressions in question did not justify the application of Article 17 ECHR. Judge Silvis held that this unusual approach *'may be seen as somewhat putting the cart before the horse'*.[105]

The indirect approach is sometimes referred to as a soft approach, because Article 17 ECHR is only used as an interpretation tool.[106] Yet, this does not mean, as some scholars rightly point out, that the indirect application is a weak approach, considering that the practical difference in outcome between the two approaches is minimal.[107] In fact, the Commission and the Court have relied on Article 17 ECHR and the necessity of the interference in a democratic society required under Articles 10(2) and 11(2) ECHR as interchangeable justifications for declaring applications inadmissible.[108]

---

102 E.g. EComHR12 May 1988, *Kühnen v. Germany*, appl. no. 12194/86; ECtHR 20 April 1999 (dec.), *Witzsch v. Germany*, appl. no. 41448/98; ECtHR 1 February 2000 (dec.), *Schimanek v. Austria*, appl. no. 32307/96.

103 See also Buyse, *Shaping Rights in the ECHR*, p. 199.

104 Additional Dissenting opinion of Judge Silvis (the Netherlands), joined by Judges Casadevall (Andorra), Berro (Monaco) and Kūris (Lithuania) in the case ECtHR 15 October 2015 (GC), *Perinçek v. Switzerland*, appl. no. 27510/08, par. 4.

105 Additional Dissenting opinion of Judge Silvis (the Netherlands), joined by Judges Casadevall (Andorra), Berro (Monaco) and Kūris (Lithuania) in the case ECtHR 15 October 2015 (GC), *Perinçek v. Switzerland*, appl. no. 27510/08, par. 7.

106 Haeck, *Handboek EVRM. Deel 2,* p. 251; Van Drooghenbroeck, *Revue trimestrielle des droits de l'homme*, p. 551.

107 Cannie and Voorhoof, *Netherlands Quarterly of Human Rights*, p. 67-68.

108 Rainey, *The ECHR*, p. 441.

For the applicant it will not make much difference whether his application is declared inadmissible as being incompatible ratione materiae with the Convention or as being manifestly ill-founded. From a legal perspective it does make a difference, though, whether an activity falls outside the scope of the right invoked by the applicant or whether the interference does not disclose a violation of that right.

4.6.3 (iii) Article 17 ECHR could have been, but was not applied

The third category consists of cases in which Article 17 ECHR seemed relevant but nevertheless was not applied.[109] These cases concern situations similar to those in which the Commission and the Court have previously applied Article 17 ECHR and this article therefore seemed relevant.[110] Nonetheless, these cases are dealt with under Article 10 (2) or Article 11(2) ECHR without any reference to the prohibition of an abuse of rights in Article 17 ECHR.

Buyse refers to the Court's decision in the case *Le Pen v. France*, which has been discussed in the previous chapter, as an example of this approach.[111] The President of the French nationalist political party Front National, Le Pen, was fined for incitement to discrimination, hatred, and violence towards a religious group, on account of statements he had made about Muslims in France in a newspaper interview.[112] Given the Commission's and the Court's earlier application of Article 17 ECHR in the cases *Glimmerveen and Hagenbeek v. the Netherlands* (in which the Commission considered the advocacy of a nationalist policy to be an activity in the sense of Article 17 ECHR and declared the application inadmissible as being incompatible with the provisions of the Convention, see in more detail the previous chapter), an evaluation of Article 17 ECHR would have been reasonable. The Court held that Le Pen's statements caused polarisation between the *'French people'* and the *'Muslim community'* in the context of a general debate on the problems linked to the integration of immigrants in their host countries. Hence, by avoiding any reference to Article 17 ECHR, the Court found that the interference with Le Pen's right to freedom of expression had been *'necessary in a democratic society'* and rejected the application as being manifestly ill-founded.[113]

Although not an admissibility decision, Haeck also refers to the case *Refah Partisi v. Turkey* in this regard. Even though the Grand Chamber held that *'no-one must be authorised to rely on the Convention's provisions in order to weaken or destroy the ideals and values of a democratic society'* and continued that the constitutional

109 Villiger, *Freedom of Expression*, p. 326.
110 Buyse, *Shaping Rights in the ECHR*, p. 202-203.
111 Buyse, p. 202, footnote 77.
112 ECtHR 20 April 2010 (dec.), *Le Pen v. France*, appl. no. 18788/09. See also EComHR 16 July 1982, *X. v. Germany*, appl. no. 9235/81, par. 4.
113 ECtHR 20 April 2010 (dec.), *Le Pen v. France*, appl. no. 18788/09, par. 1.

changes the party pursued *'were incompatible with the concept of a 'democratic society' and that the real opportunities Refah had to put them into practice made the danger to democracy more tangible and more immediate'*, the Court refrained from using or mentioning Article 17 ECHR.[114]

4.6.4 (iv) The facts in the case were not sufficiently serious for Article 17 ECHR

The fourth and final category consists of cases in which the Court found that the facts in the case were not sufficiently serious to justify the application of Article 17 ECHR.[115] In the words of Buyse, in these cases *'Article 17 is brought forward by the state, but the Court decides that the issue falls outside the clause's scope of application'*.[116] The circumstances in these cases share resemblances to those in cases in which Article 17 ECHR was previously applied. The respondent governments in these cases, therefore, argued that the activities of the applicant fell within the scope of the prohibition of abuse of rights and requested the Court to declare the application inadmissible.[117] Nonetheless, the Court considered it inappropriate to apply Article 17 ECHR and dealt with the case under Article 10(2) ECHR.

An example of this approach is found in the Court's judgment in the case *Féret v. Belgium*.[118] As chairman of the Belgian section of the nationalist party *Front National*, the applicant was convicted of publicly inciting discrimination or hatred in leaflets distributed by his party during election campaigns. Considering that in the past the Commission and the Court had applied Article 17 ECHR in the *Glimmerveen and Hagenbeek* case and the *Norwood* case, the Belgian government asked the Court to declare the application inadmissible under Article 17 ECHR. Yet, contrary to its reasoning in these earlier cases, the Court held that the content of the offending leaflet did not justify the application of Article 17 ECHR: *'le contenu des tracts incriminés ne justifie pas l'application de l'article 17 de la Convention en l'espèce'*.[119] Buyse rightly notes that differentiations like these without adequate argumentation obscure the understanding of Article 17 ECHR.[120]

---

114 ECtHR 13 February 2003 (GC), *Refah Partisi (the Welfare Party) and others v. Turkey*, appl. nos. 41340/98 et al., par. 99 and 132 respectively. See also Haeck, *Handboek EVRM. Deel 2*, p. 258.

115 Villiger, *Freedom of Expression*, p. 327.

116 Buyse, *Shaping Rights in the ECHR*, p. 202-203.

117 E.g. ECtHR 30 January 1998, *United Communist Party v. Turkey*, appl. no. 19392/92, par. 21 and 60; ECtHR 10 July 2008, *Soulas v. France*, appl. no. 15948/03.

118 ECtHR 16 July 2009, *Féret v. Belgium*, appl. no. 15615/07.

119 ECtHR 16 July 2009, *Féret v. Belgium*, appl. no. 15615/07, par. 82.

120 Buyse, *Shaping Rights in the ECHR*, p. 202-203.

4.7 Criticism of Article 17 ECHR

In the previous chapter we have seen that an analysis of the case law shows that the Strasbourg approach to Article 17 ECHR lacks consistency. In addition, the Court increasingly appears to have taken an interest in Article 17 ECHR. As a result, also the interest of legal scholars in the provision has experienced an upsurge. In legal doctrine the current interpretation of Article 17 ECHR has progressively met with criticism. Qualifying anti-democratic political ambitions as dangers and excluding them from the protection of the Convention is a controversial measure. The critique of the understanding of Article 17 ECHR in the case law of the Commission and the Court centres on several implications of this interpretation: the marginal balancing of interests under the direct application of Article 17 ECHR; the unpredictability of the application of Article 17 ECHR; and the broadening of the scope of Article 17 ECHR.

4.7.1 Restrictions in the name of protecting fundamental rights and democracy

One of the complexities associated with Article 17 ECHR relates to its role in the defence of fundamental rights and the democratic society. Scholars have argued that, symbolically, the abuse clause in the Convention sends a clear signal about the need to uphold democracy and human rights protection. In that context Buyse has argued that *'Article 17 ECHR is a microcosm for particular instances of what the Convention as a whole is meant to do on a larger scale: to protect democracy and to prevent totalitarianism'*.[121] As the Strasbourg case law has shown, however, it is very difficult to decide effectively which acts and activities aim at the destruction of the rights and freedoms guaranteed in the Convention and democracy.[122] The difference between activities that deserve protection and activities that truly pose a threat to human rights protection and democracy is an extremely complex and delicate one. It relates to the fundamental dilemma of democracy that it has to restrict freedom in order to guarantee freedom. Article 17 ECHR precludes actions which undermine the principles of democracy and fundamental rights protection. In fact, it is the provision *par excellence* that articulates that within the system of the Convention it is not allowed for anti-democratic groups and individuals to profit from fundamental rights in order to suppress or even destroy democracy. The abuse clause was included in the Convention in order to *'protect the signatory States against activities which threaten the preservation of the democratic rights and freedoms themselves'*.[123] Article 17 ECHR is consequently an explicit expression of the concept of militant democracy: a democratic system that is capable of defending itself against being overthrown from within. Later in this book we will focus on this dilemma in more detail when we

121 Buyse, *Shaping Rights in the ECHR*, p. 187.
122 Buyse, p. 204.
123 Robertson, *TP*, vol. IV, p. 26.

explore the interpretation of Article 17 ECHR in the light of the concept of militant democracy in Chapter nine.

According to Cannie and Voorhoof the abuse clause is undesirable and not necessary for defending and maintaining a democratic society, or for the protection and promotion of core democratic values such as human dignity and equality. The Court's approach in cases that are dealt with under Article 10(2) or 11(2) ECHR, they argue, shows that democracy can just as well be protected by allowing restrictions on these rights without bringing the abuse clause into play. If Article 17 ECHR is not necessary to defend democracy against other forms of hate speech or the introduction of Sharia law, then why would the abuse clause be necessary to defend democracy against Holocaust denial?[124] The same logic applies in their view to the need to apply Article 17 ECHR in order to protect or promote respect for the core values of human dignity and equality. The fact that the Court did not rely on Article 17 ECHR in several racist hate speech cases shows that applying the abuse clause is not necessary for the protection of these values. Cannie and Voorhoof therefore conclude that the abuse clause does not have any added value in this respect.[125] Moreover, they fear that the application of the abuse clause *'removes the need for States to pertinently and sufficiently justify interferences and drastically reduces the Court's role in ensuring that limitations are narrowly construed and convincingly established'*.[126] This development may open the door to an abuse of the abuse clause by the States Parties. They may try to use the abuse clause to justify restrictions on the expression of unpopular views.[127] This, they fear, may have serious consequences for the level of protection of free speech in Europe. Buyse, too, has warned against the potential negative consequences of the abuse clause as a tool to protect democracy and fundamental rights. *'If states are allowed to inflict extreme punishments on the enemies of democracy'*, he argues, *'this would be just as prone to undermine that very democracy as liberticidal activities themselves'*.[128]

4.7.2 The inconsistent interpretation of Article 17 ECHR

Also the inconsistency of the Strasbourg interpretation of Article 17 ECHR has regularly been the subject of criticism by legal scholars. In the previous chapter we have seen that the Commission and the Court have used the different methods for the application of Article 17 ECHR interchangeably.[129] Cannie and Voorhoof have

124 Cannie and Voorhoof, *Netherlands Quarterly of Human Rights*, p. 73-76.
125 Cannie and Voorhoof, p. 76-78.
126 Cannie and Voorhoof, p. 72. See also Hare, *Extreme Speech and Democracy*, p. 76-77.
127 Hare, *Extreme Speech and Democracy*, p. 79.
128 Buyse, *Shaping Rights in the ECHR*, p. 205. See also Cannie and Voorhoof, *Netherlands Quarterly of Human Rights*, p. 55; Arai, *Theory and Practice of the ECHR*, p. 621 and 1086-1087.
129 Rainey, *The ECHR*, p. 441.

observed that the way the abuse clause is used by the Strasbourg organs does not seem to be guided by some defined theory.[130] As a result it is often unclear why some activities are excluded from the protection of the Convention while others are not. Particularly illustrative of the eclectic approach to the application of Article 17 ECHR are the cases instigated by Witzsch against Germany, who has more than once been convicted of his revisionist beliefs. These cases have been discussed in the previous chapter. While in the first case the Commission considered the facts on their merits in the light of Article 10(2) ECHR and concluded that there was no appearance of a breach of Article 10 ECHR and accordingly declared the application inadmissible as being manifestly ill-founded, in the second case the Court found that *'the freedom of expression guaranteed under Article 10 of the Convention may not be invoked in conflict with Article 17, in particular in cases concerning Holocaust denial and related issues'* and declared the application inadmissible as being incompatible *ratione materiae* with the Convention.[131] Buyse concludes with regard to this inconsistency: *'[s]ame applicant, very similar context, even same outcome to the case, but a different application of Article 17: it fails to convince'*.[132] This inconsistency makes it almost impossible to distinguish clear criteria for the application of Article 17 ECHR.

The inconsistent approach seems particularly apparent in the particular status of Holocaust denial, anti-Semitism and Nazi ideology in the Strasbourg practice. The Commission and the Court have consistently considered activities related to National Socialism, Holocaust denial in particular, to be contrary to the Convention's underlying values, and thus a danger to democracy. Yet, commentators have observed that the Court seems to less readily accept the application of Article 17 ECHR when it comes to other forms of hate speech or support for other totalitarian doctrines.[133] A number of cases related to incitement to violence and the introduction of Sharia law, which can also be said to undermine the values of democracy, for instance, has been consistently dealt with under Article 10(2) ECHR, without reference to Article 17 ECHR. As an example, legal doctrine often refers to the *Refah Partisi* case, in which the Court labelled the aim of introducing Sharia law as incompatible with certain fundamental democratic values, but still considered the case under Article 11 ECHR. *'Why then can this approach under the speech-protective framework of Article 10 not be stretched to statements or activities related to other undemocratic doctrines?'*,

130 H. Cannie and D. Voorhoof, 'The Abuse Clause in International Human Rights Law: an Expedient Remedy against Abuse of Power or an Instrument of Abuse Itself', in: K. Vanhoutte, G. Fairbairn and M. Lang (eds.), *Bullying and the Abuse of Power* (Critical issues series), Oxford: Inter-Disciplinary Press, 2010, p. 122.

131 ECtHR 13 December 2005 (dec.), *Witzsch v. Germany*, appl. no. 7485/03, par. 3.

132 Buyse, *Shaping Rights in the ECHR*, p. 201.

133 Keane, *Netherlands Quarterly of Human Rights*, p. 642; Cannie and Voorhoof, *Netherlands Quarterly of Human Rights*, p. 80-82; Buyse, *Shaping Rights in the ECHR*, p. 205-206.

Cannie and Voorhoof have wondered.[134] And Buyse for his part points to the Court's approach to other debates regarding historical events. While the Commission and the Court have found that Holocaust denial falls outside the scope of Article 10 ECHR, this is not the case for other debatable perspectives of history, such as the Azeri massacre by Armenians in the early 1990s. As a consequence, *'[t]he tension remains between applying Article 17 when the Court is of the view that a historical fact is uncontested (on the one hand) and its recognition that its role does not extend to arbitrating historical issues in ongoing debates (on the other)'*.[135] The emphasis on National Socialism and related activities may be explained by the historical background of the Convention. The *'fear of history repeating itself'* was one of the main grounds for the creation of the Convention and of Article 17 ECHR in particular.[136] Yet, times have changed and commentators have questioned whether an interpretation of Article 17 ECHR which is *'in essence 'enhanced protection' against Holocaust denial'* can still be justified.[137] The inconsistency in the interpretation of the abuse clause, scholars have argued, leaves the door open for arbitrariness.[138] Eventually, this high degree of unpredictability also weakens the ability of the abuse clause to fulfil its function as the alarm bell that the drafters of the Convention intended it to be.[139]

4.7.3 Marginal balancing exercise under the direct application of Article 17 ECHR

The direct application of Article 17 ECHR allows for an exceptional restriction on the exercise of fundamental rights by excluding certain activities from the protection of the Convention. Van Drooghenbroeck is one of the few legal scholars who have argued in favour of this direct application. He considers the value of the direct application of Article 17 ECHR that it provides a stronger mechanism to protect the Convention's democratic values than the limitation of rights in accordance with Articles 10(2) and 11(2) ECHR. The second paragraphs of Article 8 to 11 ECHR merely allow for the limitation of rights, leaving the core of the rights intact. This would follow from the reference in the limitation clauses to the 'democratic society'.[140] Article 17 ECHR, however, allows for a more drastic restriction on the exercise of rights by completely excluding certain activities from the protection of the Convention. In that way, Van Drooghenbroeck argues, Article 17 ECHR offers a solution in cases in which the regular limitation of rights does not suffice to guarantee the continued protection

134 Cannie and Voorhoof, *Netherlands Quarterly of Human Rights*, p. 76.
135 Buyse, *Shaping Rights in the ECHR*, p. 206.
136 Cannie and Voorhoof, *Netherlands Quarterly of Human Rights*, p. 80.
137 Keane, *Netherlands Quarterly of Human Rights*, p. 642.
138 Cannie and Voorhoof, *Bullying and the Abuse of Power*, p. 122.
139 Buyse, *Shaping Rights in the ECHR*, p. 208; Harris et al., *Law of the ECHR*, p. 854, footnote 21.
140 Van Drooghenbroeck, *Revue trimestrielle des droits de l'homme*, p. 550.

of the fundamental rights of others. Consequently, by virtue of Article 17 ECHR democracy is protected by a well-defined shield, which categorically excludes anti-democratic actors from the protection of the Convention, rather than by an obscured case-to-case approach under Article 10 ECHR.[141]

A majority of legal scholars, however, have criticised the direct application of Article 17 ECHR for the lack of a clear balancing process, including a marginal proportionality test.[142] The limitation clause in Article 10(2) ECHR, for instance, provides for a considerate approach according to which *'formalities'*, *'conditions'*, *'restrictions'* or *'penalties'* imposed on the rights guaranteed in these provisions are only justified if they are *'prescribed by law'*, *'necessary in a democratic society'* and proportionate to the legitimate aim pursued. This requires a balancing exercise to be carried out between the right of the applicant and the legitimate grounds for its restriction. As Cannie and Voorhoof have recalled, for example, the Court has continuously underscored the particular importance of freedom of expression in a democratic society.[143] This right may, therefore, only be restricted when the conditions of the limitation clause are met. In this regard, the Court controls whether the interference was necessary in a democratic society and proportionate to the aim pursued.

In contrast, the direct application of Article 17 ECHR constitutes a far less subtle approach. The direct application of Article 17 ECHR results in the inadmissibility of the complaint based on a *prima facie* assessment, and exempts the Commission or the Court from further examining the compatibility of the interference in the right of the applicant with the second paragraphs of Article 10 ECHR. States Parties thereby enjoy a wide margin of appreciation.[144] Keane argues that in fact the application of Article 17 ECHR suggests a shift in the burden of proof required to justify interferences away from the state. It basically removes anti-democratic speech from the protection of the freedom of expression purely on the basis of its content, thereby eliminating the need for a balancing process that normally takes place under Article 10(2) ECHR.[145] In the case of the direct application of Article 17 ECHR *'[t]he State would not be required to show that there was a pressing need for an interference – it would be required to prove only the content of the speech in question and not the effect of that speech'*.[146] Also the proportionality of an interference with a right is rarely considered when Article 17 ECHR is directly applied. Even though

141 Van Drooghenbroeck, p. 546-547.
142 Tulkens, *Law in the Changing Europe*, p. 440. Cannie and Voorhoof, *Netherlands Quarterly of Human Rights*, p. 69-71; Buyse, *Shaping Rights in the ECHR*, p. 189.
143 Cannie and Voorhoof, *Netherlands Quarterly of Human Rights*, p. 64-67.
144 Cannie and Voorhoof, *Bullying and the Abuse of Power*, p. 119.
145 Keane, *Netherlands Quarterly of Human Rights*, p. 643.
146 Keane, p. 656.

case law requires that the proportionality of the national measure is reviewed under Article 17 ECHR,[147] this review is less profound that the regular proportionality test under Article 10(2) ECHR.[148] In other words, *'the application of the abuse clause takes away the democratic guarantee from applicants to see their utterances placed and judged in their specific contexts, taking into account all factual elements of the case'*.[149] Many scholars therefore consider the direct application of Article 17 ECHR to be highly problematic.

According to some scholars Article 17 ECHR can continue to play a role in the evaluation of the necessity of the interference in a democratic society. The indirect application of Article 17 ECHR as an interpretation principle is generally considered far less problematic than its direct application. From this perspective Article 17 ECHR could be an auxiliary tool for the evaluation of the necessity of the interference in a democratic society under the balancing test of Article 10(2) or 11(2) ECHR. In the words of Frowein, the indirect approach to Article 17 ECHR could silence some of the criticism against the '*guillotine*' application of the provision. *'It would seem'*, he argues, *'that the use of Article 17 within the restrictive clause of Article 10(2) is a proper method to avoid some of the dangers which Article 17 would otherwise raise'*.[150] Buyse, too, has argued in this regard that *'by balancing and thus opening up the option to look at the proportionality of the interference, state excesses could be tackled'*.[151]

Yet, Cannie and Voorhoof reject this solution. In cases of direct application, the balancing procedure is completely absent. When applied indirectly, however, they point out that Article 17 ECHR is afforded a similar impact, as the indirect application almost systematically leads to the finding that the interference was necessary in a democratic society. In these cases, too, the interests involved, the context and the relevant legal elements of the case are hardly taken into consideration.[152] So, even though the case is formally considered under Article 10 ECHR, the indirect application erases any serious evaluation of the requirements in Article 10(2) ECHR. They therefore argue that *'not only from a democratic, but also from a human rights perspective'* it would be preferable not to confer *'any decisive impact'* at all on the prohibition of abuse of rights.[153] Without taking such a strong position, other scholars have also raised the question whether the additional security measure of Article 17

147 EComHR 8 January 1960 (report), *De Becker v. Belgium*, appl. no. 214/56, par. 279.

148 Arai, *Theory and Practice of the ECHR*, p. 1086.

149 Cannie and Voorhoof, *Bullying and the Abuse of Power*, p. 123.

150 J.A. Frowein, 'How to save democracy from itself?', in: Y. Dinstein and F. Domb (eds.), *The Progression of International Law. Four Decades of the Israel Yearbook on Human Rights – An Anniversary Volume*, Leiden: Martinus Nijhof Publishers, 2011, p. 167.

151 Buyse, *Shaping Rights in the ECHR*, p. 198.

152 Cannie and Voorhoof, *Netherlands Quarterly of Human Rights*, p. 68.

153 Cannie and Voorhoof, p. 83.

ECHR is not in fact superfluous, since complaints by anti-democratic actors that pose a threat to the Convention system can also be rejected on the basis of Article 10(2) or 11(2) ECHR.[154]

4.7.4 The broadening of the scope of Article 17 ECHR

Finally, in the previous chapter we have seen that since its first application in cases related to far-right and far-left political agendas, the scope of application of Article 17 ECHR has been broadened. Commentators have observed that over the years *'the application of Article 17 has gone beyond the original intention expressed in the travaux préparatoires, which was to employ Article 17 to counter totalitarian tendencies'*.[155] In an often cited passage of the judgment in the famous *Lawless* case, the Court emphasised that *'the general purpose of Article 17 is to prevent totalitarian groups from exploiting in their own interest the principles enunciated by the Convention'*.[156] The cases in which Article 17 ECHR has been applied *'represent a gradual shift from the classic cases of totalitarian threat to broader issues (such as racism) that go against the Convention's values'*.[157] While the original realm of Article 17 ECHR was to *'protect the rights enshrined in the Convention by safeguarding the free functioning of democratic institutions'*,[158] in more recent cases the Commission and the Court have also considered activities that are '*contrary to the text and spirit of the Convention*'[159] or that run counter to the '*basic*', *'underlying'* or *'fundamental values'* or *'ideas'*[160] of the Convention to fall within the scope of Article 17 ECHR. Under these new criteria Article 17 ECHR can potentially cover an increasing amount of issues that were not foreseen by the drafters of the Convention.

This shift has been criticised in legal doctrine for stretching the definition of abuse. By stretching the scope of application, Article 17 ECHR risks becoming

---

154 Spielmann, *Mélanges en hommage à Louis Edmond Pettiti*, p. 685; Harris et al., *Law of the ECHR*, p. 854.

155 Villiger, *Freedom of Expression*, p. 328.

156 ECtHR 1 July 1961, *Lawless v. Ireland (no. 3)*, appl. no. 332/57, par. 6. See also ECtHR 9 July 2013, *Vona v. Hungary*, appl. no. 35943/10, par. 36.

157 Buyse, *Shaping Rights in the ECHR*, p. 205.

158 EComHR 20 July 1957, *German Communist Party v. Germany*, appl. no. 250/57. See also Harris et al., *Law of the ECHR*, p. 853.

159 EComHR 2 September 1994, *Ochensberger v. Austria*, appl. no. 21318/93, par. 1; EComHR 18 October 1995, *Honsik v. Austria*, appl. no. 25062/94; EComHR 24 June 1996, *Marais v. France*, appl. no. 31159/96, par. 1; EComHR 16 January 1996, *Rebhandl v. Austria*, appl. no. 24398/94, par. 3; ECtHR 13 December 2005 (dec.), *Witzsch v. Germany*, appl. no. 7485/03, par. 3.

160 EComHR 6 September 1995, *Remer v. Germany*, appl. no. 25096/94, par. 1; EComHR 18 October 1995, *Honsik v. Austria*, appl. no. 25062/94; EComHR 29 November 1995, *Nationaldemokratische Partei Deutschlands, Bezirksverband München-Oberbayern v. Germany*, appl. no. 25992/94; EComHR 24 June 1996, *Marais v. France*, appl. no. 31159/96, par. 1. See also Cannie and Voorhoof, *Bullying and the Abuse of Power*, p. 120.

'*overly broad in denying human rights protection and in preventing an assessment of the proportionality of state interference*'.[161] Moreover, criteria based on the *'text and spirit of the Convention'* or the *'basic values of the Convention'* are indeed rather vague and difficult to define. This is why Judges Sajó, Zagrebelsky, and Tsotsoria in their dissenting opinion in the *Féret* case warned against such indefinite criteria, as they would open the door to an abuse of the instrument provided in Article 17 ECHR.[162] Also Cannie and Voorhoof fear that the application of the abuse clause beyond its primary objective risks turning this clause into *'an instrument of abuse itself'*.[163] Where Article 17 ECHR originally aimed to defend the foundations of a democratic society, the provision may become a tool in the hands of repressive governments. As a result, the prohibition of abuse of rights may become counterproductive.

4.8 Conclusions

In this chapter we looked at the prohibition of an abuse of rights in the Convention from a theoretical perspective. We have studied the interpretation of Article 17 ECHR by legal scholars. Legal scholars seem to acknowledge that Article 17 ECHR sends a clear, symbolic signal about the need to uphold democracy and democratic values. Legal doctrine has stressed the role of the abuse clause in relation to groups and individuals who engage in activities or perform acts in the sense of Article 17 ECHR. The scope of Article 17 ECHR is in that sense confined to fundamental rights that, if invoked, may *'facilitate the attempt to derive therefrom a right to engage personally in activities aimed at the destruction of 'any of the rights and freedoms set forth in the Convention'*.[164] The application of Article 17 ECHR is therefore predominantly linked to cases concerning the exercise of the right to freedom of expression (Article 10 ECHR) and occasionally also the right to freedom of association (Article 11 ECHR).

Yet, legal doctrine has also repeatedly pointed to the potential negative consequences of the application of the abuse clause. Their critique is primarily directed against the direct application of Article 17 ECHR, according to which a complaint concerning activities that fall within the scope of Article 17 ECHR is declared inadmissible as being incompatible *ratione materiae* with the protection of the Convention. Under the direct application of Article 17 ECHR activities that fall within the scope of Article

161 Buyse, *Shaping Rights in the ECHR*, p. 205. See also Cannie and Voorhoof, *Netherlands Quarterly of Human Rights*, p. 83.

162 Dissenting opinion by Judge Sajó (Hungary), joined by Judges Zagrebelsky (Italy) and Tsotsoria (Georgia) in the case ECtHR 16 July 2009, *Féret v. Belgium*, appl. no. 15615/07, p. 26.

163 Cannie and Voorhoof, *Bullying and the Abuse of Power*, p. 117.

164 ECtHR 1 July 1961, *Lawless v. Ireland (no. 3)*, appl. no. 332/57, par. 6, p. 18. See also Harris et al., *Law of the ECHR*, p. 853.

17 ECHR automatically fall outside the protection of the Convention, thereby ending a case before the Strasbourg organs. This approach has been fiercely criticised for the lack of a clear balancing of the interests involved and the marginal assessment of the proportionality of the interference with the applicant's right.[165] The direct application results in the inadmissibility of a complaint based on a *prima facie* assessment, thereby exempting the Commission or the Court from further examining the compatibility of the interference with the limitation criteria in the second paragraph of Article 10 or 11 ECHR.

Furthermore, the previous chapter on the case law on Article 17 ECHR has shown that it is very difficult, if not almost impossible, to decide effectively which acts and activities aim at the destruction of the rights and freedoms guaranteed in the Convention. Scholars have warned that the difference between (controversial) activities that deserve the protection of the Convention and activities that are truly dangerous to democracy and democratic values is an extremely complex and delicate one.[166] From a practical perspective, it has also been argued that given the general criteria for limitation afforded by Articles 10(2) and 11(2) ECHR and Article 3 of the First Protocol, it is generally not necessary to resort to Article 17 ECHR to assess this necessity.[167] In addition, some scholars fear that states may try to use the abuse clause to justify restrictions on the expression of unpopular views, thereby seriously reducing the level of protection of free speech in Europe. If states are allowed to rely on Article 17 ECHR to justify serious interferences with the fundamental rights of anti-democratic actors, they risk undermining those democratic standards by violating the democratic values of the Convention themselves.

Moreover, commentators have criticised the inconsistent approach to the scope of Article 17 ECHR by the Strasbourg organs, which results in a high degree of unpredictability.[168] This is especially considered problematic since over the years case law has shown a shift in the interpretation of Article 17 ECHR from the classic threat of totalitarianism to broader issues that go against the Convention's more substantive values.[169] In the previous chapters we have seen that the original realm of Article 17 ECHR was to prevent a (re)emergence of totalitarianism by protecting *'the rights enshrined in the Convention by safeguarding the free functioning of democratic institutions'*,[170] as we have seen in Chapter three, but in more recent cases the Commission and the Court have also considered activities that are '*contrary to*

165 Tulkens, *Law in the Changing Europe*, p. 440. Cannie and Voorhoof, *Netherlands Quarterly of Human Rights*, p. 69-71; Buyse, *Shaping Rights in the ECHR*, p. 189.
166 Buyse, *Shaping Rights in the ECHR*, p. 204.
167 Harris et al., *Law of the ECHR*, p. 854.
168 Buyse, *Shaping Rights in the ECHR*, p. 203.
169 Cannie and Voorhoof, *Netherlands Quarterly of Human Rights*, p. 62-63; Harris et al., *Law of the ECHR*, p. 853; Buyse, *Shaping Rights in the ECHR*, p. 205; Villiger, *Freedom of Expression*, p. 328.
170 EComHR 20 July 1957, *German Communist Party v. Germany*, appl. no. 250/57.

the text and spirit of the Convention' or that run counter to the '*basic values'* of the Convention to fall within the scope of Article 17 ECHR. Critics have argued that by stretching the scope of Article 17 ECHR the provision risks becoming *'overly broad in denying human rights protection and in preventing an assessment of the proportionality of state interference'*.[171] Eventually, they argue, this may endanger human rights protection and respect for democracy and the rule of law.

In sum, the legal doctrine on Article 17 ECHR has stressed the fundamental and yet controversial role of Article 17 ECHR as a collective guarantee of the protection of fundamental rights and the democratic system. Given the provision's potentially far-reaching legal consequences, however, they believe that too broad an interpretation of Article 17 ECHR risks resulting in a degeneration of the human rights protection in Europe. Based on this critical perspective of the purpose and function of the abuse clause, several scholars have called for a restrictive interpretation of Article 17 ECHR Yet, legal scholars do not provide a coherent doctrine for the interpretation of the prohibition of abuse of rights in the context of the Convention. Some scholars have argued that its interpretation should be limited to the indirect application as an alternative for the much criticised direct application of the provision. Applying the abuse clause merely as an auxiliary tool for the evaluation of the necessity of the interference in a democratic society under the balancing test of Article 10(2) or 11(2) ECHR provides for a fair balancing of the interests concerned and requires an evaluation of the proportionality of the interference, which would make it possible to tackle state excesses in restricting political rights.[172] In that way some of the undesirable effects associated with the direct application of Article 17 ECHR could be avoided.[173] Cannie and Voorhoof have argued, however, that the protection of democracy and democratic values is in fact better served if this ambiguous and controversial provision is not applied at all.[174] They have rightly argued that the way in which the Commission and the Court have so far used the indirect application of the main critique of the abuse clause has not been countered. While in cases of direct application the balancing procedure is completely absent, the provision is afforded a similar impact in many cases in which it is applied indirectly, as this almost systematically leads to the finding that the interference was necessary in a democratic society. In these cases too, they argue, neither the interests involved, nor the context and all the factual and legally relevant elements of the case are seriously taken into

171 Buyse, *Shaping Rights in the ECHR*, p. 205. See also Cannie and Voorhoof, *Netherlands Quarterly of Human Rights*, p. 83.

172 Buyse, *Shaping Rights in the ECHR*, p. 198.

173 Frowein, *The Progression of International Law*, p. 167. See also e.g. P. van Dijk, F. van Hoof, A. van Rijn and L. Zwaak (eds.), *Theory and Practice of the European Convention on Human Rights*, 4th ed., Antwerp/Oxford: Intersentia, 2006, p. 1086-1087.

174 Cannie and Voorhoof, *Netherlands Quarterly of Human Rights*, p. 83.

consideration.[175] So, even though the case is formally considered in the light of one of the fundamental rights protected by the Convention, the outcome of the indirect application is practically the same as under the direct application of Article 17 ECHR, without a thorough examination of the relevant facts in view of the case as a whole.

In the following chapters, the study of the prohibition of abuse of fundamental rights will be broadened, as we will look at other sources that may help to come to a coherent interpretation of Article 17 ECHR. In the next chapter we will first explore the interpretation of equivalent abuse clauses in several other international human rights treaties, including the Universal Declaration of Human Rights, the International Covenant on Civil and Political Rights, the International Covenant on Economic, Social and Cultural Rights, the American Convention on Human Rights, and the Charter of Fundamental Rights of the European Union.

175 Cannie and Voorhoof, p. 68.

Chapter 5
Other Abuse Clauses in Human Rights Law

5.1 Introduction

The previous chapters focussed on the origin and interpretation of the abuse clause in Article 17 ECHR. We have learned that it is an ambiguous provision and that neither case law nor legal doctrine provides a uniform interpretation. The prohibition of abusing rights is not unique to the ECHR. Several international human rights documents of universal or regional application also contain an abuse of rights clause. Equivalent provisions to Article 17 ECHR are found in the Universal Declaration of Human Rights (1948),[1] the International Covenant on Civil and Political Rights (1966),[2] the International Covenant on Economic, Social and Cultural Rights (1966),[3] the American Convention on Human Rights (1969), and the Charter of Fundamental Rights of the European Union (2000). In this chapter we will explore the interpretation of these other abuse clauses.

In this chapter the interpretation of the abuse clauses in these other human rights documents will be analysed. Even though all these abuse clauses are similar in wording, these documents vary in their scope and focus (universal or regional and general or specific groups of rights). The purpose of this chapter is to explore to what extent these other abuse clauses provide interesting insights that may contribute to a better understanding of Article 17 ECHR. It will therefore not provide an in-depth study of these human rights documents in general, but will merely focus on the background and interpretation of the abuse clauses in these documents.

5.2 The Universal Declaration of Human Rights

In October 1945 the UN was established by the entry into force of the Charter of the United Nations. Motivated by the tragic experience of the Second World War and the atrocious human rights violations committed in the Holocaust, the promotion and protection of human rights is one of the core purposes of the UN. In the UN Charter the protection of human rights is mentioned in three major provisions: Articles 1(3), 55(c), and 56. These provisions impose, in broad terms, an obligation on the Member

1 UN GA, Resolution 217A (III), *UN doc.* A/RES/3/217A.
2 *UN doc.* A/6316, 999 UNTS 171, entered into force on 23 March 1976. The ICCPR provides for an optional right of individual communication. All Convention parties have accepted it except for Monaco, Switzerland, and the UK.
3 *UN doc.* A/6316, 993 UNTS 3, entered into force on 3 January 1976.

States of the UN to *'promote... universal respect for, and the observance of, human rights'* and to take *'joint and separate action in co-operation with the Organization'* to achieve that purpose.[4]

These provisions have subsequently been supplemented by the UDHR. In February 1947, a Commission on Human Rights (CHR) was set up by the UN and chaired by Eleanor Roosevelt and it began drafting a universal human rights standard. This soon turned out to be a challenging endeavour. As tensions between the East and the West drastically intensified during the Cold War, the possibilities to create a binding human rights convention were severely jeopardised. Eventually, a non-binding declaration seemed more realistic than an international convention at the time.[5] Finally, the UDHR was adopted on 10 December 1948. The adoption of the Declaration was a milestone, as it was the first time that human rights to be universally protected were set forth in such detail. The UDHR contains thirty articles. The abuse clause is found in the final provision of the Declaration. Article 30 UDHR reads: *'[n]othing in this Declaration may be interpreted as implying for any State, group or person any right to engage in any activity or to perform any act aimed at the destruction of any of the rights and freedoms set forth herein'*.

The aim of this provision – in conjunction with Article 29 UDHR, which highlights the duties and responsibilities of citizens[6] – was to meet the needs felt by the States Parties *'to redress the balance'* vis-à-vis their citizens.[7] The states involved in the drafting of the Declaration were concerned about the loss of sovereignty that the creation of the Declaration would entail. With the abuse clause states had an additional instrument to prevent the rights and freedoms guaranteed in the Declaration from being construed to allow the rise of movements that aim to overthrow their

4 T. Buergenthal, 'The Normative and Institutional Evolution of International Human Rights', *Human Rights Quarterly*, vol. 19, no. 4, 1997, p. 707.

5 Å. Samnøy, 'The Origin of the Universal Declaration of Human Rights', in: G. Alfredsson and A. Eide (eds.), *The Universal Declaration of Human Rights. A Common Standard of Achievement*, The Hague/Boston/London: Martinus Nijhoff Publishers, 1999, p. 10. Nowadays, according to the dominant view the provisions in the Declaration do have binding legal effect, either as legal principles that are part of customary international law or as the authoritative interpretation of the human rights provisions in the UN Charter and as such are binding on the Member States of the UN (see e.g. A.D. Renteln, *International Human Rights. Universalism versus Relativism*, Newbury Park/London/New Delhi: Sage Publications, 1990, p. 29).

6 Jordan Paust explicitly reads the two provisions (Articles 29(1) and 30 UDHR) in conjunction, arguing that the abuse clause in Article 30 UDHR can be linked to the private duties described in Article 29(1) UDHR. The duties implied here, he explains, *'are duties not to engage in action aimed at the destruction of the human rights of others'*: J.J. Paust, 'The Other Side of Right: Private Duties under Human Rights Law', *Harvard Human Rights Journal*, vol. 5, 1992, p. 54. See also M.S. McDougal et al, *Human Rights and World Public Order. The Basic Policies of an International Law of Human Dignity*, New Haven/London: Yale University Press, 1980, p. 807 and Renteln, *International Human Rights*, p. 41-44.

7 Alfredsson and Eide, *The Universal Declaration of Human Rights*, p. 633.

democratic governments. It has even been suggested that without such a *'safety valve'* it is unlikely that the Declaration would have been adopted.[8]

Article 30 UDHR speaks of engaging *'in any activity'* or performing *'any act'* aimed at the destruction of the rights guaranteed in the Declaration. Several commentators have suggested that with this emphasis the drafters wanted to make clear *'that the mere expressions of opinion critical of a government or of a political system were not covered by the provision, but what was required to come within its ambit was some "action", or steps taken in anticipation of "action"'.*[9] In other words, the provision would only apply if some action has actually been taken in furtherance of the objective to destroy the rights which the Declaration aims to protect. In this way the provision would be prevented from being construed as allowing for political oppression by state authorities.

The incorporation of the abuse clause was proposed by Malik (Lebanon), one of the most prominent members of the drafting committee that was established by the CHR. *'The Declaration'*, he argued, *'granted all kinds of rights to mankind. Persons who were opposed to the spirit of the Declaration or who were working to undermine the rights of men should not be given the protection of those rights.... Many Articles of the Declaration were open to such abuse and a provision of that nature was an essential protection. Its object was to prevent any persons from engaging in any subversive activities which might be in any direct or indirect manner damaging to the rights of man'.*[10] In its original version, the provision referred only to *'any person'*, but it was subsequently enlarged by referring also to states and groups. At the initiative of Hodgson (Australia) states were included in the provision because in the past states had frequently been the chief offenders against human rights.[11] Finally, at the initiative of Grumbach (France) the General Assembly added a reference to groups in the provision since experience had proven that it was often the case that groups were involved in acts that were aimed at the destruction of human rights.[12]

During the third session of the CHR an attempt was made to delete the abuse clause from the Declaration, because it was considered too vague and lacking

8 Alfredsson and Eide, p. 650.

9 T. Buergenthal, 'To Respect and to Ensure: State Obligations and Permissible Derogations', in: L. Henkin (ed.), *The International Bill of Rights. The International Covenant on Civil and Political Rights*, New York: Columbia University Press, 1981, p. 89. See also A. Verdoodt, *Naissance et Signification de la Déclaration Universelle des Droits de l'Homme*, Louvain/Paris: Éditions Nauwelaerts, 1964, p. 273; N. Robinson, *The Universal Declaration of Human Rights. Its Origin Significance, Application and Interpretation*, New York: Institute of Jewish Affairs, 1958, p. 143.

10 UN ECOSOC, Commission on Human Rights, second session, 41st meeting, 16 December 1947, UN Doc. E/CN.4/SR.41, p. 7-8.

11 UN ECOSOC, Commission on Human Rights, second session, 41st meeting, 16 December 1947, UN Doc. E/CN.4/SR.41, p. 7-9.

12 Verdoodt, *Naissance et Signification de la Déclaration Universelle des Droits de l'Homme*, p. 273.

precision.[13] The opponents of the provision argued that *'its application did not seem clear and it would be unwise to include in the Declaration an article that obscured its meaning'*.[14] Knowing whether a state, group or individual abused the rights in the Declaration calls for a difficult and controversial assessment. At the time of its drafting, however, these difficulties hardly seemed apparent to the members of the Commission, *'who were mostly concerned with the need to prevent the resurrection of nazism or its equivalents'*.[15] The French representative Ordonneau, for example, strongly argued in favour of the abuse clause as a clear signal to groups and individuals with neo-Nazi tendencies. He claimed that it was *'essential that the Declaration should at least recall the dangers of nazism; such a reference would have a legal value of its own... it would be a weapon against any possible recurrence of that doctrine. It was wrong to deny a possible recurrence, and the danger against which [the provision] was aimed was a serious one'*.[16] In the end, the attempt to delete the abuse clause was unsuccessful.[17] After some slight textual amendments,[18] the provision was subsequently unanimously adopted.[19] It seems that the drafters of the Declaration attached great importance to the abuse clause as a warning to anti-democratic actors without specifying how the difficulties involved in the interpretation of the provision were to be overcome. This has brought the commentators Opsahl and Dimitrijevic to conclude that *'[t]he drafters may have entered the article as a 'common sense savings clause' without seeing all its potential implications'*.[20]

---

13 Proposal by India, the United Kingdom, and China: UN ECOSOC, Commission on Human Rights, third session, 74th meeting, 15 June 1948, UN Doc. E/CN.4/SR.74, p. 7.

14 UN ECOSOC, Commission on Human Rights, third session, 74th meeting, 15 June 1948, UN Doc. E/CN.4/SR.74, p. 7.

15 Alfredsson and Eide, *The Universal Declaration of Human Rights*, p. 649.

16 UN ECOSOC, Commission on Human Rights, third session, 74th meeting, 15 June 1948, UN Doc. E/CN.4/SR.74, p. 9.

17 According to the report adopted at the end of the third session of the Commission, the abuse clause is found in Article 28: UN ECOSOC, Commission on Human Rights, Report of the 3rd Session of the Commission on Human Rights, 28 June 1948, UN Doc. E/800.

18 During the following session of the Third Committee of the General Assembly, two amendments to the abuse clause were accepted. A French amendment inserted the word 'group' after the word 'State' so as not only to include non-democratic individuals but also to explicitly include totalitarian groups in the provision (see UN GA, third session, third Committee, 20 November 1948, Draft International Declaration of Human Rights: Recapitulation of Amendments to Article 28 of the Draft Declaration (E/800), UN Doc. A/C.3/305/REV.1). Moreover, after the adoption of a Greek amendment, after 'to engage in any activity' also 'to perform any act' was included (see UN GA, General Assembly, 3rd session, Draft International Declaration of Human Rights: Proposal for Article 28 / Greece, 6 December 1948, UN Doc. A/C.3/406).

19 Morsink, *The Universal Declaration of Human Rights*, p. 88. In the report of the Third Committee the abuse clause is found in Article 31: UN GA, General Assembly, 3rd session, Report of the 3rd Committee, 7 December 1948, UN Doc. A/777.

20 T. Opsahl and V. Dimitrijevic, 'Articles 29 and 30', in: G. Alfredsson and A. Eide (eds.), *The Universal Declaration of Human Rights. A Common Standard of Achievement*, The Hague/Boston/ London: Martinus Nijhoff Publishers, 1999, p. 649.

As *'an integral body of principles'*,[21] the Declaration has subsequently been a major influence on the promotion and protection of human rights worldwide.[22] The Declaration served as a stimulus and an example for many international human rights instruments to follow, including the European Convention on Human Rights.[23] Furthermore, the Declaration was the inspiration for the preparations for the two human rights Covenants drafted within the context of the UN. The text of the abuse clauses in the Covenants essentially corresponds to that of Article 30 UDHR.[24]

5.3 The International Covenants on Human Rights

The original intention of the Commission on Human Rights was to propose three documents: a non-binding Declaration, which would set forth the general principles of human rights protection, a binding Convention, which would define the specific rights, and Measures of Implementation.[25] So, on the same day that it adopted the Universal Declaration, the General Assembly requested the Commission to start drafting the rest of the Bill of Rights in order to translate the content of the Declaration into the binding legal form of an international treaty.[26] Since civil and political rights and economic, social and cultural rights were *'interconnected and interdependent'*, the General Assembly considered it necessary that both were covered by the International Bill of Rights.[27] After thorough discussions, though, the General Assembly agreed to the drafting of two treaties on account of their different specificities rather than one binding convention: a Covenant dedicated to civil and political rights and a parallel Covenant providing for economic, social and cultural rights.[28] Yet, as the preparatory works show, the drafting processes of these treaties mutually inspired each other. Their background is reasonably similar, as they both emerged in the years after the Second World War with a need to reaffirm human rights after they had been flagrantly

21 M.A. Glendon, 'Knowing the Universal Declaration of Human Rights', *Notre Dame Law Review*, vol. 73, no. 5, 1997-1998, p. 1153.

22 H. Steiner and P. Alston, *International Human Rights in Context: Law, Politics, Morals*, 1996, p. 120.

23 Preparatory work on Article 17 of the European Convention on Human Rights, Information document prepared by the Secretariat of the Commission, Strasbourg, 5 March 1975, CDH(75)7 (Doc A. 38.797), p. 1.

24 M. Nowak, *U.N. Covenant on Civil and Political Rights, CCPR Commentary*, 2nd rev. ed., Kehl/Strasbourg/Arlington: N.P. Engel Publisher, 2005, p. 111.

25 R.K.M. Smith, *Textbook on International Human Rights*, 3rd ed., Oxford: Oxford University Press, 2007, p. 41.

26 OHCHR, Fact Sheet No. 2 (Rev. 1), *The International Bill of Human Rights*, p. 2: www.ohchr.org/Documents/Publications/FactSheet2Rev.1en.pdf (accessed 11 April 2016).

27 UN GA, 5th session, 4 December 1950, Resolution 421 (v) on the Draft International Covenant on Humans Rights and Measures of Implementation: Future Work of the Commission on Human Rights, UN doc. A/RES/421, section E.

28 UN GA, 6th session, 5 February 1952, Resolution 543 (VI) on the Preparation of Two Drafts International Covenants on Human Rights, UN doc. A/RES/534(VI), par. 1.

and systematically violated.[29] Subsequently, after years of preparation, in December 1966 the International Covenant on Civil and Political Rights and the International Covenant on Economic, Social and Cultural Rights were simultaneously adopted by the General Assembly. All Member States of the Council of Europe are parties to this 'International Bill of Rights'.

The two Covenants show great similarities in their structure and terminology. Especially in the initial stage, the legislative history of both Covenants overlaps considerably.[30] Article 5, which enunciates the *'rules of interpretation'* of the Covenants including a prohibition of abuse of rights in Article 5(1), is identical in both documents.[31] This provision reads *'[n]othing in the present Covenant may be interpreted as implying for any State, group or person any right to engage in any activity or to perform any act aimed at the destruction of any of the rights or freedoms recognized herein, or at their limitation to a greater extent than is provided for in the present Covenant'*. According to the explanatory text, Article 5(1) of the Covenants is based on Article 30 of the UDHR.[32] Similar to the abuse clause in the UDHR, as Nowak explains, the aim of the provision was to prevent political movements that aimed for the destruction of democracy and the rule of law, which form the basis for the rights in the Covenant, from exploiting these rights in order to come to power in a *'quasi-legal fashion'*.[33]

Even though both International Covenants contain an abuse clause, as we shall see the abuse clause plays a more significant role in the interpretation of the ICCPR than within the context of the ICESCR. This can be explained by the fact that, as Nowak explains, when talking about abuse of rights, the drafters particularly had in mind the abusive exercise of political rights and freedoms.[34]

---

29 Menon, the Indian delegate, during the 3rd session of the General Assembly, see UN GAOR, 3rd session, 181st-183rd plenary meeting, UN Doc. A.C.3/SR.181-183, p. 893. See also J. Morsink, 'World War Two and the Universal Declaration', *Human Rights Quarterly*, vol. 15, no. 2, 1993, p. 357.

30 M.J. Bossuyt, *Guide to the 'Travaux Préparatoires' of the International Covenant on Civil and Political Rights*, Dordrecht/Boston/Lancaster: Martinus Nijhoff Publishers, 1987, p. XIX.

31 M. Nowak, *U.N. Covenant on Civil and Political Rights, CCPR Commentary*, 2nd rev. ed., Kehl/Strasbourg/Arlington: N.P. Engel Publisher, 2005, p. 111.

32 UN, General Assembly, Official Records, 1 July 1955, *Annotations on the text of the draft International Covenants on Human Rights*, UN Doc. A/2929, p. 26. See also Nowak, *U.N. Covenant on Civil and Political Rights*, p. 112.

33 Nowak, *U.N. Covenant on Civil and Political Rights,* p. 115-117. Nonetheless, Nowak sees a different role for the abuse clause in the ICCPR compared to Article 17 ECHR. The latter has occasionally been applied to defend a *'liberal-democratic philosophy of human rights'*, which is not universally shared. In view of the universal character of the Covenant, Nowak therefore does not consider it appropriate to interpret Article 5(1) ICCPR in the same way.

34 Nowak, U.N. *Covenant on Civil and Political Rights*, p. 115.

5.3.1 The International Covenant on Civil and Political Rights

The incorporation of the abuse of rights clause was briefly debated during the drafting of the Covenants. The US delegation considered it *'vague, unnecessary and liable for abuse'*.[35] It was argued that by virtue of this clause, States might be invited to drastically restrict the freedom of expression. A US amendment to delete the provision, however, was rejected. Following attempts to amend the provision – to include the abuse clause in Article 19 ICCPR on the freedom of speech, or to link this prohibition to the purpose and principles set forth in the United Nations Charter and the Universal Declaration of Human Rights – also failed.[36]

As was the case for the first drafts of Article 30 UDHR, the reference to the abuse of rights by states was originally not provided for in Article 5(1) of the International Covenants.[37] In accordance with the abuse clause in the UDHR, however, a reference to the abuse of rights by states was included in the provision.[38] Any attempts to delete the reference to states from the provision failed.[39] The *travaux préparatoires* of the Covenants suggest that states were included because in the past they had frequently been the chief offenders against human rights.[40] This view is supported by a comment made by the Human Rights Committee (CCPR), the supervisory body that monitors the implementation of the ICCPR, regarding the interpretation of Article 5(1) ICCPR in the light of the freedom of expression in Article 19 ICCPR. With regard to restrictions by States on the freedom of expression according to Article 19(3) ICCPR, the CCPR found that these may not put in jeopardy the right itself. In other words, the right is the norm, and restrictions remain the exception. In this context, the Committee recalled that according to Article 5(1) ICCPR States should refrain from engaging in activities or performing acts that aim at the destruction or excessive limitation of the rights guaranteed by the Covenant.[41] Moreover, a similar interpretation of the reference to states in Article 5(1) ICCPR is offered by the Siracusa Principles on the limitation and derogation provisions in the ICCPR. According to these principles,

---

35 UN, GA, *Annotations on the text of the draft International Covenants on Human Rights*, 1 July 1955, UN Doc. A/2929, p. 26-27. See also Nowak, *U.N. Covenant on Civil and Political Rights*, p. 113.

36 UN, GA, *Annotations on the text of the draft International Covenants on Human Rights*, 1 July 1955, UN Doc. A/2929, p. 26-27.

37 Nowak, *U.N. Covenant on Civil and Political Rights*, p. 112.

38 UN, ECOSOC, Commission on Human Rights, 5th session, 10 June 1949, UN Doc. E/CN.4/315. Interesting to note, as was also pointed out by Nowak, is that in contrast to most other provisions in the International Covenants, Article 5(1) refers to *'any State'* and not merely to a state party: Nowak, *U.N. Covenant on Civil and Political Rights*, p. 113.

39 UN, GA, *Annotations on the text of the draft International Covenants on Human Rights*, 1 July 1955, UN Doc. A/2929, par. 58.

40 UN, ECOSOC, Commission on Human Rights, second session, 41st meeting, 16 December 1947, UN Doc. E/CN.4/SR.41, p. 7-9.

41 UN, CCPR, *General comment No. 34 on Article 19: Freedoms of opinion and expression*, 12 September 2011, UN doc. CCPR/C/GC/34, p. 5-6.

even in cases of a public emergency constituting a threat to the life of a nation and requiring a derogation from the rights provided in the Covenant, Article 5(1) ICCPR still applies with full force in these situations, and *'sets definite limits to actions taken [by States] under the Covenant'*.[42] In the contentious practice of the CCPR, however, the abuse of rights by States Parties does not play any role, just as it does not in the case law of the European Court of Human Rights. Finally, the provision was extended, also including the prohibition on limiting the rights guaranteed to a further extent than is provided for in the Covenant.[43] Yet, it is unclear why this element was included. Nowak suggests that it intends to prevent an abuse of the provision by governments by excessively invoking it to suppress opposition movements.[44]

5.3.1.1 Case law on the International Covenant on Civil and Political Rights

Interpretations of Article 5(1) ICCPR are very rare, but the CCPR has occasionally referred to the abuse of rights clause in its case law. First, during the early years of the CCPR a rather unusual interpretation of the Covenant's abuse of rights clause saw the light of day. In two individual communications against Uruguay, the Committee drew upon Article 5(1) ICCPR to conclude that even though Article 2(1) ICCPR limits the responsibilities of States Parties to *'all individuals within its territory and subject to its jurisdiction'*, they are responsible for violations committed by their agents on the territory of another state.[45] This extension of the scope of application of the Covenant pursuant to Article 5(1) ICCPR, however, was strongly disputed[46] and has not been repeated by the Committee ever since.

The Committee on one occasion declared a communication inadmissible based on Article 5(1) ICCPR. In the case of *M.A. v. Italy*, an Italian right-wing politician and publicist was found guilty of reorganising the dissolved fascist party *Fronte Nationale Rivoluzionario* (FNR). Before the CCPR he claimed that he had been convicted of a political offence and punished solely for his ideas. Moreover, he believed that the law on which his conviction was based was discriminatory, because it was *'purportedly enacted in order to protect public safety, but which in reality does not permit the expression of one particular ideology even by democratic and non-violent means'*.[47]

---

42 UN, ESCOR (CHR), *Siracusa Principles on the Limitation and Derogation Provisions in the International Covenant on Civil and Political Rights*, 1985, UN Doc. E/CN.4/1985/4, Annex.

43 Nowak, *U.N. Covenant on Civil and Political Rights*, p. 113.

44 Nowak, p. 115.

45 UN CCPR, 29 July 1981 (13th session), *Sergio Ruben Lopez Burgos v. Uruguay*, communication no. 52/1979 and UN CCPR, 29 July 1981 (13th session), *Lilian Celiberti de Casariego v. Uruguay*, communication no. 56/1979.

46 See e.g. the individual opinion of Tomuschat on the Committee's views in these cases.

47 UN CCPR, 10 April 1984 (21st session), *M.A. v. Italy*, communication no. 117/1981, par. 9. See also Nowak, *U.N. Covenant on Civil and Political Rights*, p. 117.

With regard to the admissibility of the communication, the Italian government argued that M.A. had been convicted *' of organizing a movement which has as its object the elimination of the democratic freedoms and the establishment of a totalitarian regime'*.[48] The Committee held that reorganising the dissolved fascist party was indeed an act aimed at the destruction of any of the rights and freedoms recognised by the Covenant. The Committee went on to specify that it would appear in this case that *'the acts of which M.A. was convicted (reorganizing the dissolved fascist party) were of a kind which are removed from the protection of the Covenant by article 5 thereof'*.[49] As a consequence, the Committee declared the communication inadmissible as being incompatible with the provisions of the Covenant.

In addition, Article 5(1) ICCPR played a role in a number of cases concerning anti-Semite hate speech and denial of the Holocaust – the kind of cases in which the ECtHR has also repeatedly referred to the prohibition of abuse of rights. The first case, *J.R.T. and the W.G. Party v. Canada*, concerned a political party that used tape-recorded messages linked up to the Toronto telephone system to warn callers *'of the dangers of international finance and international Jewry leading the world into wars, unemployment and inflation and the collapse of world values and principles'*.[50] After several complaints by Jewish groups and individuals, the party was ordered to refrain from using telephone communications for the dissemination of hate messages. The party contested this ban before the CCPR, arguing that Canada had violated the party's right to hold and express their opinions without interference (Article 19 ICCPR). The Canadian government, for its part, started its submission by objecting to the admissibility of the communication. According to the Canadian government, the ban gave effect to Article 20(2) ICCPR, which compels States to enact legislation against the advocacy of national, racial or religious hatred.[51] The 'right' to communicate racist ideas was not protected by the Covenant, as it was in fact incompatible with its provisions and the communication should therefore be declared inadmissible.[52] Without mentioning Article 5(1) ICCPR, the Committee followed the Canadian government in this line of thought and concluded that *'the opinions which Mr. T. seeks to disseminate through the telephone system clearly constitute the advocacy of racial or religious hatred which Canada has an obligation under article 20 (2) of the Covenant to prohibit. In the Committee's opinion, therefore, the communication*

48 UN CCPR, 10 April 1984 (21st session), *M.A. v. Italy*, communication no. 117/1981, par. 7.2.

49 Ibid par. 13.3.

50 UN CCPR, 6 April 1983 (18th session), *J.R.T. and W.G. Party v. Canada*, communication no. 104/1981, par. 2.1.

51 Article 20(2) ICCPR reads as follows: '*Any advocacy of national, racial or religious hatred that constitutes incitement to discrimination, hostility or violence shall be prohibited by law*'.

52 UN CCPR, 6 April 1983 (18th session), *J.R.T. and W.G. Party v. Canada*, communication no. 104/1981, par. 6.2.

is, in respect of this claim, incompatible with the provisions of the Covenant'.[53] The Committee accordingly decided that the communication was inadmissible. This restrictive approach to the admissibility of communications related to antisemitism has sometimes been cited by governments in their defence to a communication before the CCPR. So far, however, the Committee has never been inclined to repeat it.

A second hallmark case in this regard is *Faurisson v. France*. Robert Faurisson is a notorious Franco-British revisionist who publicly questioned the use of gas chambers for extermination purposes in Nazi concentration camps during the Second World War.[54] Based on the Law on the Freedom of the Press of 1881, which was amended in 1990 by the 'Gayssot Act' which made it an offence to contest crimes against humanity as defined in the London Charter of 1945 on the basis of which Nazi leaders were tried and convicted by the International Military Tribunal at Nuremberg, Faurisson was convicted in 1991. Before the CCPR Faurisson claimed that his conviction violated his right to freedom of expression as guaranteed in Article 19 ICCPR.[55] Surprisingly enough, issues regarding the incompatibility of the complaint with the provision of the Covenant and the application of Article 5(1) ICCPR were not discussed in the context of the admissibility of the communication. The communication was declared admissible and these issues were addressed in the context of the evaluation of the merits of the case.[56] In that regard the French Government recalled, among other arguments, that Article 5(1) ICCPR *'allows a State party to deny any group or individual any right to engage in activities aimed at the destruction of any of the rights and freedoms recognized in the Covenant'.*[57] Faurisson's activities within the meaning of Article 5(1) ICCPR, the French Government argued, clearly contained elements of racial discrimination, which is prohibited both under Article 20(2) of the Covenant and other international human rights instruments.[58] Further, the Committee's decision in *J.R.T. and W.G. Party v. Canada* was brought to mind in which the Committee held that the activities of J.R.T. *'clearly constituted the advocacy of racial or religious hatred'* and declared the communication inadmissible. The French Government asked the Committee to also apply this reasoning in the case of Faurisson.[59] The Committee, for its part, did not go into the application of Article 5(1) ICCPR or its earlier views in the case *J.R.T. and W.G. Party v. Canada* and dealt with the communication purely under Article 19 ICCPR. In that respect, the Committee concluded that the restriction of

---

53 Ibid, par. 8(b) and 9.
54 UN CCPR, 8 November 1996 (58th session), *Faurisson v. France*, communication no. 550/1993, par. 2.1 and 2.6.
55 Ibid, par. 7.1.
56 Ibid, par. 6.5 and 7.1-7.8.
57 Ibid, par. 7.4.
58 Ibid, par. 7.7.
59 Ibid, par. 7.8.

Faurisson's freedom of expression was permissible and necessary in the interest of the community as a whole by serving respect for the Jewish community to live free from fear of an atmosphere of anti-Semitism.[60] Even though the Committee noted that the general terms of the Gayssot Act may under different conditions lead to decisions or measures that are incompatible with the Covenant, it concluded in this case that the facts did not reveal a violation of Article 19 ICCPR by France.[61]

Finally, the case *Ross v. Canada* concerned a Canadian teacher who was removed from the classroom and assigned a non-teaching position because he had published several controversial books and had publicly made anti-Jewish statements in his spare time.[62] He filed a complaint with the CCPR, claiming that both his right to freedom of expression (Article 19 ICCPR) and his freedom of religion (Articles 18 ICCPR) – he asserted that his views were religiously motivated – had been violated by Canada. The Canadian government first raised preliminary objections to the complaint. Drawing a parallel between this case and the case *J.R.T. and W.G. Party v. Canada*, the Canadian Government submitted that the complaint should be deemed inadmissible as being incompatible with the provisions of the Covenant.[63] Referring to Article 5(1) ICCPR, the Canadian government argued that *'to interpret articles 18 and 19 as protecting the dissemination of anti-Semitic speech cloaked as Christianity denies Jews freedom to exercise their religion, instils fear in Jews and other religious minorities and degrades the Christian faith'*.[64] Yet, the Committee for its part took a different approach. While acknowledging its restrictive admissibility approach in *J.R.T. and W.G. v. Canada*, the Committee stressed that *'restrictions on expression which may fall within the scope of article 20 must also be permissible under article 19, paragraph 3, which lays down requirements for determining whether restrictions on expression are permissible. In applying those provisions, the fact that a restriction is claimed to be required under article 20 is of course relevant. In the present case, the permissibility of the restrictions is an issue for consideration on the merits'*.[65] Subsequently, the Committee declared the complaint admissible, even though it was ultimately of the view that the facts in the case did not disclose a violation of the Covenant.[66] In this case the Committee thus seems to distance itself from its earlier restrictive admissibility approach in *J.R.T. and the W.G. Party v. Canada* by not declaring these communications inadmissible, but dealing with all expressions, however objectionable, under Article 19 ICCPR based on the merits of the case.

---

60 Ibid, par. 9.6 and 9.7.
61 Ibid, par. 9.3 and 10.
62 UN CCPR, 18 October 2000 (70th session), *Ross v. Canada*, communication no. 736/1997.
63 Ibid, par. 6.2 and 6.4.
64 Ibid, par. 6.3.
65 Ibid, par. 10.5 and 10.6.
66 Ibid, par. 12.

What this brief overview of the case law on Article 5(1) ICCPR shows is that the kind of cases in which the Covenant's abuse clause plays a role is similar to the cases in which Article 17 ECHR has been applied, namely cases related to fascism, anti-Semitism and denial of the Holocaust (except for the Committee's conclusion in the 1981 cases against Uruguay, which may very well be a once only experiment by the Committee). This small number of cases, however, demonstrates that the CCPR seems to apply the prohibition of abuse of rights in the same inconsistent way as the ECtHR has done with Article 17 ECHR. The CCPR has in an exceptional case applied Article 5(1) ICCPR in a way similar to the direct application of Article 17 ECHR in order to declare a communication inadmissible (in the case *M.A. v. Italy*, and, even though the Committee did not explicitly refer to Article 5(1) ICCPR, in fact also in the case *J.R.T. and the W.G. Party v. Canada).* Later on, however, the Committee seems to have reconsidered the restrictive admissibility approach in these cases. Even though the facts in the cases of *Faurisson v. France* and *Ross v. Canada* show great similarities to the case *J.R.T. and the W.G. Party v. Canada*, as was also put forward by the defending governments, the Committee refused to repeat its earlier approach and did not declare these communications inadmissible. In the case *Ross v. Canada* the Committee even seems to explicitly reconsider its restrictive admissibility approach by emphasising that even restrictions on expressions that advocate national, racial or religious hatred must be assessed under Article 19(3) ICCPR.[67]

5.3.2 International Covenant on Economic, Social and Cultural Rights

The Committee on Economic, Social and Cultural Rights (CESCR) has not paid much attention to the prohibition of abuse of rights in Article 5(1) ICESCR. As commentators have rightly observed, given their nature *'[m]any of the rights guaranteed in the ICESCR are not easily capable of being invoked to destroy human rights'*.[68] So far, the Committee has referred to the provision twice in a General Comment. The CESCR referred to the prohibition of abuse of rights for the first time in General Comment No. 14 on the right to health in Article 12 ICESCR.[69] In this context, though, the Committee merely seems to refer to the obligation of states under Article 5(1) ICESCR not to limit the rights to a greater extent than is provided for in the present Covenant.[70] This principle is also established in Article 4

67 Ibid, par. 10.5 and 10.6.

68 B. Saul, D. Kinley and J. Mowbray, *The International Covenant on Economic, Social and Cultural Rights: Commentary, Cases, and Materials*, Oxford: Oxford University Press, 2014, p. 265.

69 UN ICESCR, General Comment No. 14 on Article 12: the Right to the Highest Attainable Standard of Health, 11 August 2000, UN Doc. E/C.12/2000/4, par. 29.

70 In paragraph 28 of General Comment No. 14, the Committee referred to Article 4 ICESCR to emphasise that *'[i]ssues of public health are sometimes used by States as grounds for limiting the exercise of other fundamental rights'* and that *'[s]uch restrictions must be in accordance with the law, including international human rights standards, compatible with the nature of the rights*

ICESCR, which provides that *'the State may subject [the rights guaranteed in the Covenant] only to such limitations as are determined by law only in so far as this may be compatible with the nature of these rights and solely for the purpose of promoting the general welfare in a democratic society'*. Sepúlveda is therefore right when she argues that the reference to the abuse clause in General Comment No. 14 *'is perhaps more closely related to the general limitation clause of article 4 ICESCR than to article 5 ICESCR'*.[71] However, this interpretation of Article 5(1) ICESCR corresponds with the interpretation given to the provision in the Limburg Principles on the Implementation of the International Covenant on Economic, Social and Cultural Rights, which provides that *'Article 5(1) underlines the fact that there is no general, implied or residual right for a state to impose limitations beyond those which are specifically provided for in the law'*.[72] In that sense, Article 5(1) ICESCR forms a coherent whole with Article 4 ICESCR and the restriction authorised on the exercise of rights under the specific rights provisions.[73] What Article 5(1) ICESCR adds to this provision, according to several commentators, is that the prohibition of abuse concerns the *'intent'* of the restrictive measure taken by the government, namely to destroy human rights.[74]

Another rare example of a reference to the prohibition of abuse of rights is found in General Comment No. 21. Here the CESCR stated that *'while account must be taken of national and regional particularities and various historical, cultural and religious backgrounds, it is the duty of States, regardless of their political, economic or cultural systems, to promote and protect all human rights and fundamental freedoms. Thus, no one may invoke cultural diversity to infringe upon human rights guaranteed by international law, nor to limit their scope'*. Article 15(1) (a) ICESCR on the right to take part in cultural life may therefore *'not be interpreted as implying for any State, group or person any right to engage in any activity or perform any act aimed at the destruction of any of the rights and freedoms recognized in the Covenant or at their limitation to a greater extent than is provided for therein'*.[75]

---

protected by the Covenant, in the interest of legitimate aims pursued, and strictly necessary for the promotion of the general welfare in a democratic society'. Subsequently, in paragraph 29 the Committee adds that *'[i]n line with article 5.1, such limitations must be proportional, i.e. the least restrictive alternative must be adopted where several types of limitations are available'*.

71 M. Sepúlveda, *The Nature of the Obligations under the International Covenant on Economic, Social and Cultural Rights*, Antwerp/Oxford/New York: Intersentia, 2003, p. 304.

72 UN ESCOR (CHR), *Limburg Principles on the Implementation of the International Covenant on Economic*, Social and Cultural Rights, 1987, UN Doc. E/CN.4/1987/17, No. 57.

73 Sepúlveda, *The Nature of the Obligations under the ICESCR*, p. 305.

74 Saul, Kinley and Mowbray, *The International Covenant on Economic, Social and Cultural Rights*, p. 264; Buergenthal, *The International Bill of Rights*, p. 87; Sepúlveda, *The Nature of the Obligations under the ICESCR*, p. 305.

75 UN, CESCR, *General Comment No. 21 on Article 15(1)(a) ICESCR: the right of everyone to take part in cultural life*, 21 December 2009, UN Doc. E/C.12/GC/21, par. 18 and 20.

5.4 The American Convention on Human Rights

In the 1940s also on the American continent steps were taken towards the creation of a regional human rights system.[76] Nowadays, the inter-American human rights system consists of two mutually interacting pillars: that of the American Declaration of the Rights and Duties of Man (1948) and that of the American Convention on Human Rights (1969). Like the Universal Declaration, the first was originally not intended to have direct legal effect but was merely considered a *'statement of moral obligations'*.[77] In addition, the Member States have the option to become a party to one or more of the human rights treaties that are drafted under the auspices of the Organisation of American States, the most important one being the American Convention on Human Rights, also referred to as the Pact of San José. The ACHR can be considered the ECHR's counterpart on the American continent.[78]

Of the 35 Member States of the OAS, 10 did not ratify the ACHR, including the USA and Canada.[79] For the states that do not participate in the Convention system, the only general regional human rights obligations emanate from the American Declaration. Moreover, because the American Declaration guarantees several rights that are not protected by the American Convention – predominantly economic, social

76 Even though the OAS basically covers the entire American continent, at least with regard to human rights, the annual reports of the Inter-American Commission on Human Rights and the judgments of the Inter-American Court of Human Rights give the impression that the system is essentially a Latin American one with the USA and Canada making only an occasional appearance. See D. Harris, 'Regional Protection of Human Rights: The Inter-American Achievement', in: D. Harris and S. Livingstone (eds.), *The Inter-American System of Human Rights*, Oxford: Clarendon Press, 1998, p. 4.

77 R.K. Goldman, 'History and Action: The Inter-American Human Rights system and the Role of the Inter-American Commission on Human Rights', *Human Rights Quarterly*, vol. 31, no. 4, 2009, p. 863. See also Harris, *The Inter-American System of Human Rights*, p. 4. As the American Declaration is considered the authoritative interpretation of the human rights provisions in the OAS Charter, however, it is nowadays considered indirectly legally binding on all the Member States of the OAS: S. Smis et al., *Handboek Mensenrechten. De internationale bescherming van de rechten van de mens [Handbook Human Rights. The international protection of human rights]*, Antwerp/Cambridge: Intersentia, 2011, p. 398. See also Inter-American Court of Human Rights, Advisory Opinion OC-10/89, *Interpretation of the American Declaration of Rights and Duties of Man within the Framework of Article 64 of the American Convention on Human Rights* (14 July 1989), par. 37-43.

78 OAS Treaty Series no. 36, 1144 UNTS 123, entered into force on 18 July 1978.

79 Argentina, Barbados, Bolivia, Brazil, Chile, Colombia, Costa Rica, Dominica, Dominican Republic, Ecuador, El Salvador, Grenada, Guatemala, Haiti, Honduras, Jamaica, Mexico, Nicaragua, Panama, Paraguay, Peru, Suriname, Trinidad and Tobago, Uruguay, and Venezuela ratified the American Convention. The Unites States of America signed the American Convention, but did not ratify it. Trinidad and Tobago denounced its ratification of the American Convention in May 1998 (effective May 1999, meaning that the Inter-American Commission and the inter-American Court are only competent to examine alleged violations of the rights contained in the American Convention with respect to events that occurred or began to occur between the ratification by Trinidad and Tobago and May 1999). Venezuela denounced its ratification of the American Convention in September 2012, effective since September 2013: www.oas.org/dil/treaties_B-32_American_Convention_on_Human_Rights_sign.htm (accessed 11 April 2016). See also Smis et al., *Handboek Mensenrechten*, p. 393.

and cultural rights – , it is argued that it remains an important subsidiary source of human rights obligations for states party to the American Convention.[80] For the purpose of this research, the focus is on the Convention pillar, as the American Convention contains an abuse clause while the American Declaration does not.

5.4.1 Individual petitions under the American Convention on Human Rights

Under the Inter-American human rights systems, individuals and organisations can submit petitions based on the American Convention.[81] The two main supervisory organs of the OAS, the Inter-American Commission on Human Rights (IACHR) and the Inter-American Court of Human Rights (IACtHR), both have a role in examining these individual petitions. To begin with, individuals can submit petitions to the IACHR against a state that is party to the Convention.[82] When a petition is declared admissible, the IACHR will first try to reach a friendly settlement between the petitioner and the State.[83] If no friendly settlement is reached, the IACHR will draw up a report containing the facts, the arguments of the parties, the research it has conducted and its conclusions. If the Commission concludes that there has been a violation of the ACHR, the State is given three months to remedy the situation. During this period, the IACHR or the State concerned may refer the matter to the Inter-American Court.[84] Individuals do not have direct recourse to the Inter-American Court. If a case is referred to the Inter-American Court, it may also try to work towards

80 Harris, *The Inter-American System of Human Rights*, p. 6.

81 C. Medina, *The American Convention on Human Rights. Crucial Rights and their Theory and Practice*, Cambridge/Antwerp/Portland: Intersentia, 2014, p. 1.

82 According to Article 41(f) in conjunction with Article 44 ACHR. See also Smis et al., *Handboek Mensenrechten*, p. 423

83 Article 48(1)(f) ACHR.

84 Article 61(s) ACHR and Article 45 Rules of Procedure of the Inter-American Commission on Human Rights. In the early days of the Inter-American Human Rights system, there was not yet an Inter-American Court and the petition would end after examination before the Commission. The Inter-American Court's jurisdiction is limited to cases with respect to those States that have ratified the American Convention and have expressly recognized the contentious jurisdiction of the Court, unless a State accepts jurisdiction expressly for a specific case. Contrary to the European system, a state is not considered to have accepted the jurisdiction of the Inter-American Court simply because it has ratified the American Convention. Pursuant to Article 62 ACHR a state may, upon ratifying or adhering to the American Convention or at any later time, expressly declare that it recognises the Inter-American Court's jurisdiction. As of this writing, 22 of the OAS Member States have accepted the jurisdiction of the Inter-American Court: Argentina, Barbados, Bolivia, Brazil, Chile, Colombia, Costa Rica, Dominican Republic, Ecuador, El Salvador, Guatemala, Haiti, Honduras, Mexico, Nicaragua, Panama, Paraguay, Peru, Suriname, Trinidad and Tobago (only for cases until May 1999, see footnote 78), Uruguay, and Venezuela (only for cases until September 2013, see footnote 78). See: www.oas.org/en/iachr/docs/pdf/HowTo.pdf (accessed 11 April 2016). See also H. Faúndez Ledesma, *The Inter-American System for the Protection of Human Rights. Institutional and procedural aspects*, 3rd ed., San José: Inter-American Institute of Human Rights, 2008, p. 572.

a friendly settlement between the parties. If no friendly settlement is reached, the IACtHR will render a judgment in which it declares whether one or more of the rights in the Convention have been violated. These judgments are final and not subject to appeal.[85] If the matter is not referred to the Court, the IACHR will eventually draw up a report outlining its findings and its recommendations to improve the situation.[86] The Commission subsequently monitors the implementation of its recommendations by the State and, if necessary, can take follow-up measures. Nevertheless, even though they are generally considered authoritative conclusions in a case, decisions taken by the IACHR are not legally binding.[87] While the Inter-American Commission has various functions and competences with regard to the protection of human rights both under the OAS Charter and the American Convention, only the decisions taken by the Inter-American Court are binding.[88]

5.4.2 Case Law on Article 29(a) American Convention on Human Rights

The American Convention was modelled after the ECHR.[89] Nonetheless, due to the different political and economic realities on the two continents, a distinct American system has evolved, which is only marginally comparable to its European counterpart.[90] This is particularly true for the abuse of rights clause in Article 29(a) ACHR. This provision reads: *'[n]o provision of this Convention shall be interpreted as: a. permitting any State Party, group, or person to suppress the enjoyment or exercise of the rights and freedoms recognized in this Convention or to restrict them to a greater extent than is provided for herein'*. In general, Article 29 ACHR is dedicated to the interpretation of the American Convention. Or, *'more specifically, Article 29 determines the ways in which the American Convention should not be interpreted'*.[91] In that respect, the abuse of rights clause in Article 29(a) prohibits an interpretation of the rights in the American Convention that would allow for the destruction of rights. Besides a prohibition of abuse of rights, Article 29 ACHR provides provisions on the interpretation of the American Convention in relation to the national law of the States Parties, to *'other rights or guarantees that are inherent in the human personality or*

85 Article 67 ACHR.

86 Article 47 Rules of Procedure of the Inter-American Commission on Human Rights.

87 Smis et al., *Handboek Mensenrechten*, p. 430.

88 Harris, *The Inter-American System of Human Rights*, p. 23.

89 T. Buergenthal, 'The American and European Conventions on Human Rights: Similarities and Differences', *American University Law Review*, vol. 30, no. 1, 1980, p. 156.

90 Buergenthal, p. 156; M. Nowak, *Introduction to the International Human Rights Regime*, Leiden/Boston: Martinus Nijhoff Publishers, 2003, p. 189-190; Steiner and Alston, *International Human Rights in Context,* p. 869; Smis et al., *Handboek Mensenrechten,* p. 394; Goldman, *Human Rights Quarterly*, p. 867.

91 L. Lixinski, 'Treaty Interpretation by the Inter-American Court of Human Rights: Expansionism at the Service of the Unity of International Law', *European Journal of International Law*, vol. 21 no. 3, 2010, p. 587.

derived from representative democracy', to the American Declaration of the Rights and Duties of Man and to international law.[92]

The application of the abuse clause in the American Convention is very rare. So far, the Inter-American Court has only mentioned the provision in a series of three cases against Trinidad and Tobago. Even though their small number makes it difficult to draw valid conclusions regarding Article 29(a) ACHR, these judgments provide an interesting alternative perspective on the notion of abuse of human rights. On 1 September 2001, the Inter-American Court delivered a series of judgments regarding the death penalty in Trinidad and Tobago.[93] Petitions were brought before the inter-American Commission – just before the denunciation of the American Convention by Trinidad and Tobago became effective[94] – complaining that Trinidad and Tobago had allegedly violated the American Convention by sentencing several petitioners to a death penalty without offering them the required procedural guarantees provided for in Article 4 ACHR.[95] In its preliminary objections, Trinidad and Tobago challenged the jurisdiction of the Court. When Trinidad and Tobago ratified the American Convention in 1991, it made a reservation recognising the jurisdiction of the Court, but only to the extent that its judgments are consistent with its national Constitution and do not infringe, create or abolish any existing rights or duties of any private citizen.[96] The Inter-American Commission had considered the reservation to be invalid, as it was contrary to the object and purpose of the Convention and would limit the ability of the Inter-American Court to interpret and apply the American Convention in all cases against Trinidad and Tobago.[97] In these circumstances, the Inter-American Court quoted Article 29(a) ACHR, arguing that

---

92 Article 29(b), (c) and (d) ACHR.

93 Inter-American Court of Human Rights, *Case of Benjamin et al. v. Trinidad and Tobago*, 1 September 2001 (preliminary objections); Inter-American Court of Human Rights, *Case of Constantine et al. v. Trinidad and Tobago*, 1 September 2001 (preliminary objections); Inter-American Court of Human Rights, *Case of Hilaire. v. Trinidad and Tobago*, 1 September 2001(preliminary objections).

94 The weak procedural safeguards accompanying the imposition of the death penalty in Trinidad and Tobago frequently resulted in a collision with the IACtHR and eventually led to Trinidad and Tobago's denunciation of the American Convention in 1998, effective since May 1999. See www.oas.org/dil/treaties_B-32_American_Convention_on_Human_Rights_sign.htm (accessed 11 April 2016).

95 While the American Convention does not forbid the death penalty, other sections of the American Convention, as well as the jurisprudence of the IACHR and the IACtHR, demonstrate that imposing this sanction is strictly regulated and shows a strong trend within the Inter-American system towards the abolition of this form of punishment. See N. Parassram Concepcion, 'The Legal Implications of Trinidad and Tobago's Withdrawal from the American Convention on Human Rights', *American University International Law Review*, vol. 16, no. 3, 2001, p. 864.

96 *Case of Benjamin et al. v. Trinidad and Tobago*, 1 September 2001 (preliminary objections), par. 42.

97 See the Vienna Convention on the Law of Treaties that requires in Article 19, paragraph c, that reservations that are incompatible with the object and purpose of the treaty in question are unacceptable; *Case of Benjamin et al. v. Trinidad and Tobago*, 1 September 2001 (preliminary objections), par. 60 and 61.

'it would be meaningless to suppose that a State which had freely decided to accept the compulsory jurisdiction of the Court had decided at the same time to restrict the exercise of its functions as foreseen in the Convention. On the contrary, the mere acceptance by the State leads to the overwhelming presumption that the state will subject itself to the compulsory jurisdiction of the Court'.[98] The Court then moved on to conclude that accepting the reservation would imply a limitation of the recognition of the Court's jurisdiction, with negative consequences for the exercise of the rights protected by the American Convention.[99] The objection by Trinidad and Tobago was therefore rejected.[100]

This brief overview of the rare examples of the interpretation of Article 29(a) ACHR shows that the interpretation of Article 29(a) ACHR is rather unique. Instead of being a mechanism to prevent the destruction of rights by individuals – the general interpretation of the prohibition of abuse of rights in international human rights law – the Inter-American Court seems to put emphasis on the prohibition on states interpreting the American Convention in a way that would put an end to the rights and freedoms it guarantees. The idea that also individuals and groups can abuse the rights guaranteed in the American Convention appears completely absent in the context of the inter-American human rights system. In that sense, the interpretation of the abuse of rights clause in the American Convention on Human Rights is very different to that of Article 17 ECHR. In fact, the interpretation of Article 29(a) ACHR seems to show more resemblance to the interpretation of the prohibition of abuse of power in Article 18 ECHR.[101]

Speculating on the reasons for the distinctive interpretation given to the abuse of rights clause in the context of the inter-American human rights system, it could be argued that it is due to the different histories of Western Europe and Latin America. The conditions under which the human rights systems on the two continents developed were radically different.[102] During a large part of the 1970s, the American continent was confronted with military dictatorships that were involved in large-scale human rights violations.[103] So, where the purpose of the ECHR was

98 *Case of Benjamin et al. v. Trinidad and Tobago*, 1 September 2001 (preliminary objections), par. 81. See also *Case of Constantine et al. v. Trinidad and Tobago*, 1 September 2001, par. 63 and *Case of Hilaire. v. Trinidad and Tobago*, 1 September 2001, par. 64.

99 *Case of Benjamin et al. v. Trinidad and Tobago*, 1 September 2001 (preliminary objections), par. 82.

100 *Case of Benjamin et al. v. Trinidad and Tobago*, 1 September 2001 (preliminary objections), par. 89.

101 For example, in a number of cases in which the ECtHR found that a state had restricted the exercise of a right for other reasons than those originally put forward, the Court found a violation of Article 18 ECHR. See e.g. ECtHR 3 July 2012, *Lutsenko v. Ukraine*, appl. no. 6492/11; ECtHR 30 April 2013, *Tymoshenko v. Ukraine*, appl. no. 49872/11; ECtHR 22 May 2014, *Ilgar Mammadov v. Azerbaijan*, appl. no. 15172/13; ECtHR 17 March 2016, *Rasul Jafarov v. Azerbaijan*, appl. no. 69981/14.

102 Steiner and Alston, *International Human Rights in Context*, p. 869.

103 Smis et al., *Handboek Mensenrechten*, p. 394.

to preserve existing post-war rights, the ACHR rather created new rights.[104] As a consequence, both historically, and presently, the OAS human rights system has to deal with very different problems than its European equivalent, including widespread poverty, systematic torture, assassination of political dissidents, and enforced disappearances.[105] For the time being, however, this reading of the difference in interpretation of the abuse clause between the ECHR and the ACHR is merely an assumption and requires further investigation.

5.5 The Charter of Fundamental Rights of the EU

Finally, also the Charter of Fundamental Rights that was drafted for the European Union also contains an abuse clause. In 1999 the European Council launched an initiative to draft a Charter of Fundamental Rights for the EU. This initiative followed after many years of discussion about whether the EU should accede to the ECHR or should have its own Bill of Rights.[106] A body of national parliamentarians, European parliamentarians and national government representatives, referred to as the 'Convention', was established to draft this Charter. Within one year, this Convention drew up a Charter of Fundamental Rights containing a list of the human rights recognised by the EU which was collectively adopted by the European Parliament, the Council of Ministers and the European Commission in 2000.[107] At that time, however, a decision on its legal status was postponed. Yet, with the entry into force of the Lisbon Treaty in December 2009, the EU Charter became legally binding upon the EU institutions, as well as on the Member States when they act within the scope of EU law.[108]

5.5.1 The abuse clause in Article 54 EU Charter

Many provisions in the EU Charter are actually based on the ECHR. The equivalent of Article 17 ECHR in the context of EU law is found in Article 54 of the EU Charter and reads as follows: *'[n]othing in this Charter shall be interpreted as implying any right to engage in any activity or to perform any act aimed at the destruction of any of the rights and freedoms recognised in this Charter or at their limitation to a greater extent than is provided for herein'.*[109] As explained in the explanatory document,

104 Goldman, *Human Rights Quarterly*, p. 867.

105 Nowak, *Introduction to the International Human Rights Regime*, p. 189.

106 P. Craig and G. de Búrca, *EU Law. Text, Cases, and Materials*, 3rd ed., Oxford: Oxford University Press, 2003, p. 358.

107 Proclaimed on 18 December 2000, *OJEC* C-364/1. Craig and De Búrca, *EU Law*, p. 43.

108 Article 51 EU Charter. At the same time, an obligation was introduced for the EU to accede to the ECHR. G. de Búrca 'The Evolution of EU Human Rights Law', in: P. Craig and G. de Búrca (eds.), *The Evolution of EU Law*, 2nd ed., Oxford: Oxford University Press, 2011, p. 480-481.

109 See for a general study of the principle the prohibition of abuse of rights under EU law chapter six.

the abuse clause in Article 54 EU Charter corresponds to Article 17 ECHR.[110] The explanatory text does not explain, however, why this provision was incorporated in the ECHR, nor why it has been reproduced in the EU Charter. It is also unclear why the reference to states, groups and persons found in Article 17 ECHR is not reproduced in Article 54 EU Charter. Like the abuse clauses in the UN International Covenants on Human Rights, Article 54 EU Charter is located amongst the general provisions, which include provisions regarding the scope of application of the EU Charter (Article 51), the scope and limitation of the rights and freedoms guaranteed herein (Article 52) and the level of protection that should be upheld within the EU and its Member States (Article 53).

5.5.2 Case Law on Article 54 EU Charter

Since the EU Charter was only granted binding legal status in December 2009, there is, as yet, not much case law on the interpretation of this provision. In fact, at the time of writing, the provision has not yet been applied by the ECJ (or by the General Court or the Civil Service Tribunal). Advocate General Bot, however, referred to the abuse clause in the EU Charter in one of his opinions. He drew upon, amongst other arguments, Article 54 EU Charter to conclude that the 'Television without Frontiers' (TVWF) Directive also covers the issue of the prohibition of a television channel, Roj TV, operated by a Danish broadcasting company in Germany.[111] Germany had prohibited the broadcasting on the grounds that the programmes of Roj TV conflicted with the 'principle of international understanding' as defined by German constitutional law. According to the German authorities, Roj TV's programmes promoted the Kurdistan Workers' Party (PKK), which is recognised as a terrorist organisation, and incited violence. The TVWF Directive aims to ensure the free movement of broadcasting services within the internal market. Based on Article 22(a) of the Directive, however, Member States are under an obligation to ensure that broadcasts do not contain incitement to hatred on the grounds of race, sex, religion or nationality. When faced with the question whether the concept of international understanding is covered by the concept of incitement to hatred in Article 22(a) of the Directive, Advocate General Bot answered this question in the affirmative.[112] In that context he argued that *'to give the concept of infringement of the principles of international*

110 EU, Explanations relating to the Charter of Fundamental Rights (2007/C 303/02), OJ EU, 14.12.2007, C303/35.

111 Council Directive 89/552/EEC of 3 October 1989 on the coordination of certain provisions laid down by law, regulation or administrative action in Member States concerning the pursuit of television broadcasting activities (OJ 1989 L 298, p. 23), as amended by Directive 97/36/EC of the European Parliament and of the Council of 30 June 1997 (OJ 1997 L 202, p. 60).

112 Opinion of Advocate General Bot delivered on 5 May 2011 in the joined cases C-244/10 and C-245/10, *Mesopotamia Broadcast A/S METV and Roj TV A/S v. Bundesrepublik Deutschland*, [2011] ECR I-08779-8796, par. 69.

understanding a broader meaning so that it would cover messages which are not likely to arouse a feeling of intolerance would go against the fundamental right to freedom of expression. In other words and according to Article 54 of the Charter, the freedom of expression guaranteed in Article 11 of the Charter ceases to operate when the message infringes other principles and fundamental rights recognised by the Charter, such as the protection of human dignity and the principle of non-discrimination'.[113]

Still, beyond a few insignificant references to the prohibition of abuse of fundamental rights under EU Law[114] this has not (yet) developed into a more autonomous and comprehensive theory. Yet, while there is no case law on Article 54 EU Charter as yet, the occasional references to the provision by Advocates General suggest that the interpretation of the provision is expected to copy that of Article 17 ECHR.[115] A parallel (yet more coherent) interpretation would indeed be applauded, given the overlap between the two documents. Also considering that the Member States of the European Union are also parties to the ECHR and the fact that Article 6(2) of the TEU still provides that the EU shall accede to the ECHR,[116] it would be unwelcome if the two supervisory bodies (the ECtHR and the CJEU) would offer a radically different interpretation of the abuse clause.

5.6 Conclusions

We started this chapter with the observation that the ECHR is not the only human rights document that contains an abuse clause. The UDHR, the ICCPR, the ICESCR, the ACHR and the EU Charter also contain an abuse clause. This chapter analysed the historical background and interpretation of these equivalents to Article 17 ECHR. As for their wording, all these abuse clauses are rather similar. Article 30 of the UDHR was the first abuse clause to be drafted and it subsequently served as an example

113 Opinion of Advocate General Bot delivered on 5 May 2011 in the joined cases C-244/10 and C-245/10, *Mesopotamia Broadcast A/S METV and Roj TV A/S v. Bundesrepublik Deutschland*, [2011] ECR I-08779-8796, par. 68.

114 In addition, Advocate General Mengozzi referred marginally to Article 54 EU Charter as the codification of the EU principle of the prohibition of abuse of rights in a footnote in the case C-83/13, *Fonnship A/S v. Svenska Transportarbetareförbundet, Facket för Service och Kommunikation (SEKO) and Svenska Transportarbetareförbundet v. Fonnship A/S*, ECLI:EU:C:2014:201, par. 71, footnote 55.

115 See also Article 52(3) Charter, which prescribes that rights in the Charter that correspond to rights guaranteed by the ECHR – without prejudice to a more generous interpretation – will have the same meaning and scope as those laid down by the ECHR. K. Lenaerts and J.A. Gutiérrez Fons, 'The Place of the Charter in the EU Constitutional Edifice', in: S. Peers et al. (eds.), *The EU Charter of Fundamental Rights. A Commentary*, Oxford/Portland: Hart Publishing, 2014, p. 1581.

116 Nevertheless, on 18 December 2014 the Court of Justice of the EU ruled negatively on the draft agreement on the accession of the EU to the ECHR (CJEU, opinion pursuant to Article 218(11) TFEU in Case C-2/13, ECLI:EU:C:2014:2454). Since then the EU's accession appears to have reached a deadlock.

for the abuse clauses in other human rights documents. Consequently, the historical background of all these abuse clauses is basically the same. As a *'safety valve'*[117] they provide an ultimate self-defensive instrument for states to prevent the rights and freedoms they guarantee from being construed to allow the rise of movements that aim to overthrow democratic legal orders.

Also the interpretation of these different abuse clauses, at least partially, runs parallel. Like Article 17 ECHR, the abuse clauses in the UDHR and the ICCPR (and, as far as can be concluded based on the limited explanation and interpretation of Article 54, also the abuse clause in the EU Charter) seem to be merely intended to protect the human rights and the democratic system against the exploitation of civil and political rights by groups and individuals with fascist or neo-Nazi aims. States have been included, because in the past they had frequently been the chief offenders against human rights.[118] In the current interpretation of these abuse clauses, however, this aspect hardly plays any role. The fact that the prohibition of abuse of rights has only marginally been touched upon in the context of the ICESCR can be explained by the nature of these rights, which are less easily capable of being invoked to destroy human rights.[119]

Finally, even though it was drafted after the example of the ECHR, the abuse clause in the ACHR seems to serve a very different purpose. While the interpretation of the abuse clauses in other human rights documents reveals a general understanding of this clause as a rampart against an abuse of human rights by groups and individuals with neo-Nazi tendencies, its interpretation in the context of the ACHR shows that the broad and ambiguous nature of the abuse clause also leaves room for a very different interpretation. A doctrine of a prohibition of abuse of rights by anti-democratic forces as developed under the other human rights documents appears to be absent within the inter-American human rights system. In the small number of cases in which the inter-American Court has found an abuse of rights in the sense of Article 29(a) ACHR, this application of the abuse of rights clause was radically different from the regular application of Article 17 ECHR. The abuse clause in the ACHR appears to primarily serve as a sanction of an abuse by States Parties of the competence to restrict the scope of application of the Convention, thereby restricting fundamental rights to a greater extent than provided for. In the following chapter the clarification of the abuse clause is continued with a study of the general concept of the abuse of rights.

---

117 Alfredsson and Eide, *The Universal Declaration of Human Rights,* p. 650.

118 UN ECOSOC, Commission on Human Rights, second session, 41st meeting, 16 December 1947, *UN DOC. E/CN.4/SR.41*, p. 7-9.

119 Saul, Kinley and Mowbray, *The International Covenant on Economic, Social and Cultural Rights*, p. 265.

Chapter 6
The Concept of Abuse of Rights

6.1 Introduction

In the previous chapter we have looked at the notion of abuse of rights in the context of human rights law. Yet, the prohibition of abuse of rights as a legal concept is found in multiple legal disciplines. It refers to the exercise of a subjective right that *prima facie* appears to be in conformity with that right, but that upon close examination turns out to be contrary to the aim of that right and therefore abusive. The concept basically aims to *'to correct the application of a rule of law on the basis of standards such as good faith, fairness, and justice if, despite formal observance of the conditions of the rule, the objective of that rule has not been achieved'*.[1] Originally developed in the area of private law in continental European jurisdictions, the prohibition of abuse of rights has increasingly been accepted in other areas of law as well, including public international law and EU law, and has given rise to a rather large amount of academic publications. In the context of international human rights law, however, the doctrine on abuse of rights only recently started to receive attention.[2] Even though the concept of abuse of rights is sometimes briefly mentioned in the legal doctrine on Article 17 ECHR, potential parallels between the interpretations of the concept in different legal areas have never been seriously explored. Yet, a study of the interpretation of the concept of abuse of rights in a different context may reveal insights that help to better understand the prohibition of abuse of rights in Article 17 ECHR.

This chapter will first focus on the concept of the prohibition of abuse of rights as it was developed in civil law systems. Continental European jurisdictions have a long tradition when it comes to prohibiting abuses of rights in the context of private law. While primarily focussing on issues of property law, over time the prohibition of abuse of rights expanded into other fields of private law – including contract law, company law, family law and procedural law – and into practically all civil law jurisdictions *'to the point of becoming a widely accepted principle of the civil*

1 A. Lenaerts, 'The General Principle of the Prohibition of Abuse of Rights: A Critical Position on Its Role in a Codified European Contract Law', *European Review of Private Law*, vol. 18, no. 6, 2010, p. 1121.

2 A. Spielmann, 'La Convention Européenne des droits de l'homme et l'abus de droit', in: *Mélanges en hommage à Louis Edmond Pettiti*, Brussels: Bruylant, 1998, p. 673.

law'.[3] This chapter will analyse the historical background and the development of the concept of abuse of rights in the context of two dominant civil law traditions: France and Germany. It will subsequently explore to what extent a concept of abuse exists in the common law tradition. It will then analyse how the concept is interpreted in several public law areas: public international law and EU law. Finally, it will explore how the concept is interpreted in human rights law.

6.2 The historical background of the prohibition of abuse of rights

Even though the doctrine of abuse of rights only seriously became the object of academic research in Europe at the beginning of the twentieth century,[4] the idea itself is much older.[5] According to Kiss, *'[t]he idea that a subject of rights and competences can misuse them seems to be inherent to legal thinking and to have roots in all legal systems and leads to the establishment of controls on the use of recognised rights'*.[6] Several authors trace back the origin of the notion of abuse of rights to ancient Roman law.[7] Other scholars, however, dispute this by pointing to contradicting ancient Roman maxims. Following Crabb, we may conclude, though, that prohibitions on abusing rights existed under Roman law, but that they were in fact merely applied ad hoc and not as a general principle.[8] These first steps in the development of this notion, however, served as a source of inspiration for the modern doctrine of abuse of rights.[9]

---

3 J. Cueto-Rua, 'Abuse of Rights', *Louisiana Law Review*, vol. 35, no. 5, 1975, p. 967. See also J. Voyaume, B. Cottier and B. Rocha, 'Abuse of Rights in Comparative Law', in: CoE, *Abuse of Rights and Equivalent Concepts: the Principle and its Present Day Application*, 19th Colloquy on European Law, Strasbourg: CoE Publishing and Documentation Service, 1990, p. 26, 43-44; H.C. Gutteridge, 'Abuse of Rights', *Cambridge Law Journal,* vol. 5, no. 1, 1933, p. 34 and V.G.A. Boll, *Misbruik van recht*, Utrecht: A. Oosthoef, 1913, p. 6-7.

4 N. Okma, *Misbruik van recht [Abuse of rights]*, Wageningen: Gebrs. Zomer en Keuning's Uitgeversmaatschappij, 1945, p. 30.

5 L. Eck, 'Controverses Constitutionelles et Abus de Droit', conference paper for the Congrès de l'Association Française de Droit Constitutionnel (A.F.D.C.), Montpellier, June 2005, www.droitconstitutionnel.org/congresmtp/textes1/ECK.pdf, p. 2-3 (accessed 11 April 2016).

6 A. Kiss, 'Abuse of Rights', in: *Max Planck Encyclopedia of Public International Law*, http://opil.ouplaw.com/view/10.1093/law:epil/9780199231690/law-9780199231690-e1371?rskey=8pckoF&result=1&prd=EPIL (accessed 11 April 2016, last updated December 2006), Rn. 34. Also V.G.A. Boll, *Misbruik van recht [Abuse of rights]*, Utrecht: A. Oosthoef, 1913, p. 1-2.

7 Eck, 'Controverses Constitutionelles et Abus de Droit', p. 2-3; Voyaume, Cottier and Rocha, 'Abuse of Rights in Comparative Law', p. 25; L. Campion, *La théorie de l'abus des droits*, Brussels/Paris: Établissements Émile Bruylant/Librairie générale de droit, 1925, p. 5-14.

8 J.H. Crabb, 'The French Concept of Abuse of Rights', *Inter-American Law Review*, vol. 6, no. 1, 1964, p. 4-5. See also D.J. Devine, 'Some Comparative Aspects of the Doctrine of Abuse of Rights', *Acta Juridica*, 1964, p. 150-153.

9 Voyaume, Cottier and Rocha, 'Abuse of Rights in Comparative Law', p. 26.

During the Enlightenment the concept of abuse of rights was practically absent. The dominant theory of rights at the time was a liberal and individualistic one, according to which all human beings possessed certain universal and unalienable rights, independent of the society in which they live.[10] Gay describes 'freedom' as the core element of the Enlightenment: *'men of the Enlightenment united on a vastly ambitious programme, a programme of secularism, humanity, cosmopolitanism, and freedom, above all, freedom in its many forms – freedom from arbitrary power, freedom of speech, freedom of trade, freedom to realize one's talents, freedom of aesthetic response, freedom, in a word, of moral man to make his own way in the world'*.[11] The individual was considered a legal subject, enjoying fundamental rights protecting him against the power of the state.[12] The French Declaration of the Rights of Man, adopted in 1789 during the French Revolution, clearly reflects the liberal ideals of the Enlightenment. This revolution resulted in a triumph of individualism and the foundation of traditional theories of liberty.

It was only after a while that the influence of the principle of solidarity put the notion of abuse of rights back on the map.[13] In the course of the nineteenth century the prohibition of abuse of rights was – in very various forms – taken up in several continental national legal orders. It was a reaction to the individualistic liberalism of the Enlightenment and reflected the growing political and intellectual concerns and dissatisfaction with the absolutism of possessive individualism.[14] Individual rights started to no longer be considered as absolute rights, but were increasingly regarded in terms of their social context.

6.2.1 Josserand: relativity and the social function of rights

The first comprehensive theory on abuse of rights was formulated by the French scholar Josserand. The core element of Josserand's theory is the social function of rights. He believed that *'[l]aw is brought into being for the benefit of the community and not for the advantage of the individual'*.[15] In his view the legislator has conferred rights upon its citizens with specific social aims in mind. The abuse of rights should therefore be sanctioned, not by reference to its benefit for the individual, but to the extent that it conforms to this social purpose and benefits the social complex as a

10 See in particular the thoughts of the Enlightenment philosopher Locke: J. Locke, (1689) *Two Treatises of Government*, reprint, Cambridge: Cambridge University Press, 1997.

11 P. Gay, *The Enlightenment: an Interpretation, vol. 1: The Rise of Modern Paganism*, 2nd ed., New York: Alfred A. Knopf, 1967, p. 3.

12 Campion, *La théorie de l'abus des droits*, p. 23.

13 Campion, p. 23.

14 A. Sajó, 'Abuse of Fundamental Rights or the Difficulties of Purposiveness', in: A. Sajó (ed.), *Abuse: The Dark Side of Fundamental Rights*, Utrecht: Eleven International Publishing, 2006, p. 38-39.

15 Gutteridge, *Cambridge Law Journal*, p. 27.

whole.[16] As Bolgár explains, *'what Josserand voiced was the vindication of the gradual process that shifted the importance of individual rights from their private, autonomous domain into the social field, and transformed the exercise of these very rights into social functions'*.[17] At the time, Josserand's rejection of the individualistic view of human rights was rather innovative.[18] Eventually his theory proved to be extremely influential in the development of the concept of abuse of rights.

In the eyes of Josserand, all rights are social products. Observed in total isolation, individuals do not even have rights in the legal sense of the word; it is only as members of society that they acquire legal personality and become the subjects of rights and interpersonal obligations.[19] The idea that rights are completely subjective and only serve a purely individual purpose is therefore a fiction, Josserand maintained. All rights, even the most individual and egoistic rights, such as property rights, are products of society and they all have a social element.[20] This also holds true for (individual) freedoms, such as the freedom of thought and expression and the freedom of association.[21] So, every right has a social purpose and has to be exercised in that light.[22] As a consequence, rights may only be exercised in a well-considered and socially acceptable way and should not be transformed into weapons against society.[23]

It is because rights serve a certain social function that they are relative and their use may amount to an abuse.[24] An abuse of a right, according to Josserand, constitutes an act contrary to the aim for which a right was created, its spirit or its purpose.[25] This notion, which has also been referred to as a violation of the spirit of a right, forms the centrepiece of Josserand's theory. It means that the use of a right turns into an abuse when it is exercised contrary to its function. So, anyone who attempts to deviate a right from its function and tries to use it in a conflicting direction, abuses his right.[26] In Josserand's theory, the concepts of the social function

16 S. Herman, 'Classical Social Theories and the Doctrine of "Abuse of Right"', *Louisiana Law Review*, vol. 37, no. 3, 1977, p. 754.
17 V. Bolgár, 'Abuse of Rights in France, Germany, and Switzerland: A Survey of a Recent Chapter in Legal Doctrine', *Louisiana Law Review*, vol. 35, no. 5, 1975, p. 1016.
18 Bolgár, *Louisiana Law Review*, p. 1016.
19 L. Josserand, *De l'esprit des droits et de leur relativité. Théorie dite de l'abus des droits*, 2nd ed., Paris: Dalloz, 1939, p. 321.
20 Josserand, *De l'esprit des droits et de leur relativité*, p. 321-322.
21 However, Josserand discusses these freedoms from a private law perspective, as freedoms towards other citizens instead of guarantees against state intervention: Josserand, *De l'esprit des droits et de leur relativité*, p. 214, 215- 231 and 254-256.
22 Josserand, *De l'esprit des droits et de leur relativité*, p. 388.
23 Josserand, p. 324.
24 Josserand, p. 415. See also J. Dabin, *Le droit subjectif*, Paris: Dalloz, 1952, p. 288.
25 Josserand, *De l'esprit des droits et de leur relativité*, p. 395.
26 Josserand, p. 322. See also Boll, *Misbruik van recht*, p. 50.

of rights and the prohibition of abuse, that serve as a sanction thereon, are closely linked and indissoluble[27] Rights are therefore not only restricted by the concrete boundaries given by legal instruments, but also by the less apparent limit that follows from their social function.[28]

The social function implies that rights should be exercised for the purpose of an interest that is adequate for its spirit and task: a legitimate interest. With Von Jhering, Josserand was of the opinion that rights are judicially protected interests.[29] The notion of the legitimate interest suggests that the contrary, an illegitimate interest, should not be protected by the law. The range of possible illegitimate interests according to Josserand is extremely wide, ranging from the intention to prejudice someone's rights and acts out of bad faith to simply wrong acts such as crimes and acts out of culpability.[30] The consequence of the absence of a legitimate interest is that the right holder can no longer enjoy the protection of that right.[31]

In case of an argument, it is the judge who has to evaluate, based on the nature and spirit of the right in question, whether the interest of the right holder was legitimate and the boundaries of the right were not overstepped.[32] He has to scrutinize his conscience and investigate with what motive the right-holder exercised his right.[33] Even though it is a delicate task, Josserand believes that it does not exceed the investigative powers of the judiciary.[34] Here some commentators have noted that Josserand might have been too optimistic about the capacities of the judge, for it is not clear how the social function of rights – and the legitimate aims deduced from it – take shape.[35] Josserand seemed to assume that it is the legislator who defines what their social function is when rights are granted. Most of the time, however, the legislator will not explicitly define the social function of rights, especially those of an individual nature, which puts the judge who has to decide on this in a difficult position.

Even before Josserand published his theory on abuse of rights, the Dutch legal scholar Boll had also argued that rights are not purely guardians of the individual, but rather have a more social nature. This social nature is what he described as the *'social or altruistic component of rights'*.[36] In his view, one of the tasks of the law

27 Josserand, *De l'esprit des droits et de leur relativité*, p. 415.
28 Josserand, p. 311.
29 Josserand, p. 388. See also Cueto-Rua, *Louisiana Law Review*, p. 995-996.
30 Josserand, *De l'esprit des droits et de leur relativité*, p. 407-411. See also J. Dabin, *Le droit subjectif*, Paris: Dalloz, 1952, p. 287.
31 Josserand, *De l'esprit des droits et de leur relativité*, p. 388.
32 Josserand, p. 399-400.
33 Josserand, p. 399.
34 Josserand, p. 410.
35 Herman, *Louisiana Law Review*, p. 755.
36 Boll, *Misbruik van recht*, p. 44 [translation is my own].

is to contribute to a fair balance of social relationships. Everyone, therefore, has to take into account the rights and interests of others when exercising his rights.[37] This is, however, reciprocal: every individual has to sacrifice some of his freedom, but at the same time benefits from the sacrifices others make in relation to him. Boll therefore speaks of abuse when an act cannot meet with approval because it violates the way people should behave towards each other.[38] From the outset, such acts rightfully appear to constitute the exercise of a right, but it is the aim for which they are exercised that eliminates their protection.[39] Boll emphasised that it is not the act itself, but the illegitimate aim for which a right is used that renders it its condemnable character.[40] Contrary to Josserand, who claimed that some rights are indeed 'absolute' and do not qualify for abuse, Boll argued that the prohibition of abuse of rights is a general principle and is therefore generally applicable to all rights. Where there is a right, he argued, there is the potential that it will be abused.[41]

Other scholars, such as Dabin, however, have proposed that the basis for the theory of abuse of rights is not a legal one, but a moral one. From a legal perspective, he argues that rights are granted to individuals to serve their individual interests and not as tools for achieving certain specific social goals, which are extremely vague.[42] By focussing on the social function of rights, freedom is basically replaced by 'controlled rights'.[43] Dabin believes that the basis for the concept of abuse of rights is found in the extra-legal notion of morality.[44] He presumes that all individuals are moral beings. Based on Christian morals, Dabin claims that men must acts according to their inner human nature.[45] From this point of view, abuse constitutes a *'violation of the general duty of solidarity and altruism required of all men towards their fellows'*.[46]

6.2.2 Criticism of the concept of abuse of rights

Josserand's theory *'marked one of the most radical changes in the ideas on the nature and the functions of law'*.[47] His innovative ideas on rights as social products that have

37 Boll, p. 4-5.
38 Boll, p. 5.
39 Boll, p. 85.
40 Boll, p. 89.
41 Boll, *Misbruik van recht*, p. 26.
42 Sajó, *Abuse*, p. 55.
43 Dabin, *Le droit subjectif*, p. 293-294.
44 Dabin, p. 289-292.
45 Dabin, p. 289-292. See also Sajó, *Abuse*, p. 55.
46 A. Spielmann and D. Spielmann, 'The Concept of Abuse of Rights and the European Convention for the Protection of Human Rights and Fundamental Freedoms', in: CoE, *Abuse of Rights and Equivalent Concepts: the Principle and its Present Day Application*, 19th Colloquy on European Law, Strasbourg: CoE Publishing and Documentation Service, 1990, p. 72.
47 Bolgár, *Louisiana Law Review*, p. 1016.

to be interpreted in the light of their social function vis-à-vis society created a heated debate among legal scholars.

Planiol, a principal antagonist of the concept of abuse of rights, considered the concept to be *'logically untenable'* and merely a *'logomachy'*.[48] According to him the notion of abuse of rights, which he refers to as 'abusive use of rights', was contradictious.[49] As Bolgár interprets Planiol's point, *'there can be no abuse of rights if they were exercised within the limits of the law that granted their rights'*.[50] An act cannot be both lawful and unlawful at the same time. While the concept of abuse of rights *'implies a distinction between the existence of an individual right and the exercise of such a right'*,[51] Planiol considers this distinction to be artificial. Not that he thinks that rights are absolute. But what others may call 'abusive use of rights', according to Planiol is just a wrong use of terminology and should be called *'an act that has taken place without right'*.[52]

In his view, if someone uses a right, his act is licit; and when it is illicit, that is because he exceeded his right and acted without a right.[53] This implies that all acts must be classified strictly as either licit or illicit, whereby the latter creates liability while the former does not.[54] He therefore believes that there is no such thing as a legal category of abuse of rights, distinct from illicit acts. Every abusive act, because it is illicit, does not constitute the exercise of a right. The minute an act attains an abusive character, it ceases to qualify as the exercise of a right.[55] In the famous words of Planiol, the right ends where the abuse begins: *'[l]e droit cesse où l'abus commence, et il ne peut pas y avoir usage abusif d'un droit quelconque par la raison irréfutable qu'un seul et même acte ne paut pas être à la fois conforme au droit et contraire au droit'*.[56]

A dichotomic approach as the one advocated by Planiol has been disputed by the Dutch legal scholar Okma, who believes that the abuse of a right and acting without a right are two clearly different things. The abuse of a right presupposes the existence of a right. Abuse indicates that an appeal to that right *prima facie* appeared to be just, but upon closer examination tuned out to be unjust. If there were not even the appearance of a right, it would not make sense to speak about abuse, Okma argues. He therefore defines the abuse of rights as *'the exercise of a rule or subjective*

---

48 Crabb, *Inter-American Law Review*, p. 3.
49 Herman, *Louisiana Law Review*, p. 747.
50 Bolgár, *Louisiana Law Review*, p. 1016. See also Herman, *Louisiana Law Review*, p. 747.
51 Kiss, 'Abuse of Rights', Rn. 3.
52 M. Planiol, *Traite élémentaire de droit civil*, 2nd ed, Paris: Librairie Générale de droit & de jurisprudence, 1926, p. 298-299. See also Cueto-Rua, *Louisiana Law Review*, p. 975.
53 Planiol, *Traite élémentaire de droit civil*, p. 298. See also Herman, *Louisiana Law Review*, p. 747.
54 Herman, *Louisiana Law Review*, p. 749.
55 Gutteridge, *Cambridge Law Journal*, p. 24.
56 Planiol, *Traite élémentaire de droit civil*, p. 298.

right that is dismissed by a judge by reason of the aim of that rule or subjective right (apparently in contradiction with its formulation) or by reason of either the circumstances or either unwritten law (apparently in contradiction to that rule or subjective right)'.[57]

Also Ripert objected to Josserand's theory of the social function of rights. He feared *'that the emphasis on the social as against the individual orientation of law will gradually deprive the individual of his subjective rights'.*[58] Moreover, he stressed that the issue of an abuse of rights is not a legal but rather a moral one.[59] The criteria for abuse of rights should not be sought in the social function of rights, but in the moral obligations that dominate the exercise of rights. *'On dit que cet acte est antisocial et je n'en disconviens pas; mais il n'est antisociale que dans une société dominée par une morale où le devoir de ne pas nuire volontairement au prochain est inscrit dans le décalogue. Car, en apparence, l'acte est parfaitement social, étant accompli dans le cercle affecté à l'activité de chacun de nous. C'est l'intention qui le rend coupable, et c'est parce qu'il y a infraction au devoir moral qu'il est déclaré contraire au droit'*, Ripert explains.[60] Other than Dabin, however, Ripert is of the opinion that the judicial scrutiny of the morality of individual actions would introduce an undesirable arbitrary element into the jurisprudence of the courts. In the words of Ripert, *'[o]n voit ainsi la satisfaction du devoir moral dominer l'exercice des droits, et, si le juge n'a pas une claire conception du devoir moral, il sera incapable de juges s'il y a abus du droit'.*[61]

In short, the critics of the concept of abuse of rights argued that what is generally referred to as abuse is in fact acting beyond the scope of a right and therefore constitutes acting without a right. The debate, however, appears to be predominantly a linguistic one, revolving around the appropriateness of the term 'abuse of right'.[62] Consequently, even the critics do not contest the results of the application of the concept of abuse of rights in actual cases, but consider ascribing them to the doctrine of abuse of rights to be incorrect.[63] Hereafter both positions will be discussed in more detail.

---

57 Okma, *Misbruik van Recht*, p. 13 [translation is my own].

58 Bolgár, *Louisiana Law Review*, p. 1017. See also G. Ripert, *La Règle Morale dans les Obligations Civiles*, 3rd ed., Paris: Pichon et Durand-Auzias, 1935, p. 195.

59 Ripert, *La Règle Morale dans les Obligations Civiles*, p. 169.

60 Ripert, p. 191.

61 Ripert, p. 191 and 193. See also Bolgár, *Louisiana Law Review*, p. 1017.

62 B.O. Iluyomade, 'The Scope and Content of a Complaint of Abuse of Right in International Law', *Harvard International Law Journal*, vol. 16, no. 1, 1975, p. 48.

63 Crabb, *Inter-American Law Review*, p. 3; Iluyomade, p. 49.

6.3 The development of the concept of abuse of rights in different legal traditions

Even though the prohibition of abuse of rights was taken up in several national legal orders, the forms in which this concept emerged vary. Several dominant traditions can be distinguished. The first was developed by the courts in France at the end of the nineteenth century. As 'the cradle' of the concept, France played an important role in the development of the prohibition of abuse of rights. For that reason early French scholars unmistakably took the lead in this debate.[64] The developments of the doctrine of abuse of rights in Germany were generally speaking similar to the developments in France.[65] Nonetheless, in Germany the interpretation of the doctrine of abuse of rights was primarily developed through legislation.[66] Finally, it has often been argued that the concept of abuse of rights has not been accepted in states adhering to common law. Hereafter we will explore to what extent that is true and whether maybe other legal concepts fulfil a similar function under common law.

6.3.1 France as the cradle of the concept

In the French Civil Code (*Code Civil* or CC) of 1804 the concept of abuse of rights was ignored.[67] This Code was based on the ideas of the Enlightenment and at that time the prohibition of abuse did not fit the liberal interpretation of rights. Nevertheless, this did not prevent French courts from introducing the concept of abuse of rights in a number of cases in the course of the nineteenth century. In fact, the courts in France played a decisive role in the development of the doctrine of abuse of rights. In the absence of a general legislative prohibition of abuse of rights, they built a standing practice based on several individual provisions in de CC.[68] Sajó describes this development as a reaction to the individualistic liberalism of the Enlightenment. It reflected the growing political and intellectual concerns and dissatisfaction with the absolutism of this individualist approach.[69] So, eventually, under the influence of the principle of solidarity the notion of abuse of rights was put back on the map.[70]

64 Bolgár, *Louisiana Law Review*, p. 1015.
65 Bolgár, p. 1023.
66 Gutteridge, *Cambridge Law Journal,* p. 36; Bolgár, *Louisiana Law Review*, p. 1023. Other states where the principle is codified include Greece, Luxembourg, the Netherlands, Portugal and Spain: Lenaerts, *European Review of Private Law*, p. 1125-1126.
67 Crabb, Inter-American Law Review, p. 5.
68 Including the Articles 1382-1386 CC on liability and the reparation of damages. Bolgár, *Louisiana Law Review*, p. 1019-1020. In Belgium too, the principle emanates primarily from case law: Lenaerts, *European Review of Private Law*, p. 1126.
69 Sajó, *Abuse*, p. 29-30.
70 Campion, *La théorie de l'abus des droits*, p. 23.

Moreover, around that same time a renewed interest in civil liability came up.[71] This meant that, as described by Boll, individual rights were no longer considered absolute and free from liability and were increasingly regarded in terms of their aims.[72]

In France, the prohibition of abuse of rights was originally created in the field of property law on the basis of delictual liability.[73] The ultimate landmark case on this topic is the 1915 decision by the Court of Cassation (*la Cour de Cassation*) in the case *Clément-Bayard*, regarding a quarrel between two neighbours in the French countryside.[74] Clément-Bayard owned several air ships (zeppelins), which were housed in hangars on his land. Coquerel, the owner of the piece of land next to the hangars, had tried to sell his land to Clément-Bayard, but the latter had been unwilling to pay the price requested. In reaction to the failed negotiations, Coquerel erected a number of sixteen-metre high wooden fences topped by tall iron spikes on his land. These spikes were clearly dangerous to Clément-Bayard's airships and on one occasion one of the airships indeed collided with the spikes and was severely damaged. Clément-Bayard sued Coquerel for damages and demanded the removal of the structures. Coquerel pleaded that he was just exercising his practically absolute property right as protected under the French CC.[75] Moreover, he claimed that his malice towards Clément-Bayard was only one of his motives. The Court, however, held that the spikes did not serve any function for the exploitation of the land by Coquerel and were erected with the single aim of harming Clément-Bayard. Moreover, given the height of the spikes, they exceeded the fencing a landowner is allowed to build on his property to protect his legitimate interests. The Court therefore

---

71 Ripert, *La Règle Morale dans les Obligations Civiles*, p. 169-170. See also Bolgár, *Louisiana Law Review*, p. 1017.

72 Boll, *Misbruik van recht*, p. 106-107 and 82.

73 Later, the principle of the prohibition of abuse of rights was also recognized in contractual matters on the basis of the duty of good faith. Lenaerts, *European Review of Private Law*, p. 1126.

74 French Court of Cassation, 3 August 1915, *Affaire Clément-Bayard*, D.P.III.1917.1.79. See for a detailed description of this case Herman, *Louisiana Law Review*, p. 751-754; Cueto-Rua, *Louisiana Law Review*, p. 981 and Gutteridge, *Cambridge Law Journal*, p. 33-34. See for an earlier example the case concerning a house owner who had erected a tall dummy chimney on his roof, blocking the access of light to his neighbour's house, Court of Appeal of Colmar, 2 May 1855, *Affaire Doerr*, D.P. 1856.2.9. Even though the court did not in fact explicitly use the term 'abuse', some scholars argue that this case represents the origin of the modern abuse of rights doctrine (Sajó, *Abuse*, p. 39; Crabb, *Inter-American Law Review*, p. 2-3). See around that same time a case concerning the excavation of mineral water, with the result that the water in the spring of another owner was drastically diminished (a situation similar to the English *Mayor of Bradford v. Pickles* case, which is discussed later on in this chapter), Court of Appeal of Lyon, 18 April 1856, D.P.1856.2.199. See also Gutteridge, *Cambridge Law Journal*, p. 33 and Cueto-Rua, *Louisiana Law Review*, p. 965-966.

75 Article 544 CC provided and still provides that *'La propriété est le droit de jouir et disposer des choses* de la manière la plus absolue, *pourvu qu'on n'en fasse pas un usage prohibé par les lois ou par les règlements'* [emphasis added]. See also J.M. Perillo, 'Abuse of Rights: A Pervasive Legal Concept', *Pacific Law Journal*, vol. 27, no. 1, 1995, p. 43.

considered that Coquerel had abused his right and ordered him, first, to pay for the damage caused to Clément-Bayard's airship, and second, to remove the iron spikes: '*dans cette situation des faits, l'arrêt a pu apprécier qu'il y avait eu par Coquerel* abus de son droit *et, d'une part, le condamner à la réparation du dommage causé à un ballon dirigeable de Clément-Bayard, d'autre part, ordonner l'enlèvement des tiges de fer surmontant les carcasses en bois'*.[76] The case is illustrative for the test that is applied in most French abuse of rights cases: did the right holder have the intention to harm someone else?[77]

6.3.2 Abuse of rights in Germany: reasonableness and fairness in contract law

In Germany, a similar development took place by which rights were increasingly interpreted based on the social context in which they operate. Under German law, however, the prohibition of abuse of rights did not emanate from property law, but was originally founded on notions of reasonableness and fairness in contract law.[78] Furthermore, whereas the prohibition of abuse of rights in France was primarily developed by the courts, in the German context the prohibition of abuse of rights finds it origin predominantly in legislation. A general provision referring to the prohibition of abuse as a general legal principle was formulated in Section 226 German Civil Code (*Bürgerliches Gesetzbuch* or CC). This famous '*Schikaneverbot*' holds that the exercise of a right is unacceptable, when its only aim is to cause harm to someone else.[79] It is important to recall that the German CC was promulgated in 1900, roughly one century after the French CC.[80] By the time it was drafted, the doctrine of abuse of rights had already been established in legislative thinking and there was less resistance towards including a provision reflecting the acceptance of the abuse of rights doctrine.[81]

At the end of the day, however, the general prohibition of abuse of rights in Section 226 CC has hardly ever been applied.[82] In reality it turned out to be almost impossible to prove that the right holder's only motive for action was to harm another person. Nonetheless, there are several other provisions in the German CC that deal

---

76 www.legifrance.gouv.fr/affichJuriJudi.do?idTexte=JURITEXT000007070363 (accessed 11 April 2016) [emphasis added].

77 Gutteridge, *Cambridge Law Journal*, p. 32.

78 Lenaerts, *European Review of Private Law*, p. 1126.

79 Section 226 CC reads: '*Die Ausübung eines Rechts ist unzulässig, wenn sie nur den Zweck haben kann, einem anderen Schaden zuzufügen*', www.gesetze-im-internet.de/englisch_bgb/ (accessed 11 April 2016).

80 The French CC came into force in 1804 and the German CC in 1900. Bolgár, *Louisiana Law Review*, p. 1023.

81 Bolgár, *Louisiana Law Review*, p. 1023.

82 Gutteridge, *Cambridge Law Journal*, p. 36.

with special cases of abuse, for example in the exercise of property rights.[83] In addition, several other provisions in the German CC indirectly affect the doctrine of the abuse of rights. These include, in the first place, Section 242 CC, which provides a general provision on good faith (*Treu und Glauben*) in the execution of obligations.[84] In addition, Section 826 CC on the restitution of damages caused by actions that are held to be contrary to morality (*Sittlichkeit*) should be mentioned in this regard.[85] Most abuse-like cases in Germany were concluded on the basis of these provisions. Instead of focusing on the behaviour of the right holder, these provisions focus on the act itself and, above all, on its results: are these, in the light of the circumstances, abnormal or excessive?[86]

6.3.3 The absence of the concept of abuse of rights in common law

As argued before, the abuse of rights seems to be predominantly a civil law doctrine.[87] As a result of the rather absolutist view of rights in states adhering to common law, the concept would be less readily comprehended in these legal systems.[88] It has been argued, for example, that English law has rejected the concept of abuse of rights.[89] This rejection would be based on a powerful perception of fundamental rights as safeguards of individual freedom: *'an act which is not illegal cannot be penalised simply because it causes harm to others'*.[90] The question in liability cases is therefore *'what the defendant has done and not why he did it'*.[91] If it is established that someone has a right, nothing should prevent him from exercising it as he sees fit, whether his motives be selfish or malicious. According to this strict interpretation of ownership and contractual rights courts in common law jurisdictions also protect protection actions taken out of greed, malice or cruelty.[92]

---

83 Gutteridge, p. 36.

84 This provision reads: *'Der Schuldner ist verpflichtet, die Leistung so zu bewirken, wie Treu und Glauben mit Rücksicht auf die Verkehrssitte es erfordern'*. See Bolgár, *Louisiana Law Review*, p. 1024; Gutteridge, *Cambridge Law Journal*, p. 38.

85 This provision reads: *'Wer in einer gegen die guten Sitten verstoßenden Weise einem anderen vorsätzlich Schaden zufügt, ist dem anderen zum Ersatz des Schadens verpflichtet'*. See Bolgár, *Louisiana Law Review*, p. 1024; Gutteridge, *Cambridge Law Journal*, p. 37-38.

86 See also Voyaume, Cottier and Rocha, 'Abuse of Rights in Comparative Law', p. 36.

87 Iluyomade, *Harvard International Law Journal*, p. 49 and 55-57.

88 Gutteridge, *Cambridge Law Journal*, p. 22 and 30 respectively. See also Voyaume, Cottier and Rocha, 'Abuse of Rights in Comparative Law', p. 39; M. Byers, 'Abuse of Rights: An Old Principle, A New Age', *McGill Law Journal*, vol. 47, no. 2, 2002, p. 395. Denmark and the other Nordic countries share a similar approach: Lenaerts, *European Review of Private Law*, p. 1125.

89 Gutteridge, *Cambridge Law Journal*, p. 30.

90 Voyaume, Cottier and Rocha, 'Abuse of Rights in Comparative Law', p. 39.

91 Gutteridge, *Cambridge Law Journal*, p. 31.

92 Cueto-Rua, *Louisiana Law Review*, p. 967.

A well-known and illustrative example of this in English law is found in the case *Mayor of Bradford v. Pickles*, decided by the House of Lords in 1895. Pickles was a landowner in Bradford. His land contained underground water that flowed down to springs, which were used to supply the city of Bradford with water. In 1892 Pickles sunk a shaft into the ground and started to drive a level through his land to divert the flow of water. As a consequence, the water supply of the city diminished considerably. Although Pickles alleged that he wanted to take advantage of some minerals, there was evidence that his primary aim was to force the city to either buy his land or pay him for the water. The city then sued Pickles to restrain him from doing anything causing the waters of the spring and streams to dry up or diminish in quantity or quality. Just like the lower courts, the House or Lords ruled in favour of Pickles. In the words of Lord Watson, *'no use of property which would be legal if due to a proper motive can become illegal because it is prompted by a motive which is improper or even malicious'*.[93] According to the House of Lords, Pickles, as the owner of the land, had acted lawfully and, however malicious his motive may have been, had the right to divert the water under his land and deprive his neighbours of it.

Yet, even though it is true in common law systems that there is no general recognition of the prohibition of abuse of rights, *'pragmatic solutions are found through the use of concepts that, in concrete situations, will lead to a similar result as the prohibition of abuse of rights would do'*.[94] Similar concepts in the context of tort law and liability, such as nuisance in the context of property rights, show that in fact *'the essence of the doctrine of abuse of right'* is also present in common law.[95] Even though the case of *Pickles v. Bradford* is classically regarded as the foundation of the formal rejection of the concept of the prohibition of abuse of rights in English law, in two subsequent cases on nuisance, the House of Lords did rely on a harmful intent on the part of the right holder to qualify the acts at hand unlawful.[96] In addition, it has also been argued that the principle of equity performs a similar function to the prohibition of abuse of rights, *'namely the "relativisation" of rights'*.[97] So, despite differences in the nature and scope of the methods used, the solutions for dealing with the potential undesirable effects of the exercise of rights adopted under English law are roughly similar to those adopted by civil law systems. Overall, the conclusion that

---

93 House of Lords, 29 July 1895, *Mayor, Aldermen and Burgesses of the Borough of Bradford v. Edward Pickles,* [1895] A.C. 587. See also Cueto-Rua, *Louisiana Law Review*, p. 967-968.

94 Lenaerts, *European Review of Private Law*, p. 1125. See also Iluyomade, *Harvard International Law Journal*, p. 49.

95 Iluyomade, *Harvard International Law Journal*, p. 58.

96 *Christie v. Davey* (1893) I CH 316 (HL) and *Hollywood Silver Fox Farm Ltd v. Emmet* (1936) 2 KB 468 (HL). See A. Saydé, *Abuse of EU Law and Regulation of the Internal Market*, Oxford/Portland: Hart Publishing, 2014, p. 35.

97 Saydé, *Abuse of EU Law*, p. 37. See also Voyaume, Cottier and Rocha, 'Abuse of Rights in Comparative Law', p. 40.

the thoughts behind the prohibition of abuse of rights are completely rejected under the common law system is therefore too simplistic.

6.4 The concept of abuse of rights in public law

The concept of abuse of rights seems to be predominantly a private law matter. In that context it operates on a national level and moderates the horizontal relations between individuals. Over time, however, the prohibition of abuse of rights also found its way into public law. In general, the terminology of abuse in public law often refers to the abuse of an administrative power or discretion for an object other than that for which it was conferred by state authorities, in civil law systems knows as *détournement de pouvoir*.[98] Yet, while the *détournement de pouvoir* is a ground for a judicial review of administrative actions, abuse of rights is generally a ground for a judicial review of the exercise of subjective rights by individuals or groups.[99] The concept is also recognised in an international context, as a moderator of the relation between states in public international law. And in EU law, the concept of abuse of rights was shaped in a vertical relation between states, on the one hand, and companies, groups and individuals on the other.

6.4.1 The prohibition of abuse of rights in public international law

Over time, the prohibition of abuse of rights has also found its way into the area of public international law. In this context, abuse of rights can be defined as *'a State exercising a right either in a way which impedes the enjoyment by other States of their own rights or for an end different from that for which the right was created, to the injury of another State'*.[100] The prohibition of abuse of rights progressively appears in international treaties and conventions.[101] In addition, the notion of abuse of

---

98 Iluyomade, *Harvard International Law Journal*, p. 51-52.

99 Iluyomade, p. 51.

100 Kiss, 'Abuse of Rights', Rn. 1.

101 The most explicit recognition of the prohibition of abuse of rights is found in Article 300 of the UN Convention on the Law of the Sea, 10 December 1982, UN Doc. A/CONF.62/121 and Article 34 of the Agreement for the Implementation of the Provisions of the United Nations Convention on the Law of the Sea, 4 December 1995, UN GA, 6th Sess., UN Doc. A/CONF.164/37. See in addition Article 34 of the Agreement for the Implementation of the Provisions of the United Nations Convention on the Law of the Sea of 10 December 1982 relating to the Conservation and Management of Straddling Fish Stocks and Highly Migratory Fish Stocks (adopted 4 August 1995, entered into force 11 December 2001, [1995] 34 ILM 1542) and Article 33 of the Convention on the Conservation and Management of Highly Migratory Fish Stocks in the Western and Central Pacific Ocean (adopted 5 September 2000, entered into force 19 June 2004, [2001] 40 ILM 278).

rights has found a modest degree of support in the judgments of international courts and tribunals as a standard for measuring and interpreting international norms.[102]

The concept appears to have been generally accepted in legal practice in the field of public international law, even though in legal doctrine it is still contested. Several scholars nowadays consider the doctrine of abuse of rights to be accepted in public international law.[103] Others, however, object to the autonomous relevance of the doctrine of abuse of rights for the area of public international law.[104] They argue, among other things, that the prohibition of abuse of rights is merely an expression of broader principles such as the principles of good faith, reasonableness or normal administration.[105] The resistance against the concept of abuse of rights in public international law may be partly explained by the fact that the acceptance of principles at the international level depends on the widespread existence of these principles at the national level. As we have seen earlier on in this chapter, whereas the prohibition of abuse of rights is a well-established concept in civil law, a formal doctrine of abuse of rights is absent in most common law countries.

6.4.2 The prohibition of abuse of rights in EU Law

In legal doctrine there is still discussion on the question whether the prohibition of abuse of law constitutes a general principle of EU law.[106] In this regard it is also considered relevant that the notion of abuse of rights is not universally recognized in

---

102 J. Crawford, *Brownlie's Principles of Public International Law*, 8th ed., Oxford: Oxford University Press, 2012, p. 562. See for a detailed description Byers, *McGill Law Journal*, p. 397-404; Iluyomade, *Harvard International Law Journal*, p. 61-66. The most recent manifestation of the notion was in the matter of the Chagos Marine Protected Area Arbitration *(Mauritius v. UK)*, award rendered on 18 March 2015 by the Arbitral Tribunal constituted under annex vii of the United Nations Convention on the Law of the Sea, par. 542-543. See for a clear formulation of this principle in international law also WTO Appellate Body, *United States – Import Prohibition of Certain Schrimp and Schrimp Products Case*, 1998.

103 Byers, *McGill Law Journal*, p. 404. See *inter alia*, H. Lauterpacht, *The Function of Law in the International Community*, Oxford: Clarendon Press, 1933, p. 284-306; A. Kiss, *L'abus de droit en droit international*, Paris: Librairie generale de droit et de jurisprudence, 1952; N. Politis, *Le Problème des Limitations de la Souveraineté et la théorie de l'Abus des Droits dans les Rapport Internationaux*, Académie de Droit International (extrait du recueil des cours), Paris: Librairie Hachette, 1926, p. 108-109; Iluyomade, *Harvard International Law Journal*, p. 72-73.

104 Byers, *McGill Law Journal*, p. 411; P. Birnie, A.E. Boyle and C. Redgwell, *International Law and the Environment*, 3rd ed., Oxford: Clarendon Press, 2009, p. 204-205.

105 See e.g. Crawford, *Brownlie's Principles of Public International Law*, p. 563; B. Cheng, *General Principles of Law as Applied by International Courts and Tribunals*, 1953, p. 121.

106 See on this issue in particular R. de la Feria and S. Vogenauer (eds.), *Prohibition of Abuse of Law. A New General Principle of EU Law?*, Oxford/Portland: Hart Publishing, 2011. See also R. de la Feria, 'Prohibition of Abuse of (Community) Law: The Creation of a New General Principle of EC Law through Tax', *Common Market Law Review*, vol. 45, no. 2, 2008, p. 396-397.

the national laws of all the Member States.[107] In practice, however, questions of abuse seem to have increasingly gained importance in the context of EU Law.[108] Prohibitions of abuse of rights are occasionally explicitly included in EU legislation.[109] Last year, for example, the European Council amended the Parent-Subsidiary Directive (2011/96/EU), which intends to ensure that profits made by cross-border companies are not taxed twice, by adding a binding anti-abuse clause to prevent tax avoidance and aggressive tax planning by corporate groups that prevents Member States from granting the benefits of the directive to arrangements that are not 'genuine' and have been put into place for the main purpose of obtaining a tax advantage without reflecting economic reality.[110]

In addition, the Court of Justice of the European Union has applied the concept of abuse of rights in a number of high-profile cases.[111] The foundation of the formal doctrine on the abuse of EU law is generally attributed to the Court of Justice's judgment in the case *Emsland-Stärke*. According to the Court of Justice, the facts of the case suggested a purely formal dispatch of goods from the territory of the European Community with the sole purpose of benefiting from export refunds. In that regard, the Court of Justice emphasised that *'it is clear from the case-law of the Court that the scope of Community regulations must in no case be extended to cover abuses on the part of a trader'*.[112] Subsequently, the Court of Justice for the first time formulated a test for the abuse of EU law by defining two elements of an abusive practice: an objective element and a subjective element. The objective element refers

---

107 De la Feria, *Common Market Law Review*, p. 395; A. Arnull, 'What is a General Principle of EU Law?', in: De la Feria and Vogenauer, *Prohibition of Abuse of Law*, p. 18.

108 H. Eidenmüller, 'Abuse of Law in the Context of European Insolvency Law' in: De la Feria and Vogenauer, *Prohibition of Abuse of Law*, p. 137; P. Schammo, 'Comments on Abuse of Rights in EU Law', in: De la Feria and Vogenauer, p. 193.

109 Article 35 of the Free Movement of Persons Directive, for example, contains an abuse of rights clause providing that *'Member States may adopt the necessary measures to refuse, terminate or withdraw any right conferred by this Directive in the case of abuse of rights or fraud, such as marriages of convenience'*: Directive 2004/38/EC of the European Parliament and of the Council of 29 April 2004.

110 Article 1(2) of Council Directive 2011/96/EU of 30 November 2011 on the common system of taxation applicable in the case of parent companies and subsidiaries of different Member States. See www.consilium.europa.eu/en/press/press-releases/2015/01/council-adopts-anti-abuse-clause/ (accessed 11 April 2016).

111 CJEU Case C-110/99, *Emsland-Stärke*, [2000] ECR I-1569; CJEU Case C-255/02, *Halifax*, [2006] ECR I-1609; CJEU Case C-456/04, *Agip Petroli*, [2006] ECR I-3395; CJEU Case C-196/04, *Cadbury Schweppes*, [2006] ECR I-7995; CJEU Case C-279/05, *Vonk Dairy Products*, [2007 ECR I-239; CJEU Case C-524/04, *Thin Cap Group Litigation*, [2007] ECR I-1; CJEU Case C-251/06, *ING AUER*, [2007] ECR I-9689; CJEU Case C-425/06, *Part Service*, [2008] ECR I-897. See also Saydé, *Abuse of EU Law*, p. 48.

112 CJEU Case C-110/99, *Emsland-Stärke*, [2000] ECR I-1569, par. 51. See also CJEU Case C-125/76, *Cremer*, [1977] ECR 1593, par. 21.

to *'objective circumstances in which, despite formal observance of the conditions laid down by the Community rules, the purpose of those rules has not been achieved'*.[113] In addition, the subjective element refers to *'the intention to obtain an advantage from the Community rules by creating artificially the conditions laid down for obtaining it. The existence of that subjective element can be established, inter alia, by evidence of collusion between the Community exporter receiving the refunds and the importer of the goods in the non-member country'*.[114]

Even though the Court increasingly used the term 'abuse' after this judgment, its approach was not yet very articulate.[115] It was only after the Halifax case that the Court adopted a more coherent approach to the prohibition of abuse of rights.[116] In this case, the Court of Justice extended the scope of the doctrine of abuse of rights to the field of EU tax law (VAT). At the same time it unlocked the potential for the doctrine to be applied to all internal abuses of law.[117] The Halifax case was about a British bank which had put in place a complex transaction structure with a number of separate companies that it had set up, with the purpose of enabling Halifax to reclaim more VAT than it would be entitled to claim if it had paid for the construction of a number of call centres directly. Since the transaction was carried out for the sole purpose of circumventing VAT regulations, the Court of Justice concluded that *'[t]he application of Community legislation cannot be extended to cover abusive practices by economic operators, that is to say transactions carried out not in the context of normal commercial operations, but solely for the purpose of wrongfully obtaining advantages provided for by Community law'*.[118]

Even though the doctrine was first developed in the areas of the free movement of services and tax law, the prohibition of abuse of rights was subsequently extended to other areas of EU law.[119] Most of the abuse of rights cases dealt with commercial law, but the Court has also kept the door ajar for application in non-commercial

---

113 CJEU Case C-110/99, *Emsland-Stärke*, [2000] ECR I-1569, par. 52. See also Saydé, *Abuse of EU Law*, p. 50-51; De la Feria, *Common Market Law Review*, p. 396.

114 CJEU Case C-110/99, *Emsland-Stärke*, [2000] ECR I-1569, par. 53.

115 De la Feria, *Common Market Law Review*, p. 397.

116 De la Feria, p. 397.

117 Finally, in the case Cadbury Schweppes, the Court of Justice extended the scope to cross-border abuses of law: CJEU Case C-196/04, *Cadbury Schweppes*, [2006] ECR I-7995. See Saydé, *Abuse of EU Law*, p. 53.

118 CJEU Case C-255/02, *Halifax plc, Leeds Permanent Development Services Ltd and County Wide Property Investments Ltd v. Commissioners of Customs & Excise*, [2006] ECR I-1609, par. 69. See for the application of this principle to corporate taxation: Case C-196/04, *Cadbury Schweppes plc, Cadbury Schweppes Overseas Ltd v. Commissioners of Inland Revenue*, [2006] ECR I-7995.

119 S. Vogenauer, 'The Prohibition of Abuse of Law: An Emerging General Principle of EU Law', in: De la Feria and Vogenauer, *Prohibition of Abuse of Law*, p. 521-522.

cases.[120] Yet, several scholars argue that the case law of the Court of Justice suggests that the doctrine of abuse of rights is less accepted in the field of the free movement of persons and citizenship rights.[121] Some scholars suggest that this seems to be consistent with the traditional dichotomy in the interpretation of the free movement of persons and of those concerning other rights or freedoms.[122] In the area of EU migration law, for example, the Court of Justice has shown that it is unwilling to accept an abuse of rights doctrine. Based on several cases concerning the rights of third country nationals who are spouses or parents of an EU citizen to reside on the territory of an EU Member State based on the right of free movement, for example, Advocate General Sharpton recalled in her Opinion in the *Ruiz Zambrano* case that the Court has repeatedly made clear *'that there is nothing reprehensible about taking advantage of a possibility conferred by law and that this is clearly distinguishable from an abuse of rights'*.[123]

Worth mentioning is that recently it has been argued by several legal scholars that the expression 'abuse' in the context of the cases discussed above aims at a different phenomenon than what is generally referred to in civil law traditions as the abuse of rights.[124] What is actually referred to, they argue, is the principle of abuse of *law*. The concept of abuse of law in the EU context is defined by Saydé as *'a gain-seeking,*

120 K. E. Sørensen, 'What is a General Principle of EU Law? A Response', in: De la Feria and Vogenauer, *Prohibition of Abuse of Law,* p. 29.

121 K.S. Ziegler, '"Abuse of Law" in the Context of the Free Movement of Workers', in: De la Feria and Vogenauer, *Prohibition of Abuse of Law,* p. 295-314; E. Spaventa, 'Comments on Abuse of Law and the Free Movement of Workers', in: De la Feria and Vogenauer, p. 315-320; C. Costello, 'Citizenship of the Union: Above Abuse?', in: De la Feria and Vogenauer, p. 321-353; M. Dougan, 'Some Comments on the Idea of a General Principle of Union Law Prohibiting Abuses of Law in the Field of Free Movement for Union Citizens', in: De la Feria and Vogenauer, p. 355-362.

122 J. Snell. 'And then there were two: products and citizens in community law', in: T. Tridimas and P. Nebbia (eds.), *European Union Law for the Twenty-First Century*, Oxford: Hart Publishing, 2004, p. 62. See also R. de la Feria, 'Introducing the Principle of Prohibition of Abuse of law', in: De la Feria and Vogenauer, *Prohibition of Abuse of Law,* p. xix.

123 Opinion of Advocate General Sharpston in the case *Ruiz Zambrano* (C-34/90), 30 September 2010, *ECR* 2001, I-01177, par. 104. See for other examples of this approach: See CJEU Case C109/01, *Akrich* [2003] ECR I9607, par. 55-57 and CJEU Case C-200/02, *Chen,* [2004] *ECR* I-9925, par. 36. See also R. de la Feria, *Prohibition of Abuse of Law,* p. xviii.

124 S. Vogenauer, *Prohibition of Abuse of Law*, p. 554-558; P. Pistone, 'Abuse of Law in the Context of Indirect Taxation: From (Before) *Emsland-Stärke 1* to *Halifax* (and Beyond)', in: De la Feria and Vogenauer, p. 381; A. Saydé, 'Defining the Concept of Abuse of Union Law', *Yearbook of European Law*, vol. 33, no. 1, 2014, p. 142-143. Others do make a distinction between these two forms of abuse, but use different terminology for them. See e.g. T. Tridimas, 'Abuse of Rights in EU Law: Some Reflections with Particular Reference to Financial Law', in De la Feria and Vogenauer, p. 171; S. Whittaker, 'Comments on "Abuse of Law" in European Private Law', in: De la Feria and Vogenauer, p. 258-259; C. Amand, 'Prohibition of Abusive Practices in European VAT: Court Aid to National Legislations Bugs?', *Intertax*, vol. 36, no. 5, 2008, p. 189.

artificial, and undesirable choice of law made by a private individual'.[125] Abuse of EU law first and foremost constitutes an attempt to 'avoid' or 'circumvent' one (national) legal order and to elect a more favourable law.[126] The artificiality of the practice refers to the lack of economic rationality of the practice, which was adopted purely to obtain a regulatory benefit.[127] Finally, in order to find an abuse of law, the choice of law made by the individual has to be illegitimate or undesirable.[128] In that sense it differs from the concept of abuse of rights, which refers to the undesirable exercise of rights. In this perspective, *'[a]buses of law constitute improper* acquisitions *of rights, and abuses of rights illegitimate* exercises *of existing rights'*.[129] Accordingly, Saydé argues, there have only been a relatively marginal number of situations under EU law that can be identified as dealing with a genuine abuse of rights, including the abuse clause in Article 54 of the EU Charter.[130] Nonetheless, whether it is defined as abuse of rights or as abuse of law, the essence of the prohibition is also in EU law that it aims to correct negative outcomes of the exercise rights if they are strictly interpreted according to the letter of the law.

6.5 Provisional observations on the doctrine of abuse of rights

This overview of the historical development and the different manifestations of the prohibition of abuse of rights have shown that ever since the liberal, almost absolute interpretation of rights which was characteristic of the Enlightenment was mitigated in the course of the nineteenth century, the prohibition of abuse of rights has increasingly gained ground in a number of legal areas. In general, the prohibition of abuse of rights functions as a corrective mechanism for any undesirable outcomes of the exercise of rights for others. A purely positivist perception of rights may allow

125 Saydé, *Yearbook of European Law*, p. 138. See also Saydé, *Abuse of EU Law*, p. 23-26.

126 This is what distinguishes abuse of law from fraud, which consists of 'concealing the fact that the conditions of application of a legal rule are not fulfilled (misinterpretation), in order to wrongfully obtain a regulatory benefit': Saydé, *Abuse of EU Law*, p. 25.

127 This element corresponds to the *subjective* element of abuse in the formal doctrine of the ECJ: cases C-110/99, *Emsland-Stärke* [2000] ECR I-11569, par. 53 and C-255/02, *Halifax* [2006] ECR I-1609, par. 75. See Saydé, *Yearbook of European Law*, p. 139 and 146.

128 Corresponding to the *objective* element of abuse in the formal doctrine of the ECJ: cases C-110/99, *Emsland-Stärke* [2000] ECR I-11569, par. 52 and C-255/02, *Halifax* [2006] ECR I-1609, par. 74. See Saydé, *Yearbook of European Law*, p. 139 and 153.

129 Saydé, *Abuse of EU Law*, p. 28.

130 Other examples referred to by Saydé involve abuses of legal proceedings (cases 338/82, *Albertini and Montagnani* [1984] ECR 2123, par. 51–52; 243/78, *Simmenthal* [1980] ECR 593, par. 10-11 and the 'Greek saga' cases C-441/93, *Pafitis* [1996] ECR I-1347; C-367/96 *Kefalas* [1998] ECR I-2843 and C-373-97 *Diamantis* [2000] ECR I-1705), abuses of tendering procedures (cases C-233/96, *Denmark v. Commission* [1998] ECR I-5759, par. 22–25; C-238/96, *Ireland v. Commission* [1998] ECR I-5801, par. 68–71), and abuses of intellectual property rights (cases C-235/89, *Commission v. Italy* [1992] ECR I-777, par. 27; 35/83, *BAT Cigaretten-Fabriken* [1985] ECR 363, par. 35; 341/87, *EMI Electrola* [1989] ECR 79, par. 8 ff). Saydé, *Yearbook of European Law*, p. 143.

for the exercise of rights in a way that is legal according to the letter of the law, but causes disproportional harm to the rights of someone else. Basically, the prohibition of abuse of rights aims to restore a kind of elementary fairness that had been violated by the abusive exercise of rights.

In civil law, the doctrine of abuse of rights emanated from the idea that rights are not an aim in themselves, but serve a bigger social purpose. This idea was principally elaborated by Josserand at the beginning of the twentieth century.[131] The social function of rights carries with it certain duties and responsibilities on the part of the right holder to exercise his right in accordance with this social function. The introduction of the concept of abuse met with fierce criticism. The concept creates an intermediate category of cases, which are covered by a right at first and legal sight, but after more profound scrutiny turn out to be abusive and therefore illegal. According to the critics, such as Planiol, the concept was *'logically untenable'*[132] as there can be no abuse if a right is exercised within the scope of that right. Moreover, as the social function of rights is often difficult to define, the grounds for restrictions allowed by the doctrine of abuse of rights are necessarily vague and abstract. In that context Herman rightly points out that the prohibition of abuse of rights in fact *'occupies the intersection of positive rights and morals'*.[133]

In the first French cases in which an abuse of rights was found, the abusive character of an activity was based on the intent or motive of the right holder. Yet, this 'subjective' test is tricky as *'[i]t involves an investigation of a psychological order into the question of motive and the introduction into the matter of an ethical element, both of which are considerations which tend to impede the effective operation of a legal rule'*.[134] It is for this reason that the 'Schikaneverbot' in Section 226 of the German CC, which considers the exercise of a right to be abusive when its only aim is to harm to someone else, proved virtually impossible to apply in practice.[135] In many legal orders, therefore, attempts have been made to complement the subjective criterion with more 'objective' criteria, such as the excessive harm caused or the lack of a legitimate interest.[136] In other words, it is more about 'what *he did and was it reasonable... and not* why *he did it'*.[137] In EU law, for example, we see that the test

131 Josserand, *De l'esprit des droits et de leur relativité*.

132 Crabb, *Inter-American Law Review*, p. 3.

133 Herman, *Louisiana Law Review*, p. 748.

134 Gutteridge, *Cambridge Law Journal,* p. 26. See also Cueto-Rua, *Louisiana Law Review*, p. 988; Devine, *Acta Juridica*, p. 149; Voyaume, Cottier and Rocha, 'Abuse of Rights in Comparative Law', p. 28-31.

135 Gutteridge, *Cambridge Law Journal*, p. 36.

136 Cueto-Rua, *Louisiana Law Review*, p. 989 and 992-996. See also Gutteridge, *Cambridge Law Journal,* p. 26-27; Lenaerts, *European Review of Private Law*, p. 1127; Voyaume, Cottier and Rocha, 'Abuse of Rights in Comparative Law', p. 31-39.

137 D.J. Devine, 'Some Comparative Aspects of the Doctrine of Abuse of Rights', *Acta Juridica*, 1964, p. 149.

developed by the CJEU in the *Emsland-Stärke* case consists of both a subjective criterion, referring to the intention of the right holder, and an objective criterion referring to the extent to which the purpose of the rules invoked by the right holder have been achieved.[138] Still, this objective criterion has a rather abstract character and is often based on the notion of morality and fairness.

In general, it seems that the social approach to the interpretation of rights and their limitations has nowadays become the dominant approach. Even though the ideas of Josserand were rather controversial, over the years the prohibition of abuse of rights developed into a cardinal legal concept that has progressively been accepted in different legal disciplines. In all the legal areas discussed above, a doctrine of abuse of rights has been developed, which provides for a general ground for restrictions on the exercise of rights based on the demands of the social context in which they are exercised. Whether it is defined as an abuse of rights (civil law), a violation of the principle of equity (common law[139]), abuse of law (EU Law[140]) or a violation of the principle of good faith (public international law[141]), in practically all legal systems instruments exist that in concrete situations produces similar results. So, even though the manifestation of the basic idea differs from one legal context to another, 'the essence of the doctrine of abuse of right' seems to be omnipresent.

6.6 The Prohibition of Abuse in Human Rights Law

Even though the concept of abuse of rights has a long tradition in other legal areas, for a long time the doctrine on abuse of rights received only little interest in the context of the protection of human rights.[142] The mention of the concept of abuse of rights in relation to human rights may seem strange at first sight. Human rights are traditionally meant as a check on the power of the state.[143] Human rights are related to the protection of individual autonomy. Individual autonomy embodies the idea that

138 CJEU Case C-110/99, *Emsland-Stärke*, [2000] ECR I-1569, par. 52-53. See also Saydé, *Abuse of EU Law*, p. 50-51; De la Feria, *Common Market Law Review*, p. 396.

139 Voyaume, Cottier and Rocha, 'Abuse of rights in Comparative Law', p. 340.

140 Saydé, *Abuse of EU Law*.

141 P. Birnie and A.E. Boyle, *International Law and the Environment*, Oxford: Oxford University Press, 1992, p. 126; Cheng, *General Principles of Law as Applied by International Courts and Tribunals*, p. 121; Crawford, *Brownlie's Principles of Public International Law*, p. 563.

142 Spielmann, *Mélanges en hommage à Louis Edmond Pettiti*, p. 673.

143 A. Spielmann and D. Spielmann, 'The Concept of Abuse of Rights and the European Convention for the Protection of Human Rights and Fundamental Freedoms', in: *Abuse of Rights and Equivalent Concepts: the Principle and its Present Day Application* (Proceedings of the nineteenth Colloquy on European Law), CoE: Strasbourg, 1990, p. 61. Sajó is one of the few scholars who have argued in favour of a doctrine of abuse of rights in constitutional law. Certain rights and freedoms are basically liberties and liberties cannot be clearly defined precisely because vagueness is needed to guarantee personal autonomy. There would therefore be a need for a proper concept of abuse in relation to constitutional rights in order to correct the improper use of such liberties: Sajó, *Abuse*, p. 34-35.

every individual is exclusively in charge of his own fate and is not accountable to the state for the choices he makes. Earlier in this chapter we have seen that the concept of abuse of rights originated in private law from the idea that rights are conferred on people with specific social aims in mind. Later, this idea also became increasingly accepted between states in public international law and in the area of commercial EU law. Yet, an interpretation of abuse as an act contrary to the aim or social function for which that right was created may seem less appropriate in the context of human rights. Sajó has argued that understanding human rights as serving a social function, would mean that *'we have a different concept of rights, values, and constitutional and social order than in case one accepts that fundamental liberties (e.g., as enabling individual self-determination) are ends in themselves'*.[144] This tension adds to the complexity of accepting a general doctrine of abuse of rights in the context of human rights law. Given the fact that fundamental rights were originally designed to guarantee individual freedom and prevent infringements of this freedom by the state, a clause restricting the scope of the rights guaranteed in the Convention on the basis of abstract notions such as the democratic society is even more problematic in that context.[145]

Nevertheless, the concept of abuse of rights did gain ground in human rights law in its own particular way: the abuse clauses that have been incorporated in several international and regional human rights documents that have been created after the Second World War. In the previous chapters, we have seen that besides the ECHR, also the UDHR, the ICCPR, the ICESCR and the EU Charter prohibit an abuse of the rights and freedoms they guarantee. In this context, however, the concept abuse of rights takes a distinct form that differs from the general understanding of the concept of abuse of rights as discussed in this chapter. These abuse clauses were incorporated to prevent civil and political rights and freedoms from exploitation by groups and individuals with anti-democratic aims. Within the framework of the abuse clauses, abuse is consequently defined in terms of an attempt to destroy the democratic system of human rights protection.[146] The abuse clauses are an expression of the idea that rights are not absolute entitlements, but privileges whose exercise is restricted by the social demands of the context in which they operate. Activities that threaten the very basis of the democratic regime or essential democratic values are considered abusive and are therefore excluded from the protection of the human rights guaranteed in these instruments. In other words, the prohibition of abuse of rights in the context of human rights law echoes some of the basic assumptions of the concept of abuse of rights in general. In accordance with Josserand's interpretation of rights based on

144 Sajó, p. 30.
145 Spielmann and Spielmann, 'The Concept of Abuse of Rights and the European Convention for the Protection of Human Rights and Fundamental Freedoms', p. 61.
146 Sajó, *Abuse*, p. 52-53.

their social function, abuse clauses in a way too are corrective mechanisms that aim to correct any undesirable outcomes of the exercise of rights that disproportionally affect the interests of the community at large. Nonetheless, in the context of the abuse clause, the interest of society refers specifically to the protection of democracy and democratic values. While the general prohibition of abuse of rights is concerned with the impact of the abusive activity on the rights of others (as is the case in, for example, private law), the prohibition of abuse of rights in Article 17 ECHR is concerned with a more fundamental threat. The abuse clauses in human rights law focus on the exercise of political rights with the aim of undermining the fundamental democratic values of the Convention and the eventual aim being to destroy them.[147] Hence, understood in this way, the central concern of Article 17 ECHR *'is not the impact on others but on the democratic regime as such, which is endangered by the improper use of fundamental human rights'*.[148] The correction of other improper uses of rights are dealt with in the context of the balancing of rights with the protection of other interests as provided in the second paragraphs of Articles 10 and 11 ECHR. No matter how improper, these activities are still evaluated in the context of what can be allowed in a democratic society. Article 17 ECHR, on the other hand, deals with activities that can under no circumstances be allowed in a democratic society, because they threaten the existence of democracy itself.

In that sense, Article 17 ECHR also differs from that other prohibition of abuse of rights in Article 35(3)(a) ECHR, which provides that the Court shall declare applications inadmissible if it considers that they are an abuse of the right of individual application. According to the Court's own admissibility guide 'abuse' within the meaning of Article 35(3)(a) ECHR *'must be understood in its ordinary sense according to general legal theory – namely, the harmful exercise of a right for purposes other than those for which it is designed'*.[149] Haeck is right when he explains that Article 17 ECHR refers to *substantive* abuses of rights, whereas Article 35(3)(a) ECHR relates to *procedural* abuse.[150] Applications considered abusive in the sense of Article 35(3)(a) ECHR include applications that are knowingly based

147 Sajó, p. 52.

148 Sajó, p. 53.

149 The Court's Admissibility guide: *Practical Guide on Admissibility Criteria*, p. 37. www.echr.coe.int/Documents/Admissibility_guide_ENG.pdf (accessed 11 April 2016). See also ECtHR 15 September 2009, *Miroļubovs and others v. Latvia*, appl. no. 798/05, par. 62 and 65.

150 Y. Haeck, 'Artikel 17 Verbod van rechtsmisbruik' ['Article 17 Prohibition of Abuse of rights'], in: Vande Lanotte, J. and Haeck, Y. (eds.), *Handboek EVRM. Deel 2. Artikelsgewijze commentaar, volume II [Handbook ECHR. Part 2. Commentary by article, volume II]*, Antwerp/Oxford: Intersentia, 2004, p. 245, footnote 8. See also L. Zwaak (rev.), 'Chapter 2 The procedure before the European Court of Human Rights' in: P. van Dijk, F. van Hoof, A. van Rijn and L. Zwaak (eds.), *Theory and practice of the European Convention on Human Rights*, 4th ed., Antwerp/Oxford: Intersentia, 2006, p. 193. In the admissibility guide, an abuse of the right of application is indeed categorised under the procedural criteria: the Court's Admissibility guide: *Practical Guide on Admissibility Criteria*, p. 37ff.

on untrue information, use offensive language, or intentionally breach the duty of confidentiality of friendly-settlement negotiations or are vexatious and manifestly ill-founded applications that are repeatedly lodged.[151] Even though the abuse referred to in Article 35(3)(a) ECHR also prohibits the exercise of rights in a way that harms society in general, these situations differ significantly from the fundamental form of abuse of rights referred to in Article 17 ECHR.

6.7 Conclusions

In this chapter we have studied the legal doctrine on abuse of rights. The concept of abuse of rights finds its origin in the growing political and intellectual dissatisfaction with the absolutism of the liberalism of the Enlightenment at the turn of the nineteenth century.[152] Individual rights were increasingly regarded in terms of their social context. The prohibition of abuse of rights functions in this regard as a corrective mechanism if the strict application of the law according to its letter allows for rights to be exercised in a way that seriously harms the interests of others.[153] It covers acts that are lawful and covered by a right at first sight, but after more profound scrutiny turn out to create an unacceptable outcome and are therefore considered unlawful after all. The first comprehensive theory on the abuse of rights by Josserand marked a radical change in the thinking about the nature and function of legal rules.[154] Innovative as it was, Josserand's theory was heavily criticised by other scholars at the time. According to the critics, such as Planiol, the concept was *'logically untenable'*[155] as there can be no abuse if a right is exercised within the scope of that right.

The concept was first developed in national legal systems, mainly those belonging to the civil law tradition. Nowadays the essence of the concept of abuse of rights seems to be omnipresent. Nevertheless, its content varies among different legal areas. In France, the 'cradle' of this idea, for example, the prohibition of abuse of rights was traditionally based on the intent or motive of the right holder to disproportionally harm someone else. Yet, this 'subjective' test is considered problematic as *'[i]t involves an investigation of a psychological order into the question of motive and the introduction into the matter of an ethical element, both of which are considerations which tend to impede the effective operation of a legal rule'*.[156] In many legal orders, therefore, attempts have been made to complement the subjective criterion with more 'objective' criteria, such as the infliction of excessive harm or the lack of a legitimate

151 The Court's Admissibility guide: *Practical Guide on Admissibility Criteria*, p. 37-40.
152 Sajó, *Abuse*, p. 29-30.
153 Voyaume, Cottier and Rocha, 'Abuse of Rights in Comparative Law', p. 45.
154 Bolgár, *Louisiana Law Review*, p. 1016.
155 Crabb, *Inter-American Law Review*, p. 3.
156 Gutteridge, '*Cambridge Law Journal*, p. 26.

interest. Still, these objective criteria have a rather abstract character and are often difficult to apply.

In the context of international human rights law, the concept of abuse of rights for a long time hardly received any attention.[157] The mention of the concept of abuse of rights in relation to human rights may indeed seem strange at first sight. Human rights are traditionally meant as a check on the power of the state.[158] The prohibition of abuse of rights is therefore still considered a peculiarity. Yet, as we have seen in the previous chapters, the concept of abuse of rights has gained ground in human rights law in the form of abuse clauses that have been incorporated in many human rights documents that have been created after the Second World War, such as Article 17 ECHR. In chapter two we have seen that Article 17 ECHR was originally incorporated into the Convention as a rampart against the exploitation of the Convention by groups with totalitarian intentions that aim to overthrow democracy. In this context the concept of abuse of rights takes a distinct form, namely as an attempt to destroy the democratic system or its underlying values and principles.[159] Contrary to the application of this concept in other areas of law, where the prohibition of abuse basically functions as a corrective mechanism for any undesirable outcomes of the exercise of rights for other individuals, the purpose of the abuse clause is a very fundamental one. Its central concern *'is not the impact on others but on the democratic regime as such'*.[160]

This is where the concept of 'militant democracy' comes in. A militant democracy is *'a democratic regime which is willing to adopt pre-emptive, prima facie illiberal measures to prevent those aiming at subverting democracy with democratic means from destroying the democratic regime'*.[161] The abuse clause is the militant provision *par excellence*, as it provides that anti-democratic groups and individuals are not allowed to profit from fundamental rights in order to engage in subversive activities with the aim of destroying democracy. The following three chapters will therefore analyse the concept of militant democracy and explore to what extent it may elucidate the understanding of Article 17 ECHR.

---

157 Spielmann, *Mélanges en hommage à Louis Edmond Pettiti*, p. 673.

158 Spielmann and Spielmann, 'The Concept of Abuse of Rights and the European Convention for the Protection of Human Rights and Fundamental Freedoms', p. 61.

159 Sajó, *Abuse*, p. 52-53.

160 Sajó, p. 53.

161 J. Müller, 'Militant Democracy', in: M. Rosenfeld and A. Sajó (eds.), *The Oxford Handbook of Comparative Constitutional Law*, Oxford: Oxford University Press, 2012, p. 1253.

Chapter 7
The Concept of Militant Democracy

7.1 Introduction

In the previous chapter we have learned that the prohibition of abuse of rights in human rights law takes a distinct form, namely as an attempt to destroy the democratic system, and its values and principles.[1] The purpose of the abuse clause is a very fundamental one, as its central concern *'is not the impact on others but on the democratic regime as such'*.[2] These abuse clauses in the different international and regional human rights instruments (with the exception of the ACHR), like Article 17 ECHR aim to prevent groups and individuals from relying on human rights for the purpose of engaging in activities aimed at the destruction of these rights. Abuse in this context is not based on the rights of others, which is the main focus of the abuse of rights in general, *'but on the democratic regime as such, which is endangered by the improper use of fundamental human rights'*, as Sajó puts it.[3] In other words, the abuse clause in human rights law reflects concern for the defence of democracy and fundamental rights, and precludes actions which undermine these principles. The legal strife against anti-democratic actors aiming to destroy democracy is the principal focus of the concept of militant democracy. To better understand Article 17 ECHR, it is therefore important to learn more about the interpretation and implications of the concept of militant democracy.

This chapter is the first of three chapters that focus on the concept of militant democracy. It examines the concept of militant democracy from a theoretical perspective. The following two chapters will subsequently explore the implementation of this concept in a concrete legal context. Chapter eight discusses the interpretation of the concept in the German constitutional order and Chapter nine explores how the concept takes shape in the context of the ECHR (in particular with regard to the interpretation of Article 17 ECHR). In what follows, we will start by examining the historical background of the concept of militant democracy. This chapter then moves on to the theoretical foundations of the concept. Subsequently, it explores how the concept of militant democracy has been put into practice in European democracies after the Second World War and how the implementation of the concept has been perceived in

1 A. Sajó, 'Abuse of Fundamental Rights or the Difficulties of Purposiveness', in: A. Sajó (ed.), *Abuse: the Dark Side of Fundamental Rights*, Utrecht: Eleven, 2006, p. 52-53.

2 Sajó, p. 53.

3 Sajó, p. 53.

legal doctrine. Finally it reflects on the criticism that has been voiced with regard to the application of the concept of militant democracy.

7.2 The concept of militant democracy

Even though there is no generally agreed upon definition of militant democracy, it can be described as a democratic system that has adopted and applies pre-emptive, *prima facie* undemocratic legal instruments to defend itself against the risk of being overthrown by anti-democratic actors that make use of political rights and democratic procedures with the aim of abolishing it. Based on this definition, a number of elements that make a democracy militant can be distinguished.[4] First, the concept of militant democracy presupposes the existence of a democratic regime. This means that states which are not democratic cannot take undemocratic measures under the pretext of militant democracy. As Thiel put it, *'only in a democracy... the question of whether enemies of democracy are allowed to use democratic structures and rights to destroy it (the "weak flank" of every liberal democracy) culminate in the dilemma and debate around the idea of a "militant democracy"'*.[5] Second, it refers to pre-emptive measures, *'meaning that states need not wait until those who aim to destroy or overturn the system have the real opportunity to do so'*.[6] These measures include, for example, (constitutional) provisions that aim to protect a 'democratic core', provisions that deal with extremist political parties and other organisations, and measures taken against groups and individuals who abuse their rights against the democratic system or its core principles.[7] Third, militant measures are aimed against a specific enemy, namely individuals and groups aiming to destroy the democratic regime. Fourth, the concept focusses on the activities by these enemies that harm democracy by making use of the rights and procedures provided to them by democracy. Fifth, the measures taken by a militant democracy have a *prima facie* undemocratic nature, because they interfere with the political rights of 'the enemies of democracy' and limit the free political competition inherent in the idea of democracy.

The concept of militant democracy departs from the assumption that democracy is the best political model and that once a democratic regime has been established it should stay democratic. At the same time, it presumes that democracy is intrinsically

4 The second, third and fourth element are based on the elements distinguished by Tyulkina: S. Tyulkina, *Militant Democracy. Undemocratic Political Parties and Beyond*, Abingdon/New York: Routledge, 2015, p. 14.

5 M. Thiel (ed.), *The Militant Democracy Principle in Modern Democracies*, Farnham/Burlington: Ashgate Publishing Company, 2009, p. 2.

6 Tyulkina, *Militant Democracy*, p. 14.

7 The concept of militant democracy does not clearly define what measures should be taken and an exhaustive account of all potentially militant measures is therefore extremely difficult to give. Thiel, however, made an attempt and distinguishes seven 'clusters of militancy': M. Thiel, 'Comparative Aspects', in: Thiel, *The Militant Democracy Principle in Modern Democracies*, p. 401-408.

vulnerable to exploitation. The concept is based on the fear that within the framework of democracy, anti-democratic actors may attempt to establish a regime that dissolves democracy by using the mechanisms of democracy itself, such as free speech, the freedom of assembly and free elections.[8] In this context the scholarly literature often refers to a quote by Joseph Goebbels, Minister of Propaganda in Nazi Germany, who allegedly gloated after the Nazis had seized power that *'[i]t will always remain one of the best jokes of democracy that it provides its own deadly enemies with the means with which it can be destroyed'*.[9] A militant democracy, therefore, aims to prevent its own destruction by consciously putting in place *'an elaborate repertoire of instruments'*[10] to protect democracy from being exploited. A democracy, in other words, that *'does not tolerate its own abolition'*.[11] The term militant democracy has never been openly used by the drafters of the Convention or the judges in Strasbourg. Nevertheless, we have seen earlier in this study that it is clear that the prohibition of abuse of rights in Article 17 ECHR is in fact a militant instrument. In Chapter two we have learned that the drafters included Article 17 ECHR with the aim of preventing the political rights and freedoms guaranteed in the Convention from being exploited by anti-democratic actors. And in Chapter four we have seen that also in legal doctrine Article 17 ECHR is interpreted as explicit expression of the concept of militant democracy.

7.3 The introduction of the concept of militant democracy

The discussion on democratic self-defence is not new. According to some, its roots can even be *'traced back to the very beginning of democratic theory itself'*.[12] Some scholars point out that ancient philosophers such as Plato and Montesquieu already reflected on the question of how to protect democracy from exploitation.[13] *'That a state is interested in defending itself against forces aiming at its destruction'*, Thiel therefore argues, *'is initially not a political, philosophical, or legal aspect, but a*

8 A. Sajó, 'From Militant Democracy to the Preventive State?', *Cardozo Law Review*, vol. 27, no. 5, 2006, p. 2262.

9 *'Das wird immer einer der besten Witze der Demokratie bleiben, dass sie ihren Todfeinden die Mittel selber stellte, durch die sie vernichtet wurde'*: J. Goebbels, *Der Angriff. Aufsätze aus der Kampfzeit*, Munich: Eher Verlag, 1935, p. 61, cited in K.D. Bracher et al. (eds.), *Nationalsozialistische Diktatur, 1933-1945: Ein Bilanz (Bonner Schriften zur Politik und Zeitgeschichte; Bd. 21)*, Düsseldorf: Droste Verlag, 1983, p. 16.

10 M. Minkenberg, 'Repression and reaction: militant democracy and the radical right in Germany and France', *Patterns of Prejudice*, vol. 40, no. 1, 2006, p. 26.

11 M. Klamt, 'Militant Democracy and the Democratic Dilemma: Different Ways of Protecting Democratic Constitutions', in: F. Bruinsma and D. Nelken (eds.), *Explorations in Legal Cultures (Recht der Werkelijkheid 28:3)*, The Hague: Elsevier, 2007, p. 134.

12 O. Pfersmann, 'Shaping Militant Democracy: Legal Limits to Democratic Stability', in: A. Sajó (ed.), *Militant democracy*, Utrecht: Eleven International Publishing, 2004, p. 47.

13 Pfersmann, p. 47; Tyulkina, *Militant Democracy*, p. 14.

simple fact'.[14] However, the first coherent theories on militant democracy came up in the 1930s. Against the rapid rise to power of Nazi and fascist movements in Western Europe, legal and political scholars started to develop comprehensive theories on how to avert this threat. The origin of the term 'militant democracy' at least in the English language is generally attributed to Karl Loewenstein, a German scholar of Jewish origin who migrated to the United States in 1933. Even though Loewenstein was not the only one who published on this topic at that time,[15] his ideas proved to be very influential and he is therefore widely seen as the *'father'* of the concept of militant democracy.[16] Not all legal scholars are happy with the term 'militant democracy', though. Thiel, for example, argues that the term has too much of a militaristic, aggressive tone: *'[i]t creates the impression that a democratic system is aiming at a dissemination of its own democratic model'*.[17] Even though perhaps better words could be found, to this day the term militant democracy is still the most commonly used.

Loewenstein introduced the term 'militant democracy' in the second half of the 1930s in a series of articles reflecting on the expansion of autocratic governments on the

---

14 M. Thiel, '"Militant Democracy" and state of emergency in Germany', in: A. Ellian and G. Molier (eds.), *The State of Exception and Militant Democracy*, Dordrecht: Republic of Letters, 2012, p. 275.

15 Interesting in this regard is also the work of the Jewish sociologist Mannheim. He analysed the situation in Europe from a sociological perspective. In one of his essays, *Diagnosis of our Time*, which was first published in 1943, he argued that democracies would eventually transform from liberal, laissez-faire democracies to planned democracies. These planned democratic societies, according to Mannheim, may take the shape of either a society ruled by dictatorship or a new form of democratic government with increased power. Instead of allowing this planned society to develop unguarded towards one of these scenarios, Mannheim proposed that democracies should be vigilant and use their knowledge and judgment to guide this process in the direction of a planned, militant democracy. According to Mannheim, *'[o]ur democracy has to become militant if it is to survive... The new militant democracy will therefore develop a new attitude to values. It will differ from the relativist laissez-faire of the previous age, as it will have the courage to agree on some basic values which are acceptable to everybody who shares the traditions of Western civilization'*, K. Mannheim, 'Diagnosis of our Time', in: *Diagnosis of our Time. Wartime Essays of a Sociologist*, London: Routledge & Kegan Paul LTD, 1950, p. 7.

16 P. Cliteur and B. Rijpkema, 'The Foundations of Militant Democracy', in: A. Ellian and G. Molier (eds.), *The State of Exception and Militant Democracy*, Dordrecht: Republic of Letters, 2012, p. 229.

17 Thiel considers the term *'self-defendant democracy'* more appropriate, because it accentuates the reactive or responsive character of the concept: Thiel, *The Militant Democracy Principle in Modern Democracies*, p. 383. Other expressions that have been suggested in legal doctrine include *'defensive democracy'* (J. Müller, 'Militant Democracy', in: M. Rosenfeld and A. Sajó (eds.), *Comparative Constitutional Law*, Oxford: Oxford University Press, 2012, p. 1253), *'fighting democracy'* (S. Avineri, 'Introduction', in: A. Sajó (ed.), *Militant democracy*, Utrecht: Eleven International Publishing, 2004, p. 1; Müller, p. 1253), *'vigilant democracy'* (P. Harvey, 'Militant democracy and the European Convention on Human Rights', *European Law Review*, vol. 29, no. 3, 2004, p. 407), *'intolerant democracy'* (G.H. Fox and G. Nolte, 'Intolerant democracies', *Harvard International Law Journal*, vol. 36, no. 1, 1995, p. 1).

European continent. Autocracy (or dictatorship, which he considers to be the same), he described as the counterpart of democracy, characterised by a concentration of power and the absence of control.[18] It was not a new phenomenon, as autocracy had been the predominant form of government throughout Europe's history.[19] Yet, he argued, at the time Europe was facing a dramatic expansion of fascism that put democracies on the defensive.[20] Because the defence mechanisms of democracy were naturally weak, he feared that European democracies would fall prey to autocracy. Fascists would have no problem in using democratic means to destroy it: *'[d]emocracy, faithful to its avowed principles, tendered to a ruthless enemy the most effective weapons for its own destruction. Fascism and National Socialism have always proudly put forward the contention that they came into power, not by revolution, but by utilization of the working machinery of democratic constitutions'*.[21] He criticised the lack of resistance of democratic governments to the attacks by fascism, contributing significantly to its success.[22] On the one hand, democracy's practice of seeking compromises made forceful action impossible. On the other hand, by offering them the protection of the freedom of speech, the freedom of assembly and the freedom of association as well as the right to participate in elections, democracy handed hostile political parties the means to openly strive for its destruction.[23] The autocratic threat could only be averted if these 'soft spots' of democracy would be fortified.[24] He believed there to be only one solution: democracy – just as its counterpart – had to become militant in order to resist the autocratic threat.

Loewenstein's following two articles entitled *Militant Democracy and Fundamental Rights I and II* published in 1937 received more attention than his first publications

18 K. Loewenstein, 'Autocracy versus Democracy in Contemporary Europe I', *The American Political Science Review*, vol. 29, no. 4, 1935, p. 571-572.

19 Loewenstein, p. 572.

20 Loewenstein focussed first and foremost on the rise of fascism, which at that time posed the largest autocratic threat (See also Cliteur and Rijpkema, *The State of Exception and Militant Democracy*, p. 231). Yet, he described militant democracy as a mechanism for responding to political extremism in a broader sense; K. Loewenstein, 'Militant Democracy and Fundamental Rights II', *The American Political Science Review*, vol. 31, no. 4, 1937, p. 650. See also K. Roach, 'Anti-Terrorism and Militant Democracy: Some Western and Eastern Responses', in: A. Sajó (ed.), *Militant democracy*, Utrecht: Eleven International Publishing, 2004, p. 176.

21 Loewenstein, 'Autocracy versus Democracy in Contemporary Europe I', *The American Political Science Review*, p. 579. Cliteur and Rijpkema rightly point out that Loewenstein does not clearly define what kind of anti-democratic actors he is pointing at. Their conclusion that Loewenstein *'seems to focus on violent parties'*, however, is less convincing, considering that Loewenstein argues that the danger of fascism lies precisely in the fact that it uses *democratic* means to eventually destroy it (see Cliteur and Rijpkema, *The State of Exception and Militant Democracy*, p. 242).

22 Loewenstein, 'Autocracy versus Democracy in Contemporary Europe I', *The American Political Science Review*, p. 592-593.

23 Cliteur and Rijpkema, *The State of Exception and Militant Democracy*, p. 233.

24 Cliteur and Rijpkema, p. 235.

on this topic.[25] Loewenstein observed that by that time the threat had become imminent as fascism had developed into a universal danger.[26] The anti-democratic movement of fascism, he argued, appealed to the emotions of the public while operating formally within the democratic system and using elections as a way towards power.[27] According to Loewenstein, fascism was not an ideology, but a political technique that parasitized on democracy. In fact, the success of fascism was based on its perfect adaptation to democracy: *'[u]nder cover of fundamental rights and the rule of law, the anti-democratic machine could be built up and set in motion legally. Calculating adroitly that democracy could not, without self-abnegation, deny to any body of public opinion the full use of the free institutions of speech, press, assembly, and parliamentary participation, fascist exponents systematically discredit the democratic order and make it unworkable by paralyzing its functions until chaos reigns'*.[28] He used the metaphor of the *'Trojan horse by which the enemy enters the city'* to describe the way fascism exploited the weaknesses of democracy to gain power with the aim of destroying the system from within.[29] In order to avert the threat of fascism, Loewenstein argued, democratic states have to cooperate and form a common front against fascism.[30] But above all, European states facing fascism could no longer remain passive and should strengthen themselves internally. Fascism could only be defeated on its own plane. A timely implementation of anti-fascist legislation, including bans against paramilitary organisations, the prosecution of incitement to violence or hatred, and the prohibition of subversive actors, was necessary to effectively defend democracies against the fascist exploitation of democracy.[31] The failure of the Weimar Republic and the collapse of other democratic regimes in Europe were according to Loewenstein due to the fact that these legal orders either lacked militant instruments, or had failed to use them adequately.[32]

25 K. Loewenstein, 'Militant Democracy and Fundamental Rights I', *The American Political Science Review*, vol. 31, no. 3, 1937, p. 417-432 and Loewenstein, 'Militant Democracy and Fundamental Rights II', *The American Political Science Review*, p. 638-658. See also Klamt, *Explorations in Legal Cultures*, p. 133.

26 Loewenstein, 'Militant Democracy and Fundamental Rights I', *The American Political Science Review*, p. 417.

27 Loewenstein, p. 417-418. See also S. Avineri, 'Introduction', in: A. Sajó (ed.), *Militant democracy*, Utrecht: Eleven International Publishing, 2004, p. 1.

28 Loewenstein, 'Militant Democracy and Fundamental Rights I', *The American Political Science Review*, p. 423. See also Cliteur and Rijpkema, *The State of Exception and Militant Democracy*, p. 236.

29 Loewenstein, 'Militant Democracy and Fundamental Rights I', *The American Political Science Review*, p. 424.

30 Loewenstein, p. 428-429. See also Cliteur and Rijpkema, *The State of Exception and Militant Democracy*, p. 237.

31 Loewenstein, 'Militant Democracy and Fundamental Rights I', *The American Political Science Review*, p. 429. See also A.K. Bourne, 'The Prohibition of Political Parties and "Militant Democracy"', *Journal of Comparative Law*, vol. 7, no. 1, 2012, p. 196.

32 Avineri, *Militant democracy*, p. 1.

The argument of democracies that they did not want to compromise their democratic nature when defending themselves he considered *'legalistic self-complacency and suicidal lethargy'*.[33] The time had come when states could no longer remain passive and had to become militant, as Loewenstein had already made clear in his previous articles. This meant first and foremost the temporary suspension of constitutional principles for the sake of democratic self-defence.[34] Here we touch upon the fundamental question of the justification of militant democracy. Because how can democracy cover these weak spots without selling out its democratic nature: *'[d]emocracy stands for fundamental rights, for fair play for all opinions, for free speech, assembly, press. How could it address itself to curtailing these without destroying the very basis of its existence and justification?'*[35]

According to Loewenstein the justification for militant measures can be found in an analogy with the state of emergency in times of war, when it is generally accepted that constitutional guarantees are suspended.[36] Analogically, in the context of militant democracy, democracy is at war with fascism and European democracies are confronted with a 'state of siege'. In such a context, *'[c]onstitutional scruples can no longer restrain from restrictions on democratic fundamentals, for the sake of ultimately preserving these very fundamentals'*.[37] The consequences of this state of siege can be far reaching. In Loewenstein's view, democracy *'must live up to the demands of the hour, and every possible effort must be made to rescue it, even at the risk and cost of violating fundamental principles'*.[38]

7.4 Militant democracy put into practice

The call to action by Loewenstein and others could not prevent European democracies from being overrun by fascism and Nazism. Although before the Second World War instruments that could be regarded as militant were available in many European states, many of these were ad hoc and none of the legal orders of these states had adopted anything resembling a coherent doctrine of democratic self-defence.[39] The Second World War, however, was a tragic learning experience that gave rise to an increased

---

33 Loewenstein, 'Militant Democracy and Fundamental Rights I', *The American Political Science Review*, p. 431.
34 Loewenstein, p. 430-432.
35 Loewenstein, p. 430-431.
36 Loewenstein, p. 430-432. See also Cliteur and Rijpkema, *The State of Exception and Militant Democracy*, p. 239.
37 Loewenstein, 'Militant Democracy and Fundamental Rights I', *The American Political Science Review*, p. 430-431. See also Cliteur and Rijpkema, *The State of Exception and Militant Democracy*, p. 238-239.
38 Loewenstein, 'Militant Democracy and Fundamental Rights I', *The American Political Science Review*, p. 432.
39 Müller, *The Oxford Handbook of Comparative Constitutional Law*, p. 1257.

interest in the concept of militant democracy. The failure of the Weimar Republic was not easily forgotten and a sentiment of 'never again' dominated democratic thinking at that time. As a result, after the Second World War the concept of militant democracy seriously became part of the constitutional thinking and militant measures were incorporated in many European constitutional orders. In post-war Europe, the justifications and techniques have become widely used.[40] One may argue that over the past decades militant democracy has gradually emerged as a new archetype of statehood.[41]

An analysis of the way the issue of democratic self-defence is addressed in different countries shows a wide diversity of more or less militant arrangements.[42] Militant democracy is *'not a universal stencil'* that can be applied in the same way in any democratic state.[43] The application of the concept of militant democracy always accommodates the distinctive characteristics of a particular democracy. The way in which elements of militant democracy are implemented in any legal order strongly depends on a country's history and legal culture. Because the concept of militant democracy does not prescribe a particular method for the protection of democracy, for example, we see that militant measures may either be provided for in a state's constitution or derive from administrative law or criminal law (or even private law, as is the case for the Dutch provision that forms the basis for outlawing political parties[44]).

Some states eagerly embraced the militant democracy rationale. Especially in Germany the concept of militant democracy strongly influenced the drafting of the Basic Law that came into force in 1949.[45] The post-war German constitution is

40 Bourne, *Journal of Comparative Law*, p. 196.

41 P. Macklem, 'Guarding the Perimeter: Militant Democracy and Religious Freedom in Europe', *Constellations*, vol. 19, no. 4, 2012, p. 576.

42 Thiel, *The Militant Democracy Principle in Modern Democracies*, p. 382.

43 Tyulkina, *Militant Democracy*, p. 35.

44 Article 2:20 of the Dutch Civil Code, which provides for the prohibition of legal persons, also covers the banning of political parties. P.P.T. Bovend'Eert and H.R.B.M. Kummeling, *Het Nederlandse Parlement [The Dutch Parliament]*, 11th ed., Deventer: Kluwer, 2010, p. 87-88. See also R. Nehmelman, 'Het partijverbod: over de grenzen van de democratie' ['The party ban: crossing the boundaries of democracy'], in: C.W. Noorlander, et al. (eds.), *Het volk regeert. Beschouwingen over de (Nederlandse) democratie in de 21e eeuw [The people rule. Reflections on the (Dutch) democracy in the 21st century]*, Nijmegen: Wolf Legal Publishers, 2008, p. 331-352; J.A.O. Eskes, *Repressie van politieke bewegingen in Nederland. Een juridisch-historische studie over het Nederlandse publiekrechtelijke verenigingsrecht gedurende het tijdvak 1798-1988 [The repression of political movements in the Netherlands. A legal-historical study on the Dutch public law on associations during the period 1798-1988]*, Zwolle: W.E.J. Tjeenk Willink, 1988.

45 P. Macklem, 'Militant democracy, legal pluralism, and the paradox of self-determination', *International Journal of Constitutional Law*, vol. 4, no. 3, 2006, p. 488; Müller, *The Oxford Handbook of Comparative Constitutional Law*, p. 1258.

imbued with militant measures that aim to prevent the rise of another anti-democratic regime, including a prohibition of abuse of rights in Article 18 Basic Law. In fact, *'Germany developed the most explicit – and the most far-reaching – theory of militant democracy'*.[46] It is therefore often referred to as the cradle of the concept of militant democracy.[47] That is why the Germany system is singled out in the context of this research and studied in more detail in the following chapter.

However, militant instruments were not only introduced in Germany. The explicit and far-reaching implementation of the concept of militant democracy in Germany is an exceptional one.[48] Nonetheless, nowadays practically all democracies have adopted certain measures to defend themselves against attacks by anti-democratic actors.[49] However, the extent to which democracies wish to defend themselves and the means by which they aim to do this varies strongly from state to state.[50] Many European states have adopted legal provisions that aim to defend the democratic structure, yet sometimes without an explicit acknowledgment of the concept of militant democracy as an overarching constitutional principle.

Militant instruments were also incorporated in several European constitutions of states that regained democracy after a totalitarian episode.[51] The Italian Constitution of 1947, for example, contains a clause prohibiting the re-establishment of the fascist party.[52] And the French Constitution of 1958 allows for the banning of political parties and associations that do not adhere to democratic principles.[53] In democracies where democracy was restored in the 1970s after years of authoritarian rule and dictatorship – including Spain after Franco, Portugal after Salazar, and Greece after the Regime

46 Müller, *The Oxford Handbook of Comparative Constitutional Law*, p. 1260.

47 Thiel, *The Militant Democracy Principle in Modern Democracies*, p. 8.

48 Thiel, p. 383.

49 Thiel, p. 384; Müller, *Comparative Constitutional Law*, p. 1266.

50 Thiel, *The Militant Democracy Principle in Modern Democracies*, p. 2.

51 Müller, *The Oxford Handbook of Comparative Constitutional Law*, p. 1254.

52 Article xii, first sentence, of the Constitution of the Italian Republic provides: *'It shall be forbidden to reorganise, under any form whatsoever, the dissolved Fascist party'*, www.senato.it/documenti/repository/istituzione/costituzione_inglese.pdf (accessed 11 April 2016). See also Fox and Nolte, *Harvard International Law Journal*, p. 36.

53 Article 4, first sentence, of the Constitution of the Fifth Republic provides: '*Political parties and groups shall contribute to the exercise of suffrage. They shall be formed and carry on their activities freely. They shall respect the principles of national sovereignty and democracy*', www.conseil-constitutionnel.fr/conseil-constitutionnel/root/bank_mm/anglais/constitution_anglais.pdf (accessed 11 April 2016). See also M. Minkenberg, 'Repression and reaction: militant democracy and the radical right in Germany and France', *Patterns of Prejudice*, vol. 40, no. 1, 2006, p. 39.

of the Colonels – we see that similar militant elements have been included in the constitution.[54]

Subsequently, while interest in militant democracy waned for a while after the 1970s,[55] the concept experienced a revival after the fall of the Iron Curtain in 1989 and the collapse of the Soviet Union, when the concept of militant democracy became a topic of interest in the new democracies in Central and Eastern Europe. In the light of transitional justice and under the mantle of the Council of Europe these states were faced with the challenge of securing democracy for the future.[56] After the fall of the Soviet Union, many of these Eastern and Central European states have banned communist ideology in a way similar to the banning of neo-Nazism in Western Europe.[57] Consistent with a militant narrative, many of these new democracies adopted measures to defend themselves against both communism and fascism, for example by banning parties – or sometimes just symbols – associated with these totalitarian movements.[58]

In addition, in the years after the War the concept of militant democracy also made its entrance on the international stage. In Chapter five we have seen that at that time various international human rights instruments were drafted within the framework of the UN and the Council of Europe, such as the Universal Declaration of Human Rights (1948), the European Convention on Human Rights (1950), and the International Covenants on respectively Civil and Political Rights and Economic, Social and

54 See e.g. Article 6 of the Spanish Constitution, which provides: *'Political parties are the expression of political pluralism, they contribute to the formation and expression of the will of the people and are an essential instrument for political participation. Their creation and the exercise of their activities are free in so far as they respect the Constitution and the law. Their internal structure and their functioning must be democratic'*, www.congreso.es/portal/page/portal/Congreso/Congreso/Hist_Normas/Norm/const_espa_texto_ingles_0.pdf (accessed 11 April 2016); Article 46(4) of the Portuguese Constitution provides: *'Armed associations, military, militarised or paramilitary-type associations and organisations that are racist or display a fascist ideology shall not be permitted'*, www.tribunalconstitucional.pt/tc/conteudo/files/constituicaoingles.pdf (accessed 11 April 2016); and finally Article 25(3) of the Constitution of Greece prohibits the abusive exercise of fundamental rights, albeit without a sanctioning mechanism such as that under the German Constitution: *'The abusive exercise of rights is not permitted'*, www.hellenicparliament.gr/UserFiles/f3c70a23-7696-49db-9148-f24dce6a27c8/001-156%20aggliko.pdf (accessed 11 April 2016). See also Fox and Nolte, *Harvard International Law Journal*, p. 36.

55 Müller, *The Oxford Handbook of Comparative Constitutional Law*, p. 1262.

56 R. O'Connell, 'Militant Democracy and Human Rights Principles', *Constitutional Law Review* (Georgian Constitutional Court), 2009, p. 85. See also A. Sajó, 'Militant Democracy and Transition towards Democracy', in: A. Sajó (ed.), *Militant Democracy*, Utrecht: Eleven Legal Publishers, 2004.

57 H.A. Welsh, 'Dealing with the Communist Past: Central and East European Experiences after 1990', *Europe-Asia Studies*, vol. 48, no. 3, 1996, p. 414.

58 Müller, *Comparative Constitutional Law*, p. 1262. The German Basic Law served as a model for the constitutions of several new democracies in Central and Eastern European, including Croatia, Lithuania, Poland, Romania and Slovenia: G.H. See also Fox and Nolte, 'Intolerant democracies', *Harvard International Law Journal*, p. 36.

Cultural Rights (1966). All these treaties breathe the ambitions of that time to create stable democracies that would not be overrun by the next anti-democratic wave.[59] As we have seen in the previous chapter, militant elements, such as an abuse of rights clause, are therefore found in all these treaties.

7.5 Reflections on the implementation of militant democracy

From an academic perspective, the development of the concept of militant democracy did not stand still after the Second World War either. In the decades after the Second World War, many scholars tried to put the practical application of the concept in a theoretical perspective. Without claiming to give a comprehensive account, the legal theories discussed here represent a broad set of different perspectives on the implementation of militant democracy.

7.5.1 Procedural, substantive, tolerant and militant democracies

Fox and Nolte used the notions of procedural and substantive democracy to investigate modern democracies. In a leading article from the 1990s they developed a complex methodical framework for examining and comparing how democracies deal with the presence of anti-democratic actors. This exercise has resulted in a two dimensional typology of democratic responses to extremism. First, they categorise democracies according to two widely accepted models of democratic government: the procedural model and the substantive model. They subsequently expand these models by adding how norms regarding anti-democratic actors are interpreted and implemented in practice by introducing a further division of democracies into tolerant and militant democracies.

7.5.1.1 The procedural model of democracy

The procedural model in the typology of Fox and Nolte (also referred to as the formal or thin perception of democracy) *'defines democracy as a set of procedures'*.[60] This model draws on Schumpeter's interpretation of democracy as the *'institutional arrangement for arriving at political decisions in which individuals acquire the power to decide by means of a competitive struggle for the people's vote'*.[61] In this perception *'[t]he views of all citizens are given equal consideration and the*

---

59 See e.g. G.H. Fox & G. Nolte, 'Fox and Nolte Response', *Harvard International Law Journal*, vol. 37, no. 1, 1996, p. 238.

60 Fox and Nolte, 'Intolerant democracies', *Harvard International Law Journal*, p. 14.

61 J. Schumpeter, *Capitalism, Socialism and Democracy*, 2nd ed., New York/London: Harper & Brothers, 1947, p. 269, cited in Fox and Nolte, 'Intolerant democracies', *Harvard International Law Journal*, p. 14.

primacy of majority rule as a basis for legitimacy limits State authority to select among competing views'.[62] According to Fox and Nolte, *'[t]his sort of democracy provides a framework for decision making, but does not prescribe the decisions themselves'*.[63] Essentially, this perception of democracy refers to democracy in the sense of the equal participation of all citizens in the process of political decision-making whereby the opinion of the majority is decisive. For good reason, all major human rights instruments require periodic elections in which citizens can express their opinion.[64] See, for example, Article 3 of the First Protocol to the ECHR in which the States Parties declare *'to hold free elections at reasonable intervals by secret ballot, under conditions which will ensure the free expression of the opinion of the people in the choice of the legislature'*. Through periodic and free elections it is decided which political conviction wins and, until the next elections, this determines the direction of political decision-making. The political decisions that result from this process are, in this procedural approach, always qualified as acceptable, since they are taken democratically.[65] The democratic quality of political decisions thus depends primarily on the procedure followed, whatever the content of the outcome may be.[66] Because it confines itself to procedural elements, procedural democracy is often considered as a 'minimum standard' of democracy that may even be imperfect or insufficient, *'because a pure procedural point of view would qualify a completely and unscrupulously corrupt, but orderly elected government as democratic'*.[67] Essential in the procedural mode is that every minority–at least in theory–can grow into a majority, even into a majority that aims for the destruction of democracy. Procedural democracy, therefore, *'cannot guarantee that supporters of democracy will always emerge victorious; that is a question of political will'*.[68] Echoing Kelsen's response to the democratic paradox, this model holds that if a popular majority have the power to create a democracy, it would follow that they should also have the power to dismantle it.[69] From this perspective, measures that interfere with that free and open process of democracy by excluding individuals and groups based on their political views are unacceptable.

---

62 Bourne, *Journal of Comparative Law*, p. 197.

63 Fox and Nolte, 'Intolerant democracies', *Harvard International Law Journal*, p. 14.

64 Fox and Nolte, p. 10.

65 Brems, *Democratie op het einde van de 20st eeuw*, p. 316.

66 S. Sottiaux, 'Democratie en grondrechten. De inhoudelijke en procedurele democratiemodellen van Dworkin en Habermas' ['Democracy and fundamental rights. The substantive and procedural models of democracy of Dworkin and Habermas'], in: M. Adams and P. Popelier (eds.), *Recht en democratie. De democratische verbeelding in het recht [Law and democracy. The democratic perception in law]*, Antwerp/New York/Oxford: Intersentia, 2004, p. 43.

67 Thiel, *The Militant Democracy Principle in Modern Democracies*, p. 386.

68 Fox and Nolte, 'Intolerant democracies', *Harvard International Law Journal*, p. 16.

69 H. Kelsen, *Vom Wesen und Wert der Demokratie*, 2nd ed., Tübingen: Verlag J.C.B. Mohr, 1929, p. 94, 98 and 102-103. See also Fox and Nolte, *Harvard International Law Journal*, p. 15-16.

7.5.1.2 The substantive model of democracy

According to the substantive (or material or thick) perception democracy is defined, however, '*not as the process of ascertaining the preferences of political majorities, but as a society in which majority rule is made meaningful*'.[70] Democracy is according to this model conceived *'as a means for creating a society where citizens enjoy core rights and liberties'*.[71] Hence, democracy relates to more than the representation of the will of the majority of the people in political decision-making. In this view, democracy is built on substantive values and principles that ought to be respected by the decision-making authorities. Fox and Nolte explain that this substantive view of democracy presumes that majorities are fluid: *'[i]n order for citizens to move in and out of the majority as issues change, they must at all times enjoy a core of political rights that ensures effective participation. In this view, democratic procedure is not an end in itself, but a means of creating a society in which citizens enjoy certain essential rights'*.[72] Therefore, political decisions in a substantive interpretation of democracy are only acceptable if these substantive requirements are respected. The process of political decision-making is therefore in this substantive democracy more or less confined by the requirements set by democracy. Yet, while there is no clear-cut definition of democracy, it is very difficult to clearly determine what the core principles of democracy are. Müller argues that *'[a] narrow definition of a set of democratic core principles... could lead to highly illiberal outcomes; but a wide one would leave the door open to supposed extremists claiming that their understanding of democracy is just radically different – but still recognizably democratic or even liberal'*.[73]

7.5.1.3 Tolerant and militant democracies

Fox and Nolte, however, believe the procedural and the substantive models of democracies to be too abstract to give a meaningful impression of states' practices. They only designate the state's formal constitutional framework, but not how norms regarding anti-democratic actors are interpreted and implemented in practice. Fox and Nolte therefore further subdivided these two categories into 'tolerant' (or passive) and 'militant' (or active) democracies. One clear line of demarcation between tolerant and militant democracies, according to Fox and Nolte, is whether a state's constitution can be amended to alter or eliminate democratic institutions.[74]

70 Fox and Nolte, 'Intolerant democracies', *Harvard International Law Journal*, p. 16. Fox and Nolte borrow this definition from R.G. Ross, 'Democracy, Party and Politics', *Ethics*, vol. 64, no. 2, 1954, p. 120-121.

71 Bourne, *Journal of Comparative Law*, p. 197.

72 Fox and Nolte, 'Intolerant democracies', *Harvard International Law Journal*, p. 16.

73 Müller, *Comparative Constitutional Law*, p. 1267.

74 Fox and Nolte, 'Intolerant democracies', *Harvard International Law Journal*, p. 24.

If a constitution contains clauses providing that certain basic structures cannot be amended, it can be categorised as militant. By categorising state practice along these lines, they arrive at a division of democracies into four categories: (1) tolerant procedural democracy; (2) militant procedural democracy; (3) tolerant substantive democracy; and (4) militant substantive democracy.[75]

	Procedural	**Substantive**
Tolerant	(1) tolerant procedural	(3) tolerant substantive
Militant	(2) militant procedural	(4) militant substantive

They then use these categories to examine the practice of a number of democratic states and international human rights documents. The UK, for example, they describe as a tolerant procedural democracy, because the British legislature is not bound by any substantive rules and is tolerant towards anti-democratic political actors. The US serves as the example for a militant procedural democracy, because, although it has implemented a procedural form of democracy, the republican form of government laid down in the constitution cannot be amended. France is referred to as a tolerant substantive democracy. French law, according to Fox and Nolte, contains several substantive elements – for instance concerning political parties – but has never really evolved into a more militant form of democracy. Finally, Germany is (not surprisingly) categorised as a militant substantive democracy. Just like the binary approach, however, these models are criticised for still relying on a binary approach, forcing an artificial distinction between 'tolerant' and 'militant' democracies.[76]

Koskenniemi in particular has objected to the model developed by Fox and Nolte. He has criticised the framing of the issues in terms of democratic government, on the one hand, and undemocratic opposition on the other. This dichotomy, he argues, assumes an external perspective on the basis of which to decide what is democratic and what is not. Yet, both the government and the opposition *'would normally argue their case in terms of democracy – a 'true,' or 'real' democracy in contrast to the opponent's distorted view'*, although they are referring to different conceptions of democracy (procedural or substantive).[77] The government may adhere to a substantive perception of democracy, while the opposition relies on a procedural perception of democracy. Or both parties may interpret the procedural and substantive standards in contrasting ways. In those situations, it is difficult to argue that the opposition aims

75 Fox and Nolte, p. 22 et seq. See also Thiel, *The Militant Democracy Principle in Modern Democracies*, p. 388.
76 Thiel, p. 395.
77 M. Koskenniemi, '"Intolerant Democracies": a Reaction', *Harvard International Law Journal*, vol. 37, no. 1, 1996, p. 231.

to replace democracy by something else. The external perspective is deceptive in that respect, as it is impossible to talk about democracy without becoming involved in this controversy as a participant.

7.5.2 Militant democracy as a linear concept

The first theoretical thoughts on militant democracy were based on a simple dichotomy according to which a democracy is either militant or not.[78] This binary approach is found in the work of Loewenstein, who urged European democracy no longer to be passive and become militant.[79] Nowadays, however, this approach is considered too narrow to adequately capture the complexity of the concept.[80] Thinking about militant democracy in a dichotomic way no longer seems relevant. Pfersmann argues that nowadays practically all democracies are *more or less* militant, as all states have introduced obstacles in response to the threat posed by anti-democratic actors. He therefore concludes that the option 'off' is deceptive.[81] Thiel, too, observes that the extremes of the totally militant or the totally pure open democracy are illusory: *'[t]he political and constitutional reality teaches that there hardly are "full-fledged" libertarian or protectionist democratic systems; most democracies only show a tendency or combine elements of both types.'*[82] The consequence of the assumption that all democracies are in some sense militant democracies is that it is impossible to know what a non-militant democracy is.[83]

Over the years, legal doctrine has therefore increasingly become to think of militant democracy as a linear concept. Pfersmann, for example, claims that militancy is a gradual scale, with the 'pure open democracy' – which is basically a procedural democracy – on the one hand, and the strict or militant democracy on the other. The open democracy, or *'the constitution of minimal stability'*, is defined by Pfersmann as *'a legal system in which the addressees participate in the production of the general norms by majoritarian decisions, directly or through the election of representatives in charge of enacting such general rules. In this "pure" setting, we do not include any other requirement but participation in the production of general*

78 Thiel, *The Militant Democracy Principle in Modern Democracies*, p. 384.

79 Loewenstein, 'Militant Democracy and Fundamental Rights, I', *The American Political Science Review* and Loewenstein, 'Militant Democracy and Fundamental Rights, II', *The American Political Science Review*. See also C. Buis, 'France', in: Thiel, *The Militant Democracy Principle in Modern Democracies*, p. 102.

80 Thiel, *The Militant Democracy Principle in Modern Democracies*, p. 384; Buis, *The Militant Democracy Principle in Modern Democracies*, p. 102; Müller, *Comparative Constitutional Law*, p. 1266.

81 Pfersmann, p. 53.

82 Thiel, *The Militant Democracy Principle in Modern Democracies*, p. 381.

83 Bourne, *Journal of Comparative Law*, p. 197.

norms'.[84] In this pure open democracy, however, as Pfersmann acknowledges, the stability of democracy is at risk. Because the legislator in this pure open democracy has unrestricted competence, it may enact legislation that abolishes the open democracy and replaces it with a totalitarian regime. States have therefore put in place obstacles to prevent this. These obstacles consist, in the first place, of non-legal strategies that promote pro-democratic beliefs and attitudes. In addition, states may adopt legal strategies which could be direct or indirect. Direct obstacles prohibit anti-democratic actions or impose obligations to identify such actions in a preventive way under the threat of sanctions and stimulate the prevention of anti-democratic actions and promote pro-democratic beliefs and attitudes. Still, these direct obstacles presuppose that the majority of the people favour democracy. In addition, indirect or higher-order obstacles restrict democratic decision-making in order to prevent a simple majority from changing the rules *'according to which rules are produced by a simple majority'*.[85] These obstacles modify the rules concerning decision-making. At the other end of the scale, we therefore find the *strict* militant democracy, *'in which absolutely no majority, not even unanimity, is entitled to modify the democratic setting'*.[86] This rigorous interpretation of militant democracy in fact impedes any form of constitutional change. The question here is to what extent such a militant democracy can still be called a 'democracy'.[87]

Thiel, however, has objected to this linear approach to the interpretation of militant democracy, as it assumes that different factors affecting the level of militancy can be weighted. It does not tell us, however, how their weight is to be determined.[88] What is, for example, the weight of the possibility of banning a political party, or the prohibition of anti-democratic speech? To what extent does it contribute to democracy becoming militant? And, Thiel argues, even on this scale between the pure open democracy and the militant democracy, there has to be a point after which a democracy is no longer considered more or less pure and open, but has shifted towards a militant democracy.[89] Since this brings us back to the challenge of differentiating between tolerant and militant democracies, he argues that this gradual approach does not solve the problems attributed to the binary approaches. Nonetheless, this method offers a more nuanced and more appropriate approach to the implementation of militant democracy.

---

84 Pfersmann, *Militant democracy*, p. 53.
85 Pfersmann, p. 56.
86 Pfersmann gives Germany, France and Italy as examples: p. 57.
87 Pfersmann, p. 58.
88 Buis, *The Militant Democracy Principle in Modern Democracies*, p. 103.
89 Thiel, *The Militant Democracy Principle in Modern Democracies*, p. 397-398.

7.5.3 Militant democracy as calculated risk aversion

In *Militant Democracy and Transitions towards Democracy* Sajó recalls that militant democracy is (at least selectively) risk averse. Militant democracy aims to avert the risk that by using the mechanisms of democracy, such as free speech, the freedom of assembly, and free elections a regime may be established that dissolves democracy.[90] He proposes a calculus for militant democracy in transitional societies – Sajó refers to the post-communist democracies in Central and Eastern Europe – recovering from communist dictatorship. Democratic risk aversion would be particularly relevant for these transitional societies, because as young democracies they face a variety of risks. Yet, Sajó acknowledges that risk-aversion is troubling in a constitutional democracy that stands for liberty, as liberty requires a certain level of risk taking.[91] Sajó recalls the position of Justice Brandeis, Associate Justice of the Supreme Court of the US from 1916 to 1939, who stated in his famous concurring opinion in the case *Whitney v. California* that liberty is for the brave: *'[t]hose who won our independence believed that the final end of the state was to make men free to develop their faculties, and that in its government the deliberative forces should prevail over the arbitrary... They believed liberty to be the secret of happiness, and courage to be the secret of liberty. They believed that freedom to think as you will and to speak as you think are means indispensable to the discovery and spread of political truth; that, without free speech and assembly, discussion would be futile;... that the greatest menace to freedom is an inert people; that public discussion is a political duty, and that this should be a fundamental principle of the American government.'*[92] For militant democracies operating under the assumption of risk aversion, however, Sajó considers this reasoning to be unattractive. Especially for states with an autocratic or dictatorial past not taking militant measures may be too perilous. He adds that *'[t]he inclination of social risk aversion increases where specific historical experiences and reasons dictate precaution. Here even low probabilities of occurrence of an anti-democratic U-turn are impermissible, or at least a matter of precautionary restriction'*.[93]

Subsequently, Sajó argues that a reasonable ground for the assumption of risk to democracy can in general be established in cases where *'the future event pertains to a class of events that have had a high observed (past) occurrence'*.[94] Risk aversion, however, presupposes that future events can be discussed in terms of statistical probabilities. But calculating the risks of democracy being dissolved is not that simple. As Sajó rightly points out, in some situations there is no basis to evaluate such probabilities. For instance, there may be too few previous cases

90 Sajó, *Militant democracy*, p. 214.
91 Sajó, p. 214.
92 US Supreme Court, *Whitney v. California*, 274 *US* 357 [1927], par. 375.
93 Sajó, *Militant democracy*, p. 215.
94 Sajó, p. 215.

where the participation of anti-democratic political parties at free elections actually resulted in the establishment of an anti-democratic regime to calculate any statistical likelihood. In these situations, probabilities are often merely based on assumptions about risk. Even though this alternative approach may be criticised, as it is not based on occurrence-related analysis, Sajó believes it to be a functional approach that *'helps to come up with solutions in situations where information is scarce or too costly'*.[95] Yet another complication is that issues of militant democracy often emerge in a context where the events according to which probabilities are calculated are not insular but interrelated. The well-known cascade effect, according to which *'one event increases the likelihood of a different second one that disproportionally increases the likelihood of an evil consequence'*, renders the calculation of consequences even more complex.[96] This potential cascade effect should therefore also be part of the probability evaluation. For risk aversion to be acceptable without compromising democracy and liberty, therefore, *'there ought to be a showing of reasonable handling of probabilities and clear identification of the evil in those cases in which such evaluation is possible at all. Furthermore, in matters where probabilities cannot be established, the tendency of the constitution to preserve the status quo would make militant democracy legitimate as a technique of risk reduction.'*[97]

7.5.4 Different paradigms for militant measures

The traditional focus of militant democracy has been on outlawing *'political parties whose programmes and activities disregard fundamental democratic principles or openly aim to destroy them'*.[98] Niesen places all attempts to ban political parties in the context of two militant paradigms. Even though Niesen focuses on party bans, his conclusions provide interesting insights about militant measures in general. Based on different underlying conceptions of what constitutes a threat, Niesen makes a distinction between anti-extremism (basically militant democracy in a traditional sense), on the one hand, and banning the former ruling party (also referred to as negative republicanism), on the other.[99] As Müller concisely puts it, this dichotomy

---

95 Sajó, p. 215.
96 Sajó, *Cardozo Law Review*, p. 2287.
97 Sajó, p. 217.
98 Tyulkina, *Militant Democracy*, p. 19.
99 In an earlier publication Niesen referred to these two paradigms as 'anti-extremism' and 'negative republicanism': P. Niesen, 'Anti-Extremism, Negative Republicanism, Civic Society: Three Paradigms for Banning Political Parties', *German Law Journal*, vol. 3, no. 7, 2002, www.germanlawjournal.com/s/GLJ_Vol_03_No_07_Niesen.pdf (accessed 11 April 2016). In the case of Rwanda, Niesen distinguishes a third paradigm, which he refers to as anti-particularism. Under this paradigm it allows for the banning of political parties that discriminate or incite hatred and violence along ethnic or similar lines: P. Niesen, 'Political party bans in Rwanda 1994–2003: three narratives of justification', *Democratization*, vol. 17, no. 4, 2010, p. 709 and 715-718.

is based on the following question: *'does a democracy work with a relatively open or even universal understanding of "extremism", where threats can emanate from different parts of the political spectrum, or is militancy more particularist, so to speak, and thus essentially aimed at preventing the return of a specific, highly problematic historical past?'.*[100] Finally, Niesen speculates on whether a new, third paradigm is emerging, which focuses on the protection of the rights and freedoms of people in a minority situation. This perception of democracy does not focus so much on traditional democratic processes, such as elections, party competition and political decision-making, but on democracy as a moral concept in which majorities and minorities can participate on the basis of reciprocal recognition.

7.5.4.1 Militant democracy as anti-extremism

The classic interpretation of militant democracy as anti-extremism refers to a democracy that aims to protect the stability of the liberal democratic system and of its constitutive principles and institutions.[101] It is a general strategy of democratic protection that targets *'anti-system'* political parties that aim to overthrow the democratic system, independent of the direction it is coming from. In this context, the justification of a party ban is found in the preservation of democracy. What this democracy exactly entails is unclear in Niesen's definition of this paradigm. As we will see, however, in the context of the Federal Republic of Germany it refers to the 'free democratic basic order', which besides democratic procedures also includes the protection of fundamental rights and the rule of law.[102] Niesen refers to the constitutional state of affairs in the Federal Republic of Germany immediately after the Second World War as the main example of this type of militant democracy.[103] He explains that the 1949 Basic Law was not merely drafted as a response to a widespread resistance against the Nazis, nor as the fruit of a struggle for self-liberation of the German people. In fact, Niesen argues that the deliberations during the drafting of this provision show that it was just as much directed against the contemporary threat of communism as against the Nazi past.[104] As a consequence, the dangers to democracy were not associated exclusively with Nazism, but threats were deemed to emanate from both the extreme right and the extreme left. Or, in the words of Müller, the instrument of the party ban was originally designed as a barrier against the rise of dangerous extremism, regardless of its direction of origin.[105] This is particularly apparent from the phrasing

100 Müller, *Comparative Constitutional Law*, p. 1263.
101 G. Frankenberg, 'The learning Sovereign', in: Sajó, *Militant democracy*, p. 124.
102 Niesen, *German Law Journal*, par. 4 and 14.
103 Niesen, par. 7 et seq. See also Frankenberg, *Militant democracy*, p. 123-126; Müller, *Comparative Constitutional Law*, p. 1263.
104 Niesen, *German Law Journal*, par. 7.
105 Müller, *Comparative Constitutional Law*, p. 1263.

of the party ban provision in Article 21(2) of the Basic Law. Based on this provision, a political party that aims for the impairment or destruction of the *'free democratic basic order'* may be declared unconstitutional by the Federal Constitutional Court.[106] Furthermore, since the introduction of this provision, the German Federal Constitutional Court has declared two political parties unconstitutional: the neo-Nazi *Sozialistische Reichspartei* (SRP) and the *Kommunistische Partei Deutschlands* (KPD). According to Niesen, the Court framed the threat posed by both parties in a similar way, namely as *'the hostile takeover of the republic by left- or right-wing extremists'*.[107] These cases, Niesen argues, *'involved little public commitment to what the politics of National Socialism had been, to what its aims and activities involved, or to what should be regarded as essential problematic features, but concentrated on the technical-instrumental level of political engineering, on how "anti-system" associations in general could be combated'*.[108] Because the paradigm of anti-extremism, constitutionally speaking, puts neo-Nazism and Communism on a par, it presupposes that the one can only be dealt with if the other is also dealt with. As a result, in its application to merely neo-Nazi and Communist political parties, the traditional interpretation of militant democracy as anti-extremism is often associated with an outdated Cold War mind-set.[109] Hence, when the threat of Communism resided to the background in the late 1980s, Niesen argues, anti-extremism no longer was perceived as the appropriate strategy for addressing the continuous threat of neo-Nazism.[110]

7.5.4.2 Militant democracy as banning the former ruling party

As a result, an alternative paradigm came up in the thinking about militant democracy in the 1990s: banning the former ruling party. Contrary to the classic interpretation of militant democracy, this paradigm finds its justification in the prevention of the reoccurrence of a specific injustice committed in the past. As Niesen describes, the features of banning the former ruling party *'are not abstract requirements of constitutional reproduction, but relate to the concrete historical problem-solving function of the constitution in question'*.[111] The goal of this paradigm is therefore, in the words of Frankenberg, *'to prevent the resurrection of a defeated historical system of injustice'*.[112] While Niesen characterises the first years of Germany's post-war

106 Article 21(2) of the German Basic Law, www.bundestag.de/blob/284870/ce0d03414872b427e57fccb703634dcd/basic_law-data.pdf (accessed 11 April 2016).
107 Niesen, *German Law Journal*, par. 8.
108 Niesen, par. 8.
109 Müller, *Comparative Constitutional Law*, p. 1267. See also C. Leggewie and H. Meier, *Republikschutz. Maßstäbe für die Verteidigung der Demokratie*, Hamburg: Rowohlt, 1995, p. 212-227.
110 Niesen, *German Law Journal*, par. 16-17; Müller, *Comparative Constitutional Law*, p. 1260.
111 Niesen, *German Law Journal*, par. 2.
112 Frankenberg, *Militant democracy*, p. 127.

democracy as an example of the classic anti-extremist paradigm of militant democracy, in the 1990s it shifted towards the paradigm of banning the former ruling party.[113] Niesen argues that the most advanced application of banning the former ruling party logic is found in the 2001 proceedings against the neo-Nazi *Nationaldemokratische Partei Deutschlands* (NPD). Drawing on the 'essential affinity' criterion from the 1952 SRP party case,[114] the requesting parties considered a ban on the NPD to be justified because of its *'affinities to the NSDAP as regards its political programme, its strategic and tactical mode of operation, its rhetoric and political language, and, finally, its explicit references to National Socialism (in, e.g., the apology of NS crimes)'*.[115] Furthermore, Niesen refers to the Italian post-war constitution as an example of banning the former ruling party. For example, in response to the experience with fascism, Article XII of the Italian Constitution contains a concrete provision that forbids the reorganisation of the fascist party in any form.[116] Contrary to the initial German approach, Niesen argues that the Italian Constitution is not directed against extremist or anti-system parties in general, but protects democracy against a revival of fascism by introducing a *'historically embedded and therefore sharply delineated exception which cannot be generalized'*.[117] Niesen therefore concludes that *'[w]hereas anti-extremism displays left-right symmetry, identifies an abstract enemy of its basic democratic order, the Italian version of negative republicanism relies on an anti-Fascist particularism, an historically specific identification of its opponent, and takes its understanding of democracy means from its confrontation.'*[118] Other examples of banning the former ruling party are according to Niesen the anti-Stalinism in several former USSR states, the De-Ba'athification in post-Saddam Hussein Iraq and Rwanda's ban on the former state party MRND in 1994.[119]

According to Niesen the legitimacy of banning the former ruling party results from a democratic learning process.[120] The justification for banning the former ruling party

113 Niesen, *German Law Journal*, par. 31. See also Müller, *Comparative Constitutional Law*, p. 1263.
114 BverfGE 2, 18 March 2003, 2 BvB 1/01, p. 65-70.
115 Niesen, *German Law Journal*, par. 31.
116 Article XII of the Italian Constitution states: *'It shall be forbidden to reorganise, under any form whatsoever, the dissolved Fascist party'*.
117 F. Lanchester, 'Die Institution des politischen Partei in Italien', in: D. Th. Tsatsos, D. Schefold, H.-P. Schneider (eds.), *Parteienrecht im europäischen Vergleich*, Baden-Baden: Nomos, 1990, p. 417, cited by Niesen, *German Law Journal*, par. 19.
118 Niesen, *German Law Journal*, par. 20.
119 Niesen, 'Banning the Former Ruling Party', *Constellations*, vol. 19, no. 4, 2012, p. 549-553. See on the Rwandese situation also Niesen, *Democratization*, p. 709-729.
120 Niesen, *German Law Journal*, par. 37-38.

as the outcome of a learning process has been further developed by Frankenberg.[121] This idea is based on the assumption that the legitimacy of democracy lies in the ultimate sovereignty of the people. This people, from whom all governing power emanates, is a *leaning sovereign.*[122] Sovereignty in this context refers to he who has the last word. Or, in the view of Frankenberg, *'[t]he sovereign is the one who learns while speaking the last word'.*[123] Learning in this context has a double meaning. First, this sovereign *must* learn. To take political decisions, the sovereign is constantly dependent on new information and is forced to take precautions to remain open to new information. Openness is therefore essential to the learning process and is therefore what separates democratic sovereignty from anti-democratic sovereignty. Second, the sovereign *may* learn. This is clearly a normative aspect meaning that the sovereign is able to explain the past and to draw conclusions for the future. This does not mean, however, as Frankenberg stressed, that militant democracy as the outcome of a constitutional learning process is free from criticism: *'[m]ore than anything, the teachings and practices of a "militant democracy" should be questioned as to whether and to what degree they betray the principle of general self-determination and cut off political learning experiences and experiments vital to the future orientation of democracy'.*[124] Like Niesen, Frankenberg recalls how the focus of militant measures in Germany shifted from anti-extremism to anti-national socialism '*regardless of the guise under which it reappears'* in the 1990s.[125] This approach, Frankenberg argues, is deeply embedded in a historical learning process: *'[o]n the grounds of normative considerations, democratic experimentalism is limited to the extent that new experiments in National Socialism are no longer tolerated. The democratic sovereign, one may infer, has come to the conclusion, based on the singularity of the crimes committed by the National Socialist terror regime that, should it reappear, regardless in what particular form, there is no further requirement for learning. Neo-Nazi organizations, whether they are clubs, associations, paramilitary groups,*

121 Niesen explains that he based the justification of banning the former ruling party as the outcome of a learning process by the people as a learning sovereign on a hint by Günter Frankenberg and Wolfgang Löwer, the authors of the petition on behalf of the German Parliament (Bundestag) to ban the NPD in 2001, who claimed that *'Der zwingende, rechtfertigende Grund für diese Einschränkung des demokratischen Experimentalismus ist die Singularität der nationalsozialistischen Verbrechen'*, www.aktiv-gegen-diskriminierung.info/sites/aktiv-gegen-diskriminierung.info/files/pdfs/NPD-Verbotsantrag_des_Bundestags_29.Ma%CC%88rz_2001.pdf (accessed 11 April 2016). This idea was subsequently elaborated by Frankenberg, *Militant democracy*, p. 113-118.

122 Frankenberg, p. 115. The term 'learning sovereign' was coined by Brunkhorst (H. Brunkhorst, *Solidarität unter Fremden*, Frankfurt: Fischer Taschenbuch, 1997, p. 119 and H. Brunkhorst, *Demokratie und Differenz: Vom klassischen zum modernen Begriff des Politischen,* Frankfurt: Fischer Taschenbuch, 1994, p. 199). Frankenberg, however, developed the concept of the learning sovereign in the context of militant democracy.

123 Frankenberg, *Militant democracy*, p. 115.

124 Frankenberg, p. 118.

125 Frankenberg, p. 129.

or political parties, are confronted with the presumption that with their operative program and practice they enter upon a criminal inheritance and therefore have absolutely nothing to contribute to a future-oriented democracy. That is why it is justified to restrict their access to the public sphere'.[126]

The justification of militant measures in the sense of banning the former ruling party has met with criticism. According to its adversaries, banning the former ruling party aims to deal with a discredited past by focussing on manifestations of that past in the present, whether they still pose a threat to democracy or not.[127] Whether an individual or group poses a real and present threat to democracy is not a criterion for intervention; the link to a past injustice is often sufficient. Yet, why the successor of the former ruling party must be banned once the specific danger of a relapse has passed is indeed a legitimate question.[128] Frankenberg warns that the paradigm of banning the former ruling party may authorise societies to translate any unpleasant memory into a party ban. Hence, *'[i]n order to prevent negative republicanism from getting out of control, learning experiences, to justify a precarious exclusion to the principle of democracy, must be qualified according to the weight of the injustice done'*.[129]

Furthermore, Niesen argues that banning the former ruling party may be particularly justified during periods of transition and consolidation, but cannot automatically be extended in a stable democracy.[130] It can indeed be argued that this paradigm for banning political parties can be particularly relevant in the context of transitional justice. Transitional justice in this context can be defined as a *'"shift in political orders" signalling "change in a liberalizing direction"'*.[131] Arguments related to preventing the resurrection of a past unjust regime underlie many of the justifications for constraining certain political activities during times of political transition and the corresponding instability.[132] The likelihood that democracy is being overturned may be bigger in democracies in their infancy that still struggle with the destructive heritage of their former ruling party, than in more mature democracies. For relatively young democracies the need to defend themselves against slipping back into this system of injustice may well be a legitimate interest that may justify militant measures. For stable democracies, on the other hand, it is questionable to

126 Frankenberg, p. 128.
127 Müller, *Comparative Constitutional Law*, p. 1267.
128 Niesen, *Constellations*, p. 548; Müller, *Comparative Constitutional Law*, p. 1267.
129 Frankenberg, *Militant democracy*, p. 129.
130 Niesen, *German Law Journal*, par. 33. See also Müller, *Comparative Constitutional Law*, p. 1267.
131 M. Hamilton, 'Transition, political loyalties and the order of the state', in: A. Buyse and M. Hamilton (eds.), *Transitional Jurisprudence and the European Convention on Human Rights. Justice, Politics and Rights*, Cambridge: Cambridge University Press, 2011, p. 152. Hamilton based his definition on R. Teitel, *Transitional Justice*, Oxford University Press, 2000, p. 5.
132 Hamilton, *Transitional Jurisprudence*, p. 159.

what extent the threat of sliding back into totalitarianism can still be an argument for outlawing political parties that are affiliated with the former ruling party.

More generally, the critics of this paradigm warn that it is *'subject to all the problems associated with thinking in historical analogies: its parameters might lead to distortions of political judgment in the present because in order to do something about a threat to democracy, that threat always has to be framed as somehow a replay of the past.'*[133] Finally, because threats are always framed in terms of the prevention of a replay of the past, negative republicanism may be blind to (other) current and future dangers to democracy.

7.6 Criticism of the concept of a militant democracy

It is safe to say that nowadays the concept of militant democracy occupies a prominent place in legal theory and militant measures have been incorporated in many European constitutional orders. However, ever since the concept was introduced it has been regarded with a certain degree of suspicion. After all, militant measures in the name of protecting democracy limit the free political competition that is inherent in the idea of democracy. In addition, the concept has been criticised for being too vague and imprecise, and too narrowly focussed on legal instruments.[134] Hereafter some main points of criticism will be discussed.

7.6.1 Complexities of intolerance and democracy

The concept of militant democracy is often placed in the context of what Popper referred to as the *'paradox of tolerance'* and, related to that, the *'paradox of democracy'*. The *'the paradox of tolerance'*, according to Popper, is that *'unlimited tolerance must lead to the disappearance of tolerance'*.[135] If unlimited tolerance would be applied even to the intolerant, the intolerant may eventually destroy the tolerant society. Accordingly, it would be a bad idea to show tolerance towards political actors who preach intolerance, as the latter will take advantage of this toleration to eventually abolish tolerance. This does not mean in the view of Popper that societies must always suppress intolerant expressions; as long as they can be countered by rational arguments, suppression would even be unwise. But in the end, Popper argued, societies have the right to suppress them, if necessary even by force. As Popper put it, *'we should therefore claim, in the name of tolerance, the right not to*

133 Müller, *Comparative Constitutional Law*, p. 1267.
134 Bourne, *Journal of Comparative Law*, p. 197.
135 K.R. Popper, (1945) *The Open Society and its Enemies*, London: Routledge, 2012, p. 581 (footnote 4).

tolerate the intolerant'.[136] Open societies should therefore actively fight the intolerant and *'[a]ny movement preaching intolerance'* should be placed outside of the law.[137]

Closely related to this is what Popper referred to as the *'paradox of democracy'*. This paradox refers to the possibility that through the process of democratic decision-making a majority may decide in favour of a non-democratic regime.[138] Popper's response to this paradox is that a true democratic government is one *'of which we can get rid without bloodshed – for example, by way of general elections; that is to say, the social institutions provide means by which the rulers may be dismissed by the ruled, and the social traditions ensure that these institutions will not easily be destroyed by those who are in power'*.[139] The essence of democracy, according to Popper, lies in its sustainable character. Democracy *'rests upon the decision, or upon the adoption of the proposal, to avoid and to resist tyranny'*.[140] In order to prevent its enemies from putting an end to democracy, political institutions should be designed in a way to guarantee that every decision in a democracy can be revoked in a non-violent way. In this perception, democracy, as Tyulkina put it, *'should not only be about procedure, but also about substance'*.[141]

Such a substantive perception of democracy is also found in the work of several other scholars. For example, Sajó considers precisely not taking militant measures to be undemocratic. Democracy should not be enforceable as a *'suicide pact'*, forcing governments to hand over power to anti-democratic parties who win electoral majorities.[142] He therefore considers the paradox to be illusory – or even hypocritical.[143] After all, the ultimate purpose of militant measures interfering with the democratic process is not to harm democracy, but rather to uphold it. Brems argues in this respect that militant democracy is not an exception to democracy, but on the

---

136 Popper, p. 581 (footnote 4).
137 Popper, p. 581 (footnote 4).
138 Popper, p. 581-582 (footnote 4).
139 Popper, p. 118.
140 Popper, p. 118.
141 Tyulkina, *Militant Democracy*, p. 14.
142 The term 'suicide pact' was used in relation to the defence of the democratic order by Justice Jackson in his dissenting opinion in the case US Supreme Court, *Terminiello v. Chicago*, 337 *U.S.* 1, 37 (1949) (Jackson J., dissenting). See also S. Issacharoff, 'Fragile democracies', *Harvard Law Review,* vol. 120, no. 6, 2007, p. 1466 and Fox and Nolte, *Harvard International Law Journal*, p. 8. Cliteur and Rijpkema criticise the analogy made between suicide and the abolition of democracy by a democratic majority: Cliteur and Rijpkema, *The State of Exception and Militant Democracy*, p. 257-258.
143 A. Sajó, 'Militant Democracy and Transition towards Democracy', in: A. Sajó (ed.), *Militant Democracy*, Utrecht: Eleven Legal Publishers, 2004, p. 211.

contrary, part of democracy itself.[144] Democracy, in the view of Brems, in essence comes down to giving the general interest preference over the individual, which she considers legitimate, because the democratic system is designed to guarantee the free development of the individual.[145] Hence, eventually a militant democracy is in the interest of all and temporary restrictions of rights are legitimate to serve the general interest.

Schmitt also proposed to make a distinction between procedural rules and substantive principles in a constitution.[146] He argued that *'the basic substantive principles such as the democratic character of the state were the result of a fundamental decision of the "pouvoir constituant" (the people) and therefore could not be simply swept aside by the "pouvoir constitué" (the elected representatives), even if the procedures for a constitutional amendment were followed'*.[147] In a democracy, the constitution therefore contains *'an implicit core of unalterable rules which embody its identity'*.[148] This unalterable core cannot be abolished by procedural rules: *'these fundamental principles contain a supralegal dignity, which raises them above every regulation of an organizational and constitutional type facilitating their preservation as well as over any individual regulations of a substantive law variety'*.[149] Subsequently, the possibilities for constitutional change are limited. Notwithstanding the controversial nature of his work, mainly due to his role as the principal legal defender of the Nazi regime during the Second World War,[150] the idea of constitutions containing an unalterable core received considerable support after the Second World War.[151] The most concrete example of this is the 'eternity clause' in Article 79(3) of the German Basic Law, which prohibits the amendment of certain fundamental constitutional provisions, namely the dignity of man and the

144 E. Brems, 'Democratie en zelfverdediging' ['Democracy and self-defence'], in: E. Brems (ed.), Democratie op het einde van de 20st eeuw. Onderzoek en probleemgericht denken over de democratie bij jonge onderzoekers in Vlaanderen *[Democracy at the end of the 20th century. Research into problem-oriented thinking about democracy among young researchers in Flanders]*, Brussels: Paleis der Academiën, 1994, p. 346.

145 Brems, p. 317.

146 Tyulkina, *Militant Democracy*, p. 17.

147 Fox and Nolte, *Harvard International Law Journal*, p. 18-19. See C. Schmitt, *Legality and Legitimacy*, trans. J. Seitzer (ed.), Durham/London: Duke University Press, 2004, p. 40-58, in particular, p. 57-58.

148 Fox and Nolte, *Harvard International Law Journal*, p. 19.

149 Schmitt, *Legality and Legitimacy*, p. 57.

150 J.W. Bendersky, *Carl Schmitt: Theorist for the Reich* (originally from 1983), Princeton: Princeton University Press, 2014, p. 195-218. See also Fox and Nolte, *Harvard International Law Journal*, p. 18-20.

151 Fox and Nolte, *Harvard International Law Journal*, p. 19.

basic democratic principles of the German legal order (democracy, the separation of powers, the rule of law, and the social federal state).[152]

Van den Bergh thought along similar lines by arguing that the unalterable core of democracy consists of its self-correcting capacity. In his 1936 inaugural lecture Van Den Bergh addressed the issue of democracy and anti-democratic political parties. He too feared the rise of fascism in Europe at that time and reflected on how democracies should react to this threat.[153] He focused on political parties that aim to put an end to democracy exclusively through lawful means: parties that through propaganda and participation in elections seek to obtain a parliamentary majority in order to turn the democratic state into a dictatorial state by amending the law and the constitution.[154] Many democrats, Van den Bergh argued, reject these parties, but at the same time are of the opinion that as long as these parties make use of only lawful methods, they should be treated equally to other political parties. After all, is it not the essence of democracy that all opinions are of equal value and everyone has the right to try to win the people for his opinions and achieve his ideals?[155] According to Van den Bergh, however, that is not the whole story. In his view, one of democracy's fundamental strengths is its self-correcting capacity.[156] Like any other constitutional order, democracy can result in bad decisions. More than any other system, however, it provides that decisions can be revised. Yet, there is but one decision that is not democratically revocable: the decision to abolish democracy itself. It is the only democratic decision that is not liable to democracy's self-correction and therefore distinct from other political ambitions. It is here that Van den Bergh found the justification for the prohibition of anti-democratic parties.[157]

Later the same idea has been elaborated by Issacharoff. In a 2007 article on 'fragile democracies' Issacharoff argued that democracy is not about *'[t]he ability of a temporally defined majority to select governors. The real definition of democracy must turn on the ability of majorities to be formed and re-formed over time and to remove from office those exercising governmental power'*.[158] He proposes to allow the *'renewability of consent'*, *'which requires periodic elections in which the*

---

152 Article 79(3) BL reads: *'Amendments to this Basic Law affecting the division of the Federation into Länder, their participation on principle in the legislative process, or the principles laid down in Articles 1 and 20 shall be inadmissible'*. See also Fox and Nolte, *Harvard International Law Journal*, p. 19.

153 His publication received considerably less (international) attention than the ideas of Loewenstein, and the fact that it was published in Dutch may be (partly) to blame for this.

154 G. van den Bergh, *De democratische Staat en de niet-democratische partijen [The democratic state and non-democratic parties]*, Amsterdam: N.V. De Arbeiderspers, 1936, p. 6.

155 Van den Bergh, p. 7-8.

156 Van den Bergh, p. 9. See also Cliteur and Rijpkema, *The State of Exception and Militant Democracy*, p. 243.

157 See also Cliteur and Rijpkema, *The State of Exception and Militant Democracy*, p. 244.

158 Issacharoff, *Harvard Law Review*, p. 1464.

governors place their continued office-holding in the hands of the governed' to be the key guideline for the settling of judicial disputes on democratic participation.[159] *'In order for consent to be meaningfully renewed'*, Issacharoff argues, *'the decisions of a majority-supported government bearing on the structure of the political process must be capable of being reversed by subsequent majorities'*.[160]

More generally, the idea that states should not tolerate intolerance also finds support in the liberal thoughts of Locke and Rawls. In his work on religious tolerance, for example, Locke argued, as Tyulkina put is, that *'state's tolerance cannot be extended to those who, in the name of religion, are not willing to be tolerant of others'*.[161] Even though Locke was a strong advocate of the freedom of belief, he believed that this liberty did not extend to denying the duty to tolerate others. Intolerant speech, Locke argued, *'undermine[s] the Foundations of Society'* and should not receive legal protection.[162] Rawls later continued this line of thought and concluded on the issue of toleration of the intolerant that the intolerant have no title to complain when they are denied an equal liberty. This conclusion is based on the assumption that *'[a] person's right to complain is limited to violations of principles he acknowledges himself.'*[163] Being intolerant is in the view of Rawls a ground for limiting someone's liberty. Based on the right of self-preservation, therefore, *'[j]ustice does not require that men must stand idly by while others destroy the basis of their existence'*.[164]

Other scholars, however, consider the acknowledgment of substantive values that restrict the possible outcome of democratic decision-making to be highly problematic. If the state interferes with the process of democratic decision-making by the majority, then can the outcome of this process still be considered democratic? In the event that a state restricts the rights of anti-democratic actors *'the suspicion is inevitable that democracy is failing to meet its own criteria: that political decisions must arise out of free political competition. After all, militant democracy limits such competition'*.[165] Kelsen, for example, vigorously defended the liberty of the enemies of democracy to express themselves as long as they would refrain from violence. Democracy should remain tolerant, even when it has to defend itself against anti-democratic opponents. Democracy cannot defend itself by abandoning its own democratic principles.

159 Issacharoff, p. 1465.
160 Issacharoff, p. 1465.
161 Tyulkina, *Militant Democracy*, p. 17.
162 J. Locke, (1689) *A Letter Concerning Toleration*, reprint, J. Tully (ed), trans. W. Popple, Indianapolis: Hackett, 1983, p. 49. See also S. Heyman, 'Hate Speech, Public Discourse, and the First Amendment', in: I. Hare and J. Weinstein (eds.), *Extreme Speech and Democracy*, Oxford: Oxford University Press, 2009, p. 168.
163 Rawls, *A Theory of Justice*, p. 217.
164 Rawls, p. 218.
165 Sajó, *Militant Democracy*, p. 211.

According to Kelsen, it is indeed this tolerance that distinguishes democracy from autocracy. Governmental intervention in the freedom of the enemies of democracy would be undemocratic and requires democracy to comprise on its essential characteristic: tolerance. Tolerating the enemies of democracy bears a risk, but, *'es ist das Wesen und die Ehre des Demokratie, diese Gefahr auf sich zu nehmen; und wenn Demokratie diese Gefahr nicht bestehen kann, dann ist sie nicht wert, verteidigt zu werden'*.[166] In other words, *'Man muß seiner Fahne treu bleiben, auch wenn das Schiff sinkt'*.[167] Kelsen believed free competition in 'the free market place of ideas' to be always preferable to the suppression of anti-democratic expressions.[168] From this perspective, the harm to democracy stemming from the prohibition of the expression of anti-democratic views is greater than any benefits of a self-defending democracy. The suppression of political speech can in that case be ineffective or even counterproductive, Issacharoff argues.[169] In addition, Issacharoff points to the rather fatalistic implications of this vision, namely that *'ultimately not much can protect the people from their doom if that is their charted course'*.[170]

7.6.2 The risk of abusing militant measures

These paradoxes and controversies surrounding the idea of a militant democracy show that militant measures also have a downside. As mentioned before, the concept of militant democracy inevitably gives rise to the suspicion that democracy is failing to meet its own criteria.[171] Both the proponents and critics of militant democracy underline that too strong an emphasis on militant measures may result in intolerance and damage the democratic society. As put by Harvey, *'an excessively narrow definition of the scope [of] legal political action to the exclusion of a number of different anti-democratic political parties endangers political pluralism and, by virtue of its constitutional status, this definition creates a priori a kind of oligarchy instead of a modern pluralist democracy'*.[172] Issacharoff takes this concern even further and argues that *'[a]s an empirical matter, it is entirely possible that democracy faces greater dangers from the promiscuous use of police powers than from domestic enemies. With respect to more stable democracies, I am willing to concede that this*

166 H. Kelsen, *Was ist Gerechtigkeit?*, 2nd ed., Vienna: Franz Deuticke, 1975, p. 42. See also Leggewie and Meier, *Republikschutz*, p. 262; B. Neuberger, 'Israel', in: Thiel, *The 'Militant Democracy' Principle in Modern Democracies*, p. 185-186.

167 H. Kelsen, (1932) *Verteidigung der Demokratie. Abhandlungen zur Demokratietheorie*, reprint, Tübingen: Mohr Siebeck, 2006, p. 237.

168 Neuberger, *The 'Militant Democracy' Principle in Modern Democracies*, p. 186. Leggewie and Meier share Kelsen's point of view: *Republikschutz. Maßstäbe für die Verteidigung der Demokratie,* p. 20.

169 Issacharoff, *Harvard Law Review,* p. 1412.

170 Issacharoff, p. 1412.

171 Sajó, *Militant Democracy,* p. 211.

172 Harvey, *European Law Review*, p. 409.

is likely the case and that the main task of legal oversight may very well be the preservation of civil liberties'.[173] Such intolerance is therefore, according to Rawls, only permitted under very limited conditions. The freedom of the intolerant, Rawls argued, *'should be restricted only when the tolerant sincerely and with reason believe that their own security and that of the institutions of liberty are in danger'*.[174]

Macklem argued that this risk presents itself most vividly in the context of broad definitions in legal (constitutional) provisions and open-ended delegations of governmental authority.[175] Militant democracy may *'"cast its net too widely" and capture far more than is needed to sustain democracy'*.[176] Militant democracy always involves the suspicion that *'the label anti-democratic is used too often as a pretext for banning those whose political activism amounts to no more than a challenge to the dominant national ideology'*.[177] An additional complication concerns knowing at what time militant measures are appropriate. How can we define the point at which democracy is sincerely endangered and militant democracy needs to be invoked to save it?[178] Militant democracy, as Noorloos rightly points out, inherently *'involves the risk of overreaction: is there a real risk to democracy or fundamental rights, or do states limit the rights of individuals or groups because they consider their views to be immoral or offensive?'*.[179] As Harvey observed, the criticism is in this regard not so much directed against the concept of militant democracy itself, but rather at its abusive application in practice. In that regard some fear that militant measures could easily be instrumentalised against legitimate opposition to the government.[180] As it is often the government which decides whether to apply militant measures to what it qualifies as anti-democratic actors, the risk is that this power may be abused to qualify members of the opposition as anti-democratic in order to exclude them from the democratic arena. In that way militant measures intended to defend democracy may also serve abusive states in suppressing their citizens.

States should therefore be wary of too easily identifying certain movements as enemies of democracy. Militant democracy always involves the suspicion that *'the label anti-democratic is used too often as a pretext for banning those whose political*

173 Issacharoff, *Harvard Law Review*, p. 1467.
174 Rawls, *A Theory of Justice*, p. 220. See also Tyulkina, *Militant Democracy*, p. 18.
175 Macklem, *International Journal of Constitutional Law*, p. 494.
176 Tyulkina, *Militant Democracy*, p. 29.
177 Harvey, *European Law Review*, p. 409.
178 Tyulkina, *Militant Democracy*, p. 30.
179 M. van Noorloos, *Hate Speech Revisited. A comparative and historical perspective on hate speech law in the Netherlands and England and Wales*, Antwerp: Intersentia, 2011, p. 16-17. See also C. Mouffe, 'The limits of liberal pluralism: towards an agonistic multipolar world order', in: Sajó, *Militant Democracy*, p. 76.
180 Müller, *Comparative Constitutional Law*, p. 1260; Macklem, *International Journal of Constitutional Law*, p. 492.

activism amounts to no more than a challenge to the dominant national ideology'.[181] Legal doctrine seems to agree that militant measures must therefore always be submitted to close legal scrutiny in order to safeguard militant democracy against such abuse. So far, however, no strong and consistent method has been developed to detect and prevent abusive militant practices.[182] Müller, however, claims that it is important that decisions about militant state action are removed from everyday decision-making by the executive and the legislature. He refers in this respect to the German system, where the monopoly of banning political parties lies with the German Federal Constitutional Court, *'an institution relatively isolated from political pressures'*, as the most justifiable approach.[183] In addition, Macklem is of the view that the international community has a significant role to play in this. Especially international human rights law may help to offer clarity regarding the justifiability of government claims based on militant democracy. Especially the ECHR and the European Court of Human Rights may provide *'some guidance on the extent to which rights and freedoms enshrined in the convention constrain a state's capacity to combat perceived threats to its democratic existence'*.[184]

7.6.3 Stretching the focus of militant democracy?

At the same time, several scholars have observed a shift in the focus of militant democracy.[185] In the past, militant measures were primarily aimed at anti-democratic political parties. Especially the classic threats to European democracies, the remains of fascism and Nazism, were targeted by militant democracy. The evolution of the concept of militant democracy shows, however, that the perceived threats that democracy has to be guarded against vary over time. Even though most states in Western Europe nowadays have stable democracies, he warns that we should not be misled because *'every generation got its own disease'*.[186] *'The discourse on the "militant democracy"'*, Thiel therefore argues, *'has by no means become obsolete with the political achievements of the last two decades'*.[187] In fact, Macklem has argued that questions relating to the nature and scope of militant democracy have acquired greater political and legal salience in recent years.[188] Yet, in the contemporary debate on the protection of democracy a trend can be identified according to which measures taken against what can be considered new anti-democratic threats are increasingly justified on the grounds of arguments that traditionally belong to the concept of

181 Harvey, *European Law Review*, p. 409.
182 Tyulkina, *Militant Democracy*, p. 30.
183 Müller, *Comparative Constitutional Law*, p. 1266.
184 Macklem, *International Journal of Constitutional Law*, p. 494.
185 Bourne, *Journal of Comparative Law*, p. 197.
186 Thiel, *The Militant Democracy Principle in Modern Democracies*, p. 379.
187 Thiel, p. 379.
188 Macklem, *Constellations*, p. 576.

militant democracy. Müller has argued in that respect that *'[w]ith the end of the cold war, definitions of the supposed enemies of democracy have become much more diffuse and difficult to establish'*.[189] From a narrow focus on fascist and communist actors, the concept has developed into a much wider range of measures against all kinds of extremist threats.[190] The definition of what is to be defended appears to have been broadened accordingly, from merely referring to the process of democratic decision-making to more substantive democratic values.

First, challenges to the principle of secularism seem to be increasingly placed within the framework of militant democracy.[191] Legal practice shows that arguments of militant democracy have been invoked more frequently in this field in recent years. In this perspective, as Macklem put it, *'secularism and liberalism go hand in hand'* and secularism therefore places limits on the role of religion in a democratic society.[192] In this context, it has been argued that pre-emptive action was taken against the exercise of political rights to dismantle secularism as one of the core features of a liberal democracy. Especially in countries with a strict separation of Church and state, such as France and Turkey, some religious practices have been considered as threats to democracy and preemptive measures have been taken against them.[193] At the same time, as Müller observes, the area of militant secularism is *'a new and complex terrain for militant democracy'*.[194] The question of to what extent the separation between state and Church is a prerequisite for democracy is still under discussion. It indeed seems to be an area in which militant democracy is progressively required to speak out, but also to clearly demarcate the boundaries of a legitimate application of militant measures to protect the principle of secularism.[195]

Second, recently (Islamic) terrorism has been increasingly studied from the perspective of militant democracy.[196] The extent to which the concept of militant democracy is relevant to the issue of terrorism, however, is highly debated.[197] It is true that the

189 Müller, *The Oxford Handbook of Comparative Constitutional Law*, p. 1256.
190 Bourne, *Journal of Comparative Law*, p. 197.
191 Müller, *The Oxford Handbook of Comparative Constitutional Law,* p. 1256; Sajó, *Cardozo Law Review*, p. 2264-2265; Macklem, *Constellations*, p. 579; Macklem, *International Journal of Constitutional Law*, p. 491; Tyulkina, *Militant Democracy*, p. 167-205.
192 Macklem, *Constellations*, p. 579.
193 Müller, *The Oxford Handbook of Comparative Constitutional Law*, p. 1256.
194 Müller, p. 1256.
195 Müller, p. 1265; Tyulkina, *Militant Democracy*, p. 179-184.
196 E.g. K. Roach, 'Anti-Terrorism and Militant Democracy: Some Western and Eastern Responses', in: Sajó, *Militant democracy*, p. 171-207; A. Ellian and G. Molier, 'Introduction: the State of Exception and Militant Democracy in a Time of Terror', in: Ellian and Molier, *The State of Exception and Militant Democracy*, p. 1-4; Macklem, *International Journal of Constitutional Law*, p. 488; Klamt, *Explorations in Legal Cultures*, p. 153.
197 Buis, *The Militant Democracy Principle in Modern Democracies*, p. 97.

two issues share certain characteristics, as terrorists – like anti-democratic actors – generally aim to overthrow the democratic society. And terrorism also raises questions regarding the extent to which democracies can drastically restrict the fundamental rights of potential terrorists in order to protect society. Both 'the war on terrorism' and militant democracy belong to the overarching issue of internal security, as observed by Thiel.[198] But even though the problems associated with combating terrorism are not completely alien to the notion of militant democracy, the challenges they raise are considerably different.[199] Even though terrorism without any doubt presents serious problems for democracy, the issue of anti-democratic actors poses a particular problem, as they operate within its framework as they pursue their political aims by following the road of democracy. They therefore confront democracies with a major dilemma: to suppress them would infringe upon democracy's bedrock principles, but to allow them endangers the survival of the democratic system itself.[200] That is why Issacharoff claims that *'[u]ltimately the greatest challenge for a democracy, at least conceptually, comes from the threat of being assaulted not from without but from within'*.[201] Terrorists, on the other hand, do not compete for power within democracy but try to subvert democracy through acts of violence from outside.[202] Terrorism, even though in close connection with the issue, is therefore generally not considered to be an object of militant democracy.[203] As a result, several scholars have felt the need to coin new terms for similar reactions to modern day movements that threaten

198 Thiel, *The Militant Democracy Principle in Modern Democracies*, p. 308.

199 Müller, *The Oxford Handbook of Comparative Constitutional Law*, p. 1255; Fox and Nolte, *Harvard International Law Journal*, p. 51.

200 Fox and Nolte, *Harvard International Law Journal*, p. 8 and 14.

201 Issacharoff, *Harvard Law Review*, p. 1442.

202 Here we must admit, though, that the distinction between anti-democratic actors operating within democracy and terrorists is not always that clear-cut. As Müller points out, terrorists could also be said to abuse civil rights and liberties and the rule of law in order to subvert democracy. Moreover, some terrorist organisations have electoral wings – *'peaceful extremism'*, in the words of Capoccia (see G. Capoccia, *Defending Democracy: Reactions to Extremism in Interwar Europe*, Baltimore: Johns Hopkins University Press, 2005, p. 232-233) – that somewhat blurs the borders between the two. Furthermore, the totalitarian movements that were the original targets of militant democracy besides their political participation also used terrorist intimidation: Sajó, *Cardozo Law Review*, p. 2265.

203 Müller, *The Oxford Handbook of Comparative Constitutional Law*, p. 1255; J. Müller, 'A "Practical Dilemma Which Philosophy Alone Cannot Resolve?" Rethinking Militant Democracy: An Introduction', *Constellations*, vol. 19, no. 4, 2012, p. 538; Thiel, *The Militant Democracy Principle in Modern Democracies*, p. 380. See also Sajó, who analyses different constitutional mechanisms of state self-defence, thereby distinguishing between the counter-terror-state (mechanisms tailored to terrorism only) and militant democracy (which is more broadly applicable): Sajó, *Cardozo Law Review*, p. 2265.

democracy.[204] Illustrative in this regard is Sajó, who refers to the preventive state as a constitutional paradigm that emerges from clusters of counter-terror techniques.[205]

7.6.3.1 Militant democracy as civic society

Niesen has referred to this new approach – at least in the German debate – as *civic society*.[206] Because of their fixation with fascism, neo-Nazism, and Communism, the old paradigms of militant democracy may not be able capture contemporary patterns of anti-democratic threats.[207] Hence, this new paradigm may provide a framework according to which contemporary threats may be addressed. Although this paradigm is still in a preliminary stage, Niesen makes an attempt to describe its general outlines.[208] This paradigm broadens the focus *'from the one-directional opposition characteristic of negative republicanism to more plural and amorphous opponents, yet without falling back into anti-extremism'*.[209] This new approach is based on a particularly moral perception of democracy. Niesen claims that in the traditional perception of militant democracy, restrictions on civil and political rights are generally considered a contradiction in terms. According to the paradigm of banning the former ruling party, however, such restrictions are interpreted as a narrow exception to the rule. In this new paradigm of civic society, however, Niesen argues, restrictions are *'neither contradictions nor exceptions, but straightforward implications of democracy'*.[210] Where classic militant democracy denies that democracy entails the right to suicide, and banning the former ruling party implies an obligation for democracy to maintain a discredited anti-democratic tradition, civic society, according to Niesen, claims that *'democratic self-determination entails a positive self-referential obligation for its reproduction'*.[211] The aim of restrictions on civil and political rights in the paradigm of civic society is not the protection of democracy itself, but that of democracy as a protector of minorities and future generations.[212] They aim to protect the 'minima

---

204 Harvey, *European Law Review*, p. 410.

205 Sajó, *Cardozo Law Review*, p. 2255.

206 Niesen has again drawn inspiration for this new paradigm from the petition on behalf of the German Parliament (Bundestag) to ban the NPD in 2001 written by Frankenberg and Löwer, who argued that *'Das grundgesetzliche Demokratieprinzip gebietet also, nicht nur einer Bürgerschaft zu jeder Zeit ein Recht auf politische Selbstbestimmung und Selbstkorrektur einzuräumen, sondern impliziert zugleich die Verpflichtung, die Integrität des demokratischen Prinzips zum Schutz der Rechte* überstimmter *Minderheiten zu wahren'*, www.aktiv-gegen-diskriminierung.info/sites/aktiv-gegen-diskriminierung.info/files/pdfs/NPD-Verbotsantrag_des_Bundestags_29.Ma%CC%88rz_2001.pdf (accessed 11 April 2016). Niesen, *German Law Journal*, par. 42.

207 See also Harvey, *European Law Review*, p. 410.

208 Niesen, par. 41.

209 Niesen, par. 41.

210 Niesen, par. 42.

211 Niesen, par. 42.

212 Niesen, par. 43.

moralia et legalia *of a democracy, without demanding that the democratic system as a whole be in danger. What matters is not a danger to the system, but a threat or violation of people in a minority situation'*, Frankenberg explains.[213] This new paradigm, Niesen argues, is based on theories of civil society. These civil society theories hold that contemporary democracy is *'centered in civic processes'*[214] and *'not in processes of political coordination through electoral campaigns, party competition, and governmental decision making'*.[215] Yet, *[d]emocracy depends not so much on the equal chance of winning political power, not even on the equal chance of exercising political liberty. It 'depends for its success on the recognition of the other as equal, on reciprocity and the capacity for discursivity'*, Niesen argues.[216] In this paradigm, citizens are required to interact on a *'level of minimal morality'*, and organized racist and anti-Semite propaganda counts as the exemplary violation of this condition.[217] These moral requirements of equal recognition serve as a condition for democratic participation.[218] Frankenberg therefore concludes that this paradigm is based on respect for human rights, whereby reciprocal recognition is key: *'[w]hoever aims to create "areas of fear" and "nationally liberated zones" (liberated from certain minorities), or whoever publicly and systematically persecutes or terrorizes those who think, live or simply look differently, violates the democratic life-form and drastically denies the civil acceptance one owes in a democracy even to opponents'*.[219] Because of its focus on the phenomena of racial discrimination and hatred, this paradigm differs from anti-extremism that focuses on political actors that reject democratic values and institutions. It also differs from the paradigm of banning the former ruling party, as it does not require new phenomena to be interpreted in the framework of historical events. The advantage of the paradigm of civic society is even though it is informed, but not determined by the anti-National Socialist stance of banning the former ruling party, as it is particularly sensitive to problems of racism and anti-Semitism, it also allows for societies that do not share the Nazi experience to adopt anti-neo-Nazi measures on civic society premises.[220]

---

213 Frankenberg, *Militant democracy*, p. 130-131.
214 U.K. Preuß, 'Die empfindsame Demokratie', in: C. Leggewie and H. Meier (eds.), *Verbot der NPD oder mit Rechtsradikalen leben*?, Frankfurt am Main: Suhrkamp, 2002, p. 104-119, cited in Niesen, *German Law Journal*, par. 43.
215 Niesen, *German Law Journal*, par. 43.
216 Preuß, *Verbot der NPD oder mit Rechtsradikalen leben?*, p. 104-119, cited in Niesen, *German Law Journal*, par. 43.
217 Preuß, p. 126f. cited in Niesen, par. 43 and 44.
218 Niesen, *German Law Journal*, par. 45.
219 Frankenberg, *Militant democracy*, p. 130-131.
220 Niesen, *German Law Journal*, par. 44.

7.6.3.2 Decline of democracy and human rights protection?

Bourne has argued that with broadening the scope of the concept of militant democracy, it has in essence become *'the victim of "concept stretching"'*.[221] Niesen warns against the problems this paradigm may cause, as it significantly broadens the category of dysfunctional political activities and lowers the threshold of restrictions on these activities: *'[t]he slippery slope from ideological expression to offence is no longer blocked, either by the need for an empirical prognosis of danger, or by the particularist self-restraint of negative republicanism'*.[222] Even though Niesen acknowledges that the civic society paradigm may contribute to a common moral response to historical national catastrophes in an international or even supranational political context, something that banning the former ruling party was not able to do, he believes that *'with its position on expressive and participatory liberties still culpably underdeveloped, the price to be paid for progressing to the new paradigm seems unacceptably high'*.[223] Niesen is not the only one who has criticised the expansion of the gradual extension of the concept of militant democracy beyond its traditional fields of application.[224] Other scholars also fear that the new approach to militant democracy may result in a loss of human rights protection. In the words of Bourne, *'an overzealous application of the instruments of militant democracy, which potentially affect a wide range of political and civil rights, may diminish the quality of democracy in practice'*.[225]

7.7 Conclusions

This chapter focussed on the concept of militant democracy from a theoretical perspective. The concept of militant democracy was introduced by Loewenstein in 1937 in reaction to the advance of Nazism and fascism on the European continent. A militant democracy is in this chapter defined as *'a democratic regime which is willing to adopt pre-emptive, prima facie illiberal measures to prevent those aiming at subverting democracy with democratic means from destroying the democratic regime'*.[226] This chapter has shown that there is no generally agreed upon theory on militant democracy. On the contrary, the concept seems to have its roots in different legal and normative traditions. What all of the proponents of militant democracy have in common, though, is that they believe that democracy should not be *'a suicide*

---

221 Bourne, *Journal of Comparative Law*, p. 197.
222 Niesen, par. 42-43.
223 Niesen, par. 44.
224 Tyulkina, *Militant Democracy*, p. 169.
225 Bourne, *Journal of Comparative Law*, p. 196-197.
226 Müller, *The Oxford Handbook of Comparative Constitutional Law*, p. 1253.

pact'[227] by allowing its enemies to take advantage of the fundamental rights and the open democratic procedures it implies.

After the Second World War the militant democracy rationale seriously became part of constitutional thinking. In the decades after 1945 militant measures have systematically been incorporated in many European constitutional orders. An analysis of the way in which the issue of democratic self-defence is addressed in different countries, however, shows a great diversity in more or less militant arrangements.[228] The implementation of the concept developed in its own way in the context of different legal orders. Some states have explicitly put in place a structure of militant measures in order to protect their democratic orders from being overthrown from within (Germany[229]), while in other states legal provisions that aim to defend the democratic structure exist without an explicit acknowledgment of the concept of militant democracy as an overarching constitutional principle (for example, the UK[230] or the Netherlands[231]). Moreover, the perceived threat that democracy has to be guarded against varies from state to state and may change over time. In sum, the application of militant democracy is therefore highly context-dependent.

At the same time, the concept of militant democracy has been criticised since the beginning. Based on opposing normative perceptions critics have argued that militant measures taken in the name of protecting democracy, such as party bans and restrictions on political speech, are *prima facie* undemocratic in the sense that they restrict the political participation of its enemies. Moreover, militant measures intended to defend democracy may be used by states to suppress their citizens. So whereas an open democracy may be structurally weak, an excessively militant democracy may eventually be no longer democratic, some scholars have warned.[232] Frankenberg therefore argues that the assumptions and practices of militant democracy should be continuously scrutinised.[233] This certainly also applies to the expansion of the concept of militant democracy beyond its traditional field of application (totalitarian doctrines, in particular fascism and Nazism) to 'new threats' including terrorism and challenges to more substantive principles such as the principle of secularism. With

227 Issacharoff, *Harvard Law Review*, p. 1466; Fox and Nolte, *Harvard International Law Journal*, p. 8.

228 Thiel, p. 382.

229 Thiel, p. 109-145.

230 R. Mullender, 'United Kingdom', in: Thiel, *The Militant Democracy Principle in Modern Democracies*, p. 311-356.

231 See about the legal measures that may be qualified as militant in the Netherlands: W. van der Woude, *Democratische waarborgen [Democratic safeguards]*, Alphen aan den Rijn: Kluwer, 2009. See also P.E. de Morree, 'De doorwerking van artikel 17 EVRM in de Nederlandse rechtsorde', in: H.R.B.M. Kummeling et al. (eds.), *De Samengestelde Besselink. Bruggen bouwen tussen nationaal, Europees en internationaal recht, recht [The Composed Besselink. Building bridges between national, European and international law]*, Nijmegen: Wolf Legal Publishers, 2012, p. 147-156.

232 Pfersmann, *Militant democracy*, p. 48.

233 Frankenberg, *Militant democracy*, p. 118.

respect to the application of militant measures, a constant balance has to be sought between the interest of preserving democracy and the protection of individual rights and freedoms.

In this chapter it has been briefly indicated that in reaction to the fall of the Weimar Republic and the horrors of the Second World War, Germany *'developed the most explicit – and the most far-reaching – theory of militant democracy'*.[234] The post-war German constitution, the Basic Law, is imbued with militant measures that aim to prevent the rise of another anti-democratic regime. One of these militant measures is the prohibition of abuse of rights in Article 18 Basic Law. The next chapter is therefore dedicated to the interpretation of the concept of militant democracy and the prohibition of abuse of rights in the German context.

234 Müller, *The Oxford Handbook of Comparative Constitutional Law*, p. 1260.

Chapter 8
The German 'Wehrhafte Demokratie'

8.1 Introduction

This is the second chapter out of three chapters that deal with the concept of abuse of rights. The previous chapter discussed the concept of militant democracy from a general, theoretical perspective. It showed that practically all democracies have adopted certain measures to defend themselves against being overthrown by anti-democratic actors. Yet, the extent to which democracies have adopted and apply militant measures in order to defend themselves varies strongly from state to state.[1] This chapter aims to provide a concrete example of the interpretation and implementation of the concept of militant democracy: Germany. In the next chapter we will subsequently explore how the concept of militant democracy takes shape in the context of the ECHR.

The German legal order is generally regarded as an archetypal militant democracy. It was the first European legal order to openly recognise the necessity of designing a democracy capable of defending itself against anti-democratic actors who use the democratic process in order to subvert it.[2] The fact that the Nazis could rely on lawful means in their quest for political power made post-war Germany particularly conscious of the need to protect its re-established democracy against anti-democratic forces.[3] The German Basic Law (BL), which entered into force some years after the end of the Second World War, is clearly modelled upon the idea of a self-defensive democracy, in German referred to as the *wehrhafte Demokratie* or *streitbare Demokratie*.[4] In fact, Germany is generally considered to have developed *'the most explicit – and the most far-reaching – theory of militant democracy'*.[5] The abuse clause in Article 18 BL, the

1 M. Thiel (ed.), *The Militant Democracy Principle in Modern Democracies*, Farnham/Burlington: Ashgate Publishing Company, 2009, p. 2 and 384. See also J. Müller, 'Militant Democracy', in: M. Rosenfeld and A. Sajó (eds.), *Comparative Constitutional Law*, Oxford: Oxford University Press, 2012, p. 1266.

2 P. Harvey, 'Militant Democracy and the European Convention on Human Rights', *European Law Review*, vol. 29, no. 3, 2004, p. 408.

3 E.M. Schnelle, *Freiheitsmißbrauch und Grundrechtsverwirkung. Versuch einer Neubestimmung von Artikel 18 GG*, Berlin: Duncker & Humblot, 2014, p. 13.

4 M. Thiel (ed.), *Wehrhafte Demokratie. Beitrage über die Regelungen zum Schutze der freiheitlichen demokratischen Grundordnung*, Tübingen: Mohr Siebeck, 2003, p. 9. Thiel also refers to the term 'abwehrbereite' Demokratie.

5 Müller, *The Oxford Handbook of Comparative Constitutional Law*, p. 1260.

German equivalent of Article 17 ECHR, is part of the militant scheme of the BL. This provision reads:

'Whoever abuses the freedom of expression, in particular the freedom of the press (paragraph (1) of Article 5), the freedom of teaching (paragraph (3) of Article 5), the freedom of assembly (Article 8), the freedom of association (Article 9), the privacy of correspondence, posts and telecommunications (Article 10), the rights of property (Article 14), or the right of asylum (Article 16a) in order to combat the free democratic basic order shall forfeit these basic rights. This forfeiture and its extent shall be declared by the Federal Constitutional Court'.[6]

Article 18 BL is unique, as it provides a court procedure in which the Federal Constitutional Court (*Bundesverfassungsgericht*) can decide to forfeit the constitutional rights of an individual who has abused these rights. Such a provision is not found in other European constitutions.[7] The German constitutional order therefore provides a particularly interesting example to exemplify the concept of militant democracy. This chapter explores the interpretation of the concept of militant democracy and the abuse clause in the context of the German constitutional order.

In what follows, first the interpretation of the *wehrhafte Demokratie* in the German context will be discussed. In this context the historical background of the Basic Law has a prominent place, as it is essential for understanding its militant character. This chapter then provides an overview of the militant structure of the Basic Law. Next, attention will also be paid to the interpretation of the notion of militant democracy by the Federal Constitutional Court. Subsequently, this chapter focuses on the abuse clause in Article 18 BL. After the introduction of Article 18 BL as a militant provision, this chapter moves on to describe the forfeiture procedure prescribed in Article 18 BL and the key elements of the provision, followed by an analysis of the few cases based on Article 18 BL that have been considered by the Federal Constitutional Court. In the concluding remarks we will reflect on the German *wehrhafte Demokratie* and the role of Article 18 BL. This will be the prelude to the next chapter where we will explore the militant nature of the European Convention on Human Rights.

---

6 www.bundestag.de/blob/284870/ce0d03414872b427e57fccb703634dcd/basic_law-data.pdf (accessed 11 April 2016).

7 The Greek Constitution also contains an abuse clause in Article 25(3), which states that *'[t]he abusive exercise of rights is not permitted'*, www.hellenicparliament.gr/UserFiles/f3c70a23-7696-49db-9148-f24dce6a27c8/001-156%20aggliko.pdf (accessed 11 April 2016). Yet, contrary to the German abuse clause it does not provide for the forfeiture of constitutional rights. See P. Dagtoglou, 'Der Missbrauch von Grundrechten in der griechischen Theorie und Praxis', in: J. Iliopoulous-Strangas (ed.), *Der Mißbrauch von Grundrechten in der Demokratie*, Baden-Baden: Nomos Verlagsgesellschaft, 1989, p. 103-117.

8.2 The role of Article 17 ECHR in the German legal order

Before we move on to a study of the militant instruments in the Basic Law, however, it is worth shedding some light on the role of Article 17 ECHR in the German legal order. The effect of the ECHR in German constitutional law is founded on a dualist model of the relationship between international and domestic law. This means that treaties, in particular those that seek to create rights or obligations for individuals, must, according to Article 59(2) BL, be approved by parliamentary statute before they become binding within the domestic legal order.[8] Accordingly, constitutional complaints cannot be directly based on an alleged violation of the ECHR. Yet, this does not mean that the ECHR is not relevant in German constitutional law. As key elements of the German constitutional order, the ECHR and the Strasbourg case-law are generally taken into account in interpreting the Basic Law.[9] Complaints with respect to human rights violations are based on the fundamental rights guaranteed by the German Basic Law, but since these largely run parallel to the guarantees provided by the ECHR they are generally interpreted in harmony with it.[10] With regard to the relation between Article 18 BL and Article 17 ECHR it has been argued that both provisions can simply exist alongside each other without any difficulties, as States Parties are granted significant room for interpretation in this regard.[11] Nonetheless, this study has not come across any cases in which Article 17 ECHR has played a role in the interpretation of Article 18 BL. This may be due to the fact that, as we will see in this chapter, the two abuse clauses function in a different way within the militant framework of the two systems.

8.3 Militant democracy in Germany: *Die Wehrhafte Demokratie*

As mentioned in the previous chapter, the concept of militant democracy basically originated in reaction to the rise of power by the Nazis in Germany. The term

---

8 See BVerfGE 74, 358 (1987), par. 370; BVerfGE 82, 106 (1990), par. 114; *Görgülü* case, BVerfGE 111, 307 (2004), par. 316; *Caroline von Hannover* case, BVerfGE 120, 180 (2008), par. 200. See also the Act of Approval of the ECHR (*Gesetz über die Konvention zum Schutze der Menschenrechte und Grundfreiheiten*) of 7 August 1952, *Bundesgesetzblatt (BGBl)* II, no. 14, 22 August 1952, p. 685. C. Tomuschat, 'The Effects of the Judgments of the European Court of Human Rights According to the German Constitutional Court', *German Law Journal*, vol. 11, no 5, 2010, p. 518, www.germanlawjournal.com/s/GLJ_Vol_11_No_05_Tomuschat.pdf (accessed 11 April 2016). Tomuschat points out that because of the particular importance of human rights some German scholars have argued that international human rights treaties, in particular the ECHR, should enjoy constitutional authority. However, he stresses, so far the Federal Constitutional Court has never accepted this line of argument.

9 BVerfGE 74, 358 (1987), par. 370. Tomuschat, *German Law Journal*, p. 519.

10 BVerfGE 74, 358 (1987), par. 370; BVerfGE 111, 307 (2004), par. 317.

11 *Maunz/Dürig, Grundgesetz-Kommentar*, suppl. 75, Art. 18, Rn. 148, available from Beck online (accessed 11 April 2016).

was coined by the German legal scholar Loewenstein who feared that European democracies would be overrun if they would remain passive and did not become militant.[12] After the Second World War the notion of militant democracy strongly influenced the drafting of the new German constitution, with the result that the German legal order contains the most explicit and far-reaching implementation of this notion.[13]

8.3.1 The drafting of a militant constitution

The Second World War had practically destroyed the German constitutional order. Consequently, after the defeat of the Third Reich a completely new constitution was created under the auspices of the Western Allied Powers.[14] This process started with a Constitutional Convention at Herrenchiemsee (Bavaria) in 1948. During this convention, German constitutional experts discussed the basis and potential problematic aspects of the new constitution. The drafting of a new constitution was not an easy task, as the War had caused a radical turn in the constitutional thinking in Germany. The drafters of the post-war Basis Law accused the Weimar Constitution that governed Germany between 1919 and 1933 of having given too much room to the enemies of democracy.[15] In the words of Kommers and Miller, *'democracy itself, enshrined and preserved in many of the rights that Hitler hastily abolished after the Reichstag fire, was just as much an accomplice to Hitler's rise to power as it was his victim'*.[16] According to the general perception, the Weimar Constitution had been defenceless against the attack by the NSDAP, which had contributed substantially to the abolition of democracy and the establishment of a brutal totalitarian regime. One of the primary weaknesses generally attributed to the Constitution of the Weimar Republic was its value neutrality (*Wertneutralität*).[17] The Weimar Constitution was based on the liberal principle that all political forces should be given a clear field. Despite their clearly totalitarian ambitions, therefore, Hitler and his Nazi movement were in the early 1930s considered as a group competing for political power just like any other.[18] Although the rise of power to Hitler and the NSDAP cannot be

12 K. Loewenstein, 'Militant Democracy and Fundamental Rights I', *The American Political Science Review*, vol. 31, no. 3, 1937.

13 Müller, *The Oxford Handbook of Comparative Constitutional Law*, p. 1258-1260.

14 The Basic Law originally only applied in West Germany, but after the reunification in 1990 became the constitution for the entire Federal Republic of Germany.

15 M. Zuleeg, 'Mißbrauch von Grundrechten vor dem Hintergrund demokratischer Strukturen in Europa', in: Iliopoulous-Strangas, *Der Mißbrauch von Grundrechten in der Demokratie*, p. 41.

16 D.P. Kommers and R.A. Miller, *The Constitutional Jurisprudence of the Federal Republic of Germany*, 3rd ed., Durham/London: Duke University Press, 2012, p. 285.

17 W. Schmitt Glaeser, *Mißbrauch und Verwirkung von Grundrechten im politischen Meinungskampf*, Bad Homburg/Berlin/Zürich: Verlag Gehlen, 1968, p. 25. See also *Maunz/Dürig, Grundgesetz-Kommentar*, suppl. 75, Art. 18, Rn. 7.

18 Schmitt Glaeser, *Mißbrauch und Verwirkung von Grundrechten im politischen Meinungskampf*, p. 29.

exclusively attributed to the failing Constitution of the Weimar Republic,[19] it is generally considered that the exceptionally tolerant nature of the Weimar Constitution significantly contributed to the defeat of democracy.[20] Moreover, in those years after the War, West Germany, like other democracies in Europe, feared the spread of communism. The re-established West-German democracy, therefore, also had to be protected against this increasing danger from the East. The 1949 Basic Law is therefore considered to be a reaction to both the fall of the Weimar Republic and the establishment of the Third Reich and the aggressive communist dictatorships that were assuming power in Eastern Europe.[21]

Based on this strongly anti-totalitarian mind-set, the drafters aimed to create a militant democracy, in German referred to as *wehrhafte Demokratie*, that would resist being overthrown by totalitarianism and this dominated the drafting process.[22] The intended draft constitution would not provide its enemies with the weapons to destroy it: *'Die neue deutsche Demokratie will ihren Feinden nicht mehr die Waffen liefern, die sie brauchen, um sie zu stürzen'*.[23] The conclusion at the Constitutional Convention was therefore that the post-war constitution would be radically different from that of the Weimar Republic. To that end, the drafters gave up on the old positivist idea that law and morality (or justice) are separate domains,[24] and created a constitution that was clearly based on normative values. Hence, Reif describes the Basic Law as the manifestation of a transition from a relativist, non-normative democracy to a normative democracy.[25]

While they agreed that fundamental rights should have a central place in the new constitution, the drafters also realised the risks involved in the exercise of certain fundamental rights. The past had shown that not only governments were potential

19 Thiel, for example, rejects the thesis that the Weimar Republic was completely defensive. He argues that *'the legal system of the Weimar Republic contained a bundle of statutory provisions protecting the state and the constitutional system'*. It was, however, not as *'fortified'* as the Basic Law's democratic system: M. Thiel, 'Germany', in: M. Thiel (ed.), *The Militant Democracy Principle in Modern Democracies*, Farnham/Burlington: Ashgate Publishing Company, 2009, p. 128.

20 Schmitt Glaeser, *Mißbrauch und Verwirkung von Grundrechten im politischen Meinungskampf*, p. 27. See for a different evaluation R.A. Kahn, 'Cross-Burning, Holocaust Denial, and the Development of Hate Speech Law in the United States and Germany', *University of Detroit Mercy Law Review*, vol. 83, no. 3, 2006, p. 183-184.

21 *Maunz/Dürig, Grundgesetz-Kommentar*, suppl. 75, Art. 18, Rn. 4 and 6.

22 G.H. Fox and G. Nolte, 'Intolerant democracies', *Harvard International Law Journal*, vol. 36, no. 1, 1995, p. 32.

23 Schmitt Glaeser, *Mißbrauch und Verwirkung von Grundrechten im politischen Meinungskampf*, p. 31.

24 Kommers and Miller, *The Constitutional Jurisprudence of the Federal Republic of Germany*, p. 1.

25 E.J. Reif, *Der Begriff der Verwirkung der Grundrechte in Artikel 18 des Grundgesetzes (unter besonderer Berücksichtigung der Lehre vom Mißbrauch der Grundrechte)*, Munich: Dissertationsdruck Schön, 1970, p. 90.

enemies of democracy and fundamental rights, but also citizens, as rights holders, could ultimately present a threat to the democratic regime. Under the new constitution, therefore, citizens had to be prevented from exploiting the rights in the Basic Law with the aim of destroying democracy. If necessary, they argued, the state should have the power to forfeit the rights of anti-democratic citizens in order to protect democracy against the threat of totalitarianism. The legal experts of the Constitutional Convention believed that a democracy that did not provide for the forfeiture of political fundamental rights that are invoked against the free and democratic order, would accept the risk of being 'suicidal'.[26] After the example of the constitutions of some of the *Länder* (states) that had just previously been adopted,[27] the Constitutional Convention decided to include an abuse clause in its draft constitution.[28]

Subsequently, the draft prepared by this Herrenchiemsee convention served as the starting point for the deliberations of the Parliamentary Council (*Parlamentarischer Rat*) in Bonn. In September 1948 the Parliamentary Council, consisting of delegates from all eleven German *Länder* (states) that were under the occupation of the three Western allied powers (France, Great Britain and the USA),

---

26 P. Bucher (ed.), *Der Parlamentarische Rat 1948-1949. Akten und Protokolle*, vol. 2 (Der Verfassungskonvent auf Herrenchiensee), Boppard am Rhein: Harald Boldt Verlag, 1981, p. 623. See also Schmitt Glaeser, *Mißbrauch und Verwirkung von Grundrechten im politischen Meinungskampf*, p. 22.

27 An abuse clause is still found in Article 17 of the Constitution of Hesse (*Hessen*) of 1 December 1946, www.hessischer-landtag.de/icc/internet/nav/fc7/fc744614-3968-d11b-9b77-912184e37345.htm (accessed 11 April 2016); in Article 10 of the Constitution of Saarland of 15 December 1947, www.saarland.de/dokumente/thema_justiz/100-1.pdf (accessed 11 April 2016); and in Article 37 of the Constitution of Berlin of 23 November 1995, http://gesetze.berlin.de/jportal/?quelle=jlink&query=Verf+BE&psml=bsbeprod.psml&max=true (accessed 11 April 2016). Because Article 31 BL provides that federal law takes precedence over state law, however, these state abuse clauses have practically become inoperative. See H. Krüger, 'Missbrauch und Verwirkung von Grundrechten', *Deutsches Verwaltungsblatt*, vol. 68, no. 4, 1953, p. 99. See on Article 31 BL *Maunz/Dürig, Grundgesetz-Kommentar*, suppl. 75, Art. 31, Rn. 8-12; W. Kahl, H.J. Abraham and R. Dolzer (eds.), *Bonner Kommentar zum Grundgesetz*, Heidelberg: Müller Verlag, 1993, p. 9. In the past, an abuse clause was also included in Article 124 of the Constitution of Baden of 22 May 1947, www.verfassungen.de/de/bw/baden/baden47.htm (accessed 11 April 2016). After the merger of the state Baden with the states Württemberg-Baden and Württemberg-Hohenzollern in 1952, this abuse clause ceased to exist. Finally, until its revision in 1991, Article 133 of the Constitution of Rhineland-Palatinate (*Rheinland-Pfalz*) of 18 May 1947 also contained an abuse clause, www.verfassungen.de/de/rlp/rlp47-index.htm (accessed 11 April 2016).

28 Article 20(1) of the Herrenchiemsee proposal, www.verfassungen.de/de/de49/chiemseerentwurf48.htm (accessed 11 April 2016). B. Pieroth, 'Die Grundrechte des Grundgesetzes in der Verfassungstradition', in: D. Merten and H. Papier, *Handbuch der Grundrechte in Deutschland und Europa*, Band II, Heidelberg: C.F. Müller Verlag, 2006, p. 37; W. Schmitt Glaeser, *Mißbrauch und Verwirkung von Grundrechten im politischen Meinungskampf*, Bad Homburg/Berlin/Zürich: Verlag Gehlen, 1968, p. 23; M. Thiel, 'Die Verwirkung von Grundrechten gemäß Art. 18 GG', in: M. Thiel (ed.), *Wehrhafte Demokratie. Beitrage über die Regelungen zum Schutze der freiheitlichen demokratischen Grundordnung*, Tübingen: Mohr Siebeck, 2003, p. 168-171.

continued the drafting process. They made several amendments to the draft prepared by the Herrenchiemsee convention. With regard to the abuse clause as it is currently found in Article 18 BL, it is interesting to note that the original Herrenchiemsee proposal only included the freedom of expression (including the freedom of the press), the freedom of assembly and the freedom of association.[29] The freedom of teaching, the privacy of correspondence, posts and telecommunications, the rights of property, and the right of asylum were added by the Parliamentary Council. The exact reasons for the incorporation of these rights are still unclear. Finally, on 8 May 1949 the Parliamentary Council adopted the Basic Law. After ratification by the parliaments of more than two-thirds of the participating *Länder*, it took effect on 23 May 1949.[30]

8.3.2 *Wehrhafte Demokratie* as adopted by the Federal Constitutional Court

The militant nature of the German Basic Law was subsequently officially confirmed by the Federal Constitutional Court in the early 1950s.[31] In a series of cases the Federal Constitutional Court unequivocally made clear that the Basic Law is equipped with the intention and the means to defend its democratic character.

The first case that is relevant in this regard is the case against the Socialist Reich Party (*Sozialistische Reichspartei* or SRP) of 1952. Even though the term *wehrhafte* or *streitbare Demokratie* is not used in this case, the Federal Constitutional Court clearly offered a militant interpretation of the Basic Law. The SRP was a political party that saw itself as the legitimate successor of Hitler's NSDAP. Convinced of its neo-Nazi orientation, the Federal Government (*Bundesregierung*) held that the SRP sought to impair the free democratic basic order and requested the Federal Constitutional Court to declare it unconstitutional and to prohibit the party in accordance with Article 21(2) BL.[32] In its response to this request, the Federal Constitutional Court stressed that *'the fundamental ideas upon which this provision is based furnish important indicators for interpreting Article 21 ... Because of the special importance of parties in a democratic state, [the court] is justified in eliminating them from the political scene if, but only if, they seek to topple supreme fundamental values of the*

29 Article 20(1) of the Herrenchiemsee proposal read *'Wer die Grundrechte der Freiheit der Meinungsäußerung (Art. 7 Abs. 1), der Pressefreiheit (Art. 7 Abs. 2), der Versammlungsfreiheit (Art. 8) oder der Vereinigungsfreiheit (Art. 9) zum Kampf gegen die freiheitliche und demokratische Grundordnung mißbraucht, verwirkt damit das Recht, sich auf diese Grundrechte zu berufen'*. See also Bucher, *Der Parlamentarische Rat 1948-1949*, vol. 2, p. 582; Kahl, Abraham and Dolzer, *Bonner Kommentar zum Grundgesetz*, p. 2a.

30 D.P. Currie, *The Constitution of the Federal Republic of Germany*, Chicago/London: University of Chicago Press, 1994, p. 10.

31 Müller, *The Oxford Handbook of Comparative Constitutional Law*, p. 1254.

32 Kommers and Miller, *The Constitutional Jurisprudence of the Federal Republic of Germany*, p. 286.

free democratic basic order which are embodied in the Basic Law'.[33] Based on the findings that former Nazis held key positions in the party, that the party's organisation was similar to that of the NSDAP and the fact that the party's programme and the behaviour of its leaders showed its commitment to a revival of the Third Reich, the Federal Constitutional Court found that it sought to eliminate the free democratic basic order.[34] In the end, based on Article 21 BL, the Federal Constitutional Court declared the SRP unconstitutional and ordered its dissolution.

Another landmark judgment in the acknowledgment of the militant nature of the Basic Law was the Federal Constitutional Court's ruling in the case against the German Communist Party (*Kommunistische Partei Deutschlands* or KPD) of 1956. It was in this case that the Federal Constitutional Court introduced the term '*streitbare Demokratie*' to describe the militant character of the Basic Law.[35] The government had initiated proceedings against the KPD in the same year as it submitted a request to declare the SRP unconstitutional. However, the case against the KPD took the Federal Constitutional Court much longer to decide.[36] While the prohibition of the SRP did not come as a surprise, because it was evident that Article 21(2) BL had been introduced to fight neo-Nazi activities, the ban on the KPD was more controversial.[37] Even though the party hardly enjoyed any popular support, the symbolic importance of the case was a product of the bitterly cold war between East and West Germany.[38] When the Federal Constitutional Court finally decided on the case, the KPD suffered the same fate as the SRP. The Federal Constitutional Court stressed that the Basic Law had decided in favour of a substantive understanding of democracy that had to be defended against its enemies.[39] Based on an investigation of the party's structure, leadership, campaign, literature, and political style, it found that the activities of the KPD were systematically directed against the existing constitutional system.[40] In a now famous passage the Court set forth the meaning of the party ban in Article 21(2) BL and concluded that the BL *'represents a conscious effort to achieve a synthesis between the principle of tolerance with respect to all political ideas and certain inalienable values of the political system. Article 21(2) does not contradict any basic principle of the constitution; it expresses the founders' conviction, based on their concrete historical experience, that the state could no longer afford to maintain an attitude of neutrality towards political parties. In this sense the Basic Law has created*

33 *Socialist Reich Party* case, BVerfGE 2, 1 (1952), translated by Kommers and Miller, p. 287.
34 Kommers and Miller, *The Constitutional Jurisprudence of the Federal Republic of Germany*, p. 288-289.
35 *German Communist Party* case, BverfGE 5, 85 (1956). See also Thiel, *Wehrhafte Demokratie*, p. 7.
36 Kommers and Miller, p. 290.
37 Thiel, *The Militant Democracy Principle in Modern Democracies*, p. 121.
38 Kommers and Miller, *The Constitutional Jurisprudence of the Federal Republic of Germany*, p. 292.
39 Müller, *The Oxford Handbook of Comparative Constitutional Law*, p. 1254.
40 Kommers and Miller, *The Constitutional Jurisprudence of the Federal Republic of Germany*, p. 290.

a "militant democracy", a constitutional value decision that is binding on the Federal Constitutional Court'.[41] This passage marked the birth of the terminology of militant democracy in German case law and it has been part of its constitutional vocabulary since. In following cases, the Federal Constitutional Court further contributed to the development of the concept of militant democracy into an overarching constitutional principle.[42] More recently, however, it has been argued that the concept of militant democracy has become less important than in the past. Due to changes in the political situation, mainly the collapse of the East German Democratic Republic and Germany's reunification in 1990, the threat presented by internal political enemies appears to be perceived as having diminished. Over the years, Germans seem to have regained confidence in the strength of their democratic institutions and processes.[43]

Nevertheless, the instruments of militant democracy have sporadically been activated in the past few decades.[44] Illustrative in this regard is the renewed interest in the concept of militant democracy in Germany in the debate revolving around the attempts to ban the extreme-right Nationalist Democratic Party (*Nationaldemokratische Partei Deutschlands* or NPD). In 2001 both houses of the German Parliament (*Bundestag* and *Bundesrat*) and the German Federal Government (*Bundesregierung*) jointly filed a motion to the German Federal Constitutional Court to ban the NPD because of its neo-fascist and therefore unconstitutional nature.[45] Before the Court, however, it turned out that the request was partly based on evidence provided by members of the party who were being supervised and paid by the secret services.[46] The Federal Constitutional Court therefore decided to dismiss the case in 2003.[47] In December 2012 the Federal Council (*Bundesrat*) again initiated a procedure to have the party banned by the Federal Constitutional Court.[48] The Federal Council has argued that

41 BvefGE 5, 85 (1956), p. 139, translated by Kommers and Miller, p. 291.

42 See e.g. with regard to the Federal Armed Forces (Bundeswehr), BVerfGE 28, 36 (1970); wiretapping, BVerfGE 30, 1 (1970); the loyalty of civil servants, BVerfGE 39, 334 (1975); and radical groups, BVerfGE 47, 198 (1978). See also Thiel, *Wehrhafte Demokratie*, p. 111-112.

43 Kommers and Miller, *The Constitutional Jurisprudence of the Federal Republic of Germany*, p. 300-301.

44 Thiel, *The Militant Democracy Principle in Modern Democracies*, p. 114. See also Müller, *Comparative Constitutional Law*, p. 1262.

45 Spiegel Online, 24 March 2012, 'Debatte über NPD-Verbot: Triumph der Demokraten?', www.spiegel.de/politik/deutschland/ist-ein-parteiverbot-die-richtige-waffe-gegen-die-npd-a-823345.html (accessed 11 April 2016).

46 See also the editor's note by Niesen: P. Niesen, 'Anti-Extremism, Negative Republicanism, Civic Society: Three Paradigms for Banning Political Parties', *German Law Journal*, vol. 3, no. 7, 2002, www.germanlawjournal.com/s/GLJ_Vol_03_No_07_Niesen.pdf (accessed 11 April 2016).

47 BverFGE 18 March 2003, *NPD-Verbotsverfahren*, 2 BvB 1/01, www.bundesverfassungsgericht.de/entscheidungen/bs20030318_2bvb000101.html (accessed 11 April 2016). See also Kommers and Miller, *The Constitutional Jurisprudence of the Federal Republic of Germany*, p. 293-300.

48 Zeit Online, 14 December 2012, 'Bundesrat startet neues NPD-Verbotsverfahren', www.zeit.de/politik/deutschland/2012-12/bundesrat-npd-verbotsverfahren (accessed 11 April 2016).

the party's object and the behaviour of its supporters are aimed at impairing or even eliminating the free democratic basic order. According to the Federal Council, the party maintains an aggressive antisemitic, racist and hostile attitude that is related to National Socialism. At the time of writing it is unclear how the Federal Constitutional Court will decide on this request.[49]

8.4 Article 18 Basic Law as an instrument of the *Wehrhafte Demokratie*

The abuse clause in Article 18 BL is the most explicit expression of the 'wehrhafte' ambitions of the German constitutional order. The provision provides for a special judicial procedure in which the Federal Constitutional Court (*Bundesverfassungsgericht*) can decide to forfeit the constitutional rights of an individual who has abused these rights. It is in Article 18 BL that the concept of the *wehrhafte Demokratie* finds its sharpest expression. Yet, the text of Article 18 BL raises many theoretical and practical questions.[50] It therefore comes as no surprise that the interpretation of the provision has generated a lively debate in (primarily German) legal doctrine. Especially during the first twenty years after the adoption of the Basic Law in 1949 numerous scholars submitted this provision to a rigorous theoretical examination. In the 1960s and 1970s the *wehrhafte Demokratie* of the new Basic Law and Article 18 BL in particular were popular subjects for academic authors.[51] After this momentary attention in the 1960s and 1970s, however, interest in the provision has decreased. This may be due to the fact that up until now the provision has led quite an uneventful existence in legal practice. The rather odd outcome of this is that the understanding of Article 18 BL is merely based on its interpretation in academic literature.[52]

Article 18 BL consists of several key elements. Legal doctrine generally distinguishes between six elements: whoever (*wer*), abuse (*Mißbrauch*), the rights that qualify for forfeiture, to combat (*zum Kampfe*), the free democratic basic order (*die freiheitliche demokratische Grundordnung),* and forfeiture (*Verwirkung*). All these elements require further interpretation, as they are neither defined by the Basic Law nor in any other law. In the following sections the interpretation of these six elements in German legal doctrine will be discussed in the order of their appearance in Article 18 BL.

49 See for the latest updates on the case: www.bundesrat.de/DE/plenum/themen/npd-verbot/npd-verbot.html (accessed 11 April 2016).

50 Schnelle, *Freiheitsmißbrauch und Grundrechtsverwirkung*, p. 14 and 292.

51 C. Knödler, *Missbrauch von Rechten, selbstwidersprüchliches Verhalten und Verwirkung im öffentlichen Recht*, Aktuelle Beiträge zum öffentlichen Recht, Band 4, Herbolzheim: Centaurus Verlag, 2000, p. 34, footnote 216.

52 T. Maunz, 'Verwirkung von Grundrechten', in: P. Badura and R. Scholz (eds.), *Wege und Verfahren des Verfassungslebens: Festschrift für Peter Lerche zum 65. Geburtstag* (reissued), 1993, p. 281; Schnelle, *Freiheitsmißbrauch und Grundrechtsverwirkung*, p. 19.

8.4.1 Whoever abuses

Article 18 BL provides that *whoever* abuses his right shall forfeit these rights. Even though neither the Basic Law nor the Law on the Federal Constitutional Court (*Gesetz* über *das Bundesverfassungsgericht*, LFCC) specify who these abusers may be, it is safe to assume that 'whoever' refers to the individuals and legal persons that can be holders of the rights enumerated in Article 18 BL.[53] Since the majority of the rights in Article 18 BL apply to individuals, they are the main addressees of the prohibition of abuse of rights. The freedom of expression (Article 5(1) BL) and the freedom of teaching (Article 5(3) BL), for example, explicitly apply to 'every person'. German nationals can abuse all rights enumerated in Article 18 BL except for the right of asylum in Article 16a BL, because only non-nationals can seek asylum in Germany. Non-German nationals, on the other hand, can abuse all of the rights in Article 18 BL except for the freedom of assembly in Article 8 BL and the freedom of association in Article 9 BL, because the rights granted by these provisions apply merely to 'all Germans'. Furthermore, public office holders and mandate holders can also be subject to a forfeiture procedure if they exercise one of the rights in Article 18 BL in an abusive manner, as long as no specific constitutional procedure applies.[54]

8.4.2 Abuse (*Missbrauch*)

One of the main questions with regard to Article 18 BL concerns the definition of the notion of abuse.[55] It has been suggested that the use of the term 'abuse' indicates that there are two ways to combat the free democratic basic order: one abusive (and prohibited) and one non-abusive (and permissible).[56] After all, the provision does not simply speak of 'use... in order to combat the free democratic basic order', but explicitly uses the term 'abuse'. Some legal scholars have therefore argued that the term abuse does not cover all uses of a right to combat the free democratic basic order. According to this interpretation, the term wants to add something by referring to a specific use of rights. Use, they claim, generally refers to the legitimate exercise of a right, while abuse refers to the exercise of a right that exceeds the boundaries of

---

53 H. Von Mangoldt and F. Klein, *Das Bonner Grundgesetz*, vol. I, Berlin/Frankfurt a.M.: Verlag Franz Vahlen GmbH, 1957, p. 519.

54 According to Article 46(3) BL permission from the Bundestag is required to initiate proceedings under Article 18 BL against a member of the Bundestag. Under Article 46(4) BL, the Bundestag can demand that any proceedings under Article 18 BL against a Bundestag member be suspended. Article 60(4) BL provides that this also applies to proceedings under Article 18 BL against the Federal President. See also Thiel, *Wehrhafte Demokratie*, p. 135.

55 Schmitt Glaeser, *Mißbrauch und Verwirkung von Grundrechten im politischen Meinungskampf*, p. 72.

56 Schmitt Glaeser, p. 73; D. Wilke, *Die Verwirkung der Pressefreiheit und das strafrechtliche Berufsverbot. Zugleich ein Betrag zur Rechtsnatur und zu den Grenzen der Grundrechte*, Berlin: Duncker and Humblot, 1964, p. 25; H. Gallwas, *Der Mißbrauch von Grundrechten, Schriften zum Öffentlichen Recht*, vol. 49, Berlin: Duncker and Humblot, 1967, p. 120.

the legal order.[57] Wilke, for example, believes that the legislature did not erroneously use the term abuse instead of use, because it emphasises that a right is used for a purpose for which that right was not created or granted.[58] This interpretation follows the interpretation of the abuse of rights in private law.[59] As we have seen in Chapter six, the abuse of rights in private law generally refers to the use of a right contrary to its aim. Because the German constitutional legislature assumed that the use of fundamental rights against the free democratic basic order was contrary to its purpose and therefore illegitimate, Wilke considers it appropriate to use the term abuse in this regard. A different interpretation would indeed suggest that the term abuse is in fact redundant.[60] This interpretation, however, represents a minority within legal doctrine.

A majority of legal scholars, however, have argued that such an interpretation would go against the meaning of the provision. They claim that the term abuse directly refers to the use of a right against the free democratic basic order and that therefore all use against the free democratic basic order amounts to a right being abused. In this view, the term abuse refers one-to-one to combating the free democratic basic order.[61] This implies that the abuse is already given when an individual uses his right to combat the free democratic basic order: *'Demgemäß ist jeder Gebrauch eines der in Art. 18 S. 1 GG genannten Grundrechte ein Mißbrauch, wenn er sich gegen die freiheitliche demokratische Grundordnung richtet'*.[62] In this interpretation the term abuse does not have an autonomous meaning, because if the provision would read *'whoever uses... in order to combat the free democratic basic order'*, the meaning of the provision would be the same.[63] If the provision would be understood otherwise, this would suggest that the normal use of a right against the free democratic basic order would be allowed, which according to a majority of legal scholars is a false assumption.

57 Wilke, *Die Verwirkung der Pressefreiheit und das strafrechtliche Berufsverbot*, p. 27. See also E.J. Reif, *Der Begriff der Verwirkung der Grundrechte in Artikel 18 des Grundgesetzes (unter besonderer Berücksichtigung der Lehre vom Mißbrauch der Grundrechte)*, Munich: Dissertationsdruck Schön, 1970, p. 93.

58 Wilke, *Die Verwirkung der Pressefreiheit und das strafrechtliche Berufsverbot*, p. 25-27. See also Schmitt Glaeser, *Mißbrauch und Verwirkung von Grundrechten im politischen Meinungskampf*, p. 74.

59 Schmitt Glaeser, *Mißbrauch und Verwirkung von Grundrechten im politischen Meinungskampf*, p. 74.

60 Maunz/Dürig, *Grundgesetz-Kommentar*, suppl. 75, Art. 18, Rn. 44; Wilke, *Die Verwirkung der Pressefreiheit und das strafrechtliche Berufsverbot*, p. 26.

61 Wilke, *Die Verwirkung der Pressefreiheit und das strafrechtliche Berufsverbot*, p. 25; Schmitt Glaeser, *Mißbrauch und Verwirkung von Grundrechten im politischen Meinungskampf*, p. 79-80; Gallwas, *Der Mißbrauch von Grundrechten*, p. 120; H. von Weber, *Der Schutz des Staates, Verhandlungen des 38. Deutschen Juristentages*, Tübingen: Verlag J.C.B. Mohr, 1950, p. E11; H. Von Mangoldt and F. Klein, *Das Bonner Grundgesetz*, vol. I, Berlin/Frankfurt a.M.: Verlag Franz Vahlen GmbH, 1957, p. 535; Kahl, Abraham and Dolzer, *Bonner Kommentar zum Grundgesetz*, p. 4; Maunz/Dürig, *Grundgesetz-Kommentar*, suppl. 75, Art. 18, Rn. 44.

62 Wilke, *Die Verwirkung der Pressefreiheit und das strafrechtliche Berufsverbot*, p. 26. See also Schmitt Glaeser, *Mißbrauch und Verwirkung von Grundrechten im politischen Meinungskampf*, p. 73.

63 Thiel, *Wehrhafte Demokratie*, p. 139.

They consider it incorrect to assume that the sheer *use* of a right against the free democratic basic order would be permitted.[64] The advocates of this interpretation stress that the German Basic Law is based on the notion of a *wehrhafte Demokratie* and that 'democratic suicide' is precluded. It is therefore out of the question that Article 18 BL would allow for any fight against its highest constitutional principles. Use against the free democratic basic order that would not constitute abuse would, therefore, be unreasonable.

8.4.3 The basic rights liable for abuse

An interesting feature of Article 18 BL is that, contrary to Article 17 ECHR and the abuse clauses in other human rights documents described in Chapter five, it explicitly lists the rights that can abused in combating democracy. This list, which is considered to be exhaustive,[65] consists of the freedom of expression (in particular the freedom of the press in Article 5(3) BL[66]), the freedom of teaching (Article 5(3) BL), the freedom of assembly (Article 8 BL), the freedom of association (Article 9 BL), the privacy of correspondence (Article 10 BL), the right to property (Article 14 BL), and the right to asylum (Article 16(a) BL). The catalogue of rights in Article 18 BL is based on historical experience that has shown that these rights in particular are vulnerable to being used to impair or destroy the free democratic basic order.[67] Thiel argues that other fundamental rights that only involve a small risk of being abused were explicitly excluded.[68] Dürig suggests, however, that also other rights than those mentioned in Article 18 BL can be abused, at least insofar as they have a political dimension.[69]

As mentioned before, the original Herrenchiemsee proposal only included the freedom of expression (including the freedom of the press), the freedom of assembly

---

64 Schmitt Glaeser, *Mißbrauch und Verwirkung von Grundrechten im politischen Meinungskampf*, p. 73; Wilke, *Die Verwirkung der Pressefreiheit und das strafrechtliche Berufsverbot. Zugleich ein Betrag zur Rechtsnatur und zu den Grenzen der Grundrechte*, p. 25; Kahl, Abraham and Dolzer, *Bonner Kommentar zum Grundgesetz*, p. 4; Gallwas, *Der Mißbrauch von Grundrechten*, p. 120; Von Weber, *Der Schutz des Staates*, p. E11.

65 Krüger, *Deutsches Verwaltungsblatt*, p. 99. See for scholars who nevertheless also accept the unwritten prohibition of abuse of (other) rights: U. Scheuner, 'Grundfragen des modernen Staats', *Recht–Staat–Wirtschaft*, vol. 3, Düsseldorf: Verlag L. Schwann, 1951, p. 160.

66 Some scholars wonder why the freedom of the press is singled out in Article 18 BL. It has no legal consequences as the freedom of expression in general is already included in the provision. The reference to the freedom of the press might have to do with the paticular danger that it involves in the sense of propaganda. See Kahl, Abraham and Dolzer, *Bonner Kommentar zum Grundgesetz*, p. 3.

67 Kahl, Abraham and Dolzer, *Bonner Kommentar zum Grundgesetz*, p. 3.

68 Thiel, *Wehrhafte Demokratie*, p. 155. See also Reif, *Der Begriff der Verwirkung der Grundrechte in Artikel 18 des Grundgesetzes*, p. 151.

69 *Maunz/Dürig, Grundgesetz-Kommentar*, suppl. 75, Art. 31, Rn. 17 and 34.

and the freedom of association.[70] This limited selection is understandable given that, according to theories on militant democracy, these rights are considered most vulnerable to abuse against the democratic regime. In particular the freedom of expression plays a dominant role in the German legal doctrine of abuse of rights.[71] In the cases regarding Article 18 BL that have been tried before the Federal Constitutional Court, the freedom of expression also played a prominent role. All four cases dealt primarily with alleged abuses of the freedom of expression and consisted of a motion to declare the forfeiture of the freedom of expression and several connected rights.[72] During the Constitutional Convention the legal experts present at Herrenchiemsee also discussed whether the freedom of religion, which also includes the freedom to belong to or practice non-religious convictions or world views, should also be included in the list of rights liable for abuse. It was considered, however, that the dissemination of dangerous religious and non-religious utterances could be better addressed in the context of the freedom of expression.[73] Hence, it was unnecessary to include a separate reference to an abuse of the freedom of religion.

The freedom of teaching, the privacy of correspondence, posts and telecommunications, the right of property, and the right of asylum were not part of the original Herrenchiemsee draft, but were added to the list by the Parliamentary Council at a later stage. Unfortunately, the available documents on the discussions in the Parliamentary Council do not provide adequate reasoning to ascertain why these rights were incorporated. With regard to the freedom of teaching, for example, it is unclear why it was added to the list in Article 18 BL. This is however found in Article 5 BL, the provision that deals with the freedom of expression.[74] And since it was the right par excellence to be abused by the Nazis to indoctrinate the young with

---

70 Herrenchiemsee Entwurf Article 20(1): *'Wer die Grundrechte der Freiheit der Meinungsäußerung (Art. 7 Abs. 1), der Pressefreiheit (Art. 7 Abs. 2), der Versammlungsfreiheit (Art. 8) oder der Vereinigungsfreiheit (Art. 9) zum Kampf gegen die freiheitliche und demokratische Grundordnung mißbraucht, verwirkt damit das Recht, sich auf diese Grundrechte zu berufen'*, www.verfassungen.de/de/de49/chiemseerentwurf48.htm (accessed 11 April 2016). See Bucher, *Der Parlamentarische Rat 1948-1949,* vol. 2, p. 582. See also Kahl, Abraham and Dolzer, *Bonner Kommentar zum Grundgesetz*, p. 2a.

71 Schmitt Glaeser, *Mißbrauch und Verwirkung von Grundrechten im politischen Meinungskampf*, p. 123-124.

72 *Otto Ernst Remer* case, BVerfGE 11, 282 (1960); *Gerhard Frey* case, BVerfGE 38, 23 (1974); *Thomas Dienel* case and *Heinz Reisz* case (1996), 2 BvA 1/92 and 2 BvA 2/92.

73 E. Pikart and W. Werner (eds.), *Der Parlamentarische Rat 1948-1949. Akten und Protokolle*, vol. 5(II) (Ausschuss für Grundsatzfragen), Boppard am Rhein: Harald Boldt Verlag, 1993, p. 756.

74 According to Wernicke the terminology 'in particular', therefore, refers to both the freedom of the press (par.1) and the freedom of teaching (par. 3) as subcategories of the general freedom of expression in Article 5 BL: Kahl, Abraham and Dolzer, *Bonner Kommentar zum Grundgesetz*, 1993, p. 3.

their National Socialist ideology,[75] this may very well explain why it is incorporated in Article 18 BL.

Yet, Article 18 BL does not merely refer to the abuse of 'communication rights'. Also the use of the right of property and the right of asylum against the free democratic basic order are prohibited.[76] Legal doctrine suggests that the right of property was included in Article 18 BL to prevent the transfer of money to a political party that is declared anti-constitutional by the Federal Constitutional Court by virtue of Article 21(2) BL.[77] More complicated, however, is the question of how the right to asylum can be abused. It is important to emphasize that the term abuse in Article 18 BL does not refer to procedural abuse or cases of fraud, but applies to situations in which the individual meets the qualifications for the protection of the right, but should not be granted this right based on substantive considerations related to the protection of the free democratic basic order.[78] For the right of asylum, it is suggested that this might be the case if someone aims to gain access to the German legal order with the sole aim of engaging in activities that pose a threat to the free democratic basic order.[79] In that case, however, the actual threat does not in fact result from the exercise of the right of asylum, but from the subsequent hazardous activities that the person in question may undertake once he has been granted asylum in Germany. The real threat is therefore posed by the political rights and freedoms to which the individual concerned will have access once he has gained access to the German legal order.[80] Some legal scholars therefore conclude that the right of asylum falsely appears in Article 18 BL.[81]

8.4.4 To combat

Article 18 BL provides for the forfeiture of rights that are used *to combat* the free democratic basic order *(zum Kampfe gegen die freiheitliche demokratische*

---

75 M.A. Glendon, *A World Made New. Eleanor Roosevelt and the Universal Declaration of Human Rights*, New York: Random House, 2002, p. 159 and 189-190.

76 Thiel, *Wehrhafte Demokratie*, p. 140.

77 Delegate Bergsträßer (Hessen) suggested that the prohibition of abusing the right of property would enable the state to intervene if someone put his property at the disposal of Hitler: Pikart and Werner, *Der Parlamentarische Rat 1948-1949*, vol. 5(II), p. 756-757. See also Reif, *Der Begriff der Verwirkung der Grundrechte in Artikel 18 des Grundgesetzes*, p. 102; Kahl, Abraham and Dolzer, *Bonner Kommentar zum Grundgesetz*, p. 6.

78 P. Lerche, 'Das Asylrecht ist unverwirkbar', in: H. Ehmke, C. Schmid and H. Scharoun (eds.): *Festschrift für Adolf Arndt: zum 65. Geburtstag*, Frankfurt am Main: Europäische Verlagsanstalt, 1969, p. 205-206.

79 M. Hollmann (ed.), *Der Parlamentarische Rat 1948-1949. Akten und Protokolle*, vol. 7 (Entwürfe zum Grundgesetz), Boppard am Rhein: Harald Boldt Verlag, 1995 at 218.

80 Lerche, *Festschrift für Adolf Arndt*, p. 207-208. See also Thiel, *Wehrhafte Demokratie*, p. 140.

81 Lerche, *Festschrift für Adolf Arndt*, p. 199-214; Wilke, *Die Verwirkung der Pressefreiheit und das strafrechtliche Berufsverbot*, p. 22-24.

Grundordnung). This terminology undeniably has an aggressive tone.[82] It emphasizes that the prohibition of abuse of rights in Article 18 BL does not apply to the conflict between political opinions that is common in a democracy.[83] It refers to a much more serious struggle against the abolition of the free democratic basic order. This fight, however, need not to be violent. On the contrary, Article 18 BL primarily deals with non-violent, intellectual battles over the preservation of the free democratic basic order.[84]

In order for the exercise of a right to come within the scope of Article 18 BL, the combat in question must be explicitly directed towards the destruction of the present-day German free democratic basic order.[85] The prospect of the actual destruction of the free democratic basic order, however, is not relevant for the application of the prohibition of abuse of rights.[86] Article 18 BL does not require that the free democratic basic order has already been damaged, as it is explicitly intended as a preventive measure of protection.[87] A serious attempt in that direction is enough for the forfeiture of rights. At the same time, however, the attack on the free democratic basic order should not appear to be a total dead letter, because in that case the right holder would not pose a serious threat (*Täter-Gefährlichkeit*).[88] Finally, the internal motivation of the abuser is not relevant for the question whether he exercised his right to combat the free democratic basic order, as the objective perception of the threat is decisive.[89]

8.4.5 The free democratic basic order

Article 18 BL prohibits attacks on the free democratic basic order *(die freiheitliche demokratische Grundordnung)*. Yet, ultimately the provision is not as such intended to protect the free democratic basic order as an objective in itself. The purpose of the protection of the democratic regime is ultimately to defend the freedom of its citizens.[90] Whether or not the free democratic basic order is at risk and needs to be

82 Schmitt Glaeser, *Mißbrauch und Verwirkung von Grundrechten im politischen Meinungskampf*, p. 71-72; Maunz/Dürig, *Grundgesetz-Kommentar*, suppl. 75, Art. 18, Rn. 54.
83 Schmitt Glaeser, *Mißbrauch und Verwirkung von Grundrechten im politischen Meinungskampf*, p. 71.
84 Thiel, *Wehrhafte Demokratie*, p. 137-138.
85 Moreover, Article 18 BL refers to the contemporary free democratic basic order in Germany. The provision does not have retrospective effect in the sense that the term free democratic basic order would also include former German constitutional orders that can be characterised as such: *Maunz/Dürig, Grundgesetz-Kommentar*, suppl. 75, Art. 18, Rn. 27. See also Schmitt Glaeser, *Mißbrauch und Verwirkung von Grundrechten im politischen Meinungskampf*, p. 71-72.
86 Schmitt Glaeser, *Mißbrauch und Verwirkung von Grundrechten im politischen Meinungskampf*, p. 72.
87 T Maunz/Dürig, *Grundgesetz-Kommentar*, suppl. 75, Art. 18, Rn. 54.
88 Schmitt Glaeser, *Mißbrauch und Verwirkung von Grundrechten im politischen Meinungskampf*, p. 72; Maunz/Dürig, *Grundgesetz-Kommentar*, suppl. 75, Art. 18, Rn. 54.
89 Schmitt Glaeser, *Mißbrauch und Verwirkung von Grundrechten im politischen Meinungskampf*, p. 72.
90 Thiel, *Wehrhafte Demokratie*, p. 2.

protected, however, clearly depends on how this notion is defined. Nevertheless, the concept of the free democratic basic order is not defined in the Basic Law nor in any other law. Still, this notion is not unique to Article 18 BL. It is referred to in several provisions in the Basic Law, often as a justification for the limitation of rights.[91] The interpretation of the concept of the free democratic basic order is generally considered to be the same in all these provisions.[92] More controversial, however, is how the free democratic basic order relates to the term 'constitutional order' (*Verfassungsmäßige Ordnung*) in Article 9(2) BL on the freedom of association.[93] The term free democratic basic order, however, is considered to be narrower than the term constitutional order. The free democratic basic order does not include all provisions in the Basic Law; it only includes those provisions that are essential elements of the free democratic basic order.[94] But still the question remains, what are these elements? Legal doctrine provides different answers to this question.

8.4.5.1 The free democratic basic order equals the elements in Article 79(3) Basic Law

In the most straight forward interpretation, the concept of the free democratic basic order equals the elements that are excluded from constitutional amendment by the eternity clause in Article 79(3) BL.[95] This provision provides that several basic elements of the German constitutional order can never be amended. These basic elements include the division of the Federation into states (*Länder*), the participation of these states in the legislative process, and the principles laid down in Article 1 BL (human dignity) and Article 20 BL (constitutional principles and the right of resistance) shall be inadmissible. This interpretation, however, is not very convincing. Papier and Durner point out in this regard that the term free democratic basic order is (perhaps deliberately) not mentioned in Article 79(3) BL. Moreover, they claim that certain elements in Article 79(3) BL do not actually fit the understanding of what is generally considered the identity of the free democratic basic order. They refer

91 See Article 10(2), Article 11(2), Article 21(2), Article 73(1)(10)(b), Article 87a(4), and Article 91(1) BL.

92 Schmitt Glaeser, *Mißbrauch und Verwirkung von Grundrechten im politischen Meinungskampf*, p. 33; Maunz/Dürig, *Grundgesetz-Kommentar*, suppl. 75, Art. 18, Rn. 56.

93 Maunz/Dürig, Grundgesetz-Kommentar, suppl. 75, Art. 18, Rn. 57.

94 *Maunz/Dürig, Grundgesetz-Kommentar*, suppl. 75, Art. 18, Rn. 57; W. Geiger, *Gesetz über das Bundesverfassungsgericht vom 12 März 1951. Kommentar*, Berlin/Frankfurt: Verlag Franz Vahlen GmbH, 1952, p. 136.

95 Thiel, *The 'Militant Democracy' Principle in Modern Democracies,* p. 116; Schmitt Glaeser, *Mißbrauch und Verwirkung von Grundrechten im politischen Meinungskampf,* p. 46.

primarily to the republican and federal character of Germany in Article 20 BL and recall that also monarchies and unitary states can be free democratic basic orders.[96]

8.4.5.2 The free democratic basic order as a liberal democracy

Many scholars therefore look for the key characteristics of the free democratic basic order in other elements. Yet, since the Basic Law provides no basis for knowing what these elements would then be, this is clearly a more complicated challenge. Nonetheless, such attempts have been made by several commentators. First, it has been argued in a negative sense that the free democratic basic order can be defined in a negative sense as the opposite of a totalitarian state.[97] This is also partly how the Federal Constitutional Court interpreted the term in its judgment concerning the constitutionality of the Socialist Reich Party, where it states that the free democratic basic order is the antitheses of a totalitarian state.[98] On the other hand, the free democratic basic order has been defined as a liberal democracy.[99] In this view, the free democratic basic order is not merely a procedural democracy but a value-bound order. It is characterised not only by free and fair elections, popular sovereignty, and majority rule, but is unmistakeably a value-conscious order with special attention for the protection of fundamental rights. Hence, in the same case regarding the Socialist Reich Party, the Federal Constitutional Court defined the free democratic basic order as an order that *'excludes any form of tyranny and arbitrariness and represents a governmental system under the rule of law, based upon self-determination of the people according to the will of the existing majority and upon freedom and equality. The fundamental principles of this order include at least: respect for the human rights given concrete form in the Basic Law, in particular for a person's right to life and free development of his personality; popular sovereignty; the separation of powers; the accountability of the government; the legality of the administration; the independence*

96 H. Papier and W. Durner, 'Streitbare Demokratie', *Archiv des öffentlichen Rechts*, vol. 128, 2003, p. 357. Most authors indeed seem to have doubts as to whether *all* the elements of Article 79(3) BL can be ascribed to the free democratic basic order: Schmitt Glaeser, *Mißbrauch und Verwirkung von Grundrechten im politischen Meinungskampf*, p. 47; Wilke, *Die Verwirkung der Pressefreiheit und das strafrechtliche Berufsverbot,* p. 32; Thiel, *Wehrhafte Demokratie,* p. 137.

97 Maunz/Dürig, *Grundgesetz-Kommentar,* suppl. 75, Art. 18, Rn. 58.

98 *Socialist Reich Party* case, BVerfGE 2, 1 (1952). In this case, the Federal Constitutional Court provided a definition of the free democratic basic order in the context of Article 21(2) BL. This interpretation, however, is also considered to be applicable to the free democratic basic order in Article 18 BL, see e.g. *Maunz/Dürig, Grundgesetz-Kommentar*, suppl. 75, Art. 18, Rn. 57 and 61.

99 M. Klamt, 'Militant Democracy and the Democratic Dilemma: Different Ways of Protecting Democratic Constitutions', in: F. Bruinsma and D. Nelken (eds.), *Explorations in Legal Cultures (Recht der Werkelijkheid 28:3)*, The Hague: Elsevier, 2007, p. 137-138. Klamt even refers to the free democratic basic order as the *liberal democratic basic order*. See also Papier and Durner, *Archiv des öffentlichen Rechts*, p. 356; Schmitt Glaeser, *Mißbrauch und Verwirkung von Grundrechten im politischen Meinungskampf*, p. 55ff.

of the judiciary; the multi-party principle; and the equality of opportunities for all political parties with regard to the right to constitutional formation and political opposition'.[100] Notwithstanding some critical remarks, German legal scholars have generally accepted this definition.[101]

8.4.6 Forfeiture (*Verwirkung*)

In response to the abuse of rights, the FCC can decide to forfeit the rights of the abuser. Like many of the other elements in Article 18 BL, the provision does not give any clues as to the interpretation of the term forfeiture and neither does any other provision in the Basic Law.[102] Several commentators, however, have made attempts to shed light on the meaning of the forfeiture of fundamental rights.

8.4.6.1 Which rights will be forfeited?

Article 18 BL does not clearly state which rights will be forfeited in the case of abuse. To begin with, the provision provides for the forfeiture of *'these basic rights'*, not of 'the abused basic right(s)'.[103] By providing for the forfeiture of *'these basic rights'*, the wording of the provision suggests that the abuse of one of the rights in Article 18 BL may result not only in the forfeiture of the abused rights, but in the forfeiture of all of them.

In addition, it is not clear whether 'these rights' only refers to the rights enumerated in Article 18 BL or also includes other rights guaranteed in the Basic Law. A few commentators have claimed that also rights that are not included in Article 18 BL can be forfeited. The aim of Article 18 BL, they have argued, is to pre-emptively prevent political threats. In order to protect democracy it may be necessary to broaden the circle of rights to be forfeited and also include others than the abused

---

100 Socialist Reich Party case, BVerfGE 2, 1 (1952), par. 12 [translation is my own]. Original text: *'Die freiheitliche demokratische Grundordnung ist eine Ordnung, die unter Ausschluß jeglicher Gewalt- und Willkürherrschaft eine rechtsstaatliche Herrschaftsordnung auf der Grundlage des Selbstbestimmung des Volkes nach dem Willen der jeweiligen Mehrheit und der Freiheit und Gleichheit darstellt. Zu den grundlegenden Prinzipen dieser Ordnung sind mindestens zu rechnen: die Achtung vor den im Grundgesetz konkretisierten Menschenrechten, vor allem vor dem Recht der Persönlichkeit auf Leben und freie Entfaltung, die Volkssouveränität, die Gewaltenteilung, die Verantwortlichkeit der Regierung, die Gesetzmäßigkeit der Verwaltung, die Unabhängigkeit der Gerichte, das Mehrparteienprinzip und die Chancengleichheit für alle politischen Parteien mit dem Recht auf verfassungsmäßige Bildung und Ausübung einer Opposition'.* See also Papier and Durner, *Archiv des öffentlichen Rechts*, p. 356; Schmitt Glaeser, *Mißbrauch und Verwirkung von Grundrechten im politischen Meinungskampf*, p. 33; Maunz/Dürig, *Grundgesetz-Kommentar*, suppl. 75, Art. 18, Rn. 61.

101 T *Maunz/Dürig, Grundgesetz-Kommentar*, suppl. 75, Art. 18, Rn. 61 footnote 2.

102 Reif, *Der Begriff der Verwirkung der Grundrechte in Artikel 18 des Grundgesetzes*, p. 97.

103 Maunz/Dürig, *Grundgesetz-Kommentar*, suppl. 75, Art. 18, Rn. 40.

right(s) listed in Article 18 BL itself.[104] Yet, legal doctrine has generally considered this interpretation to be too broad and assumes that this part of the provision must be interpreted narrowly: only the right or the rights that have actually been abused can be forfeited.[105] A broader interpretation of the provision would be problematic because of the particular importance of the protection of fundamental rights.[106] Having regard to the far-reaching consequences of the forfeiture of fundamental rights, an overly broad interpretation of this provision is indeed undesirable.

8.4.6.2 Loss of the right itself or merely a loss of the right to exercise it?

The main controversy with regard to the interpretation of the term forfeiture, however, surrounds the question of what forfeiture entails exactly. Does forfeiture result in the loss of the abused right itself or merely of the right to exercise it, in other words, to claim freedom against the state? A few legal scholars claim that forfeiture refers to the complete loss of the fundamental right itself.[107] They believe that forfeiture interferes with the fundamental right, the primary norm, itself.[108] This means that when a right is forfeited, the former right holder no longer has this right: *'Er steht, juridisch gesehen, dann so da, als existierte für ihn das betreffende Grundrecht überhaupt nicht. Damit ist er gewissermaßen "out of law"'*.[109] The advocates of this interpretation for example point to the fact that for some of the rights listed in Article 18 BL forfeiture cannot but result in the loss of the right itself, because the right and its exercise correspond. With regard to the right to vote and to stand for election, referred to in section 39(2) LFCC, and to the right of asylum, for example, this is suggested to be the case.[110] If the right to vote or to stand for election is forfeited, the individual concerned essentially entirely loses his suffrage: he can no longer vote and people can no longer vote for him. The same would apply to the right of asylum. If the Federal Constitutional Court forfeits the right of asylum, this implies that the individual concerned, even if he is being prosecuted on political grounds, may be expelled or extradited *(refoulement)*. Also the forfeiture of the freedom of the press through complete censorship in the sense that an individual must submit all his work

---

104 Lerche, *Festschrift für Adolf Arndt*, p. 210.

105 Kahl, Abraham and Dolzer, *Bonner Kommentar zum Grundgesetz*, p. 6; Von Mangoldt and F. Klein, *Das Bonner Grundgesetz*, vol. I, Berlin/Frankfurt a.M.: Verlag Franz Vahlen GmbH, 1957, p. 520.

106 Thiel, *Wehrhafte Demokratie*, p. 160.

107 See for an enumeration Reif, *Der Begriff der Verwirkung der Grundrechte in Artikel 18 des Grundgesetzes*, p. 100, footnote 19. See also Kahl, Abraham and Dolzer, *Bonner Kommentar zum Grundgesetz*, p. 6-7.

108 Reif, *Der Begriff der Verwirkung der Grundrechte in Artikel 18 des Grundgesetzes*, p. 106-107.

109 Kahl, Abraham and Dolzer, *Bonner Kommentar zum Grundgesetz*, p. 11. However, this would only apply in case of the complete forfeiture of a right. In the case of partial forfeiture, not the entire right is lost, but just a part of it.

110 Reif, *Der Begriff der Verwirkung der Grundrechte in Artikel 18 des Grundgesetzes*, p. 103-104.

to the state authorities before publication would result in the total loss of this right for the individual concerned.[111]

Nevertheless, the interpretation of forfeiture as a complete nullification of a fundamental right is generally considered problematic. The BL generally seems to consider that the rights it guarantees amount to natural rights that do not rely on codification, but originate from being human. They cannot therefore be forfeited: *'Grundrechte, die, wie es das Grundgesetz tut, als überpositiven natürliche und unveräußerliche Menschenrechte aufgefaßt und anerkannt werden, können nicht in dem Sinne verwirkt werden, daß sie untergehen'.*[112] If fundamental rights are interpreted as inherent to the human nature, it is impossible for the state to nullify these rights. Moreover, the complete nullification of a right implies that the right no longer exists in any given situation. It is hard to imagine, however, that the forfeiture of the right to freedom of expression would apply in all cases, even in a horizontal relation between individuals.

According to the dominant interpretation, therefore, forfeiture does not imply the loss of a right, leaving the individual outlawed, but merely refers to the prohibition *to exercise* that right against the state.[113] Not the content of the right, but merely the constitutional guarantee of that right is lost, rendering any appeal to that right irrelevant: *'Nicht das Recht in seiner Substanz, sonders die besondere verfassungsrechtliche Garantie des Rechts wird verwirkt. "Verwirken" hat also in Art. 18 GG die Bedeutung, durch einiges Verhalten bewirken, daß die Berufung auf die Grundrechtsgarantie unbeachtlich wird'*[114] The right holder retains his right, but he can no longer claim it. Forfeiture is therefore actually not the best term for the measure provided in Article 18 BL. Disqualification or refusal might be better terms in this regard: *'Was Art. 18 "Verwirkung" nennt, ist eine ausdrückliche, konstitutive "Aberkennung" auf Grund eines streng geregelten bundesverfassungsgerichtlichen Verfahrens'.*[115] This second interpretation largely follows the distinction between primary and secondary norms of human rights used by Geiger.[116] In this distinction,

111 W.O. Schmitt, 'Die verwirkung des Wahlrechts und der Wählbarkeit nach section 39 Abs. 2 BVerfGG', *Neue Juristische Wochenschrift*, 1966, p. 1738. See also Reif, *Der Begriff der Verwirkung der Grundrechte in Artikel 18 des Grundgesetzes*, p. 104.

112 Geiger, *Gesetz über das Bundesverfassungsgericht vom 12 März 1951. Kommentar*, p. 135.

113 See for an overview of scholars who hold this view: Wilke, *Die Verwirkung der Pressefreiheit und das strafrechtliche Berufsverbot*, p. 55 footnote 29-33 and Reif, *Der Begriff der Verwirkung der Grundrechte in Artikel 18 des Grundgesetzes*, p. 101 footnote 20. See also Krüger, *Deutsches Verwaltungsblatt*, p. 100; G. Dürig, 'Die Verwirkung von Grundrechten nach Artikel 18 des Grundgesetzes', *Juristenzeitung*, vol. 7, no. 17, 1952, p. 517; Thiel, *Wehrhafte Demokratie*, p. 145; Schnelle, *Freiheitsmißbrauch und Grundrechtsverwirkung*, p. 289.

114 Geiger, *Gesetz über das Bundesverfassungsgericht vom 12 März 1951. Kommentar*, p. 135.

115 Maunz/Dürig, *Grundgesetz-Kommentar*, suppl. 75, Art. 18, Rn. 22.

116 W. Geiger, *Gewissen, Ideologie, Widerstand, Nonkonformismus*, Munich: Verlag Anton Pustet, 1963, p. 67-68.

the claim based on an interference with individual freedom is considered a secondary norm that serves as a guarantee for the protection of the primary norm of the freedom itself. In other words, while the primary norm of a right refers to the constitutional freedom against the state, the secondary aspect refers to the capacity to actually exercise this freedom. If forfeiture only interferes with the latter, it results in the loss of a defensive claim. It does not, however, interfere directly with the freedom of the individual.[117] In the words of Dürig, therefore, the forfeiture in Article 18 BL is directed against the subjective right to legal protection with regard to the abused right.[118] Schnelle suggests in this regard that Article 18 BL should only stand in the way of protection in the individual case that a right has been abused.

This understanding of forfeiture as a disqualification to exercise a right seems to fit better with the general understanding of the Basic Law. Moreover, while the current wording of Article 18 BL provides that the right holder *'shall forfeit these basic rights'*, the original Herrenchiemsee proposal provided for the forfeiture of '*the right to invoke these fundamental rights'*.[119] During the discussions in the Parliamentary Council the text of the provision was shortened, in order for it to be brief and to the point.[120] We may assume, however, that with this amendment no different meaning of the provision was intended.[121] This is confirmed by the explanation given by the Federal Government about section 35 LFCC, where it states that the forfeiture refers to the particular constitutional protection that is inherent in the basic right: *'Der Anspruch der Verwirkung allein (Absatz 1) beseitigt den besonderen Verfassungsschutz, die besondere Rechtsgarantie, die dem Grundrecht innewohnt'*.[122] This interpretation also seems to better fit the understanding of fundamental rights in the Basic Law as natural rights that originate from the human nature.[123] Finally, forfeiture as the loss of the mere privilege to exercise a right is better understandable from a more practical perspective. The right itself remains in existence, but the right to claim it against state intervention is withdrawn in certain circumstances. It is, therefore, more convincing than the interpretation of forfeiture as the complete nullification of a right. Yet, some scholars emphasize that frictions remain, as a right that cannot be

117 Reif, *Der Begriff der Verwirkung der Grundrechte in Artikel 18 des Grundgesetzes*, p. 105-106.

118 Dürig, *Juristenzeitung*, p. 517. Others, however, have questioned whether the right to legal protection is a subjective right that can be invoked before a court; see Reif, *Der Begriff der Verwirkung der Grundrechte in Artikel 18 des Grundgesetzes*, p. 115.

119 www.verfassungen.de/de/de49/chiemseerentwurf48.htm (accessed 11 April 2016) [translation is my own]. Original text: *'verwirkt damit das Recht, sich auf diese Grundrechte zu berufen'*. See also Bucher, *Der Parlamentarische Rat 1948-1949*, vol. 2, p. 582.

120 Pikart and Werner, *Der Parlamentarische Rat 1948-1949*, vol. 5(II), p. 755.

121 Maunz/Dürig, *Grundgesetz-Kommentar*, suppl. 75, Art. 18, Rn. 74.

122 Bill concerning the Federal Constitutional Court drafted by the German federal government (*Entwurf eines Gesetzes* über *das Bundesverfassungsgericht*), 28 March 1950, Drucksache no. 788, explanation to section 35: http://dipbt.bundestag.de/doc/btd/01/007/0100788.pdf (accessed 11 April 2016).

123 Thiel, *Wehrhafte Demokratie*, p. 146.

exercised can hardly be called a right.[124] The question whether forfeiture refers to the complete loss of a right or simply to the loss of the functioning of a right is therefore merely theoretical.[125]

8.4.6.3 Is forfeiture a criminal sanction?

Finally, legal doctrine has dealt with the question whether forfeiture must be considered a criminal sanction. The wording of Article 18 BL is indeed quite similar to that of a criminal law provision, consisting of several elements that resemble the elements of a criminal offence. In the light of Article 18 BL this would imply that the elements of the criminal offence – the abuse of one of the rights listed in Article 18 BL to combat the free democratic basic order – have been met, so the right holder will be 'punished' by the forfeiture of these rights.[126] The majority of commentators reject this interpretation, however.[127] They argue that notwithstanding its criminal appearance, Article 18 BL is primarily a *preventive* norm that enables the aversion of a specific future hazard.[128] By means of forfeiting the right in question, the defendant is prevented from abusing his right against the free democratic basic order again in the future.[129] Criminal *Schutznormen*, on the other hand, generally have a repressive function and serve as a sanction against attacks on the free democratic basic order after they have taken place. Furthermore, the punitive effect which is a fundamental characteristic of criminal law provisions, is of marginal importance in the context of Article 18 BL.[130] Even though it has to be admitted that the distinction between the two is thin, German scholars stress that the forfeiture of rights therefore has to be distinguished from a criminal sanction. Rather, Article 18 BL expands the armoury to protect democracy available in criminal law by adding the possibility of *preventive* protection.[131]

---

124 Reif, *Der Begriff der Verwirkung der Grundrechte in Artikel 18 des Grundgesetzes*, p. 114; W. Wertenbruch, *Grundgesetz und Menschenwürde*, Cologne: Carl Heymanns Verlag, 1958, p. 200; G. Hönsch, *Die Verwirkung von Grundrechten nach Art. 18 GG und das Monopol des Bundesverfassungsgerichts aus Art. 18 GG*, Hamburg: Universität Hamburg, 1962, p. 79.

125 Thiel, *Wehrhafte Demokratie*, p. 145.

126 Schmitt Glaeser, *Mißbrauch und Verwirkung von Grundrechten im politischen Meinungskampf*, p. 77.

127 See e.g. Maunz/Dürig, *Grundgesetz-Kommentar*, suppl. 75, Art. 18, Rn. 47; Schmitt Glaeser, *Mißbrauch und Verwirkung von Grundrechten im politischen Meinungskampf*, p. 77 and 160; Gallwas, *Der Mißbrauch von Grundrechten*, p. 143.

128 Schmitt Glaeser, *Mißbrauch und Verwirkung von Grundrechten im politischen Meinungskampf*, p. 61-62.

129 Schmitt Glaeser, p. 70.

130 Schmitt Glaeser, p. 65-66.

131 *Maunz/Dürig, Grundgesetz-Kommentar*, suppl. 75, Art. 18, Rn. 126.

8.4.7 The procedure of Article 18 Basic Law

The procedure for a declaration of an abuse of rights and the corresponding forfeiture of fundamental rights is described in Article 18 BL and is further specified in sections 36 to 42 of the LFCC.[132] Because the decision to file a motion to declare the forfeiture of fundamental rights is an extremely controversial and political decision, this is left to the highest institutions of the republic.[133] According to section 36 LFCC, therefore, a motion to declare the forfeiture of rights may be filed by the German Parliament (*Bundestag*), the Federal Government (*Bundesregierung*) or by the government of one of the sixteen states or *Länder* (*Landesregierung*), which decide by majority. While these institutions have responsibility in upholding the democratic legal order, Article 18 BL and the relevant provisions in the LFCC do not compel these state authorities to start proceedings under Article 18 BL when they learn about an alleged abuse of rights.[134] Furthermore, Article 18 BL and section 13(1) LFCC provide that *only* the Federal Constitutional Court may pronounce the forfeiture of rights guaranteed by the Basic Law.[135] This would confirm that in the case of abuse, forfeiture does not take place *ipso iure*, but only after a decision by the Federal Constitutional Court.[136]

If the Federal Constitutional Court considers the motion well-founded and finds that one of the rights enumerated in Article 18 BL has been abused, it shall declare the forfeiture of rights and its extent. Such a decision requires a two-third majority of the panel *(Senat)* dealing with the case (section 15(4) in conjunction with section 13(1) LFCC). The forfeiture itself consists of two steps.[137] First, the Court shall establish which basic right(s) enumerated in Article 18 BL is or are to be forfeited (first sentence of section 39(1) LFCC). Second, the Federal Constitutional Court declares the scope of the forfeiture (*ihr Ausmass*). Legislation does not provide a clear explanation of

132 www.gesetze-im-internet.de/bverfgg/ (accessed 11 April 2016).

133 Geiger, *Gesetz über das Bundesverfassungsgericht vom 12 März 1951. Kommentar*, p. 138. See also the bill concerning the Federal Constitutional Court drafted by the German federal government (*Entwurf eines Gesetzes* über *das Bundesverfassungsgericht*), 28 March 1950, Drucksache no. 788, explanation to section 34, http://dipbt.bundestag.de/doc/btd/01/007/0100788.pdf (accessed 11 April 2016).

134 Thiel, *Wehrhafte Demokratie*, p. 141-142.

135 Schmitt Glaeser, *Mißbrauch und Verwirkung von Grundrechten im politischen Meinungskampf*, p. 169.

136 P.M. Huber, 'Natürliche Personen als Grundrechtsträger', in: D. Mertens and H. Papier, *Handbuch der Grundrechte in Deutschland und Europa*, Band II, Heidelberg: C.F. Müller Verlag, 2006, p. 1157. See also Schmitt Glaeser, *Mißbrauch und Verwirkung von Grundrechten im politischen Meinungskampf*, p. 163.

137 Schmitt Glaeser, *Mißbrauch und Verwirkung von Grundrechten im politischen Meinungskampf*, p. 165.

what the term 'scope' refers to in this context.[138] In legal doctrine, however, it is understood as referring to the specific kind and duration of the restrictions imposed on the abuser (second and third sentence of section 39(1) LFCC).[139] Forfeiture of the freedom of the press, for example, may include only the right holder's activities as an editor and not as a publisher.[140] Furthermore, the Federal Constitutional Court can lay down a period for the forfeiture of at least one year. This period, however, cannot be indefinite.[141] In theory, the Federal Constitutional Court could decide to only deny the abuser the protection of the abused right in the proceedings at hand and not impose any further restrictions on the exercise of rights. That would, however, nullify the preventive effect of Article 18 BL and is therefore not the most obvious result of the application of the abuse clause. By imposing restrictions on the exercise of rights, the defendant is 'disarmed', as he is precluded from engaging in certain activities in order to protect democracy against the dangers involved in these activities.[142] That is also why forfeiture based on Article 18 BL should not be understood as a limitation of rights, even though it has the characteristics thereof. Contrary to norms limiting the protection of constitutional rights, Article 18 BL provides that the Federal Constitutional Court may abolish the protection of a right.[143] If the forfeiture is not limited in time or has been pronounced for more than a year, the original applicant or the individual whose right has been abused may request the Federal Constitutional Court after two years to totally or partially annul the forfeiture or reduce its duration. Such a request for the reduction of the effects of the forfeiture may be repeated after one year (section 40 LFCC). Finally, if the Federal Constitutional Court has judged on the substance of the case, a new request can only be filed for the forfeiture of the rights of the same right holder if it relies on new facts (*ne bis in idem,*[144] section 41 LFCC).

---

138 Neither Article 18 BL nor the relevant provisions in the LFCC define the legal consequences of a forfeiture decision for the position of the individual whose rights have been forfeited vis-à-vis the judiciary, the legislature and the executive. The questions raised in this regard, though, are merely theoretical, as the practical relevance of Article 18 BL is minimal. For theoretical reflections on the potential legal consequences of forfeiture, however, see e.g. *Maunz/Dürig, Grundgesetz-Kommentar*, suppl. 75, Art. 18, Rn. 95-114; Huber, *Handbuch der Grundrechte in Deutschland und Europa*, p. 1157-1158; Thiel, *Wehrhafte Demokratie*, p. 148-150; Gallwas, *Der Mißbrauch von Grundrechten*, p. 143.

139 Kahl, Abraham and Dolzer, *Bonner Kommentar zum Grundgesetz*, p. 10.

140 Huber, *Handbuch der Grundrechte in Deutschland und Europa*, p. 1157.

141 Schmitt Glaeser, *Mißbrauch und Verwirkung von Grundrechten im politischen Meinungskampf*, p. 172-173.

142 Schmitt Glaeser, p. 166 and 170-173.

143 Thiel, *Wehrhafte Demokratie*, 2003, p. 135.

144 Maunz/Dürig, *Grundgesetz-Kommentar*, suppl. 75, Art. 18, Rn. 86.

It is generally accepted that the decision to forfeit rights has a constituent character as it decides what will be and not what is.[145] Thiel, however, is of a different opinion. Following Reif, he claims that even without a decision by the Federal Constitutional Court, Article 18 BL has a restrictive effect as an immanent limitation of the exercise of rights. This immanent limitation is only 'activated' by the decision by the Federal Constitutional Court.[146] In this view, the rights enumerated in Article 18 BL are protected only under the reserve of not being abused. The scope of protection of these rights is, therefore, restricted to their exercise in conformity with the constitution. Yet, this approach, which in fact significantly restricts the freedom that is implied by the rights guaranteed in the Basic Law, is not generally accepted.[147] According to the general interpretation of the forfeiture decision, it has *ex nunc* effect: it first interferes with the right of the defendant at the time of the decision by the Federal Constitutional Court.[148] This is also the only interpretation that would be compatible with the notion of Article 18 BL as a preventive norm that focusses on the future threat posed by the right holder.[149] Moreover, the decision to forfeit the rights of a right holder is considered to only have effect in an individual case and not to provide general forfeiting effects.[150]

8.4.8 Additional sanctions based on section 39(2) LFCC

In addition to the forfeiture of the rights mentioned in Article 18 BL, the Federal Constitutional Court may forfeit the defendant's right to vote, to stand for election and the right to hold public office or, in case the defendant is a legal person, demand its dissolution for the duration of the forfeiture (section 39(2) LFCC). Article 18 BL itself does not provide for the forfeiture of these rights. However, as German constitutional law generally considers it illegitimate to depart from the Basic Law by statutory law, several legal scholars have argued that the additional forfeiture of rights provided in section 39(2) LFCC is unconstitutional.[151] They recall that the list of rights liable for forfeiture in Article 18 BL is exhaustive. An additional forfeiture of the right to vote, to stand for election, to hold public office or to demand the

145 Kahl, Abraham and Dolzer, *Bonner Kommentar zum Grundgesetz*, p. 8; H. Lechner and R. Zuck, *Bundesverfassungsgerichtsgesetz*, 4th ed., Munich: C.H. Beck'sche Verlagsbuchhandlung, 1996, Section 36, Rn. 1 and 2, p. 246-247; *Maunz/Dürig, Grundgesetz-Kommentar*, suppl. 75, Art. 18, Rn. 87.

146 Thiel, *Wehrhafte Demokratie*, p. 150 and 152. See also Reif, *Der Begriff der Verwirkung der Grundrechte in Artikel 18 des Grundgesetzes*, p. 92.

147 Thiel, *Wehrhafte Demokratie*, p. 151.

148 Reif, *Der Begriff der Verwirkung der Grundrechte in Artikel 18 des Grundgesetzes*, p. 128.

149 Maunz/Dürig, *Grundgesetz-Kommentar*, suppl. 75, Art. 18, Rn. 87.

150 Schmitt Glaeser, *Mißbrauch und Verwirkung von Grundrechten im politischen Meinungskampf*, p. 168.

151 Huber, *Handbuch der Grundrechte in Deutschland und Europa*, p. 1158; Kahl, Abraham and Dolzer, *Bonner Kommentar zum Grundgesetz*, p. 9.

dissolution of a legal person would therefore exceed the power given to the Federal Constitutional Court. Dürig, however, has argued that Article 39(2) LFCC only confirms the interpretation of the forfeiture of rights that must have been intended by the Basic Law, namely the 'depoliticisation' of the right holder who abuses his rights. The forfeiture of the rights mentioned in section 39(2) LFCC therefore inevitably correlates with the forfeiture of rights under Article 18 BL.[152] Thiel, however, provides a more practical solution to this issue. He recalls that the withdrawal of the right to vote, to stand for election or to hold public office and the demand for the dissolution of a legal person are not forfeiture decisions in the technical sense, but merely collateral consequences of the forfeiture. They would not therefore depart from the Basic Law and be unconstitutional.[153]

8.5 Article 18 Basic Law proceedings before the Federal Constitutional Court

In contrast with the amount of theory that has been formulated with regard to Article 18 BL, its practical relevance has been very minimal. Leggewie and Meier have therefore described the provision as the *'rusty sword'* of the German militant democracy.[154] Some commentators have even argued that Article 18 BL has nowadays become practically obsolete.[155] Many reasons have been given for the insignificance of the provision in legal practice. First, it has been argued that the fact that the procedure has hardly ever been followed might be due to the complexity of the procedure.[156] Forfeiture requires a motion that can only be filed by either the Lower House of the German Parliament (*Bundestag*), the German Federal Government (*Bundesregierung*) or by the government of one of the sixteen states (*Landesregierung*). Subsequently, a declaration on the forfeiture of fundamental rights requires a two-thirds majority of the panel (*Senat)* of the Federal Constitutional Court dealing with the case. Second, the decision to file a motion to request the forfeiture of fundamental rights is a very politically delicate decision, as it basically deals with the compatibility of a specific political doctrine with the free democratic basic order. In an open and free democratic legal order, Article 18 BL should not be read as a means to suppress political opposition. Political struggle should remain possible in a wehrhafte Demokratie. State authorities should therefore guard against a misuse of the forfeiture procedure and may therefore be hesitant to initiate proceedings under Article 18 BL. Third, the consequences of

---

152 *Maunz/Dürig, Grundgesetz-Kommentar*, suppl. 75, Art. 18, Rn. 32. See also *Berufsverbot II* case BVerfGE 25, 88 (1969), par. 97.

153 Thiel, *Wehrhafte Demokratie*, p. 159.

154 C. Leggewie and H. Meier, *Republikschutz. Maßstäbe für die Verteidigung der Demokratie*, Hamburg: Rowohlt, 1995, p. 82.

155 Thiel, p. 130.

156 Huber, *Handbuch der Grundrechte in Deutschland und Europa,* p. 1157.

the application of Article 18 BL are far-reaching, as an individual may be denied the protection of one or more of the fundamental rights guaranteed in the Basic Law.[157] Since a variety of other less radical militant instruments are available in the Basic Law, the forfeiture procedure in Article 18 BL may be a last resort. Fourth, at the time of drafting the Basic Law, Article 18 BL was clearly an expression of the spirit of the time (*Zeitgeist*).[158] Since then, this spirit may have changed and the room for an abuse clause may have become smaller. The authorities concerned may not therefore be particularly eager to start a forfeiture procedure.[159] In sum, as both the practical and the ethical hurdles for initiating proceeding under Article 18 BL seem considerably high, motions to declare the forfeiture of rights are very rare. Since the entry into force of the Basic Law in 1949, only four motions have been filed at the Federal Constitutional Court. None of these four motions has led to the forfeiture of rights. Since they provide the only case law on the prohibition of the abuse of rights in the German Basic Law, these four cases will be examined in more detail.

8.5.1 The case law on Article 18 Basic Law

A first motion to declare the forfeiture of fundamental rights based on Article 18 BL was filed at the Federal Constitutional Court in 1952. The motion concerned Otto Ernst Remer, the former vice-president of the Socialist Reich Party. As we have seen, the SRP was banned after the Federal Constitutional Court had declared it unconstitutional earlier that year.[160] Subsequently, the Federal Government (*Bundesregierung*) requested the forfeiture of Remer's freedom of expression, freedom of assembly and association, active and passive voting rights, and the right to hold public office. According to the Federal Government, Remer had abused these rights against the free democratic basic order during several public propaganda speeches he gave as vice-president of the SRP. Yet, the Federal Constitutional Court concluded in 1960 that since the submission of the motion no facts had come to its attention that would suggest that Remer had continued his hostile activities versus the state after the dissolution of the SPR. On the contrary, it seemed that Remer had totally given up his political activities after the SRP was declared unconstitutional. Under these circumstances, the Federal Constitutional Court found that Remer did

157 Zuleeg, *Der Mißbrauch von Grundrechten in der Demokratie,* p. 42-43.
158 Thiel, *Wehrhafte Demokratie*, p. 130.
159 F. Matthey, 'Art. 18 (Verwirkung von Grundrechten)', in: I. von Münch (ed.), *Grundgesetz-Kommentar*, vol. 1, 3rd ed., 1985, no. 3, p. 756. See also Zuleeg, *Der Mißbrauch von Grundrechten in der Demokratie*, p. 49.
160 *Socialist Reich Party* case, BVerfGE 2, 1 (1952).

not pose a threat to the free democratic basic order and declined the request to forfeit his political rights.[161]

Subsequently, in 1969, the FCC received a motion by the Federal Government (*Bundesregierung*) to declare the forfeiture of the freedom of expression (in particular the freedom of the press), the right to vote and the right to stand for election, and the right to hold public office of the journalist Gerhard Frey and the publishing house *Druckschriften und Zeitungsverlag GmbH*, of which Frey was the sole associate. Frey's publishing house was the publisher of the *Deutsche National-Zeitung*, a journal circulating numerous nationalistic, anti-Semitist and racist articles that caused considerable turmoil both in Germany and abroad. With regard to Article 18 BL, the Federal Constitutional Court recalled that this provision was intended to avert a threat to the free democratic basic order that may arise from the activities of individuals: '*Art. 18 GG dient der Abwehr von Gefahren, die der freiheitlich demokratischen Grundordnung durch individuelle Betätigung drohen können.... Er richtet sich gegen den Einzelnen, der kraft seiner Fähigkeiten und der ihm zur Verfügung stehenden Mittel eine um der Erhaltung der Verfassung willen zu bekämpfende Gefahr schafft*'.[162] In order to assess the threat posed by the individual in question, the Federal Constitutional Court considered that a look into the future was inevitable: '*Für Art. 18 GG ist die Gefährlichkeit des Antragsgegners im Blick auf die Zukunft entscheidend*'.[163] Rights are only to be forfeited in the case that the individual concerned is likely to (continue to) pose a threat to the free democratic basic order in the future.[164] In the case of Frey, however, the Federal Constitutional Court concluded that this was not the case, because the articles that Frey had published after the motion were of a different order and did not threaten the free democratic basic order. The threat to the free democratic basic order had therefore passed.

Finally, in 1992, the Federal Government again submitted two motions to declare the forfeiture of rights based on Article 18 BL. The motions concerned the forfeiture of the right to freedom of expression, the right to freedom of the press, the right to freedom of assembly and the right to freedom of association of two neo-Nazi politicians, Thomas Dienel and Heinz Reisz. In its reasoning the Government claimed that both politicians had continuously abused these rights for the purpose of battling the free

161 *Otto Ernst Remer* case, BVerfGE 11, 282 (1960). Remer later filed a complaint with the EComHR about his conviction for Holocaust denial in the 1990s: EComHR 6 September 1995, *Remver v. Germany*, appl. no. 25096/94, see also Chapter three.

162 *Gerhard Frey* case, BVerfGE 38, 23 (1974), par. 9. See also BVerfGE 25, 44 (1969) and *Berufsverbot II*, BVerfGE 25, 88 (1969).

163 *Gerhard Frey* case, BVerfGE 38, 23 (1974), par. 9.

164 *Gerhard Frey* case, BVerfGE 38, 23 (1974), par. 9.

democratic basic order.[165] Thomas Dienel had become active in the right-extremist National Democratic Party of German (*Nationaldemokratische Partei Deutschlands*, NPD) in the 1990s. Later he founded the neo-Nazi German National Party (*Deutsch Nationale Partei*, DNP) of which he was the president and the main propagandist. In this capacity, he had frequently been guilty of the dissemination of aggressive racist and anti-Semitic beliefs. Heinz Reisz was also active in several neo-Nazi organisations. During his appearances on behalf of these organisations, he had shown himself to be aggressively anti-Semitic and had propagated the abolishment of the *'Bonner system'* (the post-war constitutional order based on the German Basic Law of 1949) and the founding of a *'Fourth Reich'*, inspired by Hitler's Third Reich.[166] Considering his aggressive anti-Semitic beliefs, his extreme xenophobia and his constant fight against the constitutional system, the Federal Government considered Reisz to be a serious threat to the free democratic basic order.[167]

The Federal Constitutional Court responded to the two motions in one decision in 1996.[168] Unfortunately the Constitutional Court refrained from giving detailed reasons for its decision.[169] The Federal Constitutional Court did find, however, that the facts and expectations presented during the criminal proceedings against both men for their right-wing extremist sentiments had shown that the two would in the future refrain from expressing and defending their extreme right sentiments in public. In the light of these findings, the Federal Constitutional Court did not consider that it had been sufficiently demonstrated that Dienel and Reisz posed a threat to the free democratic basic order under Article 18 BL and declined the request.[170]

8.5.2 Common elements

The four cases demonstrate that Article 18 BL is interpreted very restrictively. In none of the four cases did the FCC forfeit the rights of the individuals in question. The Court emphasised the relevance of Article 18 BL as a preventive norm intended to defend the free democratic basic order. Consequently, rights will only be forfeited pursuant to Article 18 BL if this is necessary to prevent the destruction of the free

165 *Verfassungsschutzbericht 1992*, Bonn: Bundesministerium des Innern, 1993, p. 102.
166 *Verfassungsschutzbericht 1992*, p. 102.
167 EComHR 20 October 1997, *Heinz Reisz v. Germany*, appl. no. 32013/96.
168 *Thomas Dienel* case and *Heinz Reisz* case (1996), 2 BvA 1/92 and 2 BvA 2/92.
169 In accordance with section 24(2) LFCC.
170 Press release only: BVerfGE Pressemitteilung Nr. 43/96 (30 July 1996). Interesting to note is that Heinz Reisz subsequently submitted an application to the European Commission of Human Rights. Before the Commission he complained under Article 6 ECHR about the length of the Article 18 BL procedure before the Federal Constitutional Court. The Commission, however, declared this application inadmissible because the forfeiture of rights concerns neither his civil rights and obligations nor any criminal charge against him and therefore fell outside the scope of Article 6 ECHR: EComHR 20 October 1997, *Heinz Reisz v. Germany*, appl. no. 32013/96 (see also Chapter three).

democratic basic order. If the Court does not consider it substantially proven that the rights holder will (continue to) exercise his rights in a way that poses a threat to the free democratic basic order, no forfeiture will take place. In other words, Article 18 BL is *'zukunftgericht'*.[171] All four motions to declare the forfeiture of rights were declined, because the Federal Constitutional Court was not convinced that the rights holders would continue to pose a threat to the free democratic basic order. In the Remer case, for example, the defendant used to engage in anti-democratic activities under the umbrella of an anti-democratic organisation that had been dissolved in the meantime. The Federal Constitutional Court subsequently found that after the SRP had been declared unconstitutional and had been dissolved, its vice-president appeared to have given up his political activities and was not expected to continue his hostile activities versus the state.[172] Schmitt Glaeser, however, warns that it is not always the case that the dissolution of a political party also constitutes the end of the political life of its active members. In this regard caution is called for, he argues.[173]

Schnelle has criticised the dominant understanding of Article 18 BL, which in her view hinders the application of the prohibition of abuse of rights in the fight against extremism. She has argued that the modern age asks for a new interpretation of Article 18 BL, one that corresponds better to the general doctrine of fundamental rights.[174] She thereby took the Strasbourg interpretation of the abuse clause in Article 17 ECHR as an example. Instead of focussing on the constitutional protective character of Article 18 BL, whereby the threat of the abuser to the free democratic basic order is decisive, she proposes to focus on the abuse of rights aspect of the provision, whereby the actions of the abuser are crucial.[175] Furthermore, forfeiture would in this perception refer merely to the denial of the protection of the abused right in that particular case and not impose restrictions on the future exercise of fundamental rights. This interpretation, she believes, would correspond better with general ideas about fundamental rights, the international framework on human rights, and the historical developments of the notion of abuse of rights in private law she argues.

8.6 Other '*Wehrhafte*' elements in the German legal order

Even though the term *wehrhafte Demokratie* itself is not constitutionalised, the Basic Law contains a number of articles that collectively express this principle. The prohibition of abuse of rights in Article 18 BL is just one of these. Besides the prohibition of abuse of rights, the Basic Law contains several other *Schutznormen*

171 Thiel, *Wehrhafte Demokratie*, p. 153.
172 *Otto Ernst Remer* case, BVerfGE 11, 282 (1960).
173 Schmitt Glaeser, *Mißbrauch und Verwirkung von Grundrechten im politischen Meinungskampf*, p. 68.
174 Schnelle, *Freiheitsmißbrauch und Grundrechtsverwirkung*, p. 21.
175 Schnelle, p. 286-287.

or norms aimed at the protection of the free democratic basic order. These militant provisions are not defined as such by the Basic Law and enumerations of the constitutional provisions that can be considered militant vary. The aim of this section is therefore not to provide an exhaustive list of all the militant instruments provided in the Basic Law, but rather to focus on the provisions that together with Article 18 BL constitute the core of the *wehrhafte Demokratie*: the prohibition of unconstitutional political parties in Article 21(2) BL, the prohibition of associations whose aims or activities contravene the criminal law, or that are directed against the constitutional order or the concept of international understanding in Article 9(2) BL.[176] Finally, militant provisions are also found outside of the Constitution, primarily in administrative and criminal legislation.

8.6.1 The party ban in Article 21(2) BL

This militant scheme of the Basic Law further includes Article 21(2) BL, which holds that political parties which *'by reason of their aims or the behaviour of their adherents, seek to undermine or abolish the free democratic basic order or to endanger the existence of the Federal Republic of Germany shall be unconstitutional'*. Earlier in this chapter we have seen that the cases in which the Federal Constitutional Court confirmed the militant nature of the Basic Law indeed concerned the interpretation of Article 21 BL. According to the first paragraph of this provision *'Political parties shall participate in the formation of the political will of the people'*. They may therefore be freely established, as long as their internal organisation conforms to democratic principles and they publicly account for their assets and for the sources and use of their funds. Political parties are distinguished from other associations on the basis of their function in the electoral process in the sense that they select and present electoral candidates and objectives between which voters can choose (*Wahlermöglichungsfunktion*).[177] Because of their important role in the political process, political parties enjoy particular protection in the German legal order. In German this is known as *Parteienprivileg*.[178] So, while the important role of political parties is 'constitutionalised' in the Basic Law, Article 21(2) BL allows for restrictions on the rights of political parties that are deemed unconstitutional.[179] In accordance with their distinctly privileged position, however, the regime for declaring a political party unconstitutional is rather strict. A request for a declaration of the unconstitutionality of a political party can only be initiated by the Lower House of the German Parliament (*Bundestag*), the Federal Council (*Bundesrat*), or the Federal

176 Leggewie and Meier, *Republikschutz*, p. 85.

177 *Epping/Hillgruber, Beck'scher Online-Kommentar Grundgesetz*, 27. Edition, Art. 21, Rn. 19-21, available from Beck online (accessed 11 April 2016).

178 Müller, *The Oxford Handbook of Comparative Constitutional Law*, p. 1258.

179 Müller, p. 1258.

Government (*Bundesregierung*), and only the Federal Constitutional Court can decide on unconstitutionality.[180] When it has found that a party is unconstitutional, the Federal Constitutional Court can dissolve the party, prohibit the creation of a substitute party and order the confiscation of its assets.[181]

Articles 21(2) and 18 BL overlap to a certain extent, as both provisions may cover political parties that combat the free democratic basic order. However, Article 21(2) BL is considered a *lex specialis* when compared to Article 18 BL. Political parties that undermine the free democratic basic order will first and foremost be considered unconstitutional under Article 21(2) BL and will be prohibited and dissolved by the Federal Constitutional Court. Once a party has been banned, the forfeiture of its rights in accordance with Article 18 BL will no longer be under discussion. When it comes to political parties, Article 18 BL will therefore practically never come into play.[182] Nevertheless, Article 18 BL can be applied against former members of the dissolved party, although case law shows that in this case it may be difficult to reasonably argue that the individual in question will continue to pose a threat to the free democratic basic order.[183]

Banning is the most severe form of the curtailment of a political party's rights and is therefore only applied as a 'last resort' in dealing with anti-democratic political parties.[184] So far, only two political parties have been banned under Article 21(2) BL: the Socialist Reich Party[185] and the German Communist Party.[186] Both bans have been discussed earlier in this chapter. These two cases show that the authorities treat the instrument of the party ban with caution.

8.6.2 The prohibition of associations in Article 9(2) BL

Next, Article 9(2) BL aims to provide protection against organisations that are not political parties. Article 9(2) BL allows for the prohibition of associations *'whose aims or activities contravene the criminal laws, or that are directed against the constitutional order or the concept of international understanding'*. The Minister of

180 Article 21(2) BL in conjunction with sections 13 and 43(1) of the Law on the Federal Constitutional Court (*Gesetz* über *das Bundesverfassungsgericht*, LFCC). According to section 43(2) LFCC, the regional government of one of the states (*Landesregierung*) can request for a declaration of unconstitutionality with regard to a political party that operates exclusively on the territory of that state.

181 Article 46(3) LFCC.

182 *Maunz/Dürig, Grundgesetz-Kommentar*, suppl. 75, Art. 18, Rn. 119.

183 In the case of a former vice-president of the SRP, for example, the Federal Constitutional Court did not consider this argument convincing: *Otto Ernst Remer* case, BVerfGE 11, 282 (1960).

184 German Communist Party case (*Kommunistische Partei Deutschlands* or KPD), BverfGE 5, 85 (1956), par. 141. See also Thiel, *The Militant Democracy Principle in Modern Democracies*, p. 123-124.

185 Socialist Reich Party case (Sozialistische Reichspartei or SRP), BVerfGE 2, 1 (1952).

186 *German Communist Party* case (*Kommunistische Partei Deutschlands* or KPD), BverfGE 5, 85 (1956). Currently, a procedure to ban the National Democratic Party of Germany (*Nationaldemokratische Partei Deutschlands* or NPD) is still pending.

the Interior[187] of the state in which an association operates can dissolve an association. For associations that operate in multiple states, it is the Federal Minister of the Interior (*Bundesminister des Innern*) who decides on the dissolution.[188]

With regard to activities directed against the constitutional order, insofar as this corresponds to the free democratic basic order, the scope of Article 9(2) BL overlaps with that of Article 18 BL. However, just like Article 21(2) BL, Article 9(2) BL too is a *lex specialis* when compared to Article 18 BL. The forfeiture of the freedom of association in Article 18 BL is generally understood to apply to the individual right of natural persons to associate with others, whereas the restriction of the freedom of association in Article 9(2) BL applies to the collective right of the association as a whole. When Article 9(2) BL applies it therefore has priority over Article 18 BL.[189]

The applicable regime for outlawing associations in Article 9(2) BL is less strict than that for banning political parties under Article 21(2) BL. Whereas political parties can only be prohibited when their aims or the behaviour of their supporters pose a serious threat to the free democratic basic order or the existence of the country, the grounds for banning other associations are less stringent. Furthermore, while a political party can only be banned by a decision of the Federal Constitutional Court, other associations can be banned by the Federal Minister of the Interior, or, if it operates in only one particular state, by the local authority of that state. While bans on political parties are extremely rare, bans on associations are less exceptional. So far, more than 400 associations have been banned on the basis of Article 9(2) BL.[190] These include numerous organisations with neo-Nazi objectives.[191]

---

187 Oficially, according to Section 3(2)(sub 1) of the Law on Associations (*Vereinsgesetz*), it is the *'oberste Landesbehörde oder die nach Landesrecht zuständige Behörde für Vereine und Teilvereine'* who can prohibit and dissolve an association. In practice, this is generally the Minister of the Interior (*Landesinnenministerium*) of the state concerned or the Senate Department of the Interior (*Senatsverwaltung für Inneres*) as it is called in the city-states of Berlin, Bremen or Hamburg. See *Erbs/Kohlhaas, Strafrechtliche Nebengesetze,* suppl. 206, Section 3, Rn. 18, available from Beck online (accessed 11 April 2016).

188 Article 9(2) BL in conjunction with Section 3(2)(sub 2) of the Law on Associations (*Vereinsgesetz*). See also *Maunz/Dürig, Grundgesetz-Kommentar*, suppl. 75, Art. 9, Rn. 132.

189 Maunz/Dürig, *Grundgesetz-Kommentar*, suppl. 75, Art. 18, Rn. 115-118; Thiel, *Wehrhafte Demokratie*, p. 164.

190 Müller, *The Oxford Handbook of Comparative Constitutional Law*, p. 1260.

191 See e.g. the ban on the Nationalist Front (*Nationalistische Front*) by the Federal Minister of the Interior on 26 November 1992, on the Free German Workers Party (*Freiheitliche Deutsche Arbeiterspartei*) by the Federal Minister of the Interior on 22 February 1995 and on the National List (*Nationale Liste*) by the Senator of the Interior of Hamburg on 23 February 1995, mentioned in Kommers and Miller, *The Constitutional Jurisprudence of the Federal Republic of Germany*, p. 16.

8.6.3 Non-constitutional militant measures

Third, militant measures are also found in other legislation.[192] These are found in administrative law, for example in the protection of the constitution by administrative measures taken by the intelligence services (*administrativer Verfassungsschutz*). They are also found in criminal restrictions on the right to freely express one's opinion in Article 5 BL, for example the penalisation of the dissemination of propaganda material by unconstitutional organisations and prohibitions on hate speech in the Criminal Code. Also the prohibition of Holocaust denial can also be considered to belong to this category. As Niesen explained, however, penal provisions against a denial of the Holocaust appear to draw primarily on related motivations and are therefore of less direct significance to the militant scheme of the BL.[193] Still, such provisions can throw some light on the understanding of the role of the abuse clause in a militant democracy, because Holocaust denial is systematically considered by the ECtHR as an activity that falls within the scope of the abuse clause in Article 17 ECHR.

8.6.3.1 The German prohibition of Holocaust denial

In Chapters three and four we have learned that by virtue of the prohibition of abuse of rights in Article 17 ECHR holocaust denial is excluded from the protection of the freedom of expression protected in Article 10 ECHR. In fact, as we have seen, cases concerning a denial of the Holocaust form the main category of cases in which the European Court of Human Rights has found an abusive exercise of rights. It is remarkable, however, that cases regarding Holocaust denial (in German referred to as *Auschwitzlüge*) are not considered under the abuse clause in Article 18 BL. For the purpose of comparison, this section will explore how Holocaust denial is dealt with in the *wehrhafte Demokratie*.

Holocaust denial was specifically made a crime in Germany in 1994.[194] Before then, Holocaust denial had been punished under more general provisions of the Criminal Code, inter alia the prohibition of insult (section 185), a violation of the memory of

192 Thiel, *The Militant Democracy Principle in Modern Democracies*, p. 131-133.

193 P. Niesen, 'Anti-Extremism, Negative Republicanism, Civic Society: Three Paradigms for Banning Political Parties', *German Law Journal*, vol. 3, no. 7, 2002, par. 3.

194 Section 130(3) of the German Criminal Code (Strafgesetzbuch or StGB) reads '*Whosoever publicly or in a meeting approves of, denies or downplays an act committed under the rule of National Socialism of the kind indicated in section 6 (1) of the Code of International Criminal Law, in a manner capable of disturbing the public peace shall be liable to imprisonment not exceeding five years or a fine*', www.gesetze-im-internet.de/englisch_stgb (accessed 11 April 2016).

the dead (section 189) and incitement to hatred (section 130 in its original form).[195] The application of these provisions to Holocaust denial, however, was criticised for excessively stretching the interpretation of these provisions.[196] Moreover, the application of these provisions did not in all cases produce a satisfactory outcome. In March 1994, for instance, the German Federal Court of Justice (*der Bundesgerichtshof*, the highest court in civil and criminal cases) decided that the prohibition of incitement to racial hatred in section 130 of the Criminal Code, which required that the accused had damaged the human worth of the victim, applied to the accusation that the Jews invented the Holocaust, but not to the outright denial of the use of gas chambers by the Nazis.[197] These circumstances prompted the Federal Government to enact legislation to specifically facilitate the criminalization of Holocaust denial.[198] In October 1994, section 130 of the Criminal Code was accordingly amended to explicitly criminalize any denial of the Holocaust as such.[199]

8.6.3.2 The Irving case

The first and only time the Federal Constitutional Court has decided on a denial of the Holocaust was in 1994 in a case on an administrative ruling preventing the British historian and Holocaust denier David Irving from speaking about the Holocaust at a conference organized by the local branch of the far-right-wing NPD in Munich.[200] When learning about the plans of the NPD to organise a public meeting where Irving would speak, the municipal authorities of Munich issued an order to prevent the participants in the meeting from denying the persecution of Jews by the Nazi

195 D. Grimm, 'The Holocaust Denial Decision of the Federal Constitutional Court of Germany', in: I. Hare and J. Weinstein (eds.), *Extreme Speech and Democracy*, Oxford: Oxford University Press, 2009, p. 557.

196 Grimm, p. 557.

197 BGH, 15 March 1994, *Deckert*, 1 StR 179/93, *NJW* 1994, 1421. See R. Kahn, *Holocaust Denial and the Law: A Comparative Study*, New York/Houndmills: Palgrave Macmillan, 2004, p. 71.

198 Kahn, *Holocaust Denial and the Law: A Comparative Study*, p. 71.

199 R.A. Kahn, 'Cross-Burning, Holocaust Denial, and the Development of Hate Speech Law in the United States and Germany', *University of Detroit Mercy Law Review*, vol. 83, no. 3, 2006, p. 190; Grimm, '*Extreme Speech and Democracy*, p. 557.

200 Before then, all cases concerning Holocaust denial had involved interpretations of the Criminal Code. The Iriving case was the first time Holocaust denial was considered in the constitutional context of the freedom of expression as protected in Article 5 BL. This case was decided, however, before the amendment of section 130 Criminal Code. See Kahn, *University of Detroit Mercy Law Review*, p. 192; Grimm, *Extreme Speech and Democracy*, p. 558.

regime.[201] After having unsuccessfully opposed the order in the administrative courts, the NPD filed a constitutional complaint under the freedom of expression in Article 5 BL and the freedom of assembly in Article 8 BL.[202]

The Federal Constitutional Court focussed first and foremost on the constitutionality of the order in the light of Article 5 BL. Article 5 BL protects the right to freely express and disseminate an opinion in speech, writing and pictures. In contrast, statements of fact are not covered under Article 5 BL. Opinions in this regard can be characterised as *'personal assessments of a matter or value judgments, whereas statements of facts are characterised by an objective relationship between the expression and its object... Hence, opinions as subjective expressions cannot be qualified as right or false, while statements of facts can'*.[203] In the *Irving* case, the Federal Constitutional Court applied this distinction, which had been made long before in other cases for that matter,[204] and found that the denial of the Holocaust was a false statement of fact. The fact that the Holocaust had actually happened was undoubtedly established in numerous reports from eyewitnesses, the findings of courts in numerous criminal proceedings, and the insights based on historical research.[205] As such, the Federal Constitutional Court held that Holocaust denial is not protected under the freedom of opinion in Article 5 BL. The same applied to the right of freedom of assembly in Article 8 BL. For the sake of completeness, the Court added that even if the denial of the Holocaust in this specific situation would be regarded as an opinion, the weight of an evidently false statement is outweighed by the harm it would cause to the interests protected by statute on which the order was based.[206] Grimm, a former Justice on the Federal Constitutional Court who was Judge Rapporteur in the *Irving* case, concludes that *'it is the German responsibility for the Holocaust that explains the decision. It has become part of the identity of post-war Germany that atrocities like these should never happen again under the responsibility of the German state'*.[207]

201 The order was based on section 5(4) of the Statute on Assemblies (*Versammlungsgesetz*). This provision *'allows for a prohibition of an assembly if there is evidence that the organizer or his followers will express opinions or allow utterances that constitute a crime. The municipal authorities were of the view that Holocaust denial consituted a crime punishable under the provisions of the Penal Code'*, in the words of Grimm, *Extreme Speech and Democracy*, p. 558. See also Kommers and Miller, *The Constitutional Jurisprudence of the Federal Republic of Germany*, p. 493-497.

202 *Auschwitzlüge* case, BVerfGE 90, 241 (1994). See also P.R. Teachout, 'Making "Holocaust Denial" A Crime: Reflections on European Anti-negationist Laws from the Perspective of U.S. Constitutional Experience', *Vermont Law Review*, vol. 30, no. 3, 2006, p. 671.

203 Grimm, *Extreme Speech and Democracy*, p. 558.

204 BverfGE 54, 208 (1980), par. 219; BverfGE 61, 1 (1982), par. 8; BverfGE 85, 1 (1991), par. 15. See Grimm, *Extreme Speech and Democracy*, p. 559.

205 BVerfGE 90, 241 (1994).

206 Grimm, *Extreme Speech and Democracy*, p. 560.

207 Grimm, p. 560.

8.6.3.3 Holocaust denial under the German Basic Law and the ECHR compared

In comparison to the interpretation of Article 17 ECHR, it is interesting to note that both under the ECHR and the German Basic Law, Holocaust denial is not protected. The way that this type of expression is placed outside the scope of the protection of the freedom of expression, however, is a different one. In the context of the ECHR, Holocaust denial, which is at the outset formally covered by Article 10 ECHR, is in the second instance excluded from the protection of the Convention on substantive grounds by virtue of Article 17 ECHR. Under German Law, a denial of the Holocaust constitutes a false statement of fact and is therefore not covered by the freedom to give one's opinion in Article 5 BL. This diversity in approaches is understandable, given the different function of the abuse clause in the ECHR and the Basic Law. Article 17 ECHR serves as a last resort clause to prevent that rights protected under the Convention may be used in a way that undermines the fundamental values of the Convention. Article 18 BL, on the other hand, serves as a preventive instrument to protect the free democratic basic order against future violations. Even though Article 18 BL could play a role in prohibiting notorious holocaust deniers from again expressing such false statements, the provision does not apply when such a statement is made in the first place. It therefore makes sense that these kinds of expressions are first and foremost addressed on the basis of sanctioning provisions in the Criminal Code, potentially in the light of Article 5 BL.

8.7 Conclusions

We have seen in Chapter seven that the concept of militant democracy was initially developed as a reaction to European democracies being overthrown by Nazism and fascism. After the Second World War, many European democracies adopted a doctrine of democratic self-defence.[208] This is especially true for Germany, where the concept of militant democracy strongly influenced the drafting of the Basic Law that came into force in 1949.[209] The fact that the Nazis could rely on political rights on their way to political power made post-war Germany particularly conscious of the need to protect its regained democracy against anti-democratic forces. The militant structure of the Basic Law consists of a collection of provisions that together aim to form a rampart surrounding the free democratic basic order *(die freiheitliche demokratische Grundordnung)*.

208 Müller, *The Oxford Handbook of Comparative Constitutional Law*, p. 1257.

209 P. Macklem, 'Militant democracy, legal pluralism, and the paradox of self-determination', *International Journal of Constitutional Law*, vol. 4, no. 3, 2006, p. 488; Müller, *The Oxford Handbook of Comparative Constitutional Law*, p. 1258.

In the abuse clause in Article 18 Basic Law, the *wehrhafte Demokratie* finds its sharpest expression.[210] The provision provides for a special judicial procedure that can be instigated by the Lower House of the German Parliament (*Bundestag*), the German Federal Government (*Bundesregierung*) or the government of one of the sixteen *Länder* (*Landesregierung*) and in which the Federal Constitutional Court (*Bundesverfassungsgericht*) decides on the forfeiture of constitutional rights. In legal practice, however, this strongest of the militant measures in the Basic Law hardly plays any role. Its lack of practical relevance has been ascribed to both practical hurdles (the procedure in Article 18 BL is rather complex) and ethical reasons. A request for the forfeiture of the constitutional rights of an anti-democratic actor is politically charged. Moreover, Article 18 BL is clearly an expression of the spirit of the time (*Zeitgeist*) and some have wondered whether the room for an abuse clause may be smaller nowadays.

If the German authorities intervene in the exercise of political rights by anti-democratic actors, they seem to do so primarily on the basis of other, less far-reaching instruments of the *wehrhafte Demokratie*.[211] These include in the first place Article 21(2) BL, which provides that unconstitutional political parties that *'by reason of their aims or the behaviour of their adherents, seek to undermine or abolish the free democratic basic order or to endanger the existence of the Federal Republic of Germany'* may be banned. Yet, given the important role of political parties in the democratic process, this provision is applied with the greatest restraint. So far, only two applications for party bans have been successful. In 1952, the Federal Constitutional Court declared the Socialist Reich Party (*Sozialistische Reichspartei* or SRP), a right-wing extremist party founded in 1949 as the successor to Hitler's NSDAP, unconstitutional and dissolved it.[212] Four years later the German Communist Party (*Kommunistische Partei Deutschlands* or KPD) met with the same fate.[213] A second important militant provision in the BL is Article 9(2), which allows for the

210 Article 18 BL reads: *'Whoever abuses the freedom of expression, in particular the freedom of the press (paragraph (1) of Article 5), the freedom of teaching (paragraph (3) of Article 5), the freedom of assembly (Article 8), the freedom of association (Article 9), the privacy of correspondence, posts and telecommunications (Article 10), the rights of property (Article 14), or the right of asylum (Article 16a) in order to combat the free democratic basic order shall forfeit these basic rights. This forfeiture and its extent shall be declared by the Federal Constitutional Court'*, www.bundestag.de/blueprint/servlet/blob/284870/ce0d03414872b427e57fccb703634dcd/basic_law-data.pdf (accessed 11 April 2016).

211 Schnelle, *Freiheitsmißbrauch und Grundrechtsverwirkung*, p. 19. Given the privileged status that political parties enjoy under German law because of their important role in the democratic process, militant interventions seem to be based principally on the prohibition of unconstitutional associations in Article 9(2) BL.

212 Socialist Reich Party case (Sozialistische Reichspartei or SRP), BVerfGE 2, 1 (1952).

213 *German Communist Party* case (*Kommunistische Partei Deutschlands* or KPD), BverfGE 5, 85 (1956). Currently, a procedure to ban the National Democratic Party of Germany (*Nationaldemokratische Partei Deutschlands* or NPD) is still pending.

prohibition of associations that are not political parties and whose aims or activities are directed against the constitutional order. In addition, the German democratic order is protected by a multitude of sub-constitutional provisions, such as criminal law provisions restricting the right to freely express one's opinion in the case of hostile propaganda or hate speech. These instruments play a far more prominent role within the militant structure of the BL.

So, contrary to the abuse clause in Article 17 ECHR, which is increasingly applied by the ECtHR, the abuse clause in Article 18 BL has hardly any practical relevance. Within the militant scheme of the German legal order Article 18 BL appears to be *'a prominent political warning more than anything else'*.[214] The next chapter will explore the understanding of the concept of militant democracy in the context of the ECHR and the role that Article 17 ECHR may fulfil in this regard.

214 Müller, *The Oxford Handbook of Comparative Constitutional Law*, p. 1258.

Chapter 9
Militant Democracy in the Context of the ECHR

9.1 Introduction

This is the last chapter in a series of three on the concept of militant democracy. This chapter will explore to what extent the understanding of the concept of militant democracy as a fundamental feature of the ECHR can help us to interpret the abuse clause in Article 17 ECHR. In the previous two chapters we have seen that militant democracy is a diffuse concept. Chapter seven has shown that there is no uniform theory on militant democracy. This has resulted in a wide range of approaches to and interpretations of the concept of militant democracy, both in theory and in practice. At the same time, several legal scholars have pointed out that militant measures taken in the name of protecting democracy, such as party bans and restrictions on political speech, are *prima facie* undemocratic in the sense that they restrict the political participation of anti-democratic enemies. So, whereas an open democracy may be structurally weak, an excessively militant democracy may eventually no longer be democratic, some of them have warned.[1] The assumptions and practices of militant democracy should therefore be continuously scrutinised.[2]

Chapter eight has provided an illustration of the interpretation of the concept of militant democracy in the concrete context of Germany. The German legal order represents the most explicit and far-reaching implementation of the concept of militant democracy.[3] The German *wehrhafte Demokratie* finds its sharpest expression in the abuse clause in Article 18 Basic Law, which provides for a special judicial procedure in which the Federal Constitutional Court (*Bundesverfassungsgericht*) can decide to forfeit certain constitutional rights of individuals and groups that use these rights *'to combat the free democratic basic order'*.[4] Yet, as we have seen, the German 'free democratic basic order' is first and foremost defended by other militant instruments that are considered less far-reaching, such as the prohibition of associations and restrictions on free speech. Within the militant scheme of the German legal order the

1 O. Pfersmann, 'Shaping Militant Democracy: Legal Limits to Democratic Stability', in: A. Sajó (ed.), *Militant democracy*, Utrecht: Eleven International Publishing, 2004, p. 48.

2 G. Frankenberg, 'The learning Sovereign', in: A. Sajó (ed.), *Militant democracy*, Utrecht: Eleven International Publishing, 2004, p. 118.

3 J. Müller, 'Militant Democracy', in: M. Rosenfeld and A. Sajó (eds.), *The Oxford Handbook of Comparative Constitutional Law*, Oxford: Oxford University Press, 2012, p. 1260.

4 Article 18 BL, www.bundestag.de/blueprint/servlet/blob/284870/ce0d03414872b427e57fccb703634dcd/basic_law-data.pdf (accessed 11 April 2016).

abuse clause in Article 18 BL therefore appears to be *'a prominent political warning more than anything else'*.[5]

Finally, as questions of self-defence are vital to every democratic system, these issues have also proven to be relevant to the ECHR. In Chapter two we have seen that the Convention came into being at a critical moment in European history. After the ruthless way in which human rights had been violated by totalitarian regimes during the Second World War, Western European democracies collectively avowed to protect democracy and against its enemies.[6] In fact, the idea behind the Convention was that surpassing the nation State was necessary to guarantee peace across the European continent and prevent gross human rights violations in the future.[7] In the words of the drafters, the purpose of the Convention was originally, therefore, to *'ensure that the states of the Members of the Council of Europe are democratic, and remain democratic'*.[8] The ECHR therefore allows states to actively defend their democratic institutions and procedures against anti-democratic actors aiming to overthrow democracy by adopting and applying militant measures. Because, as the Court put it, *'[p]luralism and democracy are based on a compromise that requires various concessions by individuals or groups of individuals, who must sometimes agree to limit some of the freedoms they enjoy in order to guarantee greater stability of the country as a whole'*.[9] Over the years a distinct doctrine of militant democracy has been developed in the context of the ECHR.[10] This chapter addresses the question of how the concept of militant democracy takes shape in the context of the Convention and how the Convention's interpretation of this concept may help to understand the role of the abuse clause in Article 17 ECHR. For that aim it will first describe the evolution of this concept in the case law of the ECtHR and legal doctrine. Next, it will show how the Commission and the Court have dealt with the controversies surrounding the concept of militant democracy.

---

5 Müller, *The Oxford Handbook of Comparative Constitutional Law*, p. 1258.

6 See on the relation between the ECHR and democracy also P.E. de Morree, 'Het Europees Hof voor de Rechten van de Mens als hoeder van de democratie' ['The European Court of Human Rights as guardian of democracy'], in: M. Duchateau and P. Kingma (eds.), *Regt spreken volgens de wet? Bijdragen over de staatsrechtelijke positie van de (Europese) rechter [Adjudication in accordance with the law? Contributions regarding the constitutional position of the (European) judge]*, Nijmegen: Wolf Legal Publishers, 2013, p. 51-72.

7 Bates, *The Evolution of the ECHR*. p. 47.

8 A. Robertson (ed.), *Collected edition of the 'Travaux Préparatoires' (hereafter referred to as 'TP')*, vol. II, The Hague: Martinus Nijhof, 1975-1985, p. 60 (Ungoed-Thomas).

9 ECtHR 13 February 2003 (GC), *Refah Partisi (the Welfare Party) and other v. Turkey*, appl. nos. 41340/98 et al., par. 99.

10 A.K. Bourne, 'The Prohibition of Political Parties and "Militant Democracy"', *Journal of Comparative Law*, vol. 7, no. 1, 2012, p. 196.

9.2 The militant interpretation of the European Convention on Human Rights

Even though the Commission and the Court have never used the term 'militant democracy' as such,[11] the Strasbourg case law confirms that the doctrine of militant democracy is an explicit feature of the ECHR.[12] Democracy and human rights have always been closely linked in the context of human rights protection. In the preamble to the Convention, for example, the Signatory States emphasise that the fundamental rights the Convention aims to protect *'are best maintained... by an effective political democracy'*. The Strasbourg organs have subsequently reaffirmed the Convention's commitment to democracy by holding that it *'appears to be the only political model contemplated by the Convention and, accordingly, the only one compatible with it'*.[13] They are nevertheless well aware that this political model is not a quiet possession. Anti-democratic actors, the Court recognised, *'might do away with democracy, after prospering under the democratic regime, there being examples of this in modern European history'*.[14] In a number of cases the Commission and the Court accordingly referred to the notion of democratic self-defence as a legitimate ground for the restriction of the fundamental rights of anti-democratic actors. The dissolution and banning of political parties are the most common measures that the Strasbourg organs considered justified from the perspective of militant democracy.[15] Other examples of militant measures allowed by the Court include barring individuals adhering to a certain ideology from running for public office[16] or holding a varying range of offices in the public sectorm[17] restrictions on political speech,[18] racist speech,[19] the

---

11 The term only appears in a Chamber judgment in the *Refah Partisi* case when the Court refers tot he submissions of the Turkish government: ECtHR 31 July 2001, *Refah Partisi (the Welfare Party) and others v. Turkey*, appl. nos. 41340/98 et al., par. 62.

12 P. Macklem, 'Militant democracy, legal pluralism, and the paradox of self-determination', *International Journal of Constitutional Law*, vol. 4, no. 3, 2006, p. 508.

13 ECtHR 30 January 1998 (GC), *United Communist Party of Turkey and others v. Turkey*, appl. no. 19392/92, par. 45. See also ECtHR 13 February 2003 (GC), *Refah Partisi (the Welfare Party) and others v. Turkey*, appl. nos. 41340/98 et al., par. 86-89; ECtHR 5 April 2007, *Church of Scientology Moscow v. Russia, appl. no. 18147/02*, par. 74.

14 ECtHR 13 February 2003 (GC), *Refah Partisi (the Welfare Party) and others v. Turkey*, appl. nos. 41340/98 et al., par. 99.

15 E.g. EComHR 20 July 1957, *German Communist Party v. Germany*, appl. no. 250/57 and ECtHR 13 February 2003 (GC), *Refah Partisi (the Welfare Party) and others v. Turkey*, appl. nos. 41340/98 et al.

16 E.g. ECtHR 16 March 2006 (GC), Ždanoka v. Latvia, appl. no. 58278/00.

17 E.g. ECtHR 26 September 1995 (GC), *Vogt v. Germany*, appl. no. 17851/91.

18 E.g. ECtHR 16 July 2009, *Féret v. Belgium*, appl. no. 15615/07.

19 E.g. ECtHR 20 February 2007 (dec.), *Ivanov v. Russia*, appl. no. 35222/04.

prohibition of certain symbols,[20] and the prosecution for Nazi activities.[21] Hereafter this chapter explores the evolution of the militant interpretation of the ECHR.

9.2.1 Militant democracy during the early years of the Convention

In Chapter seven we have seen that the concept of militant democracy was established in the second half of the 1930s in reaction to the expansion of fascism on the European continent. Loewenstein, who introduced the term, described how fascism exploited the weaknesses of democracy to gain power with the aim of destroying the system from within.[22] He believed there to be only one solution: democracy – just as its counterpart – had to become militant in order to resist the autocratic threat. By becoming militant, Loewenstein referred to the fortification of the 'soft spots' of democracy by restricting the political rights of fascist political actors, such as the freedom of speech, the freedoms of assembly and association and their right to participate in elections. *'[c]onstitutional scruples'*, Loewenstein argued, *'can no longer restrain from restrictions on democratic fundamentals, for the sake of ultimately preserving these very fundamentals'*.[23] This traditional interpretation of militant democracy focussed primarily on the danger of fascism as an authoritarian, anti-democratic ideology.

Immediately after the War, a similar militant narrative influenced the drafting of the Convention. In Chapter two we have seen that the ECHR was a reaction to the atrocities committed by the Nazi regime during the Second World War on the one hand and the rising post-war threat tensions between European democracies and the Communist Soviet Union under Stalin on the other.[24] This initial understanding of the Convention as a militant rampart against Nazi, fascist and communist exploitation of the democratic regime is clearly reflected in the early case law of the Commission and the Court. During the first decades of the Convention, the interpretation of its militant role was primarily framed in the context of the fight against totalitarianism.[25] In a number of early judgments and admissibility decisions the Commission and the Court reaffirmed that states are allowed to take measures to restrict the exercise of fundamental rights in the name of protecting their democratic orders against Nazi, fascist and communist groups and individuals that aimed to overthrow it.

---

20 E.g. ECtHR 8 July 2008, *Vajnai v. Hungary*, appl. no. 33629/06.

21 E.g. EComHR 12 May 1988, *Kühnen v. Germany*, appl. no. 12194/86.

22 K. Loewenstein, 'Militant Democracy and Fundamental Rights I', *The American Political Science Review*, vol. 31, no. 3, 1937, p. 424.

23 Loewenstein, p. 432.

24 E. Bates, *The Evolution of the European Convention on Human Rights. From its Inception to the Creation of a Permanent Court of Human Rights*, Oxford: Oxford University Press, 2010, p. 46.

25 S. Marks, 'The European Convention on Human Rights and its "Democratic Society"', in: *British Yearbook of International Law*, London: Oxford University Press, 1995, p. 211.

9.2.1.1 National Socialism

The Strasbourg organs have from the very start consistently confirmed their militant stance against supporters of National Socialism. The Commission and the Court have repeatedly held that *'National Socialism is a totalitarian doctrine incompatible with democracy and human rights'* which is not protected by Article 10 or 11 ECHR.[26] As we have seen in Chapter three, the Commission consistently declared applications by neo-Nazis and neo-Nazi organisations inadmissible. In the same line of thought as the *Glasenapp* case, for example, the Court refused to consider the refusal to appoint an applicant as a university lecturer because of his activities for the far-right National Democratic Party of Germany (*Nationaldemokratische Partei Deutschlands* or NPD) as an interference with the right to freedom of expression protected in Article 10 ECHR.[27] Illustrative in this regard is also the case *Kühnen v. Germany*. In this case, the Commission found that by advocating the reinstitution of the NSDAP and the National Socialist regime that existed in Germany between 1933 and 1945, Kühnen had aimed to impair *'the basic order of freedom and democracy'*.[28] His activities *'thus ran counter to one of the basic values underlying the Convention, as expressed in its fifth preambular paragraph, namely that the fundamental freedoms enshrined in the Convention "are best maintained... by an effective political democracy"'*.[29]

During the first decades of the Convention militant measures seem to only come into play in the case of considerably serious activities that threaten the preservation of democracy at its core. Measures restricting the exercise of political rights were only justified from the perspective of militant democracy if the activities the applicant had engaged in threatened the protection of democracy as the institutional arrangement for political decision-making in which all individuals are allowed to compete in political competition. As commentators have argued, this interpretation of militant democracy suggests *'an extremely narrow, protective view of democracy,*

26 EComHR 12 October 1989, *B.H., M.W., H.P. and G.K. v. Austria*, appl. no. 12774/87, par. 2. See also ECtHR 1 February 2000 (dec.), *Schimanek v. Austria*, appl. no. 32307/96. Here too there are rare exceptions of similar cases in which the Commission and the Court did not evaluate similar cases in the light of Article 17 ECHR, e.g. EComHR 1 December 1963, *X. v. Austria*, appl. no. 1747/62; ECtHR 28 August 1986, *Kosiek v. Germany*, appl. no. 9704/82; ECtHR 25 November 2003 (dec.), *R.L. v. Switzerland*, appl. no. 43874/98. See also Y. Haeck, 'Artikel 17 Verbod van rechtsmisbruik' ['Article 17 Prohibition of Abuse of rights'], in: Vande Lanotte, J. and Haeck, Y. (eds.), *Handboek EVRM. Deel 2. Artikelsgewijze commentaar, volume II [Handbook ECHR. Part 2. Commentary by article, volume II]*, Antwerp/Oxford: Intersentia, 2004, p. 254; H. Cannie and D. Voorhoof, 'The Abuse Clause and Freedom of Expression in the European Human Rights Convention: An Added Value for Democracy and Human Rights Protection?', *Netherlands Quarterly of Human Rights*, vol. 29, no. 1, 2011, p. 59.

27 ECtHR 28 August 1986, *Kosiek v. Germany*, appl. no. 9704/82, par. 39.

28 EComHR 12 May 1988, *Kühnen v. Germany*, appl. no. 12194/86, par. 1.

29 Ibid, par. 1.

in which democracy was a means for protecting citizens from the worst abuses of State power'.[30] Furthermore, the scrutiny of the necessity of militant measures by the Commission and the Court in these early years was rather marginal. As Harvey has argued, it appears that restrictions on the rights of anti-democratic actors at the time hardly required any justification in the sense of actual proof of the threat they posed to democracy. Restrictions were generally considered valid *'by virtue of the fact that it applied to anti-democratic actors'.*[31]

9.2.1.2 Communism

As we have previously seen, the drafting of the ECHR was a response not merely to Europe's past experience with Nazism, but also to the fears of a communist future.[32] This is the background against which the Commission for the first time applied the rationale of the concept of militant democracy. Inspired by the fear of Communism as a totalitarian regime that dominated the general political climate in the 1950s, in 1957 the Commission upheld the ban on *German Communist Party* (KPD) (see for a more detailed analysis of this case Chapter three). Recalling the *travaux préparatoires*, in which the drafters set out that totalitarian movements are prohibited from exploiting the Convention in their own interest, the Commission referred to the abuse clause in Article 17 ECHR. This fundamental provision, the Commission emphasised, was designed to safeguard the rights listed in the Convention *'by protecting the free operation of democratic institutions'.*[33] Subsequently, the Commission found that the German Communist Party's goal, a proletarian dictatorship, was incompatible with the Convention.[34] In order words, the ambitions of the German Communist Party posed such a serious threat to democracy that the German legal order was allowed to defend itself against it.

In subsequent cases the Court initially retained this militant stance vis-à-vis communism. In the case *Glasenapp v. Germany*, concerning an applicant who was denied a permanent position as a secondary schoolteacher because of her support for the KPD, the Court reaffirmed that State's power to protect its democratic order against the threat of Communist activities.[35] According to the German domestic authorities the applicant's refusal to dissociate herself from the KPD proved that she was not willing to consistently uphold the principles of the German free democratic basic order (*die freiheitliche demokratische Grundordnung),* a vow that all civil servants

---

30 Marks, *British Yearbook of International Law*, p. 231-232.

31 Harvey, *European Law Review*, p. 414.

32 Bates, *The Evolution of the ECHR*, p. 5.

33 EComHR 20 July 1957, *German Communist Party v. Germany*, appl. no. 250/57.

34 Ibid.

35 P. Harvey, 'Militant Democracy and the European Convention on Human Rights', *European Law Review*, vol. 29, no. 3, 2004, p. 414.

were required to take.[36] According to the German authorities it was clear that the KPD rejected the free democratic basic order in the Basic Law as it aimed to establish a dictatorship of the proletariat. Support for the KPD was therefore incompatible with loyalty to the free democratic system. The Court, for its part, held that such a requirement could not in itself be considered incompatible with the Convention.[37] Yet, without explicitly going into the question of the lawfulness of militant measures in this regard, the Court appeared to support Germany's claim to self-defence by refusing to accept the applicant's complaint that there had been an interference with Article 10 ECHR (the Court concluded that access to the civil service was not covered by the right to freedom of expression).[38]

Over the years, however, this strong militant stance seems to have loosened with regard to the alleged threat to democracy in Western European states posed by sympathisers of communism. In 1995 the Court was certainly more critical of the incompatibility of support for a communist party with the vow to actively uphold the free democratic basic order at all times that all German civil servants had to take. In the case *Vogt v. Germany,* concerning a secondary schoolteacher who was dismissed from her job because of her political activities for the DKP (the successor party to the KPD), the Court found that even though *'the refusal to appoint a person as a civil servant cannot as such provide the basis for a complaint under the Convention'*, as it had earlier concluded in the Glasenapp case, this did not mean that *'a person who has been appointed as a civil servant cannot complain of being dismissed if that dismissal violates one of his or her rights under the Convention'*.[39] The Court therefore found an interference with the right to freedom of expression and dealt with the case under Articles 10(2) and 11(2) ECHR.[40] The German government had argued that given its past Germany had *'a special responsibility in the fight against all forms of extremism, whether right-wing or left-wing'* and that the duty of political loyalty was the cornerstone of its *'democracy capable of defending itself'*.[41] The Court acknowledged that a democratic state is entitled to demand that civil servants promise their loyalty to the constitutional principles on which it is founded. In that context the Court specifically took into account Germany's experience with the overthrow of the Weimar Republic and considered it legitimate that *'Germany wished to avoid a repetition of those experiences by founding its new State on the idea that it should be a "democracy capable of defending itself"'*.[42] Yet, the Court considered

36 ECtHR 28 August 1986, *Glasenapp v. Germany*, appl. no. 9228/80, par. 29.
37 Ibid, par. 52.
38 Harvey, *European Law Review*, p. 414.
39 ECtHR 26 September 1995 (GC), *Vogt v. Germany*, appl. no. 17851/91, par. 43.
40 ECtHR 26 September 1995 (GC), *Vogt v. Germany*, appl. no. 17851/91, par. 44. See also ECtHR 24 November 2005, *Otto v. Germany*, appl. no. 27574/02, par. 1.
41 ECtHR 26 September 1995 (GC), *Vogt v. Germany*, appl. no. 17851/91, par. 54.
42 Ibid, par. 59.

this justification, although relevant, not sufficient to establish convincingly that it was necessary in a democratic society to dismiss the applicant from her post and found a violation of Articles 10 and 11 ECHR.[43] This more tolerant approach, however, was not unanimously supported – the judgment was rendered by a majority of ten votes to nine. The dissenters were of the opinion that the KPD at the material time still posed a serious threat to the German democratic constitutional order and that the state was *'entitled to dismiss civil servants, including school teachers, who are actively engaged in activities on behalf of anti-democratic parties'*.[44]

9.2.2 The Convention's militant democracy in the context of democratisation

With the end of the Cold War and the fall of the USSR the Strasbourg interpretation of the concept of militant democracy entered a new phase in the context of the process of democratisation in Central and Eastern Europe. Commentators have observed that the historical merits of the concept of militant democracy lay in its response to the challenges of the transition from totalitarian government to democracy. With the fall of the Weimar Republic in mind, the Convention aimed to prevent a repetition of the collapse of democratic orders as experienced in the build up to the Second World War. The first decades of the militant interpretation of the Convention therefore seemed to primarily reaffirm the militant measures taken by Western European democracies, first and foremost Germany, to protect their regained democratic orders against a reoccurrence of the totalitarian experience. It has consequently been argued that the concept of militant democracy should be understood as belonging to the realm of the process of democratic transition *'when "closer judicial vigilance" is warranted given the fragility of democratic institutions'*.[45] It is therefore no surprise that the end of communist rule and the transition to democratic governance in this part of Europe raised questions regarding the legitimacy of militant measures taken by these newly established democracies. Many post-communist states faced serious challenges involved in the process of democratisation. Several of these states introduced restrictions on the exercise of rights by political actors that sought to return to the past, including the dissolution of (successor) communist parties and other political associations, the exclusion of (former) members of the communist party from

---

43 Ibid, par. 61.

44 Joint dissenting opinion of Judges Bernhardt (Germany), Gölcüklü (Turkey), Matscher (Austria), Loizou (Cyprus), Mifsud Bonnici (Malta), Gotchev (Bulgaria), Jungwiert (Czech Republic) and Kūris (Lithuania), par. 2. See also the dissenting opinion Judge Jambrek (Slovenia), in particular par. 3. See also Harvey, *European Law Review*, p. 415.

45 R. Teitel, 'Militating Democracy: Comparative Constitutional Perspectives', *Michigan Journal of International Law*, vol. 29, no. 1, 2007, p. 49. See also M. Hamilton, 'Transition, political loyalties and the order of the state', in: A. Buyse and M. Hamilton (eds.), *Transitional Jurisprudence and the European Convention on Human Rights. Justice, Politics and Rights*, Cambridge: Cambridge University Press, 2011, p. 159.

running for political office and lustration laws that prohibit the use of communist symbols.[46] From the 1990s the Court faced several claims from Central and Eastern European states arguing for the need for such militant measures to protect their young democracies.[47]

9.2.2.1 Militant democracy as a temporary instrument during transition

The Court's judgment in the case *Rekvényi v. Hungary* suggests that the Court in general is willing to endorse such claims. The Hungarian Constitution was amended in 1993 to prohibit members of the armed forces, the police and security services from engaging in any political activity. The applicant, a police officer, alleged that the prohibition unduly restricted his rights to freedom of expression (Article 10 ECHR) and his right to freedom of association (Article 11 ECHR). The Hungarian government contended that the restrictions on the applicant's rights were necessary in a democratic society. In the context of the process of democratisation the government argued that it was *'necessary to depoliticise, inter alia, the police and restrict the political activities of its members so that the public should no longer regard the police as a supporter of the totalitarian regime but rather as a guardian of democratic institutions'*.[48] The Court appeared sensitive to this argument and found that especially against Hungary's historical background, these militant measures could be seen as necessary in a democratic society and did not constitute a violation of Article 10 or 11 ECHR.[49]

Even though the Court in the years that followed maintained that militant measures restricting the political participation of supporters of communism may be allowed in the context of democratisation, it also started to emphasise that such measures can only be justified for a limited period of time.[50] While militant measures may be justified to protect new democratic legal orders, they do not automatically continue to be allowed in more mature democracies. In the case *Partidul Comunistilor v. Romania* concerning the refusal of the Romanian authorities to register a new communist party (PCN), for example, the Court held that it could not *'accept the Government's argument that Romania cannot allow the emergence of a new communist party to form the subject of a democratic debate'*.[51] Albeit taking into account Romania's experience of totalitarian communism, the Court observed '*that that context cannot*

46 See also Hamilton, *Transitional Jurisprudence and the ECHR*, p. 151.
47 Harvey, *European Law Review*, p. 415.
48 ECtHR 20 May 1999 (GC), *Rekvényi v. Hungary*, appl. no. 25390/94, par. 44.
49 ECtHR 20 May 1999 (GC), *Rekvényi v. Hungary*, appl. no. 25390/94, par. 48 and 62.
50 Harvey, *European Law Review*, p. 415.
51 ECtHR 3 February 2005, *Partidul Comunistilor (Nepeceristi) (PCN) and Ungureanu v. Romania*, appl. no. 46626/99, par. 55.

by itself justify the need for the interference, especially as communist parties adhering to Marxist ideology exist in a number of countries that are signatories to the Convention'.[52] As there were no grounds to assume that the applicants' political programme was incompatible with a democratic society, the Court observed that there was no *'pressing social need'* to refuse the party's registration, let alone that there was evidence of a sufficiently imminent risk to democracy. In addition, since nothing in the constitution and programme of the PCN justified the conclusion that it relied on the Convention to engage in activity or perform acts aimed at the destruction of any of the rights and freedoms set forth therein, the Court rejected the request of the Romanian government to bring Article 17 ECHR into play.[53] The Court accordingly found a violation of Article 11 ECHR.

This line of thought was subsequently continued in other cases concerning restrictions on the political participation of supporters of the communist ideology in Central and Eastern Europe. In the case *Ždanoka v. Latvia,* for example, the Court was called upon to consider the disqualification of former members of the *Communist Party of Latvia (CPL)* from standing for election about a decade after Latvia's independence. The Latvian government stressed that the disqualification was a preventative measure to protect the new democratic order and underlined *'that the principle of a "democracy capable of defending itself" was compatible with the Convention, especially in the context of the post-communist societies of central and Eastern Europe'*.[54] The Court, for its part, differentiated between the legitimacy of such measures in firmly established democracies and in developing democracies.[55] It recalled that states are to a certain extent allowed to take measures to protect themselves against groups and persons attempting to destroy the democratic order.[56] At the same time, however, the Court stressed that *'[e]very time a State intends to rely on the principle of 'a democracy capable of defending itself' in order to justify interference with individual rights, it must carefully evaluate the scope and consequences of the measure under consideration, to ensure that the aforementioned balance is achieved'*.[57] In view of the historico-political context of the new democracy of Latvia, the Court therefore found that the applicant's exclusion from standing as a candidate in national elections because of her former position in the CPL was in line with the requirements of Article 3 First Protocol to the ECHR.[58] Nevertheless, the Court took the opportunity to stress

52 Ibid, par. 58.

53 Ibid, par. 58.

54 ECtHR 16 March 2006 (GC), Ždanoka v. Latvia, appl. no. 58278/00, par. 87.

55 J.L.W. Broeksteeg, Case note to ECtHR 16 March 2006 (GC), *Ždanoka v. Latvia*, appl. no. 58278/00, *EHRC* 2006/57, par. 6.

56 ECtHR 16 March 2006 (GC), Ždanoka v. Latvia, appl. no. 58278/00, par. 110.

57 Ibid, par. 100.

58 Ibid, par. 132.

that such measures may only be acceptable in new democracies given the threat *'posed by the resurgence of ideas which, if allowed to gain ground, might appear capable of restoring the former regime'* and may scarcely be considered acceptable in states with long-standing democratic traditions.[59] The Court, therefore, considered it important that the restriction of the right to stand for election of (former) members of the CPL is periodically reviewed *'with a view to bringing it to an early end'*.[60]

The same applied to the banning of the use of communist symbols in the public arena. In the case *Vajnai v. Hungary* the Court held that the banning of the display of a five-pointed red star during a lawful demonstration constituted a violation of Article 10 ECHR. The Hungarian government argued that *'[t]o wear this symbol in public amounted to identification with, and the intention to propagate, the ideologies of a totalitarian nature which characterised communist dictatorships'*.[61] Having regard to Hungary's historical experience with communism, the government considered that the ban was a response to a 'pressing social need' in pursuit of a legitimate aim. The Court found that the circumstances of the case had to be distinguished from the case *Rekvényi v. Hungary*. On the one hand, Vajnai was a politician and not a police officer participating in the exercise of powers as Rekvényi had been. On the other hand, the Court took into account that *'almost two decades have elapsed since Hungary's transition to pluralism and the country has proved to be a stable democracy'*.[62] The Court observed that Hungary had fully integrated into the value system of the Council of Europe and the Convention and had become a member of the European Union. In other words, it could now be considered a mature democracy. Under these circumstances, there was no evidence to suggest that there was a real and present danger of any political movement or party restoring the communist dictatorship.[63] Even though the Court showed that it is well aware that the systematic terror involved in the communist rule in several Central and Eastern European countries *'remains a serious scar in the mind and heart of Europe'*, it nevertheless considered that *'such sentiments, however understandable, cannot alone set the limits of freedom of expression. Given the well-known assurances which the Republic of Hungary provided legally, morally and materially to the victims of communism, such emotions cannot be regarded as rational fears. In the Court's view, a legal system which applies restrictions on human rights in order to satisfy the dictates of public feeling – real or*

59 Ibid, par. 133.

60 Ibid, par. 134.

61 ECtHR 8 July 2008, *Vajnai v. Hungary*, appl. no. 33629/06, par. 40.

62 ECtHR 8 July 2008, *Vajnai v. Hungary*, appl. no. 33629/06, par. 49. See also the case note by J. van der Velde to this case, *EHRC* 2008/105.

63 ECtHR 8 July 2008, *Vajnai v. Hungary*, appl. no. 33629/06, par. 49. See also ECtHR 3 November 2011, *Fratanoló v. Hungary*, appl. no. 29459/10, par. 25. A. Buyse, 'Dangerous expressions: the ECHR, Violence and Free Speech', *International and Comparative Law Quarterly*, vol. 63, no. 2, 2014, p. 501.

imaginary – cannot be regarded as meeting the pressing social needs recognised in a democratic society, since that society must remain reasonable in its judgement'.[64]

In this context the interpretation of the concept of militant democracy shows a similarity with the derogations allowing states to temporarily adjust their obligations under the Convention in times of emergency as provided in Article 15 ECHR.[65] As regards these derogations, Article 15 ECHR provides that measures derogating from the normal operation of fundamental rights are allowed *'to the extent strictly required by the exigencies of the situation'*. In other words, derogations must be proportionate to the actual crisis facing the government at the time.[66] This implies a requirement of temporariness, as derogations which in normal circumstances would infringe the Convention may only be allowed for as long as the emergency exists.[67] In the light of militant measures protecting the democratic order in periods of transition from communist rule, the Court appears to follow a similar line of thought by stressing that such measures are only temporarily justified after the transition to a democratic society and may be less easily justified once a democracy has proven to be stable.

9.2.2.2 The continued justification of militant measures against neo-Nazis

A different approach has been adopted by the Court when it comes to cases related to neo-Nazism, anti-Semitism and denial of the Holocaust. In the case law of the Commission and the Court discussed in Chapter three we have seen that cases concerning Holocaust denial, neo-Nazism and anti-Semitism have consistently been inadmissible. In these cases the element of a transition to a stable democracy does not seem to play a role in the justification of militant measures and the Court has maintained its readiness to accept restrictions on the exercise of the political rights of supporters of fascist and Nazi ideologies. Involvement in activities related to Nazism appears to be a reason as such to justify the application of militant measures. Hence, it is clear that the Court continues to consider extreme right-wing groups and individuals a threat to democracy and democratic values. This perception is widely shared within the Council of Europe. In 2000, the Parliamentary Assembly of the

---

64 ECtHR 8 July 2008, *Vajnai v. Hungary*, appl. no. 33629/06, par. 57.

65 In Chapter four we have learned that both provisions are related in the sense that Article 15 ECHR may apply if *'the life of the nation'*, including its democratic form of government, is at risk. Nevertheless, it has been argued that both provisions come into play at different stages on the 'slide down towards totalitarianism': Article 17 ECHR can be relied upon by states in situations that pose a threat to the democratic society but that are not yet so severe as to justify the proclamation of a state of emergency under Article 15 ECHR. See also D.J. Harris et al. (eds.), *Harris, O'Boyle and Warbrick. Law of the European Convention on Human Rights*, 3rd ed., Oxford: Oxford University Press, 2014, p. 856-857.

66 Harris et al., *Law of the ECHR*, p. 837.

67 Harris et al., p. 837.

Council of Europe stressed that '*extremist movements and parties that pose one of the greatest threats to democracy in member states are those of the far right and, more generally, those that encourage intolerance, xenophobia and racism. Even if they do not directly advocate violence, they nevertheless create a climate that encourages its development'*.[68]

We could say that the tragic experience with fascism and National Socialism, culminating in the Holocaust, has shown that these ideologies are incompatible with the fundamental principles of democracy and respect for human rights. The Strasbourg approach seems to suggest that for that reason alone, the application of militant measures against the supporters of these ideologies continues to be justified. The militant paradigm of what Niesen referred to as 'banning the former ruling party' clearly explains this mechanism. In Chapter seven we have seen that Niesen has characterised restrictions on political association and repression of free speech based on their affiliation with great injustice committed in the past as a distinct paradigm of militant democracy. Militant measures are in this context aimed at preventing *'the resurrection of a defeated historical system of injustice'*.[69] In this understanding of the concept of militant democracy militant measures are embedded in a historical learning process.[70] This learning process is in this case based on what could be described as the collective memory of Europe regarding its experience with fascism and National Socialism. In the context of the ECHR, Nazism was evidently the political system that was at the root of gross injustice and human rights violations. This historical injustice would justify the restriction of any use of rights entailing the defence, glorification or denial of the horrors caused by Nazism.

Many of the early neo-Nazi cases focussed on the special significance of the concept of militant democracy in the German context (and occasionally the Austrian context). Yet, in the case *Heinz Reisz* the Commission explicitly acknowledged that the notion of a *'democracy capable of defending itself'* is also a guiding principle for the interpretation of the Convention. The case was brought to Strasbourg by an applicant who complained about the length of the national proceedings in which the German Federal Constitutional Court was called upon to decide on the forfeiture of his political rights on account of his participation in several neo-Nazi organisations.[71] The

68 CoE, Parliamentary Assembly, *Recommendation No. 1438 on the threat posed to democracy by extremist parties and movements in Europe*, Strasbourg, 25 January 2000, par. 3.

69 Niesen also referred to this as 'negative republicanism'. See P. Niesen, 'Anti-Extremism, Negative Republicanism, Civic Society: Three Paradigms for Banning Political Parties', *German Law Journal*, vol. 3, no. 7, 2002, par. 18, www.germanlawjournal.com/s/GLJ_Vol_03_No_07_Niesen.pdf (accessed 11 April 2016).

70 See also G. Frankenberg, 'The learning Sovereign', in: A. Sajó (ed.), *Militant democracy*, Utrecht: Eleven International Publishing, 2004, p. 127.

71 The proceedings before the German Federal Constitutional Court have been discussed in more detail in Chapter eight.

Commission recalled that the German Weimar Republic nightmare had resulted in a post-War German Basic Law that is based on the idea of a '*wehrhafte Demokratie*'. Subsequently, the Commission concluded that *'The defence of an effective political democracy is also a concept underlying the system of the Convention*'.[72] According to the Commission, the function of Article 17 ECHR is similar to that of Article 18 of the Basic Law, which prohibits abuse and authorizes the forfeiture of rights: *'similarly to Article 18 of the Basic Law, it is the purpose of Article 17 (Art. 17) of the Convention, insofar as it refers to groups or to individuals, to prevent them from deriving from the Convention a right to engage in any activity or perform any act aimed at destroying any of the rights and freedoms set forth in the Convention'*.[73]

9.2.3 Towards a new militant paradigm?

In Chapter seven we have seen that legal scholars have observed that *'[w]ith the end of the cold war, definitions of the supposed enemies of democracy have become much more diffuse and difficult to establish'*.[74] They have argued that measures taken against what can be considered new anti-democratic threats are increasingly justified on the grounds of arguments that traditionally belong to the concept of militant democracy. The same trend can be distinguished in the context of the ECHR. Commentators have noted that the Court has increasingly accepted militant measures in cases that go beyond this traditional paradigm of militant democracy.[75] The Convention that was signed in 1950 was very much a product of its time. Now, more than 60 years later, times have changed. The risk of states sliding down into totalitarianism is perceived as less of a threat than before. In recent years the Court has increasingly taken a militant stance in cases concerning *'transformative political projects that do not pose a threat to democratic processes but which, instead, threaten substantive conceptions of what democracy means to a political community'*.[76] The protection of fundamental rights under the Convention has always been strongly linked to the concept of democracy. Yet, neither the Convention nor the Commission or the Court has ever provided a clear definition of this concept. As Boyle observed, the Court rather *'confined itself to specific dimensions and statements of principle, asserted without much elaboration'*.[77] The militant interpretation of the Convention suggests that over time the focus of the interpretation of the notion of democracy has shifted.

72 EComHR 20 October 1997, *Reisz v. Germany*, appl. no. 32013/96.
73 EComHR 20 October 1997, *Reisz v. Germany*, appl. no. 32013/96.
74 Müller, *The Oxford Handbook of Comparative Constitutional Law*, p. 1256.
75 P. Macklem, 'Guarding the Perimeter: Militant Democracy and Religious Freedom in Europe', *Constellations*, vol. 19, no. 4, 2012, p. 577; Harvey, *European Law Review*, p. 410-411; Marks, *British Yearbook of International Law*, p. 231-232; Macklem, *Constellations*, p. 575.
76 Macklem, *Constellations*, p. 577.
77 K. Boyle, 'Human Rights, Religion and Democracy: The Refah Party Case', *Essex Human Rights Review*, vol. 1, no. 1, 2004, p. 8.

More recent interpretations of militant democracy reveal a wider view of the concept of democracy. While democracy is still associated with democratic institutions and procedures of decision-making, democracy is progressively also identified with values such as *'pluralism, tolerance and broadmindedness'*, which *'urge to constrain the majoritarian tendencies of liberal democracy to respect individual difference'*.[78]

In Chapter seven we have seen that Niesen has referred to this new paradigm of militant democracy as 'civic society'. The aim of restrictions on civil and political rights according to this paradigm is not the protection of democracy itself, but that of democracy as a system for the protection of minorities and future generations.[79] This new paradigm, Niesen argues, is based on theories of civil society. These civil society theories hold that contemporary democracy is *'centered in civic processes'*[80] and *'not in processes of political coordination through electoral campaigns, party competition, and governmental decision making'*.[81] Yet, he also warns against the consequences of this new paradigm, as it broadens the category of subversive political activities and lowers the threshold of restrictions on these activities which may eventually result in a serious reduction in the protection of political rights and liberties.[82]

As we have seen in Chapter seven, one area in which the broadening of the scope of the concept of militant democracy is noticeable is that of political parties and organisations that advocate the replacement of democracy by a theocratic regime. Such challenges to the principle of secularism seem to be increasingly placed within the framework of militant democracy.[83] This trend is also visible in the context of the ECHR. Probably the most striking example of this new paradigm is the Court's judgment in the case concerning the ban on the Turkish Welfare Party (*Refah Partisi*). The main issue raised in this case concerned the ambition of this political party to establish a theocratic regime based on Sharia law. In 1998 the Turkish Constitutional Court dissolved the Welfare Party on the grounds that its activities were contrary

78 Marks, *British Yearbook of International Law*, p. 232.
79 P. Niesen, 'Anti-Extremism, Negative Republicanism, Civic Society: Three Paradigms for Banning Political Parties', *German Law Journal*, vol. 3, no. 7, 2002, par. 43, www.germanlawjournal.com/s/GLJ_Vol_03_No_07_Niesen.pdf (accessed 11 April 2016). See also Frankenberg, *Militant democracy*, p. 130-131.
80 U.K. Preuß, 'Die empfindsame Demokratie', in: C. Leggewie and H. Meier (eds.), *Verbot der NPD oder mit Rechtsradikalen leben*?, Frankfurt am Main: Suhrkamp, 2002, p. 104-119, cited by Niesen, *German Law Journal*, par. 43.
81 P. Niesen, *German Law Journal*, par. 43.
82 Niesen, par. 42-43.
83 Müller, *The Oxford Handbook of Comparative Constitutional Law*, p. 1256; A. Sajó, 'From Militant Democracy to the Preventive State?', *Cardozo Law Review*, vol. 27, no. 5, 2006, p. 2264-2265; Macklem, *Constellations*, p. 579; Macklem, *International Journal of Constitutional Law*, p. 491; S. Tyulkina, *Militant Democracy. Undemocratic Political Parties and Beyond*, Abingdon/New York: Routledge, 2015, p. 167-205.

to the constitutional principle of secularism.[84] In the procedure before the Chamber the Turkish government argued that the party had become a *'centre of activities contrary to the principle of secularism'* and was therefore a threat to Turkey's secular democracy.[85] The dissolution of the Welfare Party, the government asserted, was in that regard a *'preventive measure to protect democracy'*.[86] The government emphasised that *'when confronted with the risk which political Islam represented for a democratic regime based on human rights, that regime was entitled to take measures to protect itself from the danger. "Militant democracy", in other words a democratic system which defended itself against all political movements which sought to destroy it.... In the Government's submission, militant democracy required political parties, its indispensable protagonists, to show loyalty to democratic principles, and accordingly to the principle of secularism'*.[87] The Court upheld the ban on the grounds that the party's objectives were incompatible with the requirements of a democratic society.[88] Even though the Court did not use the term militant democracy, its militant interpretation of the Convention stems from the following passage in which it explains that *'[i]n view of the very clear link between the Convention and democracy..., no one must be authorised to rely on the Convention's provisions in order to weaken or destroy the ideals and values of a democratic society. Pluralism and democracy are based on a compromise that requires various concessions by individuals or groups of individuals, who must sometimes agree to limit some of the freedoms they enjoy in order to guarantee greater stability of the country as a whole'*.[89] This case shows that the Court agrees with states defending their democratic values against abolishment, thereby suggesting that such 'militant secularism' *'is an acceptable form of militant democracy'*.[90]

The interpretation of the abuse clause in Article 17 ECHR, the Convention's most far-reaching militant instrument, has also followed this trend. In Chapters three and four we have seen that commentators have observed that the case law on Article 17 ECHR shows *'a gradual shift from the classic cases of totalitarian threat to broader issues*

84 ECtHR 31 July 2001, *Refah Partisi (The Welfare Party) and others v. Turkey*, appl. nos. 41340/98 et al., par. 12. See also Bader on how secularism and militant democracy are linked in Turkey and India: V. Bader, 'Constitutionalizing secularism, alternative secularisms or liberal-democratic constitutionalism? A critical reading of some Turkish, ECtHR and Indian Supreme Court cases on 'secularism'', *Utrecht Law Review*, vol. 6, no. 3, 2010, p. 13 and 15.

85 ECtHR 13 February 2003 (GC), *Refah Partisi (the Welfare Party) and others v. Turkey*, appl. nos. 41340/98 et al., par. 23.

86 ECtHR 31 July 2001, *Refah Partisi (The Welfare Party) and others v. Turkey*, appl. nos. 41340/98 et al., par. 63.

87 Ibid, par. 62.

88 Ibid, par. 132. Macklem, *Constellations*, p. 581.

89 ECtHR 13 February 2003 (GC), *Refah Partisi (the Welfare Party) and others v. Turkey,* appl. nos. 41340/98 et al., par. 99.

90 Macklem, *Constellations*, p. 581.

(such as racism) that go against the Convention's values'.[91] Although the original realm of Article 17 ECHR was to *'protect the rights enshrined in the Convention by safeguarding the free functioning of democratic institutions'*,[92] in more recent cases, the Commission and the Court have also considered activities that are *'contrary to the text and spirit of the Convention'*[93] or that run counter to the *'basic'*, *'underlying'* or *'fundamental'* *'values'* or *'ideas'*[94] of the Convention to fall within the scope of Article 17 ECHR. Bates has observed in this regard that the Convention in general is no longer merely a *'last protector of basic human rights values against the backdrop of Nazi atrocities and Stalinism'*, but serves a greater ambition as a defender of *'European human rights and democratic values'*.[95]

9.3 Balancing the protection of fundamental rights and democracy

The Convention's approval of the notion of democratic self-defence as a legitimate ground for the restriction of the fundamental rights of anti-democratic actors is a complex one. As Harvey put it, *'while the relationship between democracy and human rights may be symbiotic, the Court has always understood there to be an inherent tension between the two'*.[96] We have seen earlier that the potentially paradoxical effect of militant measures has frequently been the subject of scholarly debate. On the one hand, the Convention is clearly an expression of concerns for the defence of democracy and its institutions.[97] As Fox and Nolte put it, the Convention *'favours the long-term survival of democracy over the short-term negative effects of*

91 A. Buyse, 'Contested contours. The limits of freedom of expression from an abuse of rights perspective – Articles 10 and 17 ECHR', in: E. Brems and J. Gerards (eds.), *Shaping Rights in the ECHR. The Role of the European Court of Human Rights in Determining the Scope of Human Rights*, Cambridge: Cambridge University Press, 2014, p. 205.

92 EComHR 20 July 1957, *German Communist Party v. Germany*, appl. no. 250/57. See also D.J. Harris, M. O'Boyle, E.P. Bates and C.M. Buckley (eds.), *Harris, O'Boyle and Warbrick. Law of the European Convention on Human Rights*, 3rd ed., Oxford: Oxford University Press, 2014, p. 853.

93 EComHR 2 September 1994, *Ochensberger v. Austria*, appl. no. 21318/93, par. 1; EComHR 18 October 1995, *Honsik v. Austria*, appl. no. 25062/94, par. 1; EComHR 24 June 1996, *Marais v. France*, appl. no. 31159/96, par. 1; EComHR 16 January 1996, *Rebhandl v. Austria*, appl. no. 24398/94, par. 3; ECtHR 13 December 2005 (dec.), *Witzsch v. Germany*, appl. no. 7485/03 at par. 3.

94 EComHR 6 September 1995, *Remer v. Germany*, appl. no. 25096/94, par. 1; EComHR 18 October 1995, *Honsik v. Austria*, appl. no. 25062/94; EComHR 29 November 1995, *Nationaldemokratische Partei Deutschlands, Bezirksverband München-Oberbayern v. Germany*, appl. no. 25992/94; EComHR 24 June 1996, *Marais v. France*, appl. no. 31159/96, par. 1.

95 Bates, *The Evolution of the ECHR*, p. 387.

96 Harvey, *European Law Review*, p. 410-411. See also Marks, *British Yearbook of International Law*, p. 216.

97 Concurring opinion of Judge Jambrek (Slovenia) in the case ECtHR 23 September 1998 (GC), *Lehideux and Isorni v. France*, appl. no. 24662/94, par. 2-3.

the deprivation of political rights of anti-democratic actors'.[98] On the other hand, an excessively militant democracy may eventually no longer be democratic.[99] The Strasbourg organs also seem to be well aware of these complexities. In the case *Klass v. Germany* the Court, therefore, stressed that even though states are allowed to adopt legislation in order to protect their democratic legal order, *'being aware of the danger such a law poses of undermining or even destroying democracy on the ground of defending it'* states may not, in the name of the struggle against anti-democratic movements, *'adopt whatever measures they deem appropriate'*.[100] The Court has stressed in a number of cases that states have to show restraint when it comes to restricting rights in the name of protecting democracy and democratic values. In the case *Stankov v. Bulgaria*, the Court warned that *'Sweeping measures of a preventive nature to suppress freedom of assembly and expression other than in cases of incitement to violence or rejection of democratic principles – however shocking and unacceptable certain views or words used may appear to the authorities, and however illegitimate the demands made may be – do a disservice to democracy and often even endanger it'*.[101] Hence, the precedence of democratic principles may not go as far as rendering the fundamental rights enshrined in the Convention meaningless. Within the system of the Convention, states are therefore urged to exercise restraint when applying militant measures to protect the democratic order. Also interferences with the rights guaranteed in the Convention with the aim of preserving the democratic system require *'a clearly established need'*.[102]

Accordingly, in a number of cases the Commission and the Court have identified transformative political projects that a state cannot prevent in the name of defending democracy.[103] For militant measures to be justified, the political agenda of the applicant should pose a fundamental threat to the democratic nature of the state. Support for modification of the legal and constitutional order of a state is in itself not incompatible with the principles of democracy.[104] The Court, for example, considered that the refusal to register a political party because of its support for the fight against impunity of those who had collaborated with the former totalitarian

---

98 Fox and Nolte, *Harvard International Law Journal*, p. 2 and 38ff. For an understanding of the paradigms of procedural and substantive democracy, see Chapter seven on the theoretical foundations of the militant democracy.

99 Pfersmann, *Militant democracy*, p. 48.

100 ECtHR 6 September 1978, *Klass and others v. Germany*, appl. no. 5029/71, par. 49.

101 ECtHR 2 October 2001, *Stankov and the united Macedonian Organisation Llinden v. Bulgaria*, appl. nos. 29221/95 and 29225/95, par. 97.

102 EComHR 11 May 1984 (report), *Glasenapp v. Germany*, appl. no. 9228/80, par. 110 [emphasis added]. See also EComHR 30 November 1993 (report), *Vogt v. Germany*, appl. no. 17851/91, par. 71. See also Harvey, *European Law Review*, p. 413.

103 Macklem, *Constellations*, p. 577.

104 Ü. Kilinç, 'La conception de la démocratie militante dans la jurisprudence de la Cour Européenne des Droits de l'Homme', *Revue trimestrielle des droits de l'homme*, vol. 23, no. 90, 2012, p. 321-322.

regime constituted a breach of the right to freedom of association in Article 11 ECHR.[105] Likewise, the Court found a violation of Article 11 ECHR in the refusal to register an association that campaigned for the restoration of the monarchy in Bulgaria and the opening of the border with the Former Yugoslav Republic of Macedonia.[106] In the same vein, the Court considered that the disqualification of a senior judge for expressing a controversial legal opinion regarding the jurisdiction of the constitutional court constituted a violation of Article 10 ECHR.[107] And in a series of cases against Turkey, the Court consistently found that militant measures against political parties that advocated self-determination and the constitutional recognition of the Kurdish people were unjustified.[108] The Turkish government had argued that such an undermining of *'the territorial integrity of the State and the unity of the nation'* justified the dissolution of these political parties. The Court stressed, for its part, that *'an association, including a political party, is not excluded from the protection afforded by the Convention simply because its activities are regarded by the national authorities as undermining the constitutional structures of the State and calling for the imposition of restrictions'*.[109]

9.4 The margin of appreciation with regard to militant measures

A final issue relates to the role of the Convention, as an international instrument, in defining the boundaries of the concept of militant democracy. Harvey considers this role to be a complicated one.[110] The concept of militant democracy is *'not a universal stencil'*[111] and the measures that may be taken to protect democracy depend on the specific characteristics of the State Party concerned. In defining when and how to defend the democratic regime the boundaries of a state's possibilities to take a militant stance are therefore classic issues to be dealt with by the authorities of the State Parties that are bound to uphold a particular constitutional order *'which often explicitly sets out the blueprint for militant democracy and specific procedures for its operation'*.[112] The difficulty for the ECtHR, however, is that it is not bound to uphold

105 ECtHR 7 December 2006, *Linkov v. Czech Republic*, appl. no. 10504/03, par. 40-46.

106 ECtHR 21 June 2007, *Zhechev v. Bulgaria*, appl. no. 57045/00, par. 47-50.

107 ECtHR 28 October 1999 (GC), *Wille v. Lichtenstein*, appl. no. 28396/95, par. 67-70.

108 ECtHR 30 January 1998 (GC), *United Communist Party of Turkey and Others v. Turkey*, appl. no. 19392/92; ECtHR 25 May 1998 (GC), *Socialist Party and others v. Turkey*, appl. no. 21237/93; ECtHR 8 December 1999 (GC), *Freedom and Democracy Party (Özdep) v. Turkey*, appl. no. 23885/94; ECtHR 9 April 2002, *Yazar and others v. Turkey*, appl. nos. 22723/93, 22724/93 and 22725/93. See also Macklem, *Constellations*, p. 577, footnote 13.

109 ECtHR 30 January 1998, *United Communist Party of Turkey and Others v. Turkey*, appl. no. 19392/92, par. 27.

110 See also Cannie and Voorhoof, *Netherlands Quarterly of Human Rights*, p. 71-72.

111 S. Tyulkina, *Militant Democracy. Undemocratic Political Parties and Beyond*, London/New York: Routledge, 2015, p. 35.

112 Harvey, *European Law Review*, p. 411.

an existing constitutional order.[113] Its task is to monitor States' compliance with the rights and freedoms guaranteed by the ECHR. Therefore, when it comes to measures belonging to the narrative of militant democracy, the Court allows states a relatively generous margin of appreciation.[114]

At the same time, it is ultimately for the Court to determine whether or not states have acted in accordance with their obligations under the ECHR. This also means that the Court has to decide whether a state's claim that restrictions on the exercise of fundamental rights were necessary in the name of defending democracy or democratic values was justified. As we have seen in Chapter seven, the concept of militant democracy assumes the existence of a democratic regime. This means that states which are not democratic cannot take undemocratic measures under the pretext of militant democracy. In that context some scholars have warned that even though all Member States of the Council of Europe are in theory supposed to meet European standards of respect for democracy and human rights, some states are considered to occupy some sort or *'"gray zone" between authoritarianism and consolidated liberal democracy'*.[115] Even though such *'illiberal democracies'*[116] masquerade as liberal democracies by creating formal democratic institutions and simulate respect for civil and political rights and liberties, they essentially have authoritarian traits. In the hands of such states, Harvey fears that the tutelary powers that states possess under the concept of militant democracy may be used to keep these illiberal regimes in power. Despite the generous margin of appreciation in this context, they argue, the Court has to be wary of the illegitimate use of the narrative of militant democracy as a justification for restrictions on the exercise of fundamental political rights and freedoms.

9.5 Conclusions

In this chapter we studied the interpretation of the concept of militant democracy in the context of the ECHR. We have seen that democracy and human rights protection are intrinsically linked under the ECHR. The importance of maintaining the ideals and values of a democratic society have been translated into a militant stance against political actors who use their fundamental rights protected under the Convention to advance an anti-democratic political agenda. Over the years a distinct concept of militant democracy has been developed within the context of the ECHR.

The case law discussed in this chapter has shown that questions related to the concept of militant democracy are principally addressed in the context of

113 Harvey, p. 411.
114 R. de Lange, Case note to ECtHR 6 January 2011, *Paksas v. Lithuania*, appl. no. 34932/04, *EHRC* 2011/47, par. 12.
115 Harvey, *European Law Review*, p. 410.
116 F. Zakaria, 'The Rise of Illiberal Democracy', *Foreign Affairs*, vol. 76, no. 6, 1997, p. 22-43.

the limitation of the right to freedom of association. In many cases in which the Commission or the Court accepted a claim of self-defence in the name of democracy by one of the States Parties to the Convention, the abuse clause in Article 17 ECHR was not involved in the justification of militant measures. The hallmark case with regard to the Convention's approach to the concept of militant democracy, the *Refah Partisi* case, is illustrative in this regard. In this case the Court did not seek recourse to Article 17 ECHR, but evaluated the ban on this anti-democratic political party within the framework of the limitation clause in Article 11(2) ECHR. This shows that the realisation of the Convention's ambition to protect the democratic systems in the Member States of the Council of Europe certainly does not depend exclusively on the application of Article 17 ECHR. It can be argued that the abuse clause in Article 17 ECHR, as the most far-reaching tutelary instrument, is the tailpiece of the Convention's militant democracy.[117] Yet, since complaints by anti-democratic actors that pose a threat to the Convention system can also be rejected on the basis of Article 10(2) or 11(2) ECHR, some scholars have wondered whether the additional security measure of Article 17 ECHR is not in fact superfluous.[118]

Furthermore, commentators have observed that the interpretation of the concept of militant democracy in the context of the ECHR has been stretched. Commentators have noted that over the years the Court has increasingly accepted militant measures in cases that go beyond this traditional paradigm of militant democracy as a rampart against totalitarianism.[119] As Macklem put it, *'militant democracy appears to have migrated from a principle that authorizes a state to act in a militant manner to preserve democratic processes to one that entitles a state to establish perimeters and guard against threats of a different kind'*.[120] Where the Convention's militant stance traditionally focussed on the protection of democracy institutions and the democratic decision-making process, nowadays also the protection of democratic values of a more substantive nature, such as *'pluralism, tolerance and broadmindedness'*, has progressively been accepted in the name of democratic self-defence.[121] At the same time, activities related to Holocaust denial, anti-Semitism and neo-Nazism have consistently – and practically without further ado – been considered incompatible with the Convention.

---

117 Kilinç, *Revue trimestrielle des droits de l'homme*, p. 302; S. Van Drooghenbroeck, 'L'Article 17 de la Convention Européenne des Droits de l'Homme est-il indispensable ?', *Revue trimestrielle des droits de l'homme,* vol. 12, no. 46, 2001, p. 542.

118 A. Spielmann, 'La Convention Européenne des droits de l'homme et l'abus de droit', in: *Mélanges en hommage à Louis Edmond Pettiti*, Brussels: Bruylant, 1998, p. 685.

119 Macklem, *Constellations*, p. 575; Harvey, *European Law Review*, p. 410-411; Marks, *British Yearbook of International Law*, p. 231-232.

120 Macklem, *Constellations*, p. 575.

121 Marks, *British Yearbook of International Law,* p. 232.

In that context the same concerns are voiced as in the general debate on the concept of militant democracy. While the Convention is an expression of the ambition to defend democracy and its underlying values and principles, embracing an excessively broad militant interpretation may endanger human rights protection. The Convention demands that a fair compromise is reached between the requirements for defending the democratic order and protecting individual rights.[122] The precedence of democratic principles may not go as far as rendering the rights and freedoms in the Convention meaningless. The Court increasingly appears to demand that interferences with the rights guaranteed in the Convention with the aim of preserving the democratic system satisfy *'a clearly established need'*.[123] While the Commission and the Court initially hardly required any kind of proof of the threat to democracy posed by applicants adhering to a totalitarian ideology, the subsidiarity and proportionality nowadays appears to receive more attention. Even though in some cases the presumption that a democracy should be able to defend itself against activities that violate its foundations and fundamental values remains in itself enough to justify militant measures, in a number of cases an objective criterion is added to the assessment of the justification of militant measures.

122 ECtHR 6 September 1978, *Klass and others v. Germany*, appl. no. 5029/71, par. 59. See also ECtHR 23 July 1968, *Case 'relating to certain aspects of the laws on the use of languages in education in Belgium' v. Belgium ('Belgian Linguistic' case)*, appl. nos. 1474/62 et al., par. 5.

123 EComHR 11 May 1984 (report), *Glasenapp v. Germany*, appl. no. 9228/80, par. 110 [emphasis added]. See also EComHR 30 November 1993 (report), *Vogt v. Germany*, appl. no. 17851/91, par. 71. See also Harvey, *European Law Review*, p. 413.

Chapter 10
Conclusions

'A force de sacrifier l'essentiel pour l'urgence, on finit par oublier l'urgence de l'essentiel'
Edgar Morin, *La Méthode*[1]

10.1 Introduction

This study focused on the prohibition of abuse of rights in Article 17 ECHR. This provision, also referred to as the abuse clause, prohibits an abuse of the fundamental rights guaranteed in the Convention. It provides that *'[n]othing in this Convention may be interpreted as implying for any State, group or person any right to engage in any activity or perform any act aimed at the destruction of any of the rights and freedoms set forth herein or at their limitation to a greater extent than is provided for in the Convention'*.

The abuse clause in Article 17 ECHR is one of the most fundamental provisions of the Convention.[2] It embodies one of its main principles: its commitment to democracy and democratic values. By preventing groups and individuals with anti-democratic aims from successfully invoking fundamental rights and freedoms, *'Article 17 ECHR is a microcosm for particular instances of what the Convention as a whole is meant to do on a larger scale: to protect democracy and to prevent totalitarianism'*.[3]

At the same time it is also one of the Convention's most controversial provisions. It is phrased in rather ambiguous terms and it remains unclear what exactly it aims to defend. Democracy and democratic values are abstract notions that are not clearly defined in the ECHR or in the Strasbourg case law. In addition, there unmistakably exists an inherent tension between human rights protection and the

---

1 E. Morin, *La Méthode*, vol. 6, Éthique, 2004.

2 Y. Arai (rev.), 'Prohibition of abuse of the rights and freedoms set forth in the convention and of their limitation to a greater extent than is provided for in the convention (Article 17)', in: P. van Dijk, F. van Hoof, A. van Rijn and L. Zwaak (eds.), *Theory and practice of the European Convention on Human Rights*, 4th ed., Antwerp/Oxford: Intersentia, 2006, p. 1084.

3 A. Buyse, 'Contested contours. The limits of freedom of expression from an abuse of rights perspective – Articles 10 and 17 ECHR', in: *Shaping Rights in the ECHR. The Role of the European Court of Human Rights in Determining the Scope of Human Rights*, E. Brems and J. Gerards (eds.), Cambridge: Cambridge University Press, 2014, p. 187.

abuse clause.[4] While human rights essentially aim to promote freedom by affirming the basic rights and freedoms citizens enjoy vis-à-vis state authorities, the abuse clause primarily aims to protect democracy and democratic values against groups and individuals invoking these rights with the aim of undermining the democratic organisation of the state. The question when the use of a fundamental right turns into abuse is therefore an extremely complicated one, both for academics and for courts required to adjudicate on it. This makes the interpretation and the application of the abuse clause a highly delicate and controversial matter.

For a long time, Article 17 ECHR received little attention in academic literature and was seldom invoked or applied in the case law of the EComHR and the ECtHR. Recent years, however, have seen an increase in the interest in the abuse clause, both from courts and legal scholars and political scientists. Yet, an analysis of this growing body of case law shows that the interpretation of Article 17 ECHR is far from unequivocal. While based on Article 17 ECHR subversive, anti-democratic activities may be excluded from the protection of the Convention, clear criteria for determining which activities fit this description are lacking. Interpretations of the provision in both legal doctrine and case law point in a variety of different directions. The inconsistent application of the abuse clause shows that there is a need to shed light on the provision in order to contribute to a more coherent interpretation. The central research question that has been addressed in this study is accordingly:

How has the prohibition of abuse of rights in Article 17 of the European Convention on Human Rights to date been interpreted by the European Commission of Human Rights and the European Court of Human Rights and how can this provision be applied in the future?

This research started with a retrospective look at the interpretation of Article 17 ECHR. It looked at the drafting history of the Convention in order to analyse why the drafters decided to include an abuse clause. Next, it elaborated on the case law of the EComHR and the ECtHR concerning Article 17 ECHR and revealed a number of unclarities and inconsistencies in the Strasbourg interpretation of the abuse clause. In search of clarification, it subsequently explored different perspectives in order to shed light on the meaning and relevance of Article 17 ECHR. First, it examined the understanding of the abuse clause in the context of the ECHR by legal scholars. Next, it analysed the interpretation of other abuse clauses in international and regional human rights law. It then moved on to a study of the general concept of abuse of rights. Finally, it explored the concept of militant democracy.

4 Buyse, *Shaping Rights in the ECHR*, p. 184.

10.2 Background and interpretation of the abuse clause

Article 17 ECHR is very much a product of its time. The Convention was drafted in the first years after the Second World War. The drafters feared that totalitarian currents of Nazi, fascist or communist tendencies would (again) attempt to overthrow Western European democracies. With the atrocities of the Second World War still fresh in the mind and faced with advancing communism from the East, the drafters aimed to *'create an international mechanism by which "free Europe" could protect itself against the rise of another Hitler, or the installation of a totalitarian regime'*.[5] The abuse clause in Article 17 ECHR is the most explicit expression of this ambition. Following the example of the UDHR, the provision was included in the Convention to prevent fundamental rights from being exploited by totalitarian groups and individuals.

The original realm of Article 17 ECHR as a rampart against totalitarian currents exploiting democracy and democratic values with the aim of overthrowing them was initially clearly reflected in the Strasbourg case law. Until the 1990s the abuse clause was primarily referred to in relation to extreme political views related to the totalitarian threats identified at the time of drafting the Convention: communism and neo-Nazism. Over time, however, the scope of the abuse clause has been broadened beyond its original focus on totalitarianism. Since the end of the Cold War Article 17 ECHR has increasingly been applied to broader issues that are considered contrary to the *'basic'*, *'underlying'* or *'fundamental' 'values'* or *'ideas'* or the *'text and spirit'* of the Convention, such as racial discrimination or hostility towards a religious group.[6]

The contemporary application of Article 17 ECHR has resulted in an obscure and inconsistent case-to-case approach. First, even though the EComHR and the ECtHR have stressed that the abuse clause is *'only applicable on an exceptional basis and in extreme cases'*,[7] so far they have failed to stipulate clear criteria for determining which cases fit this description. The abuse clause covers a wide variety of activities that are allegedly aimed at the destruction of the rights and freedoms set forth in the Convention, ranging from, *inter alia*, Holocaust denial, support for communist ideology, hate speech, challenges to the principle of secularism, and incitement to

5 E. Bates, *The Evolution of the European Convention on Human Rights. From its Inception to the Creation of a Permanent Court of Human Rights*, Oxford: Oxford University Press, 2010, p. 6.

6 See e.g. EComHR 6 September 1995, *Remer v. Germany*, appl. no. 25096/94, par. 1; EComHR 18 October 1995, *Honsik v. Austria*, appl. no. 25062/94; EComHR 29 November 1995, *Nationaldemokratische Partei Deutschlands, Bezirksverband München-Oberbayern v. Germany*, appl. no. 25992/94; EComHR 24 June 1996, *Marais v. France*, appl. no. 31159/96, par. 1; ECtHR 16 November 2004 (dec.), *Norwood v. the United Kingdom*, appl. no. 23131/03; ECtHR 14 March 2013, *Kasymakhunov and Saybatalov v. Russia*, appl. nos. 26261/05 and 26377/06, par. 113.

7 ECtHR 15 October 2015 (GC), *Perinçek v. Switzerland*, appl. no. 27510/08, par. 114. See also ECtHR 6 January 2011 (GC), *Paksas v. Lithuania*, appl. no. 34932/04, par. 87.

violence. At the same time, the case law is not sufficiently able to justify why the EComHR and the ECtHR refused to address other extreme activities under Article 17 ECHR. For example, while the principal aim of the abuse clause according to its drafters was to uphold the democratic system the Court did not refer to this provision when assessing the banning of a political party whose *'aim to set up a theocratic regime based on sharia was incompatible with democracy'*.[8] In addition, the Commission and the Court have in some cases considered that racist hate speech *'clearly constitutes an activity within the meaning of Article 17 of the Convention'*[9] while in other cases they found that comparable racist utterances were not sufficiently serious to justify the application of Article 17 ECHR.[10]

Second, it is unclear how Article 17 ECHR should be applied. Is the abuse clause a tool to assess the scope of the protection of the rights and freedoms guaranteed by the Convention or rather a principle of interpretation for the assessment of the necessity of an interference with the exercise of these rights and freedoms? Under the direct application of Article 17 ECHR an activity that is considered an abuse of rights is excluded from the protection of the Convention. The indirect application, on the other hand, means that Article 17 ECHR serves as a compass to assess whether an interference with a right was necessary in a democratic society. Yet, in a number of cases the indirect application of Article 17 ECHR did not just contribute to the Commission or the Court not finding a violation, but it rendered the application manifestly ill-founded. Through a detour, the indirect application of Article 17 ECHR in those cases still resulted in the inadmissibility of the complaint, exempting the Commission or the Court from a profound examination of the case on its merits. Meanwhile, the Strasbourg approach in a number of other cases suggests that applications by anti-democratic actors could just as well be dealt with without explicitly relying on the abuse clause. In a few cases the EComHR and the ECtHR followed a reasoning comparable to that adopted under Article 17 ECHR without openly referring to this provision and in some cases they even completely ignored the abuse clause and the accompanying case law in cases where the provision logically seemed relevant. The choice for one method or the other seems rather arbitrary and the often relatively marginal argumentation with regard to the applicability of Article 17 ECHR fails to convincingly explain these differences.

---

8 ECtHR 13 February 2003 (GC), *Refah Partisi (the Welfare Party) and other v. Turkey*, appl. nos. 41340/98 et al., par. 125.

9 EComHR 11 October 1979, *Glimmerveen and Hagenbeek v. the Netherlands*, appl. nos. 8348/78 and 8406/78.

10 ECtHR 16 July 2009, *Féret v. Belgium*, appl. no. 15615/07.

10.3 In search of a clarification of Article 17 ECHR

Given the inconsistent application of the abuse clause by the Strasbourg organs, it is clear that there is a need for clarification on this topic. For that reason, this study aimed to shed light on the interpretation of Article 17 ECHR. It explored a broad range of perspectives with the aim of collecting relevant insights that may help to come to a better understanding of the Convention's abuse clause. This study first of all analysed the current academic debate on Article 17 ECHR. It subsequently took a broad approach by adding new perspectives to the discussion on the Convention's abuse clause. In that regard three interesting frameworks have been explored: the interpretation of other abuse clauses in international and regional human rights law, the principle of abuse of rights, and the concept of militant democracy.

10.3.1 The scholarly interpretation of Article 17 ECHR

Notwithstanding its limited practical relevance in the judgments and decisions of the Commission and the Court, the provision has frequently been the subject of academic debate. While legal scholars generally acknowledge that Article 17 ECHR sends a clear signal about the need to uphold democracy and democratic values, they have repeatedly called attention to the potential negative consequences of the application of this clause. The abuse clause has paradoxical implications: if states are allowed to rely on Article 17 ECHR to justify serious interferences with the fundamental rights of anti-democratic actors, they risk undermining the democratic standards of the Convention themselves.[11] Some states may even abuse the abuse clause by relying on it in order to justify restrictions on (political) views that run counter to the view adopted by the government.[12] The distinction between (controversial) activities that deserve the protection of the Convention and activities that are truly dangerous to democracy and democratic values is indeed an extremely complex and delicate one. The incoherent Strasbourg case law, however, is far from helpful in clarifying this issue. It is therefore doubtful whether the current way in which the Court applies the abuse clause is able to succeed in protecting democracy and democratic values. Given the far-reaching consequences that the application of Article 17 ECHR may have for the protection of the fundamental rights of the applicant, one may wonder whether the current application of Article 17 ECHR is not just counterproductive. Especially considering the expansion of the scope of application of Article 17 ECHR,

11 H. Cannie and D. Voorhoof, 'The Abuse Clause and Freedom of Expression in the European Human Rights Convention: an Added Value for Democracy and Human Rights Protection?', *Netherlands Quarterly of Human Rights*, vol. 29, no. 1, 2011, p. 76-78; Buyse, *Shaping Rights in the ECHR*, p. 205; Arai, *Theory and Practice of the ECHR*, p. 1086-1087.

12 Cannie and Voorhoof, *Netherlands Quarterly of Human Rights*, p. 72; I. Hare, 'Extreme Speech under International and Regional Human Rights Standards', in: I Hare and J. Weinstein (eds.), *Extreme Speech and Democracy*, Oxford: Oxford University Press, 2009, p. 79.

the provision risks becoming *'overly broad in denying human rights protection and in preventing an assessment of the proportionality of state interference'.*[13] This may have serious consequences for the level of protection of dissenting (political) views in Europe.

The direct application of Article 17 ECHR, according to which a complaint concerning activities that fall within the scope of Article 17 ECHR is declared inadmissible as being incompatible *ratione materiae* with the provisions of the Convention, is the most problematic. The direct application results in the inadmissibility of the complaint based on a *prima facie* assessment, exempting the Commission or the Court from examining the compatibility of the interference with the limitation criteria in the second paragraph of the Articles 10 and 11 ECHR, the provisions most often associated with abuse. This approach has been rightly criticised for the lack of a clear balancing of the interests involved and the marginal assessment of the proportionality of the interference with the applicant's right. It should be remembered that the limitation clauses in the Convention have an important function. They make clear that restrictions on fundamental rights and freedoms are the exception and that they are only justified under strict conditions. The limitation clauses require the Court to make a balanced and substantiated assessment. Moreover, given the broad criteria for limitation afforded by Articles 10(2) and 11(2) ECHR, it is generally not necessary to resort to Article 17 ECHR to assess the permissibility of an interference with the rights and freedoms of an anti-democratic political actor. In the case of a serious threat to democracy or democratic principles, the restriction of a right is likely to meet a pressing social need and will probably be justified under the limitation clause.

10.3.2 Abuse clauses in other human rights documents

The ECHR is not the only human rights document that prohibits an abuse of the rights and freedoms it guarantees. Abuse clauses equivalent to Article 17 ECHR are found in the UDHR, the ICCPR, the ICESCR, the ACHR, and the EU Charter. In this study we have seen that the historical background and the original purpose of these abuse clauses are rather similar. Comparable to Article 17 ECHR, the inclusion of an abuse clause in the UDHR, the ICCPR, and the ICESCR was primarily motivated by the Second World War experience with totalitarian rule. At the time of their creation, similar concerns were raised as those surrounding Article 17 ECHR. Some experts involved in the drafting of the UDHR and the two International Covenants, for example, warned that the abuse clause lacked precision and called for an almost impossible assessment to distinguish the use of a right from abuse.[14] Yet, these difficulties seemed hardly apparent to the majority of the drafters at that time, who

13 Buyse, *Shaping Rights in the ECHR*, p. 205.

14 UN ECOSOC, Commission on Human Rights, third session, 74th meeting, 15 June 1948, *UN DOC. E/CN.4/SR.74*, p. 7.

seemed to be predominantly concerned with the need to prevent a resurrection of Nazism.[15] Attempts to delete the abuse clause from the draft documents were consequently unsuccessful.

Despite the fact that the wording and the background of the abuse clauses in these various human rights documents are quite similar, their interpretation has gone in different directions. Some differences are worth mentioning. The first difference concerns the application of Article 5(1) ICCPR, Article 17 ECHR's counterpart at UN level. While the scope of application of Article 17 ECHR seems to be expanding, the interpretation of Article 5(1) ICCPR in contrast appears to have become more restrictive.[16] Initially, the CCPR occasionally applied Article 5(1) ICCPR to declare a communication based on the right to freedom of expression inadmissible, just as the ECtHR has done under the direct application of Article 17 ECHR. Later, however, it appears to have reconsidered this approach. In the case *Ross v. Canada*, about a teacher who was removed from the classroom because of his anti-Jewish statements, the Committee emphasised that restrictions on the right to freedom of expression, even in the case of national, racial, or religious hatred, must be assessed under Article 19 ICCPR.[17] With this conclusion, the Committee seems to reject the application of the abuse clause and chose a balanced approach based on the limitation criteria provided in Article 19(3) ICCPR. The Committee has not referred to the abuse clause in Article 5(1) ICCPR to declare a communication inadmissible ever since.

The second difference worth mentioning concerns the abuse clause in Article 29(a) ACHR. Even though it was drafted after the example of the ECHR,[18] the interpretation and application of the abuse clause in the ACHR seems to differ significantly from that of Article 17 ECHR. On the one hand, in the few cases in which the IACtHR ruled on Article 29(a) ACHR it found an abuse of rights on the side of the State Party for interpreting the American Convention in a way that would put an end to the rights and freedoms it guarantees.[19] This is interesting, given that the relevance of the abuse clause for the obligations of states is practically negligible in the context of Article 17 ECHR. Article 17 ECHR seems to not play a role in the protection against state abuse,[20] as abuse of the Convention's provisions by State

15 Alfredson and Aide, *The Universal Declaration of Human Rights*, p. 649.

16 Given the small number of communications on Article 5(1) ICCPR, however, it is difficult to draw hard and fast conclusions in this regard.

17 See in particular UN CCPR 18 October 2000 (70th session), *Ross v. Canada*, communication no. 736/1997, par. 10.5 and 10.6.

18 T. Buergenthal, 'The American and European Conventions on Human Rights: Similarities and Differences', *American University Law* Review, vol. 30, no. 1, 1980, p. 156.

19 IACtHR, *Case of Benjamin et al. v. Trinidad and Tobago*, 1 September 2001 (preliminary objections), par. 81; IACtHR, *Case of Constantine et al. v. Trinidad and Tobago*, 1 September 2001, par. 63; IACtHR, *Case of Hilaire. v. Trinidad and Tobago*, 1 September 2001, par. 64.

20 Buyse, *Shaping Rights in the ECHR*, p. 188. In the context of the ECHR, the protection against state abuse seems to be primarily offered by Article 18 ECHR.

Parties is generally sanctioned in accordance with the prohibition of *detournement de pouvoir* in Article 18 ECHR. On the other hand, a doctrine on the prohibition of abuse by individuals and groups as developed under Article 17 ECHR seems absent in the context of the ACHR. This suggests that cases concerning extreme speech are considered under the right to freedom of expression and the limitations allowed by Article 13(2) and (5) ACHR. So, the interpretation of the abuse clauses in other international and regional human rights instruments basically confirms that cases regarding anti-democratic and potentially dangerous expressions can indeed be assessed without having recourse to the prohibition of abuse of rights.

10.3.3 The concept of abuse of rights

This study subsequently broadened its view beyond human rights law and explored to what extent the legal framework of the principle of abuse of rights provides relevant insights for the understanding of Article 17 ECHR. The prohibition of abuse of rights is a concept found in several legal disciplines. It basically aims to *'to correct the application of a rule of law on the basis of standards such as good faith, fairness, and justice if, despite formal observance of the conditions of the rule, the objective of that rule has not been achieved'*.[21] It finds its origin in private law in the growing political and intellectual dissatisfaction with the absolutism of the liberalism of the Enlightenment at the beginning of the nineteenth century.[22] The introduction of the concept of abuse of rights marked a radical change in the thinking about the nature and function of rights.[23] As a result, the concept was not immediately embraced by legal scholars at that time. According to the critics the concept was *'logically untenable'*[24] as there can be no abuse if an activity falls within the scope of a right. In the words of Planiol, *'[l]e droit cesse où l'abus commence'*.[25]

The concept was first developed in national legal systems, mainly those belonging to the civil law tradition. Even though it has nowadays been accepted as a general legal principle in civil private law, its content varies among states. In France, the 'cradle' of the concept, for example, the prohibition of abuse of rights was traditionally based on the intent or motive of the right holder to disproportionally harm

---

21 A. Lenaerts, 'The General Principle of the Prohibition of Abuse of Rights: A Critical Position on Its Role in a Codified European Contract Law', *European Review of Private Law*, vol. 18, no. 6, 2010, p. 1121.

22 A. Sajó, 'Abuse of Fundamental Rights or the Difficulties of Purposiveness', in: A. Sajó (ed.), *Abuse: The Dark Side of Fundamental Rights*, Utrecht: Eleven International Publishing, 2006, p. 29-30.

23 V. Bolgár, 'Abuse of Rights in France, Germany, and Switzerland: A Survey of a Recent Chapter in Legal Doctrine', *Louisiana Law Review*, vol. 35, no. 5, 1975, p. 1016.

24 J.H. Crabb, 'The French Concept of Abuse of Rights', *Inter-American Law Review*, vol. 6, no. 1, 1964, p. 3.

25 M. Planiol, *Traite élémentaire de droit civil*, 2nd ed, Paris: Librairie Générale de droit & de jurisprudence, 1926, p. 298.

someone else. Yet, this 'subjective' test is considered problematic as *'[i]t involves an investigation of a psychological order into the question of motive and the introduction into the matter of an ethical element, both of which are considerations which tend to impede the effective operation of a legal rule'*.[26] In many legal orders, therefore, attempts have been made to complement this subjective criterion with more objective criteria, such as the infliction of excessive harm or the lack of a legitimate interest to justify the action. Still, these objective criteria, too, are not unproblematic, as they are rather abstract and often difficult to apply.

The principle has subsequently been referred to in an international context, primarily in public international law and EU law. In the context of international human rights law, however, the concept of abuse of rights only recently started to receive attention.[27] The mention of the concept of abuse of rights in relation to human rights may seem strange at first sight. Human rights are traditionally meant as a check on the power of the state, and not on the activities of individuals and groups. On the contrary, their purpose is to grant citizens the freedom to live their lives as they please as much as possible. Yet, the concept of abuse of rights has gained ground in human rights law in the form of abuse clauses that have been incorporated into many human rights documents that were created after the Second World War, such as Article 17 ECHR. It can be argued that, like the prohibition of abuse of rights in general, these clauses correct the anti-social exercise of rights based on the motive or intention of the right holder. Some of the concerns associated with identifying an abuse of rights in general are echoed in the context of these abuse clauses. Also in the context of human rights law the prohibition of abuse of rights has a controversial connotation as activities that are strictly covered by a right according to its letter are subsequently excluded from its protection based on a subjective element: the subversive intention behind the activity. Moreover, where the prohibition of abuse of rights in general aims to correct the unfair consequences that a formal observance of the law would otherwise have, this is different in human rights law. Human rights instruments allow rights to be restricted under strict conditions, at least those rights generally associated with an abuse such as the right to freedom of expression and the right to freedom of association. Unlike in private law, therefore, the objective of the law in human rights law can be achieved by legitimately restricting a right and without having recourse to the concept of abuse. So, in the context of human rights law the prohibition of abuse of rights has more of a symbolic meaning, setting the normative framework according to which the rights and freedoms in the Convention are to be interpreted.

26 H.C. Gutteridge, 'Abuse of Rights', *Cambridge Law Journal,* vol. 5, no. 1, 1933, p. 26.
27 A. Spielmann, 'La Convention Européenne des droits de l'homme et l'abus de droit', in: *Mélanges en hommage à Louis Edmond Pettiti*, Brussels: Bruylant, 1998, p. 673.

10.3.4 Article 17 ECHR and the concept of militant democracy

Contrary to private law, where the central concern of the concept of abuse is the impact of the abuse on other individuals, abuse in the context of the abuse clauses in human rights law is characterised by its impact *'on the democratic regime as such'*.[28] Abuse in this context is defined as an attempt to destroy the democratic system or democratic values.[29] The abuse clause is therefore generally associated with the concept of 'militant democracy'. The last part of this study explored to what extent the normative framework of the concept of militant democracy can help with the interpretation of Article 17 ECHR. The study of the concept of militant democracy consisted of three parts: a study of the doctrine on the concept of militant democracy, an analysis of the implementation of this concept in Germany, and an exploration of the role of this concept in the context of the ECHR and the interpretation of Article 17 ECHR.

10.3.4.1 The concept militant democracy

A militant democracy has been identified in this study as a democratic system that has adopted and applies pre-emptive, *prima facie* undemocratic legal instruments to defend itself against the risk of being overthrown by anti-democratic actors that make use of political rights and democratic procedures with the aim of abolishing it. The concept was developed by Loewenstein in the second half of the 1930s in a series of articles reflecting on the expansion of fascism on the European continent.[30] Yet, it was only after the Second World War that the militant democracy rationale seriously became part of constitutional thinking. Nowadays practically all European democracies are to some extent militant. Yet, the concept of militant democracy is *'not a universal stencil'* that can be applied in the same way in any democratic state.[31] Its implementation is highly context-dependent and always accommodates the distinctive characteristics of a particular democratic legal order.

The idea of a militant democracy is highly debated. This is owing to its inherently paradoxical nature. The concept of militant democracy addresses the concern of every democracy that through the exercise of political rights and the process of democratic decision-making a majority may decide in favour of a non-

28 Sajó, *Abuse*, p. 53.

29 Sajó, p. 52-53.

30 K. Loewenstein, 'Autocracy versus Democracy in Contemporary Europe, I', *The American Political Science Review*, vol. 29, no. 4, 1935, p. 593; K. Loewenstein, 'Militant Democracy and Fundamental Rights, I', *The American Political Science Review*, vol. 31, no. 3, 1937, p. 417-432 and K. Loewenstein, 'Militant Democracy and Fundamental Rights, II', *The American Political Science Review*, vol. 31, no. 4, 1937, p. 638-658.

31 S. Tyulkina, *Militant Democracy. Undemocratic Political Parties and Beyond*, London/New York: Routledge, 2015, p. 35.

democratic regime. For democracy to survive, therefore, a militant democracy assumes that anti-democratic actors may be denied the right to participate in the democratic arena. This idea is grounded on a perception of democracy that is based on the acknowledgment of substantive values that restrict the possible outcome of democratic decision-making. Meanwhile, restrictions on the participation of anti-democratic actors inevitably raise the suspicion *'that democracy is failing to meet its own criteria: that political decisions must arise out of free political competition'*.[32] After all, militant measures limit such competition. This is especially problematic if the substantive values and principles based on which militant measures are taken are not clear. An excessively militant democracy may therefore be counterproductive, as it is neither tolerant, nor democratic. For that reason the successful implementation of the concept of militant democracy always depends on a precarious balance between respect for democratic rights and processes, on the one hand, and the protection of the system as such on the other.

10.3.4.2 The 'wehrhafte Demokratie' in Germany

Even though practically all democratic states have adopted certain measures to defend themselves against anti-democratic political actors, the German legal order provides a particularly relevant example in this regard. The fact that the Nazis could use democratic rights and elections on their way to political power made post-war Germany particularly conscious of the need to protect its democratic system against exploitation by anti-democratic forces. The German Basic Law, which entered into force in 1949, is considered to contain the *'the most explicit – and the most far-reaching – theory of militant democracy'*.[33] In an attempt to learn from this strongly developed militant democracy, in the constitutional context of Germany referred to as the '*wehrhafte Demokratie*', the German approach was singled out in this study.

The German legal order has openly recognised the need to design a democratic order capable of defending itself against anti-democratic groups and individuals (predominantly political parties and other associations) who use democracy in order to subvert it.[34] In the abuse clause in Article 18 Basic Law the *wehrhafte Demokratie*

32 A. Sajó, 'Militant Democracy and Transition towards Democracy', in: A. Sajó (ed.), *Militant Democracy*, Utrecht: Eleven Legal Publishers, 2004, p. 211.

33 J. Müller, 'Militant Democracy', in: M. Rosenfeld and A. Sajó (eds.), *The Oxford Handbook of Comparative Constitutional Law*, Oxford: Oxford University Press, 2012, p. 1260.

34 P. Harvey, 'Militant Democracy and the European Convention on Human Rights', *European Law Review*, vol. 29, no. 3, 2004, p. 408.

finds its sharpest expression.[35] This provision offers a special judicial procedure that can be instigated by the Lower House of the German Parliament (*Bundestag*), the German Federal Government (*Bundesregierung*) or the government of one of the sixteen states (*Landesregierung*) and in which the Federal Constitutional Court (*Bundesverfassungsgericht*) decides on the abuse and forfeiture of constitutional rights. Article 18 BL is intended as a preventive instrument that should only be applied if it is substantially proven that the right holder will otherwise (continue to) exercise his rights in a way that poses a serious threat to the free democratic basic order (*freiheitliche demokratische Grundordnung*). In legal practice, however, the strongest of the militant measures in the Basic Law hardly plays any role. So far all motions to declare the forfeiture of rights have been declined. Its lack of practical relevance has been ascribed to both practical hurdles (the procedure in Article 18 BL is rather complex and the threshold for considering activities to be abusive is high), and ethical reasons (a request for the forfeiture of the constitutional rights of an anti-democratic actor is highly politically charged). Moreover, Article 18 BL is clearly an expression of the spirit of the time (*Zeitgeist*) and some have wondered whether the room for an abuse clause may be smaller in the contemporary, stable German democratic order. As a result, the interest in the abuse clause seems to be declining.

Hence, legal practice shows that the German free democratic basic order is first and foremost protected through other, less far-reaching instruments of the *wehrhafte Demokratie,* such as the dissolution of democratic parties that *'seek to undermine or abolish the free democratic basic order or to endanger the existence of the Federal Republic of Germany'* (Article 21(2) BL) and the prohibition of associations that are not political parties and whose aims or activities are directed against the constitutional order (Article 9(2) BL). In addition, the German democratic order is protected by a multitude of sub-constitutional provisions, such as criminal law provisions restricting the freedom to freely express one's opinion in the case of hostile propaganda or hate speech. In practice, these instruments appear to be more important to the protection of democracy and democratic values than the abuse clause. So, whereas the interest in the abuse clause in Article 17 ECHR has increased, Article 18 BL has practically become a dead letter and appears to be nothing more than a political warning.[36]

---

35 Article 18 BL reads: *'Whoever abuses the freedom of expression, in particular the freedom of the press (paragraph (1) of Article 5), the freedom of teaching (paragraph (3) of Article 5), the freedom of assembly (Article 8), the freedom of association (Article 9), the privacy of correspondence, posts and telecommunications (Article 10), the rights of property (Article 14), or the right of asylum (Article 16a) in order to combat the free democratic basic order shall forfeit these basic rights. This forfeiture and its extent shall be declared by the Federal Constitutional Court'*, www.bundestag.de/blueprint/servlet/blob/284870/ce0d03414872b427e57fccb703634dcd/basic_law-data.pdf (accessed 11 April 2016).

36 See also Müller, *The Oxford Handbook of Comparative Constitutional Law*, p. 1258.

10.3.4.3 Militant democracy and the ECHR

The ECHR also clearly breathes the spirit of militant democracy. As we have seen in Chapter two, the purpose of the Convention was to *'ensure that the States of the Members of the Council of Europe are democratic, and remain democratic'*.[37] Even though neither the Commission nor the Court has ever explicitly used the term 'militant democracy', they did confirm that the Convention is based on the idea of a self-defensive democratic order. In the famous *Refah Partisi* case, the Court found that in considering the strong link between the Convention and democracy *'no one must be authorised to rely on the Convention's provisions in order to weaken or destroy the ideals and values of a democratic society'*.[38] The Convention therefore allows states to take militant measures in order to protect democracy and democratic values.

Notwithstanding the relevance of the concept of democracy and democratic values to the Convention, both as the framework and the condition in which it operates, the Commission and the Court have failed to define these terms. Subsequently, over the years we have seen that the situations in which the Court has allowed states to rely on the concept of militant democracy to justify measures that interfere with the rights and freedoms set forth in the Convention have shifted. In the early days of the Convention, its militant stance was principally framed in terms of the Cold War dichotomy between democracy and totalitarianism. The first cases in which the Commission and the Court sought recourse to a militant narrative concerned applications by groups and individuals adhering to extreme left-wing (communist) or extreme right-wing (neo-Nazi) ideology. Next, the fall of the USSR and the transition to democratic governance in post-communist states in Central and Eastern Europe raised questions regarding the legitimacy of militant measures taken by these newly established democracies. Even though the Court in general seemed willing to endorse such claims in the context of the process of democratisation, it started to stress that such measures can only be justified for a limited period of time.[39] The Court seems increasingly aware of the paradoxical aspect of the concept of militant democracy and found that a totalitarian experience in the past does not justify the continuous application of militant measures. In a case concerning the disqualification of a former member of the Communist Party of Latvia from standing for election the court asserted that *'[e]very time a State intends to rely on the principle of 'a democracy capable of defending itself' in order to justify interference with individual rights, it must carefully evaluate the scope and consequences of the measure under*

37 A. Robertson (ed.), *Collected edition of the 'Travaux Préparatoires' (hereafter referred to as 'TP')*, vol. II, The Hague: Martinus Nijhof, 1975-1985, p. 60 (Ungoed-Thomas).

38 ECtHR 13 February 2003 (GC), *Refah Partisi (the Welfare Party) and others v. Turkey,* appl. nos. 41340/98 et al., par. 99.

39 Harvey, *European Law Review*, p. 415.

consideration'.[40] These nuances, however, hardly seem to play a role in the Court's position vis-à-vis neo-Nazism and Holocaust denial. Here the Court continues to consider militant measures to be justified based merely on the content of the activities, without evaluating whether the applicant seriously poses a threat to democracy.

Then, in recent years the scope of the Strasbourg interpretation of the concept of militant democracy appears to have broadened. The concept of militant democracy seems to have gradually developed beyond its traditional focus as the Court has increasingly allowed militant measures against *'transformative political projects that do not pose a threat to democratic processes but which, instead, threaten substantive conceptions of what democracy means to a political community'*.[41] As a result, definitions of the supposed enemies of democracy have become much more difficult to establish. With the lack of a coherent theory of militant democracy and confronted with a wide range of interpretations of this concept in the States Parties to the Convention, the Court's interpretation of militant democracy is necessary diffuse. Yet, when the line between democratic and anti-democratic activities is based on vague and undefined substantive values, it becomes even more difficult to define when militant measures are justified.

For the application of Article 17 ECHR this means that the Court has increasingly sought to apply the abuse clause to new categories of activities that run counter to the Convention. This expansion of the focus of the abuse clause, however, is based on extremely vague criteria that the Court does not define, such as the *'spirit'* and the *'underlying values'* of the Convention. Case law shows that it has always been difficult to establish which acts and activities threaten to destroy democracy. Even if states decide not to allow democracy to be enforceable as a *'suicide pact'*, as the original understanding of the abuse clause suggests, it is very hard to draw the line between (controversial) activities that deserve the protection of the Convention and totalitarian activities that are truly dangerous.[42] Considerably stretching the definition of abuse in the context of the ECHR to cover a wide range of allegedly anti-democratic activities that are not related to totalitarianism makes this assessment even more complicated. The vague criteria the Court uses to identify abusive activities make it increasingly difficult to determine when the abuse clause should be applied. By broadening the scope of anti-democratic activities, the Court's current approach may *'"cast its net too widely" and capture far more than is needed to sustain democracy'*.[43] Subsequently, the threshold for state interference with the exercise of fundamental

40 ECtHR 16 March 2006 (GC), Ždanoka v. Latvia, appl. no. 58278/00, par. 100.

41 P. Macklem, 'Guarding the Perimeter: Militant Democracy and Religious Freedom in Europe', *Constellations*, vol. 19, no. 4, 2012, p. 577.

42 Buyse, *Shaping Rights in the ECHR*, p. 204.

43 Tyulkina, *Militant Democracy*, p. 29.

political rights becomes lower with the risk that democracy is on a *'slippery slope'* towards becoming anti-democratic itself.[44]

10.4 When and how can Article 17 ECHR be applied?

Given the different perspectives explored in this study the question is to what extent the prohibition of abuse of rights is still appropriate in the context of the ECHR. The direct application of Article 17 ECHR has proven to be problematic. It completely excludes certain activities from the protection of the Convention, leaving the applicant empty handed. Based on a *prima facie* assessment of the facts and interests involved, the direct application exempts the Commission or the Court from further examining the compatibility of an interference with the conditions for the legitimate restriction of rights. As Keane pointed out, the direct approach to Article 17 ECHR generally does not require a state to prove that the interference met a pressing social need, since *'it would be required to prove only the content of the speech in question and not the effect of that speech'*.[45] As a result, the balancing of the interests involved is marginal and the proportionality of an interference with a right is hardly taken into account.[46] This is difficult to reconcile with the Court's generally strict scrutiny of restrictions on political rights, precisely because of their importance to the functioning of a healthy democracy. To uphold a high level of fundamental rights protection, any interference with the exercise of a right protected by the Convention deserves to be closely scrutinised.[47] A *prima facie* assessment under Article 17 ECHR, which does not allow for a proper assessment of the interests involved or the proportionality of the interference with the applicant's right, is not sufficient in this regard.

Also from the perspective of militant democracy, the direct application of Article 17 ECHR is questionable. Like all militant measures, the application of the abuse clause is *prima facie* undemocratic in the sense that it restricts the political participation of groups and individuals with controversial political ideas. An excessively militant democracy may eventually no longer be democratic.[48] Militant measures must therefore be applied with great restraint. It is dubious whether the application of a far-reaching measure such as not granting certain

44 Niesen, *German Law Journal*, par. 42-43.

45 D. Keane, 'Attacking hate speech under Article 17 of the European Convention on Human Rights', *Netherlands Quarterly of Human Rights*, vol. 25 no, 4, 2007, p. 656.

46 F. Tulkens, 'Les Relations entre le Négationnisme et les Droits de l'Homme. La Jurisprudence de la Cour Européenne des Droits de l'Homme' in: *Law in the Changing Europe, Liber Amicorum Pranas Kuris*, Vilnius: Mykolo Romerio universietas, 2008, p. 440. Cannie and Voorhoof, *Netherlands Quarterly of Human Rights*, p. 69-71; Buyse, *Shaping Rights in the ECHR*, p. 189.

47 See also Buyse, *Shaping Rights in the ECHR*, p. 205. See also See also Arai, *Theory and Practice of the ECHR*, p. 621 and 1086-1087.

48 O. Pfersmann, 'Shaping Militant Democracy: Legal Limits to Democratic Stability', in: A. Sajó (ed.), *Militant democracy*, Utrecht: Eleven International Publishing, 2004, p. 48.

activities any protection whatsoever is necessary in this regard, especially since the Convention allows for the restriction of rights and freedom in order to protect interests – including those covered by the concept of militant democracy – under the regular restriction clauses. The lack of practical relevance of the abuse clauses in other human rights documents and in the German Basic Law shows that at least in these systems recourse to the abuse clause does not appear to be necessary to uphold democracy and democratic values. Moreover, the Court itself has shown in cases such as *Refah Partisi* that it can protect democracy and democratic values without declaring an application inadmissible on the basis of Article 17 ECHR. The focus of the Convention's approach towards anti-democratic groups and individuals should therefore first and foremost focus on the regular limitation clauses that are available in the Convention.

However, there is still room for the indirect application of Article 17 ECHR. In cases in which the protection of democracy and core democratic values is at stake, the abuse clause can still have a role as a principle of interpretation in the light of the assessment whether the interference meets the limitation criteria. As the expression of one of the Convention's core values it may help to interpret the other rights and freedoms more coherently in the spirit of the Convention as a whole.[49] At the same time, by focussing on the indirect application of Article 17 ECHR the interpretation of the abuse clause can do justice to the balancing exercise between the right of the applicant and the legitimate grounds for its restriction that is required under human rights law. In that way the interpretation of the abuse clause enables the Court to take into account the difficulties and nuances involved in the balance between defending democracy and democratic values, on the one hand, and the protection of (political) fundamental rights and freedoms, on the other. In this context the Court should also consider the proportionality of a militant measure taken by a State Party. This means that the Court should take into account objective criteria, such as the risk that democracy is indeed significantly harmed by the activities of the applicant. In that regard the Court should also bear in mind that militant measures may be less easily justified in mature and stable democracies. Even though the Court argued along these lines in cases concerning militant measures taken in the context of the process of democratisation in Central and Eastern Europe in the 1990s, so far this element has hardly played a role in the interpretation of other militant measures in the light of Article 17 ECHR.

This means, however, that the indirect application of Article 17 ECHR should not lead to the conclusion that the application is manifestly ill-founded, as has often happened in the past. The cases in which the Commission and the Court declared applications

---

49 See also Cannie and Voorhoof, *Netherlands Quarterly of Human Rights*, p. 83.

manifestly ill-founded after indirectly applying Article 17 ECHR have shown that the interests involved, the context and the relevant legal elements of the case were hardly taken into consideration.[50] Even though these cases were formally considered under Article 10 ECHR, the indirect application erased any serious evaluation of the requirements in Article 10(2) ECHR and basically came down to a disguised direct application.

Furthermore, a restrictive interpretation of Article 17 ECHR does not mean that the function of the ECHR in protecting and promoting democracy and democratic values is weakened. The German context has shown that even in Europe's most militant democracy the prohibition of abuse of rights is practically never invoked. Militant measures can also consist of less far-reaching restrictions on the exercise of fundamental political rights, such as allowing for sanctions on anti-democratic speech or restrictions on the rights of political parties. Moreover, militant measures are first of all adopted and imposed at the national level of the States Parties to the Convention. The role of the Strasbourg mechanism is subsidiary to the role of the States Parties to the Convention that have the primary responsibility to secure the rights and freedoms defined, but also to uphold democracy and democracy values. This means that the Court can only retrospectively evaluate whether the measures taken by a State Party were justified from the perspective of militant democracy.

In sum, by confining its attention to the indirect application of the abuse clause in Article 17 ECHR, the Strasbourg Court can face the divergent contemporary challenges to democracy and democratic values in a way that does justice to their complexity by on the one hand providing a framework for the interpretation of the limits of political rights in a democratic society, while on the other hand doing justice to the protection of fundamental rights and freedoms.

50 Cannie and Voorhoof, p. 68.

Bibliography

Books

Bates, E., *The Evolution of the European Convention on Human Rights. From its Inception to the Creation of a Permanent Court of Human Rights*, Oxford: Oxford University Press, 2010

Bendersky, J.W., (1983) *Carl Schmitt: Theorist for the Reich*, reprint, Princeton: Princeton University Press, 2014

Birnie, P., Boyle, A.E. and Redgwell, C., *International Law and the Environment*, 3rd ed., Oxford: Clarendon Press, 2009

Boll, V.G.A., *Misbruik van recht [Abuse of rights]*, Utrecht: A. Oosthoek, 1913

Bossuyt, M.J., *Guide to the 'Travaux Préparatoires' of the International Covenant on Civil and Political Rights*, Dordrecht/Boston/Lancaster: Martinus Nijhoff Publishers, 1987

Bovend'Eert, P.P.T. and Kummeling, H.R.B.M., *Het Nederlandse Parlement [The Dutch Parliament]*, 11th ed., Deventer: Kluwer, 2010

Bracher, K.D. et al. (eds.), *Nationalsozialistische Diktatur, 1933-1945: Ein Bilanz* (Bonner Schriften zur Politik und Zeitgeschichte; Bd. 21), Düsseldorf: Droste Verlag, 1983

Bucher, P. (ed.), *Der Parlamentarische Rat 1948-1949. Akten und Protokolle*, vol. 2 (Der Verfassungskonvent auf Herrenchiensee), Boppard am Rhein: Harald Boldt Verlag, 1981

Campion, L., *La théorie de l'abus des droits*, Brussels/Paris: Établissements Émile Bruylant/ Librairie générale de droit, 1925

Capoccia, G., *Defending Democracy: Reactions to Extremism in Interwar Europe*, Baltimore: Johns Hopkins University Press, 2005

Cheng, B., *General Principles of Law as Applied by International Courts and Tribunals*, 1953

Crawford, J., *Brownlie's Principles of Public International Law*, 8th ed., Oxford: Oxford University Press, 2012

Currie, D.P., *The Constitution of the Federal Republic of Germany*, Chicago/London: The University of Chicago Press, 1994

Dabin, J., *Le droit subjectif*, Paris: Dalloz, 1952

Eskes, J.A.O., *Repressie van politieke bewegingen in Nederland. Een juridisch-historische studie over het Nederlandse publiekrechtelijke verenigingsrecht gedurende het tijdvak 1798-1988 [The repression of political movements in the Netherlands. A legal-historical study on the Dutch public law on associations during the period 1798-1988]*, Zwolle: W.E.J. Tjeenk Willink, 1988

Faúndez Ledesma, H., *The Inter-American System for the Protection of Human Rights. Institutional and procedural aspects*, 3rd ed., San José: Inter-American Institute of Human Rights, 2008

Fawcett, J.E.S., *The Application of the European Convention on Human Rights*, Oxford: Clarendon Press, 1987

Frowein, J.A. and Peukert, W., *Europaïsche MenschenRechtsKonvention*, 3rd ed., Kehl am Rhein: N.P. Engel Verlag, 2009

Gallwas, H., *Der Mißbrauch von Grundrechten*, Schriften zum Öffentlichen Recht, vol. 49, Berlin: Duncker and Humblot, 1967

Gay, P., *The Enlightenment: an Interpretation. vol. 1: The Rise of Modern Paganism*, 2nd ed., New York: Alfred A. Knopf, 1967

Geiger, W., *Gesetz über das Bundesverfassungsgericht vom 12 März 1951. Kommentar*, Berlin/Frankfurt: Verlag Franz Vahlen GmbH, 1952

Geiger, W., *Gewissen, Ideologie, Widerstand, Nonkonformismus*, Munich: Verlag Anton Pustet, 1963

Gerards, J., *EVRM – Algemene beginselen [ECHR – General principles]*, The Hague: Sdu Uitgevers, 2011

Glendon, M.A., *A World Made New. Eleanor Roosevelt and the Universal Declaration of Human Rights*, New York: Random House, 2002

Craig, P. and De Búrca, G., *EU Law. Text, Cases, and Materials*, 3rd ed., Oxford: Oxford University Press, 2003

Hare, I. and Weinstein, J. (eds), *Extreme Speech and Democracy*, Oxford: Oxford University Press, 2009

Harris, D.J., O'Boyle, M., Bates, E.P. and Buckley, C.M. (eds.), *Harris, O'Boyle and Warbrick. Law of the European Convention on Human Rights*, 3rd ed., Oxford: Oxford University Press, 2014

Hennebel L. and Hochmann, T., *Genocide Denials and the Law*, Oxford: Oxford University Press, 2011

Hollmann, M. (ed.), *Der Parlamentarische Rat 1948-1949. Akten und Protokolle*, vol. 7 (Entwürfe zum Grundgesetz), Boppard am Rhein: Harald Boldt Verlag, 1995

Hönsch, G., *Die Verwirkung von Grundrechten nach Art. 18 GG und das Monopol des Bundesverfassungsgerichts aus Art. 18 GG*, Hamburg: Universität Hamburg, 1962

Jacobs F.G. and White, R.C.A., *The European Convention on Human Rights*, 2nd ed., Oxford: Clarendon Press, 1996

Josserand, L., *De l'esprit des droits et de leur relativité. Théorie dite de l'abus des droits*, 2nd ed., Paris: Dalloz, 1939

Kahl, W., Abraham, H.J. and Dolzer, R. (eds.), *Bonner Kommentar zum Grundgesetz*, Heidelberg: Müller Verlag, 1993

Kahn, R.A., *Holocaust Denial and the Law: A Comparative Study*, New York: Palgrave Macmillan, 2004

Kelsen, H., *Vom Wesen und Wert der Demokratie*, 2nd ed., Tübingen: Verlag J.C.B. Mohr, 1929

Kelsen, H., (1932) *Verteidigung der Demokratie. Abhandlungen zur Demokratietheorie, reprint*, Tübingen: Mohr Siebeck, 2006

Kelsen, H., *Was ist Gerechtigkeit?*, 2nd ed., Vienna: Franz Deuticke, 1975

Leggewie, C. and Meier, H., *Republikschutz. Maßstäbe für die Verteidigung der Demokratie*, Hamburg: Rowohlt, 1995

Knödler, C., *Missbrauch von Rechten, selbstwidersprüchliches Verhalten und Verwirkung im öffentlichen Recht*, Aktuelle Beiträge zum öffentlichen Recht, Band 4, Herbolzheim: Centaurus Verlag, 2000

Kommers, D.P. and Miller, R.A., *The Constitutional Jurisprudence of the Federal Republic of Germany*, 3rd ed., Durham/London: Duke University Press, 2012

Lauterpacht, H., *The Function of Law in the International Community*, Oxford: Clarendon Press, 1933

Lechner, H. and Zuck, R., *Bundesverfassungsgerichtsgesetz*, 4th ed., Munich: C.H. Beck'sche Verlagsbuchhandlung, 1996

Kiss, A., *L'abus de droit en droit international*, Paris: Librairie generale de droit et de jurisprudence, 1952

Locke, J., (1689) *Two Treatises of Government*, reprint, Cambridge: Cambridge University Press, 1997

Locke, J., (1689) *A Letter Concerning Toleration*, reprint, J. Tully (ed.), trans. W. Popple, Indianapolis: Hackett, 1983

Logeman, A., *Grenzen der Meschenrechte in demokratischen Gesellschaften, die 'demokratische Gesellschaft' als Determinante der Grundrechtsschranken in der Europäischen Menschenrechtskonvention*, Baden-Baden: Nomos Verlagsgesellschaft, 2004

Mannheim, K., *Diagnosis of our Time. Wartime Essays of a Sociologist*, London: Routledge and Kegan Paul LTD, 1950

Maunz, T. and Dürig, G. (eds.), *Maunz/Dürig, Grundgesetz-Kommentar*, available from Beck online (accessed 11 April 2016)

McDougal, M.S., Lasswell, H.D. and Chen, L., *Human Rights and World Public Order. The Basic Policies of an International Law of Human Dignity*, New Haven/London: Yale University Press, 1980

Medina, C., *The American Convention on Human Rights. Crucial Rights and their Theory and Practice*, Cambridge/Antwerp/Portland: Intersentia, 2014

Nowak, M., *Introduction to the International Human Rights Regime*, Leiden/Boston: Martinus Nijhoff Publishers, 2003

Nowak, M., *U.N. Covenant on Civil and Political Rights, CCPR Commentary*, 2nd rev. ed., Kehl/Strasbourg/Arlington: N.P. Engel Publisher, 2005

Mowbray, A.R., *The development of positive obligations under the European Convention on Human Rights by the European Court of Human Rights*, Oxford: Hart Publishing, 2004

Okma, N., *Misbruik van Recht [Abuse of rights]*, Wageningen: Gebrs. Zomer en Keuning's Uitgeversmaatschappij, 1945

Pikart, E. and Werner, W. (eds.), *Der Parlamentarische Rat 1948-1949. Akten und Protokolle*, vol. 5(II) (Ausschuss für Grundsatzfragen), Boppard am Rhein: Harald Boldt Verlag, 1993

Planiol, M., *Traite élémentaire de droit civil*, 2nd ed, Paris: Librairie Générale de droit et de jurisprudence, 1926

Politis, N., *Le Problème des Limitations de la Souveraineté et la théorie de l'Abus des Droits dans les Rapport Internationaux, Académie de Droit International (extrait du recueil des cours)*, Paris: Librairie Hachette, 1926

Popper, K.R., (1945) *The Open Society and its Enemies*, reprint, London: Routledge, 2012
Rainey, B., Wicks, E. and Ovey, C., *Jacobs, White and Ovey. The European Convention on Human Rights*, 6th ed., Oxford: Oxford University Press, 2014
Rawls, J., *A Theory of Justice*, Cambrdige/London: The Belknap Press of Harvard University Press, 1971
Reif, E.J., *Der Begriff der Verwirkung der Grundrechte in Artikel 18 des Grundgesetzes (unter besonderer Berücksichtigung der Lehre vom Mißbrauch der Grundrechte)*, Munich: Dissertationsdruck Schön, 1970
Renteln, A.D., *International Human Rights. Universalism versus Relativism*, Newbury Park/London/New Delhi: Sage Publications, 1990
Ripert, G., *La Règle Morale dans les Obligations Civiles*, 3rd ed., Paris: Pichon et Durand-Auzias, 1935
Robertson, A., (ed.), *Collected edition of the 'Travaux Préparatoires'*, vol. I-V, The Hague: Martinus Nijhof, 1975-1985
Robinson, N., *The Universal Declaration of Human Rights. Its Origin Significance, Application and Interpretation*, New York: Institute of Jewish Affairs, 1958
Saul, B., Kinley, D. and Mowbray, J., *The International Covenant on Economic, Social and Cultural Rights: Commentary, Cases, and Materials*, Oxford: Oxford University Press, 2014
Saydé, A., *Abuse of EU Law and Regulation of the Internal Market*, Oxford/Portland: Hart Publishing, 2014
Schmitt, C., (1932) *Legality and Legitimacy*, reprint, trans. J. Seitzer (ed.), Durham/London: Duke University Press, 2004
Schmitt Glaeser, W., *Mißbrauch und Verwirkung von Grundrechten im politischen Meinungskampf*, Bad Homburg/Berlin/Zürich: Verlag Gehlen, 1968
Schumpeter, J., *Capitalism, Socialism and Democracy*, 2nd ed., New York/London: Harper & Brothers, 1947
Sepúlveda, M., *The Nature of the Obligations under the International Covenant on Economic, Social and Cultural Rights*, Antwerp/Oxford/New York: Intersentia, 2003
Smis, S., Janssens, C., Mirgaux, S. and Van Laethem, K., *Handboek Mensenrechten. De internationale bescherming van de rechten van de mens [Handbook Human Rights. The international protection of human rights]*, Antwerp/Cambridge: Intersentia, 2011
Smith, R.K.M., *Textbook on International Human Rights*, 3rd ed., Oxford: Oxford University Press, 2007
Schnelle, E.M., *Freiheitsmißbrauch und Grundrechtsverwirkung. Versuch einer Neubestimmung von Artikel 18 GG*, Berlin: Duncker and Humblot, 2014
Staal, C.J., *De vaststelling van de reikwijdte van de rechten van de mens [The definition of the scope of human rights]*, Nijmegen: Ars Aequi Libri, 1995
Steiner H. and Alston, P., *International Human Rights in Context: Law, Politics, Morals*, 1996
Tyulkina, S., *Militant Democracy. Undemocratic Political Parties and Beyond*, Abingdon/New York: Routledge, 2015
Van den Bergh, G., *De democratische Staat en de niet-democratische partijen [The democratic state and non-democratic parties]*, Amsterdam: N.V. De Arbeiderspers, 1936

Van der Woude, W., *Democratische waarborgen [Democratic safeguards]*, Alphen aan den Rijn: Kluwer, 2009

Van Noorloos, M., *Hate Speech revisited. A comparative and historical perspective on hate speech law in the Netherlands and England and Wales*, Antwerp: Intersentia, 2011

Velaers, J., *De beperkingen van de vrijheid van meningsuiting [The restrictions on the freedom of expression]*, Antwerp: Maklu, 1991

Velu J. and Ergec, R., *La Convention européenne des droits de l'homme*, Brussels: Bruylant, 1990

Verdoodt, A., *Naissance et Signification de la Déclaration Universelle des Droits de l'Homme*, Louvain/Paris: Éditions Nauwelaerts, 1964

Von Mangoldt, H. and Klein, F. (eds.), *Das Bonner Grundgesetz*, vol. I, Berlin/Frankfurt a.M.: Verlag Franz Vahlen GmbH, 1957

Von Münch, I. and Kunig, P. (eds.), *Grundgesetz-Kommentar*, vol. 1, 3rd ed., Munich: C.H. Beck'sche Verlagsbuchhandlung, 1985

Von Weber, H., *Der Schutz des Staates*, Verhandlungen des 38. Deutschen Juristentages, Tübingen: Verlag J.C.B. Mohr, 1950

Wertenbruch, W., *Grundgesetz und Menschenwürde*, Cologne: Carl Heymanns Verlag, 1958

Wilke, D., *Die Verwirkung der Pressefreiheit und das strafrechtliche Berufsverbot. Zugleich ein Betrag zur Rechtsnatur und zu den Grenzen der Grundrechte*, Berlin: Duncker and Humblot, 1964

Chapters in books

Arai, Y. (rev.), 'Prohibition of abuse of the rights and freedoms set forth in the convention and of their limitation to a greater extent than is provided for in the convention (Article 17)', in: P. van Dijk et al. (eds.), *Theory and practice of the European Convention on Human Rights*, 4th ed., Antwerp/Oxford: Intersentia, 2006, p. 1083-1092

Arnull, A., 'What is a General Principle of EU Law?', in: De la Feria, R. and Vogenauer, S. (eds.), *Prohibition of Abuse of Law. A New General Principle of EU Law?*, Oxford/ Portland: Hart Publishing, 2011, p. 7-24

Avineri, S., 'Introduction', in: Sajó, A. (ed.), *Militant democracy*, Utrecht: Eleven International Publishing, 2004, p. 1-14

Bates, E., 'The birth of the European Convention on Human Rights', in: Christoffersen, J., and Madsen, M. (eds.), *The European Court of Human Rights between Law and Politics*, Oxford: Oxford University Press, 2011, p. 17-42

Brems, E., 'Democratie en zelfverdediging' ['Democracy and self-defence'], in: M.C. Snippe et al (eds.), *Democratie op het einde van de 20ste eeuw. Onderzoek naar probleemgericht denken over de democratie bij jonge onderzoekers in Vlaanderen [Democracy at the end of the 20th century. Research into problem-oriented thinking about democracy among young resrarch in Flanders]*, Brussels: Koninklijke Academie voor Wetenschappen, Letteren en Schone Kunsten, 1994, p. 315-347

Buergenthal, T., 'To Respect and to Ensure: State Obligations and Permissible Derogations', in: Henkin, L. (ed.), *The International Bill of Rights. The International Covenant on Civil and Political Rights*, New York: Columbia University Press, 1981, p. 72-91

De Búrca, G., 'The Evolution of EU Human Rights Law', in: Craig, P. and De Búrca, G. (eds.), *The Evolution of EU Law*, 2nd ed., Oxford: Oxford University Press, 2011, p. 465-497

Buyse, A., 'Contested contours. The limits of freedom of expression from an abuse of rights perspective – Articles 10 and 17 ECHR', in: Brems, E. and Gerards, J. (eds.), *Shaping Rights in the ECHR. The Role of the European Court of Human Rights in Determining the Scope of Human Rights*, Cambridge: Cambridge University Press, 2014, p. 183-208

Cannie, H. and Voorhoof, D., 'The Abuse Clause in International Human Rights Law: an Expedient Remedy against Abuse of Power or an Instrument of Abuse Itself', in: Vanhoutte, K., Fairbairn, G. and Lang, M. (eds.), *Bullying and the Abuse of Power* (Critical issues series), Oxford: Inter-Disciplinary Press, 2010, p. 117-124

Cliteur P. and Rijpkema, B., 'The Foundations of Militant Democracy', in: Ellian, A. and Molier, G. (eds.), *The State of Exception and Militant Democracy*, Dordrecht: Republic of Letters, 2012, p. 227-272

Costello, C., 'Citizenship of the Union: Above Abuse?', in: De la Feria, R. and Vogenauer, S. (eds.), *Prohibition of Abuse of Law. A New General Principle of EU Law?*, Oxford/Portland: Hart Publishing, 2011, p. 321-354

Dagtoglou, P., 'Der Missbrauch von Grundrechten in der griechischen Theorie und Praxis', in: Ilioupoulos-Strangas, J. (ed.), *Der Missbrauch von Grundrechten in der Demokratie*, Baden-Baden: Nomos Verlagsgesellschaft, 1989, p. 103-111

De la Feria, R., 'Introducing the Principle of Prohibition of Abuse of law', in: De la Feria, R. and Vogenauer, S. (eds.), *Prohibition of Abuse of Law. A New General Principle of EU Law?*, Oxford/Portland: Hart Publishing, 2011, p. xv-xxv

De Lange, R., 'Gutmann's Dilemma: democratie, minderheden en fundamentele Rechten' ['Gutmann's Dilemma: democracy, minorities and fundamental rights'], in: in: C.W. Noorlander et al. (eds.), *Het volk regeert. Beschouwingen over de (Nederlandse) democratie in de 21e eeuw [The people rule. Reflections on the (Dutch) democracy in the 21st century]*, Nijmegen: Wolf Legal Publishers, 2008, p. 187-211

De Morree, P.E., 'De doorwerking van artikel 17 EVRM in de Nederlandse rechtsorde' ['The implementation of Article 17 ECHR in the Dutch legal order'], in: Kummeling, H.R.B.M. et al. (eds.), *De Samengestelde Besselink. Bruggen bouwen tussen nationaal, Europees en internationaal recht [The Composed Besselink. Building bridges between national, European and international law]*, Nijmegen: Wolf Legal Publishers, 2012, p. 147-156

De Morree, P.E., 'Het Europees Hof voor de Rechten van de Mens als hoeder van de democratie' ['The European Court of Human Rights as guardian of democracy'], in: M. Duchateau and P. Kingma (eds.), *Regt spreken volgens de wet? Bijdragen over de staatsrechtelijke positie van de (Europese) rechter [Adjudication in accordance with the law? Contributions regarding the constitutional position of the (European) judge]*, Nijmegen: Wolf Legal Publishers, 2013, p. 51-72

Dougan, M., 'Some Comments on the Idea of a General Principle of Union Law Prohibiting Abuses of Law in the Field of Free Movement for Union Citizens', in: De la Feria, R. and Vogenauer, S. (eds.), *Prohibition of Abuse of Law. A New General Principle of EU Law?*, Oxford/Portland: Hart Publishing, 2011, p. 355-364

Eidenmüller, H., 'Abuse of Law in the Context of European Insolvency Law' in: De la Feria, R. and Vogenauer, S. (eds.), *Prohibition of Abuse of Law. A New General Principle of EU Law?*, Oxford/Portland: Hart Publishing, 2011, p. 137-156

Ellian A. and Molier, G., 'Introduction: the State of Exception and Militant Democracy in a Time of Terror', in: Ellian, A. and Molier, G. (eds.), *The State of Exception and Militant Democracy*, Dordrecht: Republic of Letters, 2012, p. 1-19

Frankenberg, G., 'The learning Sovereign', in: Sajó, A. (ed.), *Militant democracy*, Utrecht: Eleven International Publishing, 2004, p. 113-132

Frowein, J.A., 'How to save democracy from itself?', in: Dinstein, Y. and Domb, F. (eds.), *The Progression of International Law. Four Decades of the Israel Yearbook on Human Rights – An Anniversary Volume*, Leiden: Martinus Nijhof Publishers, 2011, p. 163-178

Haeck, Y., 'Artikel 17 Verbod van rechtsmisbruik' ['Article 17 Prohibition of Abuse of rights'], in: Vande Lanotte, J. and Haeck, Y. (eds.), *Handboek EVRM. Deel 2. Artikelsgewijze commentaar, volume II [Handbook ECHR. Part 2. Commentary by article, volume II]*, Antwerp/Oxford: Intersentia, 2004, p. 242-272

Haeck, Y. and De Vylder, H., 'Art. 35 EVRM' ['Article 35 ECHR'], in: J.H. Gerards et al. (eds.), *SDU Commentaar EVRM, Deel II – Procedurele Rechten [SDU Commentary ECHR, Part II – Procedural Rights]*, Den Haag: SDU Uitgevers, 2014, p. 170-217

Hamilton, M., 'Transition, political loyalties and the order of the state', in: Buyse, A. and Hamilton, M. (eds.), *Transitional Jurisprudence and the European Convention on Human Rights. Justice, Politics and Rights*, Cambridge: Cambridge University Press, 2011, p. 151-184

Harris, D., 'Regional Protection of Human Rights: The Inter-American Achievement', in: Harris, D. and Livingstone, S. (eds.), *The Inter-American System of Human Rights*, Oxford: Clarendon Press, 1998, p. 1-29

Huber, P.M., 'Natürliche Personen als Grundrechtsträger', in: Mertens, D. and Papier, H., *Handbuch der Grundrechte in Deutschland und Europa*, vol. II, Heidelberg: C.F. Müller Verlag, 2006, p. 1129-1162

Klamt, M., 'Militant Democracy and the Democratic Dilemma: Different Ways of Protecting Democratic Constitutions', in: Bruinsma, F. and Nelken, D. (eds.), *Explorations in Legal Cultures (Recht der Werkelijkheid 28:3)*, The Hague: Elsevier, 2007, p. 133-159

Le Mire, P., 'Article 17', in: Pettiti, L.E., Decaux, E. and Imbert, P.H. (eds.), *La Convention Européenne des Droits de l'Homme. Commentaire Article par Article*, 2nd ed., Paris: Economica, 1999, p. 509-522

Lenaerts, K. and Gutiérrez Fons, J.A., 'The Place of the Charter in the EU Constitutional Edifice', in: Peers, S., Hervey, T., Kenner, J. and Ward, A. (eds.), *The EU Charter of Fundamental Rights. A Commentary*, Oxford/Portland: Hart Publishing, 2014, p. 1559-1593

Lerche, P., 'Das Asylrecht ist unverwirkbar', in: Ehmke, H., Schmid, C. and Scharoun, H. (eds.), *Festschrift für Adolf Arndt: zum 65. Geburtstag*, Frankfurt am Main: Europäische Verlagsanstalt, 1969, p. 199-214

Loof, J.P., 'On Emergency-proof Human Rights and Emergency-proof Human Rights Procedures', in: A. Ellian and G. Molier (eds.), *The State of Exception and Militant Democracy in a Time of Terror*, Dordrecht: Republic of Letters Publishing, 2012, p. 135-175

Marks, S., 'The European Convention on Human Rights and its "Democratic Society"', in: *British Yearbook of International Law*, London: Oxford University Press, 1995, p. 209-238

Maunz, T., 'Verwirkung von Grundrechten', in: Badura, P. and Scholz, R. (eds.), *Wege und Verfahren des Verfassungslebens: Festschrift für Peter Lerche zum 65. Geburtstag*, 1993, p. 281-288

Mouffe, C., 'The limits of liberal pluralism: towards an agonistic multipolar world order', in: Sajó, A. (ed.), *Militant Democracy*, Utrecht: Eleven Legal Publishers, 2004, p. 69-79

Mullender, R., 'United Kingdom', in: Thiel, M. (ed.), *The Militant Democracy Principle in Modern Democracies*, Farnham/Burlington: Ashgate Publishing Company, 2009, p. 311-356

Müller, J., 'Militant Democracy', in: Rosenfeld, M. and Sajó, A. (eds.), *The Oxford Handbook of Comparative Constitutional Law*, Oxford: Oxford University Press, 2012, p. 1253-1269

Nehmelman, R., 'Het partijverbod: over de grenzen van de democratie' ['The party ban: crossing the boundaries of democracy'], in: C.W. Noorlander et al. (eds.), *Het volk regeert. Beschouwingen over de (Nederlandse) democratie in de 21e eeuw [The people rule. Reflections on the (Dutch) democracy in the 21st century]*, Nijmegen: Wolf Legal Publishers, 2008, p. 331-352

Neuberger, B., 'Israel', in: Thiel, M. (ed.), *The Militant Democracy Principle in Modern Democracies*, Farnham/Burlington: Ashgate Publishing Company, 2009, p. 183-207

Pech, L., 'The Law of Holocaust Denial in Europe', in: Hennebel, L. and Hochmann, T. (eds.), *Genocide Denials and the Law*, Oxford: Oxford University Press, 2011, p. 185-234

Pfersmann, O., 'Shaping Militant Democracy: Legal Limits to Democratic Stability', in: Sajó, A. (ed.), *Militant democracy*, Utrecht: Eleven International Publishing, 2004, p. 47-68

Pieroth, B., 'Die Grundrechte des Grundgesetzes in der Verfassungstradition', in: Merten, D. and Papier, H. (eds.), *Handbuch der Grundrechte in Deutschland und Europa*, vol. II, Heidelberg: C.F. Müller Verlag, 2006, p. 3-40

Pistone, P., 'Abuse of Law in the Context of Indirect Taxation: From (Before) *Emsland-Stärke 1* to *Halifax* (and Beyond)', in: De la Feria, R. and Vogenauer, S. (eds.), *Prohibition of Abuse of Law. A New General Principle of EU Law?*, Oxford/Portland: Hart Publishing, 2011, p. 381-394

Roach, K., 'Anti-Terrorism and Militant Democracy: Some Western and Eastern Responses', in: Sajó A. (ed.), *Militant democracy*, Utrecht: Eleven International Publishing, 2004, p. 171-207

Sajó, A., 'Militant Democracy and Transition towards Democracy', in: Sajó, A. (ed.), *Militant Democracy*, Utrecht: Eleven Legal Publishers, 2004, p. 209-230

Sajó, A., 'Abuse of Fundamental Rights or the Difficulties of Purposiveness', in: A. Sajó, A. (ed.), *Abuse: The Dark Side of Fundamental Rights*, Utrecht: Eleven International Publishing, 2006, p. 29-98

Samnøy, Å., 'The Origin of the Universal Declaration of Human Rights', in: Alfredsson, G. and Eide, A. (eds.), *The Universal Declaration of Human Rights. A Common Standard of Achievement*, The Hague/Boston/London: Martinus Nijhoff Publishers, 1999, p. 3-22

Schammo, P., 'Comments on Abuse of Rights in EU Law', in: De la Feria, R. and Vogenauer, S. (eds.), *Prohibition of Abuse of Law. A New General Principle of EU Law?*, Oxford/Portland: Hart Publishing, 2011, p. 193-202

Snell, J., 'And then there were two: products and citizens in community law', in: Tridimas, T. and Nebbia, P. (eds.), *European Union Law for the Twenty-First Century, vol. 2: Internal Market and Free Movement Community Policies,* Oxford: Hart Publishing, 2004, p. 49-72

Sørensen, K.E., 'What is a General Principle of EU Law? A Response', in: De la Feria, R. and Vogenauer, S. (eds.), *Prohibition of Abuse of Law. A New General Principle of EU Law?*, Oxford/Portland: Hart Publishing, 2011, p. 25-32

Sottiaux, S., 'Democratie en grondrechten. De inhoudelijke en procedurele democratiemodellen van Dworkin en Habermas' ['Democracy and fundamental rights. The substantive and procedural models of democracy of Dworkin and Habermas'], in: M. Adams & P. Popelier (eds.), *Recht en democratie. De democratische verbeelding in het recht [Law and democracy. The democratic perception in law]*, Antwerp/New York/Oxford: Intersentia, 2004, p. 39-60

Spaventa, E., 'Comments on Abuse of Law and the Free Movement of Workers', in: De la Feria, R. and Vogenauer, S. (eds.), *Prohibition of Abuse of Law. A New General Principle of EU Law?*, Oxford/Portland: Hart Publishing, 2011, p. 315-320

Spielmann, A. 'La Convention Européenne des droits de l'homme et l'abus de droit', in: *Mélanges en hommage à Louis Edmond Pettiti*, Brussels: Bruylant, 1998, p. 573-686

Thiel, M., 'Zur Einführung: Die 'wehrhafter Demokratie' als verfassungsrechtliche Grundentscheidung', in: M. Thiel (ed.), *Wehrhafte Demokratie. Beitrage über die Regelungen zum Schutze der freiheitlichen demokratischen Grundordnung*, Tübingen: Mohr Siebeck, 2003, p. 1-24

Thiel, M., 'Die Verwirkung von Grundrechten gemäß Art. 18 GG', in: Thiel, M. (ed.), *Wehrhafte Demokratie. Beitrage über die Regelungen zum Schutze der freiheitlichen demokratischen Grundordnung*, Tübingen: Mohr Siebeck, 2003, p. 129-172

Thiel, M, 'Introduction', in: Thiel, M. (ed.), *The Militant Democracy Principle in Modern Democracies*, Farnham/Burlington: Ashgate Publishing Company, 2009, p. 1-13

Thiel, M, 'Germany', in: Thiel, M. (ed.), *The Militant Democracy Principle in Modern Democracies*, Farnham/Burlington: Ashgate Publishing Company, 2009, p. 109-145

Thiel, M, 'Comparative Aspects', in: Thiel, M. (ed.), *The Militant Democracy Principle in Modern Democracies*, Farnham/Burlington: Ashgate Publishing Company, 2009, p. 379-424

Thiel, M., '"Militant Democracy" and state of emergency in Germany', in: Ellian, A. and Molier, G. (eds.), *The State of Exception and Militant Democracy*, Dordrecht: Republic of Letters, 2012, p. 273-327

Tridimas, T., 'Abuse of Rights in EU Law: Some Reflections with Particular Reference to Financial Law', in: De la Feria, R. and Vogenauer, S. (eds.), *Prohibition of Abuse of Law. A New General Principle of EU Law?*, Oxford/Portland: Hart Publishing, 2011, p. 169-192

Tulkens, F., 'Les Relations entre le Négationnisme et les Droits de l'Homme. La Jurisprudence de la Cour Européenne des Droits de l'Homme', in: *Law in the Changing Europe, Liber Amicorum Pranas Kuris*, Vilnius: Mykolo Romerio universietas, 2008, p. 425-445

Villiger, M.E., 'Article 17 ECHR and freedom of speech in Strasbourg practice', in: Casadevall, J., Myjer, E., O'Boyle, M. and Austin, A. (eds.), *Freedom of Expression. Essays in Honour of Nicolas Bratza*, Oisterwijk: Wolf Legal Publishers, 2012, p. 321-329

Vogenauer, S., 'The Prohibition of Abuse of Law: An Emerging General Principle of EU Law', in: De la Feria, R. and Vogenauer, S. (eds.), *Prohibition of Abuse of Law. A New General Principle of EU Law?*, Oxford/Portland: Hart Publishing, 2011, p. 521-572

Whittaker, S., 'Comments on "Abuse of Law" in European Private Law', in: De la Feria, R. and Vogenauer, S. (eds.), *Prohibition of Abuse of Law. A New General Principle of EU Law?*, Oxford/Portland: Hart Publishing, 2011, p. 253-260

Woods, L., 'Article 54 – Abuse of Rights', in: Peers, S., Hervey, T., Kenner, J. and Ward, A. (eds.), *The EU Charter of Fundamental Rights. A Commentary*, Oxford/Portland: Hart Publishing, 2014, p. 1539-1554

Ziegler, K.S., '"Abuse of Law" in the Context of the Free Movement of Workers', in: De la Feria, R. and Vogenauer, S. (eds.), *Prohibition of Abuse of Law. A New General Principle of EU Law?*, Oxford/Portland: Hart Publishing, 2011, p. 295-314

Zuleeg, M., 'Mißbrauch von Grundrechten vor dem Hintergrund demokratischer Strukturen in Europa', in: Iliopoulous-Strangas, J. (ed.), *Der Mißbrauch von Grundrechten in der Demokratie*, Baden-Baden: Nomos Verlagsgesellschaft, 1989, p. 41-59

Zwaak L. (rev.), 'The procedure before the European Court of Human Rights' in: P. van Dijk, F. van Hoof, A. van Rijn and L. Zwaak (eds.), *Theory and practice of the European Convention on Human Rights*, 4th ed., Antwerp/Oxford: Intersentia, 2006, p. 95-290.

Periodicals

Amand, C., 'Prohibition of Abusive Practices in European VAT: Court Aid to National Legislations Bugs?', *Intertax*, vol. 36, no. 5, 2008, p. 189–200

Bolgár, V., 'Abuse of Rights in France, Germany, and Switzerland: A Survey of a Recent Chapter in Legal Doctrine', *Louisiana Law Review*, vol. 35, no. 5 (special issue), 1975, p. 1015-1057

Bourne, A.K., 'The Prohibition of Political Parties and "Militant Democracy"', *Journal of Comparative Law*, vol. 7, no. 1, 2012, p. 196-213

Boyle, K. 'Human Rights, Religion and Democracy: The Refah Party Case', *Essex Human Rights Review*, vol. 1, no. 1, 2004, p. 1-16

Buergenthal, T., 'The American and European Conventions on Human Rights: Similarities and Differences', *American University Law Review*, vol. 30, no. 1, 1980, p. 155-166

Buergenthal, T., 'The Normative and Institutional Evolution of International Human Rights', *Human Rights Quarterly*, vol. 19, no. 4, 1997, p. 703-723

Buyse A., 'Dangerous expressions: the ECHR, Violence and Free Speech', *International and Comparative Law Quarterly*, vol. 63, no. 2, 2014, p. 491-503

Byers, M., 'Abuse of Rights: An Old Principle, A New Age', *McGill Law Journal*, vol. 47, no. 2, 2002, p. 389-431

Cannie, H. and Voorhoof, D., 'The Abuse Clause and Freedom of Expression in the European Human Rights Convention: an Added Value for Democracy and Human Rights Protection?', *Netherlands Quarterly of Human Rights*, vol. 29, no. 1, 2011, p. 54-83

Crabb, J.H., 'The French Concept of Abuse of Rights', *Inter-American Law Review*, vol. 6, no. 1, 1964, p. 1-24

Cueto-Rua, J., 'Abuse of Rights', *Louisiana Law Review*, vol. 35, no. 5 (special issue), 1975, p. 965-1013

De la Feria, R., 'Prohibition of Abuse of (Community) Law: The Creation of a New General Principle of EC Law through Tax', *Common Market Law Review*, vol. 45, no. 2, 2008, p. 395-441

Devine, D.J., 'Some Comparative Aspects of the Doctrine of Abuse of Rights', *Acta Juridica*, 1964, p. 148-186

Dreier, H., 'Grenzen demokratischer Freiheit im Verfassungsstaat', *Juristenzeitung*, vol. 49, no. 15-16, 1994, p. 741-752

Dürig, G., 'Die Verwirkung von Grundrechten nach Artikel 18 des Grundgesetzes', *Juristenzeitung*, vol. 7, no. 17, 1952, p. 513-518

Flauss, JF., 'L'abus de droit dans le cadre de la Convention européenne des droits de l'homme', *Revue Universelle des Droits de l'Homme*, vol 4, no. 12, 1992, p. 461-168

Flauss, JF., 'The European Court of Human Rights and the Freedom of Expression', *Indiana Law Journal*, vol. 84, no. 3, 2009, p. 809-849

Fox G.H. and Nolte, G., 'Intolerant democracies', *Harvard International Law Journal*, vol. 36, no. 1, 1995, p. 1-70

Fox G.H. and Nolte, G., 'Fox and Nolte Response', *Harvard International Law Journal*, vol. 37, no. 1, 1996, p. 238-242

Glendon, M.A., 'Knowing the Universal Declaration of Human Rights', *Notre Dame Law Review,* vol. 73, no. 5, 1997-1998, p. 1153-1190

Goldman, R.K., 'History and Action: The Inter-American Human Rights system and the Role of the Inter-American Commission on Human Rights', *Human Rights Quarterly*, vol. 31, no. 4, 2009, p. 856-887

Gutteridge, H.C., 'Abuse of Rights', *Cambridge Law Journal,* vol. 5, no. 1, 1933, p. 22-45

Harvey, P., 'Militant democracy and the European Convention on Human Rights', *European Law Review*, vol. 29, no. 3, 2004, p. 407-420

Herman, S., 'Classical Social Theories and the Doctrine of "Abuse of Right"', *Louisiana Law Review,* vol. 37, no. 3 (special issue), 1977, p. 747-760

Hinghofer-Szalkay, S.G., 'Extreme Meinungen und Meinungsäußerungsfreiheit: Die Schranke des Artikel 17 EMRK. Die Straßburger Rechtsprechung und ihre Struktur', *Journal für Rechtspolitik*, vol. 20, no. 2, 2012, p. 106-114

Iluyomade, B.O., 'The Scope and Content of a Complaint of Abuse of Right in International Law', *Harvard International Law Journal*, vol. 16, no. 1, 1975, p. 47-92

Issacharoff, S., 'Fragile Democracies', *Harvard Law Review*, vol. 120, no. 6, 2007, p. 1405-1467

Kahn, R.A., 'Cross-Burning, Holocaust Denial, and the Development of Hate Speech Law in the United States and Germany', *University of Detroit Mercy Law Review*, vol. 83, no. 3, 2006, p. 163-194

Keane, D., 'Attacking hate speech under Article 17 of the European Convention on Human Rights', *Netherlands Quarterly of Human Rights,* vol. 25 no, 4, 2007, p. 641-663

Kilinç, Ü., 'La conception de la démocratie militante dans la jurisprudence de la Cour Européenne des Droits de l'Homme', *Revue trimestrielle des droits de l'homme*, vol. 23, no. 90, 2012, p. 297-328

Kiss, A., 'Abuse of Rights', in: *Max Planck Encyclopedia of Public International Law*, online available at: http://opil.ouplaw.com/view/10.1093/law:epil/9780199231690/law-9780199231690-e1371?rskey= 8pckoF&result=1&prd=EPIL (accessed 11 April 2016, last updated December 2006)

Koskenniemi, M., '"Intolerant Democracies": a Reaction', *Harvard International Law Journal*, vol. 37, no. 1, 1996, p. 231-235

Krüger, H., 'Missbrauch und Verwirkung von Grundrechten', *Deutsches Verwaltungsblatt*, vol. 68, no. 4, 1953, p. 97-101

Lenaerts, A., 'The General Principle of the Prohibition of Abuse of Rights: A Critical Position on Its Role in a Codified European Contract Law', *European Review of Private Law*, vol. 18, no. 6, 2010, p. 1121-1154

Lixinski, L., 'Treaty Interpretation by the Inter-American Court of Human Rights: Expansionism at the Service of the Unity of International Law', *European Journal of International Law*, vol. 21 no. 3, 2010, p. 585-604

Loewenstein, K., 'Autocracy versus Democracy in Contemporary Europe, I', *The American Political Science Review*, vol. 29, no. 4, 1935, p. 571-593

Loewenstein, K., 'Autocracy versus Democracy in Contemporary Europe, II', *The American Political Science Review*, vol. 29, no. 5, 1935, p. 744-784

Loewenstein, K., 'Militant Democracy and Fundamental Rights, I', *The American Political Science Review*, vol. 31, no. 3, 1937, p. 417-432

Loewenstein, K., 'Militant Democracy and Fundamental Rights, II', *The American Political Science Review*, vol. 31, no. 4, 1937, p. 638-658

Macklem, P., 'Guarding the Perimeter: Militant Democracy and Religious Freedom in Europe', *Constellations*, vol. 19, no. 4, 2012, p. 575-590

Macklem, P., 'Militant democracy, legal pluralism, and the paradox of self-determination', *International Journal of Constitutional Law*, vol. 4, no. 3, 2006, p. 488-516

Minkenberg, M., 'Repression and reaction: militant democracy and the radical right in Germany and France', *Patterns of Prejudice*, vol. 40, no. 1, 2006, p. 25-44

Morsink, J., 'World War Two and the Universal Declaration', *Human Rights Quarterly*, vol. 15, no. 2, 1993, p. 357-405

Müller, J., 'A "Practical Dilemma Which Philosophy Alone Cannot Resolve"? Rethinking Militant Democracy: An Introduction', *Constellations*, vol. 19, no. 4, 2012, p. 536-539
Müller, J., 'Beyond Militant Democracy?', *New Left Review*, vol. 73, no. 1, 2012, p. 39-47
Niesen, P., 'Anti-Extremism, Negative Republicanism, Civic Society: Three Paradigms for Banning Political Parties', *German Law Journal*, vol. 3, no. 7, 2002, online available at: www.germanlawjournal.com/s/GLJ_Vol_03_No_07_Niesen.pdf (accessed 11 April 2016)
Niesen, P., 'Political party bans in Rwanda 1994–2003: three narratives of justification', *Democratization*, vol. 17, no. 4 (special issue), 2010, p. 709-729
Niesen, P., 'Banning the Former Ruling Party', *Constellations*, vol. 19, no. 4, 2012, p. 540-561
O'Connell, R., 'Militant Democracy and Human Rights Principles', *Constitutional Law Review* (Georgian Constitutional Court), 2009, p. 84-90
Oetheimer, M., 'Protecting freedom of expression: the challenge of hate speech in the European Court of Human Rights case law', *Cardozo Journal of International and Comparative Law*, vol. 17, no. 3, 2009, p. 427-443
Papier, H. and Durner, W., 'Streitbare Demokratie', *Archiv des öffentlichen Rechts*, vol. 128, 2003, p. 340-371
Parassram Concepcion, N., 'The Legal Implications of Trinidad & Tobago's Withdrawal from the American Convention on Human Rights', *American University International Law Review*, vol. 16, no. 3, 2001, p. 847-890
Paust, J.J., 'The Other Side of Right: Private Duties under Human Rights Law', *Harvard Human Rights Journal*, vol 5, 1992, p. 51-63
Perillo, J.M., 'Abuse of Rights: A Pervasive Legal Concept', *Pacific Law Journal*, vol. 27, no. 1, 1995, p. 37-97
Ross, R.G., 'Democracy, Party and Politics', *Ethics*, vol. 64, no. 2, 1954, p. 100-125
Sajó, A., 'From Militant Democracy to the Preventive State?', *Cardozo Law Review*, vol. 27, no. 5, 2006, p. 2255-2294
Saydé, A., 'Defining the Concept of Abuse of Union Law', *Yearbook of European Law*, vol. 33, no. 1, 2014, p. 138-162
Schmitt, W.O., 'Die verwirkung des Wahlrechts und der Wählbarkeit nach section 39 Abs. 2 BVerfGG', *Neue Juristische Wochenschrift,* 1966, p. 1734-1739
Sottiaux, S., 'Anti-democratic Associations: Content and Consequences in Article 11 Adjudication', *Netherlands Quarterly of Human Rights*, vol. 22, no. 4, 2004, p. 585-599
Teachout, P.R., 'Making "Holocaust Denial" A Crime: Reflections on European Anti-negationist Laws from the Perspective of U.S. Constitutional Experience', *Vermont Law Review,* vol. 30, no. 3, 2006, p. 656-692
Teitel, R., 'Militating Democracy: Comparative Constitutional Perspectives', *Michigan Journal of International Law*, vol. 29, no. 1, 2007, p. 49-70
Tomuschat, C., 'The Effects of the Judgments of the European Court of Human Rights According to the German Constitutional Court', *German Law Journal*, vol. 11, no. 5, 2010, pp. 513-526, www.germanlawjournal.com/s/GLJ_Vol_11_No_05_Tomuschat.pdf (accessed 11 April 2016)

Van Drooghenbroeck, S., 'L'Article 17 de la Convention Européenne des Droits de l'Homme est-il indispensable?', *Revue trimestrielle des droits de l'homme,* vol. 12, no. 46, 2001, p. 541-566

Weil, G.L., 'Decisions on Inadmissible Applications by the European Commission of Human Rights', *American Journal of International Law*, vol. 54, no. 4, 1960, p. 874-881

Weil, G.L., 'The Evolution of the European Convention on Human Rights', *The American Journal of International Law*, vol. 57, no. 4, 1963, p. 804-827

Welsh, H.A., 'Dealing with the Communist Past: Central and East European Experiences after 1990', *Europe-Asia Studies*, vol. 48, no. 3, 1996, p. 413-428

Williams, A.M., 'The European Convention on Human rights: a new use?', *Texas International Law Journal*, vol. 12, 1977, p. 279-292

Zakaria, F., 'The Rise of Illiberal Democracy', *Foreign Affairs*, vol. 76, no. 6, 1997, p. 22-43

Case notes

Broeksteeg, J.L.W., Case note to ECtHR 16 March 2006 (GC), *Ždanoka v. Latvia*, appl. no. 58278/00, *EHRC* 2006/57

De Lange, R., Case note to ECtHR 6 January 2011 (GC), *Paksas v. Lithuania*, appl. no. 34932/04, *EHRC* 2011/47

De Morree, P.E., Case note to ECtHR 20 October 2015 (dec.), *M'Bala M'Bala v. France*, appl. no. 25239/13, *EHRC* 2016/45

Gerards, J.H., Case note to ECtHR 15 January 2009, *Orban and others v. France*, appl. no. 20985/05, *EHRC* 2009/30

Nieuwenhuis, A., Case note to ECtHR 9 February 2012, *Vejdeland and other v. Sweden*, appl. no. 1813/07, *ECHR* 2012/85

Van der Velde, J., Case note to ECtHR 8 July 2008, *Vajnai v. Hungary*, appl. no. 33629/06, *EHRC* 2008/105

Voorhoof, D., Case note to ECtHR 16 July 2009, *Féret v. Belgique*, appl. no. 15615/07, *ECHR* 2009/111

Conference papers

Eck, L., *Controverses Constitutionelles et Abus de Droit*, conference paper for the Congrès de l'Association Française de Droit Constitutionnel (A.F.D.C.), Montpellier, 2005, www.droitconstitutionnel.org/congresmtp/textes1/ECK.pdf (accessed 11 April 2016)

Spielmann, A., and Spielmann, D., 'The Concept of Abuse of Rights and the European Convention for the Protection of Human Rights and Fundamental Freedoms', in: *Abuse of Rights and Equivalent Concepts: the Principle and its Present Day Application* (Proceedings of the nineteenth Colloquy on European Law), Strasbourg: Council of Europe Publishing and Documentation Service, 1990

Voyaume, J., Cottier, B. and Rocha, B., 'Abuse of Rights in Comparative Law', in: Council of Europe, *Abuse of Rights and Equivalent Concepts: the Principle and its Present Day Application* (Proceedings of the nineteenth Colloquy on European Law), Strasbourg: Council of Europe Publishing and Documentation Service, 1990

Policy documents

EU, *Explanations relating to the Charter of Fundamental Rights* (2007/C 303/02), OJ EU, 14.12.2007, C303/35

CoE, Committee of Ministers, *Recommendation No. R(97)20 on 'hate speech'*, Strasbourg, 30 October 1997

CoE, Committee of Ministers, *Vienna Declaration*, Vienna, 9 October 1993

CoE, ECRI, *General Policy Recommendation No. 7 on national legislation to combat racism and racial discrimination*, Strasbourg, 13 December 2002 (CRI(2003)8)

CoE, ECRI, *General Policy Recommendation No. 9 on the fight against anti-Semitism*, Strasbourg, 25 June 2004

CoE, Parliamentary Assembly, *Recommendation No. 1222 on the fight against racism, xenophobia and intolerance*, Strasbourg, 29 September 1993

CoE, Parliamentary Assembly, *Recommendation No. 1275 on the fight against racism, xenophobia, anti-Semitism and intolerance*, Strasbourg, 28 June 1995

CoE, Parliamentary Assembly, *Recommendation No. 1438 on the threat posed to democracy by extremist parties and movements in Europe*, Strasbourg, 25 January 2000

CoE, Parliamentary Assembly, *Recommendation No. 1543 on racism and xenophobia in cyberspace*, Strasbourg, 8 November 2001

CoE, Parliamentary Assembly, *Recommendation No. 1495 on combating the resurrection of Nazi ideology*, Strasbourg, 12 April 2006

CoE, Parliamentary Assembly, *Resolution No. 1308 on restrictions on political parties in the Council of Europe member states*, Strasbourg, 18 November 2002

CoE, Parliamentary Assembly, *Resolution No. 1481 on the need for international condemnation of crimes of totalitarian communist regimes*, Strasbourg, 25 January 2006

CoE, Parliamentary Assembly, *Resolution No. 1563 on Combating Anti-Semitism in Europe*, Strasbourg, 27 June 2007

CoE, Venice Commission, *Guidelines on prohibition and dissolution of political parties and analogous measures*, Venice, 10-11 December 1999, CDL-INF(2000)001

CoE, Venice Commission and OSCE/ODIHR, *Guidelines on Political Party Regulation*, Venice, 15-16 October 2010, CDL-AD(2010)024

Declaration on Crimes of Communism, Prague, 25 February 2010

OSCE, Parliamentary Assembly, *Vilnius Declaration*, Vilnius, 29 June-3 July 2009

UN, CCPR, *General Comment No. 34 on Article 19 ICCPR: Freedoms of opinion and expression*, 12 September 2011, UN doc. CCPR/C/GC/34

UN, ESCOR (CHR), *Limburg Principles on the Implementation of the International Covenant on Economic, Social and Cultural Rights*, 1987, UN Doc. E/CN.4/1987/17

UN, ESCOR (CHR), *Siracusa Principles on the Limitation and Derogation Provisions in the International Covenant on Civil and Political Rights*, 1985, UN Doc. E/CN.4/1985/4

UN, CESCR, *General Comment No. 14 on Article 12 ICESCR: the Right to the Highest Attainable Standard of Health*, 11 August 2000, UN Doc. E/C.12/2000/4

UN, CESCR, *General Comment No. 21 on Article 15(1)(a) ICESCR: the right of everyone to take part in cultural life*, 21 December 2009, UN Doc. E/C.12/GC/21

UN, GA, *Annotations on the text of the draft International Covenants on Human Rights*, 1 July 1955, UN Doc. A/2929

UN, GA, *Resolution on Holocaust denial*, 22 March 2007, *UN Doc.* A/RES/61/255

Table of Cases

European Commission of Human Rights

ECommHR 20 July 1957, *German Communist Party v. Germany*, appl. no. 250/57
EComHR 8 January 1960 (report), *De Becker v. Belgium*, appl. no. 214/56
EComHR 1 December 1963, *X. v. Austria*, appl. no. 1747/62
EComHR 5 November 1969 (report), *Denmark, Norway, Sweden and the Netherlands v. Greece (The Greek case)*, appl. nos. 3321/67 et al.
EComHR 14 December 1973 (report), *East African Asians v. the United Kingdom*, appl. nos. 4403/70 et al.
EComHR 11 October 1979, *Glimmerveen and Hagenbeek v. the Netherlands*, appl. nos. 8348/78 and 8406/78
EComHR 16 July 1982, *X v. Germany*, appl. no. 9235/81
EComHR 14 July 1983, *T. v. Belgium*, appl. no. 9777/82
EComHR 12 May 1988, *Kühnen v. Germany*, appl. no. 12194/86
EComHR 12 October 1989, *B.H., M.W., H.P. and G.K. v. Austria*, appl. no. 12774/87
EComHR 29 March 1993, *F.P. v. Germany*, appl. no. 19459/92
EComHR 2 September 1994, *Ochensberger v. Austria*, appl. no. 21318/93
EComHR 11 January 1995, *Walendy v. Germany*, appl. no. 21128/92
EComHR 2 September 1994, *Ochensberger v. Austria*, appl. no. 21318/93
EComHR 6 September 1995, *Remer v. Germany*, appl. no. 25096/94
EComHR 18 October 1995, *Honsik v. Austria*, appl. no. 25062/94
EComHR 29 November 1995, *Nationaldemokratische Partei Deutschlands, Bezirksverband München-Oberbayern v. Germany*, appl. no. 25992/94
EComHR 16 January 1996, *Rebhandl v. Austria*, appl. no. 24398/94
EComHR 24 June 1996, *Marais v. France*, appl. no. 31159/96
EComHR 26 June 1996, *D.I. v. Germany*, appl. no. 26551/95
EComHR 20 October 1997, *Reisz v. Germany*, appl. no. 32013/96
EComHR 9 September 1998, *Herwig Nachtmann v. Austria*, appl. no. 36773/97
EComHR 20 April 1999, *Witzsch v. Germany*, appl. no. 41448/98.

European Court of Human Rights

ECtHR 1 July 1961, *Lawless v. Ireland (no. 3)*, appl. no. 332/57
ECtHR 23 July 1968, *Case 'relating to certain aspects of the laws on the use of languages in education in Belgium' v. Belgium ('Belgian Linguistic' case)*, appl. nos. 1474/62 et al.
ECtHR 7 December 1976, *Handyside v. the United Kingdom*, appl. no. 5493/72
ECtHR 18 January 1978, *Ireland v. the United Kingdom*, appl. no. 5310/71

ECtHR 6 September 1978, *Klass and others v. Germany*, appl. no. 5029/71
ECtHR 25 April 1978, *Tyrer v. the United Kingdom*, appl. no. 5856/72
ECtHR 26 April 1979, *Sunday Times v. the United Kingdom (no. 1)*, appl. no. 6538/74
ECtHR 28 August 1986, *Kosiek v. Germany*, appl. no. 9704/82
ECtHR 28 August 1986, *Glasenapp v. Germany*, appl. no. 9228/80
ECtHR 2 March 1987, *Mathieu-Mohin and Clerfayt v. Belgium*, appl. no. 9267/81
ECtHR 24 March 1988, *Olsson v. Sweden (no. 1)*, appl. no. 10465/83
ECtHR 25 May 1993, *Brannigan and McBride v. the United Kingdom*, appl. nos. 14553/89 and 14554/89
ECtHR 23 September 1994 (GC), *Jersild v. Denmark*, appl. no. 15890/89
ECtHR 26 September 1995 (GC), *Vogt v. Germany*, appl. no. 17851/91
ECtHR 25 November 1996, *Wingrove v. the United Kingdom*, appl. no. 17419/90
ECtHR 18 December 1996, *Aksoy v. Turkey*, appl. no. 21987/93
ECtHR 30 January 1998 (GC), *United Communist Party of Turkey and others v. Turkey*, appl. no. 19392/92
ECtHR 25 May 1998 (GC), *Socialist Party and others v. Turkey*, appl. no. 21237/93
ECtHR 23 September 1998 (GC), *Lehideux and Isorni v. France*, appl. no. 24662/94
ECtHR 20 May 1999 (GC), *Rekvényi v. Hungary*, appl. no. 25390/94
ECtHR 8 July 1999 (GC), *Sürek v. Turkey (no. 1)*, appl. no. 26682/95
ECtHR 28 October 1999 (GC), *Wille v. Lichtenstein*, appl. no. 28396/95
ECtHR 8 December 1999 (GC), *Freedom and Democracy Party (*Özdep*) v. Turkey*, appl. no. 23885/94
ECtHR 1 February 2000 (dec.), *Schimanek v. Austria*, appl. no. 32307/96
ECtHR 12 April 2001 (dec.), *Kaptan* v. *Switzerland*, appl. no. 55641/00
ECtHR 2 October 2001, *Stankov and the united Macedonian Organisation Llinden v. Bulgaria*, appl. nos. 29221/95 and 29225/95
ECtHR 9 April 2002, *Podkolzina v. Latvia*, appl. no. 46726/99
ECtHR 9 April 2002, *Yazar and others v. Turkey*, appl. nos. 22723/93, 22724/93 and 22725/93
ECtHR 31 July 2001, *Refah Partisi (the Welfare Party) and others v. Turkey*, appl. nos. 41340/98 et al.
ECtHR 13 February 2003 (GC), *Refah Partisi (the Welfare Party) and other v. Turkey*, appl. nos. 41340/98 et al.
ECtHR 24 June 2003 (dec.), *Garaudy v. France*, appl. no. 65831/01
ECtHR 25 November 2003 (dec.), *R.L. v. Switzerland*, appl. no. 43874/98
ECtHR 4 December 2003, *Gündüz v. Turkey*, appl. no. 35071/97
ECtHR17 February 2004, *Gorzelik and others v. Poland*, appl. no. 44158/98
ECtHR 18 May 2004 (dec.), *Seurot v. France*, appl. no. 57383/00
ECtHR 29 June 2004, *Chauvy and others v. France*, appl. no. 64915/01
ECtHR 2 September 2004 (dec.), *W.P. and others v. Poland*, appl. no. 42264/98
ECtHR 16 November 2004 (dec.), *Norwood v. the United Kingdom*, appl. no. 23131/03
ECtHR 3 February 2005, *Partidul Comunistilor (Nepeceristi) (PCN) and Ungureanu v. Romania*, appl. no. 46626/99
ECtHR 6 October 2005 (GC), *Hirst v. the United Kingdom (no. 2)*, appl. no. 74025/01

ECtHR 24 November 2005, *Otto v. Germany*, appl. no. 27574/02
ECtHR 13 December 2005 (dec.), *Witzsch v. Germany*, appl. no. 7485/03
ECtHR 31 January 2006, *Giniewski v. France*, appl. no. 64016/00
ECtHR 16 March 2006 (GC), *Ždanoka v. Latvia*, appl. no. 58278/00
ECtHR 6 July 2006, *Erbakan v. Turkey*, appl. no. 59405/00
ECtHR 21 September 2006, *Monnat v. Switzerland*, appl. no. 73604/01
ECtHR 7 December 2006, *Linkov v. Czech Republic*, appl. no. 10504/03
ECtHR 20 February 2007 (dec.), *Ivanov v. Russia*, appl. no. 35222/04
ECtHR 5 April 2007, *Church of Scientology Moscow v. Russia*, appl. no. 18147/02
ECtHR 21 June 2007, *Zhechev v. Bulgaria*, appl. no. 57045/00
ECtHR 8 July 2008, *Vajnai v. Hungary*, appl. no. 33629/06
ECtHR 8 July 2008 (GC), *Yumak and Sadak v. Turkey*, appl. no. 10226/03
ECtHR 10 July 2008, *Soulas and others v. France*, appl. no. 15948/03
ECtHR 2 October 2008, *Leroy v. France*, appl. no. 36109/03
ECtHR 4 November 2008, *Balsytė-Lideikienė v. Lithuania*, appl. no. 72596/01
ECtHR 15 January 2009, *Orban and others v. France*, appl. no. 20985/05
ECtHR 19 February 2009 (GC), *A. and others v. the United Kingdom*, appl. no. 3455/05
ECtHR 30 June 2009, *Herri Batasuna and Batasuna v. Spain*, appl. nos. 25803/04 and 25817/04
ECtHR 16 July 2009, *Willem v. France*, appl. no. 10883/05
ECtHR 16 July 2009, *Féret v. Belgium*, appl. no. 15615/07
ECtHR 15 September 2009, *Miroļubovs and others v. Latvia,* appl. no. 798/05
ECtHR 20 April 2010 (dec.), *Le Pen v. France*, appl. no. 18788/09
ECtHR 22 April 2010, *Fatullayev v. Azerbaijan*, appl. no. 40984/07
ECtHR 14 September 2010, *Dink v. Turkey*, app. nos. 2668/07 et al.
ECtHR 6 January 2011 (GC), *Paksas v. Lithuania*, appl. no. 34932/04
ECtHR 13 January 2011, *Hoffer and Annen v. Germany*, appl. nos. 397/07 and 2322/07
ECtHR 7 June 2011 (dec.), *Gollnisch v. France*, appl. no. 48135/08
ECtHR 3 November 2011, *Fratanoló v. Hungary*, appl. no. 29459/10
ECtHR 9 February 2012, *Vejdeland and other v. Sweden*, appl. no. 1813/07
ECtHR 12 June 2012 (dec.), *Hizb Ut-Tahrir and others v. Germany*, appl. no. 31098/08
ECtHR 24 July 2012, *Fáber v. Hungary*, appl. no. 40721/08
ECtHR 8 November 2012, *PETA Deutschland v. Germany*, appl. no. 43481/09
ECtHR 5 March 2013, *Varela Geis v. Spain*, appl. no. 61005/09
ECtHR 14 March 2013, *Kasymakhunov and Saybatalov v. Russia*, appl. nos. 26261/05 and 26377/06
ECtHR 9 July 2013, *Vona v. Hungary*, appl. no. 35943/10
ECtHR 15 October 2015 (GC), *Perinçek v. Switzerland*, appl. no. 27510/08
ECtHR 20 October 2015 (dec.), *M'Bala M'Bala v. France*, appl. no. 25239/13

UN Human Rights Committee (CCPR)

CCPR, 29 July 1981 (13th session), *Sergio Ruben Lopez Burgos v. Uruguay*, communication no. 52/1979

CCPR, 29 July 1981 (13th session*), Lilian Celiberti de Casariego v. Uruguay*, communication no. 56/1979

CCPR, 10 April 1984 (21st session), *M.A. v. Italy,* communication no. 117/1981

CCPR, 6 April 1983 (18th session), *J.R.T. and W.G. Party v. Canada*, communication no. 104/1981

CCPR, 8 November 1996 (58th session), *Faurisson v. France*, communication no. 550/1993

CCPR, 18 October 2000 (70th session), *Ross v. Canada*, communication no. 736/1997

Inter-American Court of Human Rights

IACtHR, *Case of Benjamin et al. v. Trinidad and Tobago*, 1 September 2001 (preliminary objections)

IACtHR, *Case of Constantine et al. v. Trinidad and Tobago*, 1 September 2001 (preliminary objections)

IACtHR, *Case of Hilaire. v. Trinidad and Tobago*, 1 September 2001(preliminary objections)

Court of Justice of the European Union

Case C-110/99, *Emsland-Stärke*, [2000] ECR I-1569

Case C109/01, *Akrich* [2003] ECR I9607

Case C-200/02, *Chen,* [2004] *ECR* I-9925

Case C-255/02, *Halifax*, [2006] ECR I-1609

Case C-456/04, *Agip Petroli*, [2006] ECR I-3395

Case C-196/04, *Cadbury Schweppes*, [2006] ECR I-7995

Case C-279/05, *Vonk Dairy Products*, [2007] ECR I-239

Case C-524/04, *Thin Cap Group Litigation*, [2007] ECR I-1

Case C-251/06, *ING AUER*, [2007] ECR I-9689

Case C-425/06, *Part Service*, [2008] ECR I-897

Case C-34/90, *Ruiz Zambrano* [2010] ECR I-01177

Case C-244/10 and C-245/10, *Mesopotamia Broadcast A/S METV and Roj TV A/S v. Bundesrepublik Deutschland*, [2011] ECR I-08779-8796

Opinion of AG Mengozzi in Case C-83/13, *Fonnship A/S v. Svenska Transportarbetareförbundet and Facket för Service och Kommunikation (SEKO) and Svenska Transportarbetareförbundet v. Fonnship A/S*, [2014] ECLI:EU:C:2014:201

Arbitral Tribunal under annex vii UN Convention on the Law of the Sea

Chagos Marine Protected Area Arbitration *(Mauritius v. UK),* 18 March 2015

France

Affaire Doerr, Court of Appeal of Colmar, 2 May 1855, D.P. 1856.2.9
Affaire Saint Galmier, Court of Appeal of Lyon, 18 April 1856, D.P.1856.2.199
Affaire Clément-Bayard, Court of Cassation, 3 August 1915, D.P.III.1917.1.79

England

Christie v. Davey (1893) I CH 316 (HL)
Bradford Corporation v. Pickles (1895), Appeal Cases 587 (HL)
Hollywood Silver Fox Farm Ltd v. Emmet (1936) 2 KB 468 (HL)

Germany

BVerfGE 2, 1 (1952), *SRP-Verbot [ban of the Socialist Reich Party]*
BVerfGE 5, 85 (1956), *KPD Verbot [ban of the German Communist Party]*
BVerfGE 11, 282 (1960), *Otto Ernst Remer*
BVerfGE 25, 44 (1969), *Flugblatt zur Unterstützung der KPD*
BVerfGE 25, 88 (1969). *Berufsverbot II*
BVerfGE 28, 36 (1970), *Zitiergebot*
BVerfGE 30, 1 (1970), *Abhör-Urteil*
BVerfGE 38, 23 (1974), *Gerhard Frey*
BVerfGE 39, 334 (1975), *Treuepflicht des Beamten*
BVerfGE 47, 198 (1978), *Wahlwerbesendung*
BVerfGE 54, 208 (1980), *Böll*
BVerfGE 61, 1 (1982), *Meinungsäußerung im Wahlkampf*
BVerfGE 74, 358 (1987)
BVerfGE 82, 106 (1990), *Unschuldsvermutung*
BVerfGE 85, 1 (1991), *Bayer-Aktionäre*
BVerfGE, *Thomas Dienel* and *Heinz Reisz* (1996), 2 BvA 1/92 and 2 BvA 2/92
BVerfGE 90, 241 (1994), *Auschwitzlüge*
BVerfGE, *NPD-Verbotsverfahren* (2003), 2 BvB 1/01
BVerfGE 111, 307 (2004), *Görgülü*
BVerfGE 120, 180 (2008), *Caroline von Monaco III (St. Moritz)*
BGH, 15 March 1994, *Deckert,* 1 StR 179/93, *NJW* 1994, 1421

United States of America

US Supreme Court, *Whitney v. California*, 274 *US* 357, 1927

Samenvatting

1 Inleiding

In 1956 oordeelde het Duitse Constitutionele Hof dat de *Kommunistische Partei Deutschlands* met haar communistische denkbeelden een bedreiging vormde voor de vrije democratische rechtsorde. De partij werd onconstitutioneel verklaard en verboden. De partij klaagde vervolgens voor de Europese Commissie voor de Rechten van de Mens (ECRM of Commissie) dat het verbod een schending betekende van het recht op vrijheid van meningsuiting en de verenigingsvrijheid. De Commissie oordeelde dat de partij pleitte voor de vestiging van een communistische samenleving door middel van een proletarische dictatuur. Het promoten van een dictatuur voor de vestiging van een regime was volgens de Commissie onverenigbaar met het Verdrag.[1]

In 1990 werd de Franse filosoof en voormalig politicus Roger Garaudy veroordeeld voor het tegenspreken van misdaden tegen de menselijkheid, belastering van de Joodse gemeenschap en het aanzetten tot rassenhaat. In zijn boek *The Founding Myths of Modern Israel* trekt hij openlijk de Holocaust in twijfel en omschrijft hij de gaskamers als een mythe. Garaudy diende een klacht in bij het Europees Hof voor de Rechten van de Mens (EHRM of Hof) en claimde dat zijn veroordeling een schending was van zijn vrijheid van meningsuiting. Het Hof was echter van mening dat Garaudy met de revisionistische toon van het boek trachtte af te wijken van de ware bedoeling van het recht op vrijheid van meningsuiting door dit recht te gebruiken voor een doel dat onverenigbaar is met de tekst en de geest van het Europees Verdrag voor de Rechten van de Mens (EVRM of Verdrag).[2]

Recentelijk verbood de Duitse federale minister van Binnenlandse Zaken de internationale Islamitische organisatie Hizb Ut-Tahrir. Deze organisatie promoot de samenvoeging van alle staten in het Midden-Oosten tot één Islamitisch kalifaat bestuurd volgens de regels van de Sharia. Daarbij bepleit de organisatie de gewelddadige vernietiging van de staat Israël en zijn inwoners. Dit was volgens de minister in strijd met het beginsel van internationale verstandhouding (*Gedanken der Völkerverständigung*). Voor het EHRM klaagde de organisatie over een schending van haar recht op vrijheid van vereniging. Het EHRM oordeelde dat het promoten van de gewelddadige vernietiging van Israël en zijn inwoners indruist tegen de waarden

1 ECRM 20 juli 1957, *German Communist Party t. Duitsland*, appl. nr. 250/57.
2 EHRM 24 juni 2003 (beslissing), *Garaudy t. Frankrijk*, appl. nr. 65831/01.

van het Verdrag, in het bijzonder de eerbiedwaardigheid van het menselijk leven en de verplichting om internationale conflicten op een vreedzame wijze op te lossen.[3]

Wat deze uiteenlopende zaken met elkaar gemeen hebben is dat in al deze gevallen het EHRM oordeelde dat de klagers geen beroep toekwam op de rechten die zij inriepen, omdat zij deze rechten hadden misbruikt in de zin van artikel 17 EVRM. Dit artikel, ook wel de misbruikclausule genoemd, stelt dat *'[g]een der bepalingen van dit Verdrag mag worden uitgelegd als zou zij voor een Staat, een groep of een persoon een recht inhouden enige activiteit aan de dag te leggen of enige daad te verrichten met als doel de rechten of vrijheden die in dit Verdrag zijn vermeld teniet te doen of deze verdergaand te beperken dan bij dit Verdrag is voorzien'*. Op grond van deze bepaling hebben de Straatsburgse instituties geoordeeld dat activiteiten die onverenigbaar zijn met het Verdrag geen bescherming genieten.

2 Onderzoeksvraag

Artikel 17 EVRM belichaamt één van de belangrijkste uitgangspunten van het Verdrag: de handhaving van democratie en democratische waarden. Door te voorkomen dat antidemocratische groepen en individuen met succes een beroep kunnen doen op fundamentele rechten en vrijheden, doet artikel 17 EVRM in het klein wat het Verdrag beoogt te bewerkstelligen op een grotere schaal: het beschermen van de democratie en het voorkomen van totalitarisme.[4] Tegelijkertijd is artikel 17 EVRM ook één van de meest controversiële bepalingen in het Verdrag. De groeiende hoeveelheid jurisprudentie laat zien dat de interpretatie van artikel 17 EVRM ver van eenduidig is. Op grond van artikel 17 EVRM kunnen subversieve, antidemocratische activiteiten worden uitgesloten van de bescherming van het Verdrag. Duidelijke criteria om vast te stellen welke activiteiten hiervoor in aanmerking komen ontbreken echter. Om te kunnen komen tot een meer coherente interpretatie is er behoefte aan opheldering van de betekenis van artikel 17 EVRM. De centrale onderzoeksvraag in deze studie is daarom:

Hoe is het verbod van misbruik van recht in artikel 17 van het Europees Verdrag voor de Rechten van de Mens tot op heden geïnterpreteerd door de Europese Commissie voor de Rechten van de Mens en het Europees Hof voor de Rechten van de Mens en hoe kan deze bepaling in de toekomst worden toegepast?

---

3 EHRM 12 juni 2012 (beslissing), *Hizb Ut-Tahrir e.a. t. Duitsland*, appl. nr. 31098/08.

4 A. Buyse, 'Contested Contours. The limits of freedom of expression from an abuse of rights perspective – Articles 10 and 17 ECHR', in: E. Brems en J. Gerards (red.), *Shaping Rights in the ECHR. The Role of the European Court of Human Rights in Determining the Scope of Rights*, Cambridge: Cambridge University Press, 2014, p. 187.

In de zoektocht naar het antwoord op deze vraag begon deze studie met een overzicht van de huidige interpretatie van artikel 17 EVRM. Deze bestond uit een terugblik op de totstandkoming van het Verdrag om te onderzoeken waarom de opstellers besloten een misbruikclausule op te nemen. Vervolgens is gekeken naar de jurisprudentie van de Commissie en het Hof met betrekking tot artikel 17 EVRM, waarbij de onduidelijkheden en inconsistenties in de interpretatie van artikel 17 EVRM werden blootgelegd. Op zoek naar opheldering is vervolgens een aantal verschillende perspectieven bestudeerd die inzicht kunnen geven in de betekenis van de misbruikclausule in het licht van het EVRM. In de eerste plaats is gekeken naar de interpretatie van artikel 17 EVRM door juridische geleerden. Vervolgens is gekeken hoe de misbruikclausules in andere internationale en regionale mensenrechtensystemen worden begrepen. Daarop volgde een bestudering van het concept 'misbruik van recht', dat behalve in artikel 17 EVRM ook is terug te vinden in andere juridische disciplines. Omdat het verbod van misbruik van recht in het EVRM wordt gezien als een uiting van de gedachte dat een democratisch systeem in staat moet zijn zichzelf tegen omverwerping te beschermen is tot slot aandacht besteed aan het concept 'weerbare democratie'.

3 Achtergrond en interpretatie van de misbruikclausule

Artikel 17 EVRM is duidelijk een uitdrukking van een tijdsgeest. Het Verdrag kwam net na de Tweede Wereldoorlog tot stand. De opstellers van het Verdrag vreesden dat totalitaire stromingen van Nazistische, fascistische of communistische aard (opnieuw) zouden proberen om de West-Europese democratieën omver te werpen. Met de wreedheden van de Tweede Wereldoorlog nog vers in het geheugen en geconfronteerd met het oprukkende communisme uit het oosten hadden de opstellers de bedoeling om een internationaal mechanisme te creëren *'by which 'free Europe' could protect itself against the rise of another Hitler, or the installation of a totalitarian regime'*.[5] Artikel 17 EVRM is de meest expliciete uitdrukking van deze ambitie.

In eerste instantie kwam de originele betekenis van artikel 17 EVRM als een barrière tegen totalitaire stromingen die de democratie en democratische waarden uitbuiten met de bedoeling om deze omver te werpen duidelijk tot uitdrukking in de Straatsburgse jurisprudentie. Tot de jaren '90 werd de misbruikclausule primair toegepast in het licht van de totalitaire dreigingen waar de opstellers van het verdrag voor vreesden: communisme en neonazisme. Later is de reikwijdte van de misbruikclausule echter opgerekt. Sinds het einde van de Koude Oorlog is artikel 17 EVRM steeds vaker toegepast op activiteiten die indruisen tegen de *'basis'*, *'onderliggende'* of

5 E. Bates, *The Evolution of the European Convention on Human Rights. From its Inception to the Creation of a Permanent Court of Human Rights*, Oxford: Oxford University Press, 2010, p. 6.

'fundamentele' 'waarden' of *'ideeën'* of de *'tekst en geest'* van het Verdrag, zoals rassendiscriminatie en vijandigheid ten opzichte van een bepaalde (religieuze) groep.[6]

Deze ontwikkeling heeft geleid tot een obscure en inconsistente casuïstische benadering. In de eerste plaats, hoewel de ECRM en het EHRM hebben benadrukt dat de misbruikclausule alleen bij hoge uitzondering in extreme gevallen van toepassing is, hebben ze nagelaten om duidelijke criteria te formuleren voor welke gevallen aan deze omschrijving voldoen. Artikel 17 EVRM bestrijkt een diversiteit aan activiteiten die potentieel gericht zijn op de vernietiging van de rechten en vrijheden in het Verdrag, variërend van ontkenning van de Holocaust, communistische sympathieën, *hate speech*, anti-seculiere ideeën, en het aanzetten tot geweld. Merkwaardig genoeg hebben de ECRM en het EHRM echter andere antidemocratische activiteiten niet willen beoordelen in het licht van artikel 17 EVRM. Hoewel het voornaamste doel van artikel 17 EVRM is om de democratie hoog te houden, liet het Hof na om naar deze bepaling te verwijzen toen het oordeelde dat de bedoeling van een politieke partij om een theocratisch regime op te zetten op basis van de Sharia ondemocratisch was.[7] Daarnaast oordeelden de ECRM en het EHRM in een aantal zaken dat de racistische uitlatingen van de klager overduidelijke onder artikel 17 EVRM vielen,[8] terwijl het in andere zaken vond dat vergelijkbare uitlatingen niet ernstig genoeg waren om de toepassing van artikel 17 EVRM te rechtvaardigen.[9]

In de tweede plaats is onduidelijk hoe artikel 17 EVRM toegepast dient te worden. Op basis van de directe toepassing van artikel 17 EVRM wordt een activiteit die als misbruik wordt gekwalificeerd uitgesloten van de bescherming van een recht of vrijheid. Deze directe toepassing van artikel 17 EVRM leidt tot de niet-ontvankelijkheid van een klacht op basis van een oppervlakkige beoordeling waarna geen grondige beoordeling in het licht van de beperkingscriteria meer plaatsvindt. Deze benadering is terecht bekritiseerd vanwege het gebrek aan een duidelijke afweging van de betrokken belangen en de marginale beoordeling van de proportionaliteit van de beperking van het recht van de klager. Bij een indirecte toepassing, daarentegen, werkt artikel 17 EVRM in feite als een kompas bij de beoordeling of een beperking van een recht noodzakelijk was in een democratische samenleving in het licht van

---

6 Zie bijvoorbeeld ECRM 6 september 1995, *Remer t. Duitsland*, appl. nr. 25096/94, par. 1; ECRM 18 oktober 1995, *Honsik t. Oostenrijk*, appl. nr. 25062/94; ECRM 29 november 1995, *Nationaldemokratische Partei Deutschlands, Bezirksverband München-Oberbayern t. Duitsland*, appl. nr. 25992/94; ECRM 24 juni 1996, *Marais t. Frankrijk*, appl. nr. 31159/96, par. 1; EHRM 16 november 2004 (beslissing), *Norwood t. het Verenigd Koninkrijk*, appl. nr. 23131/03; EHRM 14 maart 2013, *Kasymakhunov and Saybatalov t. Rusland*, appl. nrs. 26261/05 en 26377/06, par. 113.

7 EHRM 13 februari 2003 (GK), *Refah Partisi (the Welfare Party) e.a. t. Turkije*, appl. nrs. 41340/98 et al., par. 125.

8 Zie bijvoorbeeld ECRM 11 oktober 1979, *Glimmerveen en Hagenbeek t. Nederland*, appl. nrs. 8348/78 en 8406/78.

9 Zie bijvoorbeeld EHRM 16 juli 2009, *Féret t. België*, appl. nr. 15615/07.

de beperkingsclausule. Tot slot resulteerde de indirecte toepassing van artikel 17 EVRM in een aantal zaken niet tot het niet vinden van een schending, maar zelfs tot het oordeel dat de klacht kennelijk ongegrond was. Middels een omweg via de beperkingssystematiek resulteerde dit alsnog in de niet-ontvankelijk van de klacht. Tegelijkertijd laat de Straatsburgse benadering in een aantal andere zaken zien dat klachten van antidemocratische politieke actoren net zo goed kunnen worden afgedaan zonder expliciet naar de misbruikclausule te verwijzen. De keuze voor de ene of de andere benadering lijkt nogal arbitrair en de vaak beperkte argumentatie met betrekking tot de toepassing van artikel 17 EVRM is niet voldoende in staat om deze verschillen te verklaren.

4 De interpretatie van artikel 17 EVRM in de doctrine

Ondanks dat artikel 17 EVRM slechts een beperkte rol speelt in de jurisprudentie van de Commissie en het Hof is de bepaling regelmatig onderwerp geweest van academisch debat. Hoewel juridische auteurs het er over het algemeen over eens zijn dat artikel 17 EVRM een duidelijk signaal afgeeft over het belang van de handhaving van democratie en democratische waarden hebben ze ook regelmatig de aandacht gevestigd op de potentieel negatieve gevolgen van de toepassing van deze bepaling. De misbruikclausule heeft paradoxale implicaties: als de toepassing van artikel 17 EVRM staten toestaat om vergaande beperkingen van fundamentele rechten te rechtvaardigen, lopen ze het risico om zelf de democratische standaarden van het Verdrag te ondermijnen.[10] Het onderscheid tussen (controversiële) ideeën die de bescherming van het Verdrag verdienen en denkbeelden die daadwerkelijk een gevaar vormen voor de democratie of democratische waarden is extreem ingewikkeld. Het gevaar bestaat zelfs dat staten de misbruikclausule proberen te misbruiken om (politieke) denkbeelden die afwijken van die van de regering uit te sluiten.[11] Gelet op de vergaande gevolgen die de toepassing van artikel 17 EVRM kan hebben voor de bescherming van de rechten van de klager moet men zich bewust zijn van de mogelijk averechtse werking van de misbruikclausule en de potentieel negatieve gevolgen voor de democratie en democratische waarden. Vooral nu de reikwijdte van artikel 17 EVRM ruimer is geworden loopt de bepaling het risico te ruimhartig

10 H. Cannie en D. Voorhoof, 'The Abuse Clause and Freedom of Expression in the European Human Rights Convention: an Added Value for Democracy and Human Rights Protection?', *Netherlands Quarterly of Human Rights*, vol. 29, no. 1, 2011, p. 76-78; Buyse, *Shaping Rights in the ECHR*, p. 205; Y. Arai (rev.), 'Prohibition of abuse of the rights and freedoms set forth in the convention and of their limitation to a greater extent than is provided for in the convention (Article 17)', in: P. van Dijk, F. van Hoof, A. van Rijn en L. Zwaak (red.), *Theory and practice of the European Convention on Human Rights*, 4th ed., Antwerpen/Oxford: Intersentia, 2006, p. 1086-1087.

11 Cannie en Voorhoof, *Netherlands Quarterly of Human Rights*, p. 72; I. Hare, 'Extreme Speech under International and Regional Human Rights Standards, in: I Hare en J. Weinstein (red.), *Extreme Speech and Democracy*, Oxford: Oxford University Press, 2009, p. 79.

te worden in het ontnemen van de bescherming van fundamentele rechten. Dit kan uiteindelijk serieuze gevolgen hebben voor bescherming van afwijkende (politieke) denkbeelden in Europa.

5 Misbruikclausules in andere mensenrechtendocumenten

Het EVRM is niet het enige mensenrechtendocument dat misbruik van de rechten en vrijheden die het garandeert verbiedt. Misbruikclausules vergelijkbaar met artikel 17 EVRM zijn ook te vinden in de Universele Verklaring van de Rechten van de Mens (UVRM), het Internationaal Verdrag inzake Burgerrechten en Politieke Rechten (IVBPR), het Internationaal Verdrag inzake Economische, Sociale en Culturele Rechten (IVESCR), de Amerikaanse Conventie voor de Rechten van de Mens (ACRM) en het Handvest van de Grondrechten van de EU.

Hoewel de formulering en de achtergrond van de misbruikclausules in al deze mensenrechtendocumenten grotendeels vergelijkbaar zijn, is hun interpretatie duidelijk een eigen weg gegaan. Een aantal verschillen is de moeite van het beschrijven waard. Het eerste verschil betreft de toepassing van artikel 5, eerste lid, IVBPR, de tegenhanger van artikel 17 EVRM op VN-niveau. Terwijl de reikwijdte van artikel 17 EVRM zich uitbreidt, lijkt de interpretatie van artikel 5, eerste lid, IVBPR juist steeds restrictiever te worden. Oorspronkelijk paste het Mensenrechtencomité artikel 5, eerste lid, IVBPR bij gelegenheid toe om een individuele petitie wegens misbruik niet-ontvankelijke te verklaren. Later lijkt het Mensenrechtencomité echter van deze benadering te zijn afgestapt. In de zaak *Ross t. Canada*, betreffende een leraar die niet meer voor de klas mocht staan na diverse anti-Joodse uitlatingen, oordeelde het Mensenrechtencomité dat iedere beperking van de vrijheid van meningsuiting, zelfs haatuitingen op grond van nationaliteit, ras of religie, beoordeeld dient te worden in het licht van het recht op vrijheid van meningsuiting in artikel 19 IVBPR.[12] Met deze conclusie lijkt het Mensenrechtencomité de directe toepassing van de misbruikclausule expliciet af te wijzen en te kiezen voor een benadering op basis van de beperkingscriteria in artikel 19, derde lid, IVBPR.

Het tweede interessante verschil heeft betrekking op de misbruikclausule in artikel 29, sub a, ACRM. Hoewel de ACRM is gemodelleerd naar het EVRM, verschilt de interpretatie van de misbruikclausule in dit verdrag significant van die van artikel 17 EVRM. Aan de ene kant heeft het Inter-Amerikaanse Hof voor de Rechten van de Mens in de paar zaken waarin het een oordeel heeft gegeven over artikel 29, sub a, ACRM geoordeeld dat juist de staat misbruik had gemaakt van het verdrag, omdat het de ACRM interpreteerde op een manier die een einde zou maken

12 UN Mensenrechtencomité, 18 oktober 2000 (70ᵉ sessie), *Ross t. Canada*, nr. 736/1997, par. 10.5 en 10.6.

aan de rechten en vrijheden die het verdrag beschermt.[13] Dit is interessant aangezien artikel 17 EVRM eigenlijk geen rol speelt bij het sanctioneren van misbruik door staten. Aan de andere kant lijkt een doctrine van het verbieden van misbruik door individuen en groepen zoals ontwikkeld in het licht van artikel 17 EVRM afwezig in de context van de ACRM. Kortom, de interpretatie van de misbruikclausules in andere mensenrechtendocumenten bevestigt dat zaken betreffende antidemocratische uitlatingen kunnen worden beoordeeld zonder beroep te doen op de misbruikclausule.

6 Het verbod van misbruik van recht

In deze studie is tevens onderzocht in hoeverre het algemene beginsel van het verbod van misbruik van recht inzicht kan bieden in de betekenis van artikel 17 EVRM. Het verbod van misbruik van recht is te vinden in verschillende juridische disciplines. De bedoeling van het verbod is in essentie om de toepassing van een rechtsregel te corrigeren op basis van standaarden zoals goede trouw, redelijkheid en billijkheid, en rechtvaardigheid indien met de formele toepassing van een rechtsregel het doel daarvan niet wordt gehaald.[14] Het beginsel vindt zijn oorsprong aan het begin van de 19^{e} eeuw in de groeiende politieke en intellectuele ontevredenheid met het absolutisme van het liberalisme dat domineerde ten tijde van de Verlichting.[15] In het begin werd het concept fel bekritiseerd omdat het logisch onhoudbaar zou zijn. Als een activiteit valt binnen de reikwijdte van een recht zou er geen sprake kunnen zijn van misbruik. Inmiddels is het verbod van misbruik van recht echter algemeen erkend als privaatrechtelijk rechtsbeginsel in nationale rechtsordes die behoren tot de *civil law* traditie.

In Frankrijk, de bakermat van dit concept, was het verbod van misbruik van recht oorspronkelijk gebaseerd op de intentie of het motief van de rechthebbende. Echter, deze 'subjectieve' test wordt over het algemeen als problematisch gezien, omdat het een psychologisch onderzoek vereist naar het motief van de rechthebbende en een moralistisch element introduceert. In verschillende rechtsordes zijn daarom pogingen gedaan om deze subjectieve criteria aan te vullen met meer objectieve criteria, zoals het resulteren in excessief leed of het gebrek aan een legitiem belang ter rechtvaardiging van een handeling. Ook deze objectieve criteria zijn echter niet onproblematisch, omdat ze abstract en moeilijk toe te passen zijn.

---

13 Inter-Amerikaans Hof voor de Rechten van de Mens (IAHRM), *Benjamin e.a. t. Trinidad en Tobago*, 1 september 2001 (preliminary objections), par. 81; IAHRM, *Constantine e.a. t. Trinidad en Tobago*, 1 september 2001, par. 63; IAHRM, *Hilaire t. Trinidad en Tobago*, 1 september 2001, par. 64.

14 A. Lenaerts, 'The General Principle of the Prohibition of Abuse of Rights: A Critical Position on Its Role in a Codified European Contract Law', *European Review of Private Law*, vol. 18, no. 6, 2010, p. 1121.

15 A. Sajó, 'Abuse of Fundamental Rights or the Difficulties of Purposiveness', in: A. Sajó (red.), *Abuse: The Dark Side of Fundamental Rights*, Utrecht: Eleven International Publishing, 2006, p. 29-30.

Het beginsel heeft vervolgens ook zijn weg gevonden naar het internationale niveau, in het bijzonder het internationaal publiekrecht en het EU recht. Ook in de context van internationale mensenrechten heeft het concept misbruik van recht recent meer aandacht gekregen. Misbruik van recht in relatie tot mensenrechten mag op het eerste gezicht vreemd lijken. Mensenrechten zijn oorspronkelijk bedoeld als bescherming tegen de macht van de staat, en niet tegen activiteiten van individuen en groepen. Ze zijn daarentegen juist bedoeld om burgers de vrijheid te bieden om zoveel mogelijk hun leven te leven zoals hen goeddunkt. Ook in de context van mensenrechten heeft het verbod van misbruik van recht daarom een controversiële connotatie. Activiteiten die strikt genomen op basis van de letter van de wet bescherming genieten worden bij nader inzien hiervan uitgesloten op basis van een subjectief element: de subversieve intentie van de rechthebbende. Bovendien, waar het verbod van misbruik van recht in het privaatrecht tot doel heeft om de oneerlijke gevolgen die een formele toepassing van het recht te corrigeren anders zou hebben, is dit in het geval van mensenrechten anders. Mensenrechteninstrumenten staan onder strenge voorwaarden beperkingen van deze rechten toe, in ieder geval van die rechten die worden geassocieerd met misbruik, zoals het recht op vrijheid van meningsuiting en het verenigingsrecht. Anders dan in het privaatrecht kan dus op basis van de beperkingsclausules in deze verdragen het doel van deze rechten worden gehaald zonder een toevlucht te nemen tot het concept misbruik van recht.

7 De weerbare democratie

Bovendien heeft misbruik in het kader van de misbruikclausules in mensenrechtenverdragen een andere betekenis dan in het privaatrecht. Waar het concept misbruik van recht in het privaatrecht ziet op de impact van het misbruik op andere individuen, wordt misbruik in het licht van mensenrechtenverdragen gekenmerkt door de impact op het democratische systeem.[16] Misbruik wordt in deze context gedefinieerd als een poging om de democratie of democratische waarden te vernietigen. De misbruikclausule wordt dan ook geassocieerd met het concept 'weerbare democratie'; een democratie die in staat is zichzelf te beschermen tegen omverwerping. In het laatste deel van deze studie is daarom onderzocht in hoeverre het concept van de weerbare democratie een kader kan bieden voor de interpretatie van artikel 17 EVRM. Deze studie bestond uit drie onderdelen: een studie van de doctrine omtrent de weerbare democratie, een analyse van de interpretatie van dit concept in Duitsland, en een studie van de rol van dit concept in de context van het EVRM en de interpretatie van artikel 17 EVRM in het bijzonder.

16 Sajó, *Abuse*, p. 53.

7.1 *Het concept weerbare democratie*

Een weerbare democratie is een democratisch systeem dat preventieve, op het eerste gezicht ondemocratische juridische instrumenten toepast om zich te beschermen tegen het risico omver te worden geworpen door antidemocratische groepen en individuen die gebruik maken van politieke rechten en democratische procedures met de bedoeling deze teniet te doen. Het concept werd voor het eerst uitgewerkt in de tweede helft van de jaren '30 door Loewenstein in een serie artikelen waarin hij zijn bezorgdheid uitte over de toename van het fascisme in Europa.[17] Het was echter pas na de Tweede Wereldoorlog dat het idee van de weerbare democratie serieus onderdeel werd van het Europese constitutionele denken. Tegenwoordig kunnen we vaststellen dat alle Europese democratieën zich in feite in meer of mindere mate weerbaar opstellen.

Toch is het idee van een weerbare democratie omstreden. Dit heeft te maken met de inherent paradoxale aard van het concept. Het idee van een weerbare democratie ziet op de ongerustheid van iedere democratie dat door gebruik te maken van politieke rechten en democratische besluitvorming een meerderheid kan kiezen voor een niet-democratisch regime. Om te overleven gaat een weerbare democratie er daarom vanuit dat antidemocratische actoren mogen worden geweerd uit de politieke arena. Ondertussen wekt de beperking van de deelname van antidemocratische actoren de argwaan dat de democratie niet aan haar eigen criteria voldoet, namelijk dat politieke besluiten voortkomen uit een vrije politieke competitie.[18] Weerbaarheidsmaatregelen beperken immers deze vrije competitie. Een excessief weerbare democratie loopt daarom het risico een averechtse uitwerking te hebben door tolerant noch democratisch te zijn. De succesvolle implementatie van het concept weerbare democratie is daarom afhankelijk van de precaire balans tussen respect voor politieke rechten en democratische procedures aan de ene kant, en de bescherming van het democratische systeem en democratische waarden aan de andere kant.

7.2 *De Duitse 'wehrhafte Demokratie'*

Hoewel vrijwel alle democratieën instrumenten hebben om zich te verdedigen tegen antidemocratische politieke actoren vormt de Duitse rechtsorde in dit geval een bijzonder voorbeeld. Het feit dat de Nazi's gebruik konden maken van democratische

17 K. Loewenstein, 'Autocracy versus Democracy in Contemporary Europe, I', *The American Political Science Review*, vol. 29, no. 4, 1935, p. 593; K. Loewenstein, 'Militant Democracy and Fundamental Rights, I', *The American Political Science Review*, vol. 31, no. 3, 1937, p. 417-432 and K. Loewenstein, 'Militant Democracy and Fundamental Rights, II', *The American Political Science Review*, vol. 31, no. 4, 1937, p. 638-658.

18 A. Sajó, 'Militant Democracy and Transition towards Democracy', in: A. Sajó (red.), *Militant Democracy*, Utrecht: Eleven Legal Publishers, 2004, p. 211.

rechten en verkiezingen in hun weg naar politieke macht heeft het naoorlogse Duitsland buitengewoon bewust gemaakt van de noodzaak het democratische systeem te bescherming tegen uitbuiting door antidemocratische stromingen. De Duitse Grondwet (*Grundgesetz*), die in 1949 in werking trad, omvat de meest expliciete en vergaande implementatie van het concept weerbare democratie, in het Duitse constitutionele recht ook wel aangeduid als *'wehrhafte Demokratie'*.

De misbruikclausule in artikel 18 Grondwet is hiervan de meest expliciete uitdrukking.[19] Deze bepaling biedt een speciale procedure die kan worden gestart door de Bondsdag, de federale regering of de regering van één van de zestien staten en waarin het Federale Constitutionele Hof beslist over de verwerking van constitutionele rechten. Artikel 18 Grondwet is bedoeld als een preventief instrument dat alleen zou moeten worden toegepast als voldoende is bewezen dat de rechthebbende anders zijn recht zal (blijven) uitoefening op een manier die een serieus gevaar vormt voor de vrije democratische rechtsorde. In de rechtspraktijk speelt dit meest zware weerbaarheidsinstrument nauwelijks een rol. Tot op heden zijn alle verzoeken tot de verwerking van een grondrecht afgewezen.

De rechtspraak laat zien dat de Duitse democratie in de eerste plaats wordt beschermd door andere, minder vergaande instrumenten van de *wehrhafte Demokratie*, zoals het beperken van het verenigingsrecht van politieke partijen die trachten de vrije democratische rechtsorde te ondermijnen of af te schaffen of een gevaar vormen voor het bestaan van de Bondsrepubliek (artikel 21(2) Grondwet) of van andere politieke organisaties wiens doelen en activiteiten zijn gericht tegen de constitutionele orde (artikel 9(2) Grondwet). Daarnaast wordt de Duitse democratische rechtsorde beschermd door een verscheidenheid aan sub-constitutionele bepalingen, waaronder strafrechtelijke verboden van vijandelijke propaganda of discriminatoire uitlatingen. In de praktijk blijken deze instrumenten belangrijker voor de bescherming van de democratie en democratische waarden dan de misbruikclausule. Dus, waar de interesse in artikel 17 EVRM de laatste jaren is toegenomen lijkt artikel 18 Grondwet juist een dode letter te zijn geworden. Artikel 18 van de Duitse Grondwet is in feite niets meer dan een politieke waarschuwing.[20]

19 Artikel 18 van de Duitse Grondwet luidt: *'Wer die Freiheit der Meinungsäußerung, insbesondere die Pressefreiheit (Artikel 5 Abs. 1), die Lehrfreiheit (Artikel 5 Abs. 3), die Versammlungsfreiheit (Artikel 8), die Vereinigungsfreiheit (Artikel 9), das Brief-, Post- und Fernmeldegeheimnis (Artikel 10), das Eigentum (Artikel 14) oder das Asylrecht (Artikel 16a) zum Kampfe gegen die freiheitliche demokratische Grundordnung mißbraucht, verwirkt diese Grundrechte. Die Verwirkung und ihr Ausmaß werden durch das Bundesverfassungsgericht ausgesprochen'* www.bundestag.de/bundestag/aufgaben/rechtsgrundlagen/grundgesetz/gg_01/245122 (bekeken op 11 April 2016).

20 Zie ook Müller, *The Oxford Handbook of Comparative Constitutional Law*, p. 1258.

7.3 De weerbare democratie en het EVRM

Ook het EVRM ademt de geest van de weerbare democratie. Hoewel de Commissie noch het Hof expliciet de term 'weerbare democratie' hebben gebezigd, bevestigt de jurisprudentie dat het Verdrag is gebaseerd op het idee van een zichzelf verdedigende democratische rechtsorde. In de beroemde *Refah Partisi*-uitspraak oordeelde het Hof dat gelet op de sterke connectie tussen het Verdrag en de democratie *'no one must be authorised to rely on the Convention's provisions in order to weaken or destroy the ideals and values of a democratic society'*.[21] Het Verdrag staat staten daarom toe om weerbaarheidsmaatregelen te nemen om de democratie en democratische waarden te beschermen.

Gedurende de eerste jaren van het Verdrag was de weerbare houding van het Hof geformuleerd in termen van de dichotomie van de Koude Oorlog tussen democratie en totalitarisme. De eerste zaken waarin de Commissie en het Hof zich weerbaar opstelden hadden betrekking op klachten van aanhangers van extreemlinkse (communistische) of extreemrechtse (neonazistische) ideologieën. De val van de Sovjet-Unie en de transitie naar democratie in diverse postcommunistische staten in Centraal en Oost Europa deed vervolgens de vraag rijzen naar de legitimiteit van weerbaarheidsmaatregelen door deze nieuwe democratieën. Het Hof was in beginsel welwillend om dergelijke maatregelen in de context van een democratiseringsproces te beoordelen in het licht van de weerbare democratie. Het lijkt zich echter meer en meer bewust van het paradoxale aspect van het concept weerbare democratie en benadrukte dat zulke maatregelen slechts gedurende een bepekte periode gerechtvaardigd zijn.[22] In een zaak over de uitsluiting van een voormalig lid van de Letse Communistische Partij van kandidaatstelling voor de verkiezingen benadrukte het Hof dat *'[e]very time a State intends to rely on the principle of "a democracy capable of defending itself" in order to justify interference with individual rights, it must carefully evaluate the scope and consequences of the measure under consideration'*.[23] Deze nuancering lijkt echter nauwelijks een rol te spelen in de houding van het Hof tegenover neonazisme en ontkenning van de Holocaust. In deze zaken blijft het Hof de toepassing van weerbaarheidsmaatregelen rechtvaardigen enkel op basis van de inhoud van de activiteit, zonder in te gaan op de noodzaak en proportionaliteit van dergelijke maatregelen ter bescherming van de democratie of democratische waarden.

---

21 EHRM 13 februari 2003 (GK), *Refah Partisi (the Welfare Party) e.a. t. Turkije*, appl. nrs. 41340/98 et al., par. 99.

22 Harvey, *European Law Review*, p. 415.

23 EHRM 16 maart 2006 (GK), Ždanoka t. Letland, appl. nr. 58278/00, par. 100.

De laatste jaren zijn de situaties waarin het Hof een beroep op het concept weerbare democratie heeft toegestaan ter rechtvaardiging van beperkingen van fundamentele rechten verruimd. Het Hof heeft in toenemende mate weerbaarheidsmaatregelen toegestaan tegen politieke projecten die geen gevaar opleveren voor het democratische systeem *an sich*, maar een gevaar vormen voor meer materiële democratische waarden. Voor de toepassing van artikel 17 EVRM betekent dit dat het Hof deze bepaling in toenemende mate is gaan toepassen op activiteiten die gericht zijn tegen de *'geest'* en de *'onderliggende waarden'* van het EVRM. De jurisprudentie laat zien hoe lastig het is om onderscheid te maken tussen (controversiële) activiteiten die de bescherming van het Verdrag genieten en activiteiten die daadwerkelijk een gevaar vormen. Vage criteria zoals de *'geest'* of de *'fundamentele waarden'* van het Verdrag die het Hof gebruikt om misbruik te definiëren maken het nog moeilijker om te vast te stellen wanneer de misbruikclausule dient te worden toegepast. De drempel voor staten om de uitoefening van politieke rechten te beperken wordt daardoor lager, wat het gevaar met zich meebrengt dat de democratie zich op een hellend vlak bevindt.

8 Hoe nu verder?

Gelet op de verschillende perspectieven die in deze studie zijn bestudeerd is de vraag in hoeverre het verbod van misbruik van recht gepast is in de context van het EVRM. De directe toepassing van artikel 17 EVRM in het bijzonder is problematisch gebleken vanuit mensenrechtenperspectief, omdat het bepaalde activiteiten uitsluit van de bescherming van het Verdrag en er geen verdere beoordeling plaatsvindt van de rechtmatigheid van de beperking in het licht van de beperkingscriteria. Ten gevolge hiervan is de afweging van de betrokken belangen zeer marginaal en wordt nauwelijks rekening gehouden met de proportionaliteit van de beperking van het recht van de klager. Dit is moeilijk te rijmen met het doorgaans strenge toezicht van het Hof op de beperking van politieke rechten, juist omdat deze rechten zo belangrijk zijn voor het functioneren van de democratie. Om fundamentele rechten op een hoog niveau te kunnen beschermen dient elke beperking van een recht dat door het Verdrag wordt beschermd aan een strenge controle te worden onderworpen.[24] Een *prima facie* beoordeling op basis van artikel 17 EVRM is in dit licht onvoldoende.

Ook vanuit het perspectief van de weerbare democratie is de directe toepassing van artikel 17 EVRM bedenkelijk. Zoals alle weerbaarheidsmaatregelen is de misbruikclausule op het eerste gezicht ondemocratisch in die zin dat zij de politieke deelname van groepen en individuen beperkt. Weerbaarheidsmaatregelen moeten daarom met grote terughoudendheid worden toegepast. Het is twijfelachtig of de toepassing van een vergaande maatregel zoals het ontzeggen van de bescherming

24 Zie ook Buyse, *Shaping Rights in the ECHR*, p. 205 en Arai, *Theory and Practice of the ECHR*, p. 621 en p. 1086-1087.

van fundamentele rechten in dit licht vereist is. Vooral omdat de beperkingsclausules in het Verdrag ook al voorzien in de beperking van rechten en vrijheden om andere zwaarwegende belangen te beschermen. Het gebrek aan praktische relevantie van de misbruikclausules in andere mensenrechtenverdragen en in de Duitse Grondwet laat zien dat het in ieder geval in deze systemen niet nodig blijkt te zijn om terug te grijpen op de misbruikclausule om de democratie en democratische waarden effectief te beschermen. Bovendien heeft het Hof zelf in zaken zoals *Refah Partisi* laten zien dat het in staat is om de democratie en democratische waarden bescherming te bieden zonder een klacht niet-ontvankelijk te verklaren op basis van artikel 17 EVRM. De aanpak van antidemocratische groepen en individuen door het Hof zou zich daarom in de eerste plaats moeten richten op de reguliere beperkingsclausules in het EVRM.

Binnen deze benadering is er echter nog wel ruimte voor een indirecte toepassing van artikel 17 EVRM. In zaken betreffende activiteiten die een aanval vormen op de democratie of democratische waarden kan de misbruikclausule nog steeds een rol spelen als een beginsel bij de beoordeling of een beperking voldoet aan de beperkingscriteria. Als een uiting van één van de kernwaarden van het Verdrag kan de misbruikclausule helpen om de rechten en vrijheden in het Verdrag op een meer coherente manier te interpreteren in het licht van de bedoeling van het Verdrag als geheel.[25] Tegelijkertijd kan de interpretatie van artikel 17 EVRM door de nadruk te leggen op de indirecte toepassing recht doen aan de balans tussen het recht van de klager en de gronden voor een rechtmatige beperking die gebruikelijk is in het licht van mensenrechtenbescherming. Op die manier biedt de interpretatie van de misbruikclausule het Hof de mogelijkheid om de moeilijkheden en nuances die een rol spelen bij de afweging tussen de bescherming van de democratie en democratische waarden, aan de ene kant, en de bescherming van politieke rechten en vrijheden, aan de andere kant, in ogenschouw te nemen. Het Hof dient daarbij ook te kijken naar de proportionaliteit van een door een staat genomen weerbaarheidsmaatregel. Dit betekent dat het Hof ook objectieve criteria, zoals het risico dat de democratie daadwerkelijk schade wordt toegebracht door de activiteiten van de klager, dient mee te nemen in zijn beoordeling. In dat licht dient het Hof tevens in acht te nemen dat weerbaarheidsmaatregelen wellicht minder gerechtvaardigd zijn in volwassen en stabiele democratieën. Hoewel het Hof deze redenering volgde in zaken betreffende de weerbaarheidsmaatregelen genomen in de context van democratiseringsprocessen in Centraal en Oost Europa in de jaren '90, speelt dit element tot op heden nog nauwelijks een rol in het kader van de beoordeling van andere weerbaarheidsmaatregelen in het licht van artikel 17 EVRM.

25 Zie ook Cannie en Voorhoof, *Netherlands Quarterly of Human Rights*, p. 83.

Kortgezegd, een indirecte toepassing van de misbruikclausule in artikel 17 EVRM stelt het Hof in staat om de verscheidenheid aan hedendaagse uitdagingen voor de democratie en democratische waarden tegemoet te treden op een manier die recht doet aan hun complexiteit. Aan de ene kant wordt zo een kader geschapen voor de interpretatie van de grenzen van politieke rechten in een democratische samenleving, terwijl aan de andere kant recht wordt gedaan aan de bescherming van fundamentele rechten en vrijheden.

Curriculum Vitae

Paulien de Morree was born in 1983 in Assen, the Netherlands. In 2005 she graduated with a MSc in Interdisciplinary Social Science and in 2009 she completed an LLM (*cum laude*), both from Utrecht University, the Netherlands. During her studies she spent a semester at the Université de Toulouse, France. After her studies she participated in a research project on parliamentary immunity in several European legal orders funded by the Netherlands Organisation for Scientific Research (NWO) and she worked for the Meijers Committee, the Standing Committee of Experts on International Immigration, Refugee and Criminal Law. In 2012 Paulien commenced her PhD research at the Institute for Constitutional and Administrative Law at Utrecht University. She authored a number of texts that were published in various national and international books and academic journals and taught several courses on constitutional and administrative law and human rights. In 2013 and 2014 she presided over the PhD Council of the Faculty of Law, Economics and Governance. During her PhD research she was a visiting scholar at the European Court of Human Rights in Strasbourg, France, and at the Max Planck Institute for Comparative Public Law and International Law in Heidelberg, Germany. Paulien became a SIM Fellow at the Netherlands Institute of Human Rights in 2015. That same year she became the president of Stichting Initiatives for Peace and Human Rights, a Dutch NGO that supports local initiatives related to human rights education and legal aid in Africa's Great Lakes Region. In 2016 Paulien was appointed an assistant professor at Utrecht University.

School of Human Rights Research Series

The School of Human Rights Research is a joint effort by human rights researchers in the Netherlands. Its central research theme is the nature and meaning of international standards in the field of human rights, their application and promotion in the national legal order, their interplay with national standards and the international supervision of such application. The School of Human Rights Research Series only includes English titles that contribute to a better understanding of the different aspects of human rights.

For previous volumes in the series, please visit http://shr.intersentia.com.

Published titles within the Series:

70. Helen Beckmann-Hamzei, *The Child in ICC Proceedings.*
    ISBN 978-1-78068-339-3
71. Karel De Meester, *The Investigation Phase in International Criminal Procedure: In Search of Common Rules.*
    ISBN 978-1-78068-305-8
72. Nelleke Koffeman, *Morally sensitive issues and cross-border movement in the EU. The cases of reproductive matters and legal recognition of same-sex relationships.*
    ISBN 978-1-78068-349-2
73. Roland Moerland, *The Killing of Death. Denying the Genocide against the Tutsi.*
    ISBN 978-1-78068-351-5
74. Andrea Broderick, *The Long and Winding Road to Disability Equality and Inclusion. The United Nations Convention on the Rights of Persons with Disabilities.*
    ISBN 978-1-78068-358-4
75. Christina Peristeridou, *The principle of legality in European criminal law.*
    ISBN 978-1-78068-357-7
76. Emilie Ellen Kuijt, *Humanitarian Assistance and State Sovereignty in International Law. Towards a Comprehensive Framework.*
    ISBN 978-1-78068-366-9
77. Lize R. Glas, *The Theory, Potential and Practice of Procedural Dialogue in the European Convention on Human Rights System.*
    ISBN 978-1-78068-375-1

www.ingramcontent.com/pod-product-compliance
Ingram Content Group UK Ltd.
Pitfield, Milton Keynes, MK11 3LW, UK
UKHW051920100926
8556IPUK00021B/1292

9 781780 68418